# DEVELOPMENT AS FREEDOM

## AMARTYA SEN

OXFORD
UNIVERSITY PRESS

# OXFORD
UNIVERSITY PRESS

Great Clarendon Street, Oxford OX2 6DP

Oxford University Press is a department of the University of Oxford.
It furthers the University's objective of excellence in research, scholarship,
and education by publishing worldwide in

Oxford New York

Athens Auckland Bangkok Bogotá Buenos Aires Calcutta
Cape Town Chennai Dar es Salaam Delhi Florence Hong Kong Istanbul
Karachi Kuala Lumpur Madrid Melbourne Mexico City Mumbai
Nairobi Paris São Paulo Shanghai Singapore Taipei Tokyo Toronto Warsaw

with associated companies in Berlin Ibadan

Oxford is a registered trade mark of Oxford University Press
in the UK and in certain other countries

First published in the United States
by Alfred A. Knopf

©Amartya Sen 1999

The moral rights of the author have been asserted
Database right Oxford University Press (maker)

First published 1999

First published as an Oxford University Press paperback 2001

A catalogue record for this title is available from the British Library

ISBN 0-19-289330-0

7

Typeset in the United States of America
Printed in Great Britain by
Clays Ltd, St Ives plc

# DEVELOPMENT AS FREEDOM

**Amartya Sen** is the Master of Trinity College,
Cambridge, and the winner of the 1998 Nobel
Prize in Economic Science. He has been
President of the Indian Economic Association,
the American Economic Association, the
International Economic Association and the
Econometric Society. He has taught at Calcutta,
Delhi, Oxford, Cambridge, the London School
of Economics, and Harvard.

'Amartya Sen develops elegantly, compactly,
and yet broadly the concept that economic
development is in its nature an increase in
freedom. By historical examples, empirical
evidence, and forceful and rigorous analysis, he
shows how development, broadly and properly
conceived, cannot be antagonistic to liberty but
consists precisely in its increase.'
*Kenneth J. Arrow, Nobel Laureate in Economic
Science*

'The perspective that Mr. Sen describes and
advocates has great attractions. Chief among
them is that, by cutting through the sterile
debate for or against the market, it makes it
easier to ask sharper questions about public
policy.'
*The Economist*

'Indispensable. ... Informed, insightful,
compassionate and optimistic.'
*The Nation*

'A new approach. ... Refreshing, thoughtful,
and human. Sen's optimism and no-nonsense
proposals leave one feeling that perhaps there is
a solution.'
*Business Week*

'[Sen] proposes a theory of global economic development that is powerful, grand and eloquently simple at the same time. ... An exhilarating work by one of the great masters of the social sciences.'
*The Boston Book Review*

'It is hard to disagree with Sen.... Together [his arguments] constitute a useful corrective to the conventional wisdom, and should feature increasingly in current debate.'
*Financial Times*

'Amartya Sen harks back to the older and richer tradition of evaluating the considerations of economic efficiency—which dominate most modern economic analyses—with respect to their general social consequences.... His thesis has radical implications.'
*Foreign Affairs*

'Unlike most Nobel Prize-winning economists, Sen has focused on the well-being of those at the bottom of society, not the efficiency of those at the top.'
*Chicago Tribune*

'[Development as Freedom] exudes a refreshing reasonableness and a willingness to acknowledge rival points of view.'
*The Atlantic Monthly*

*To Emma*

# CONTENTS

▼

# ILLUSTRATIONS

▼

▼

We live in a world of unprecedented opulence, of a kind that would have been hard even to imagine a century or two ago. There have also been remarkable changes beyond the economic sphere. The twentieth century has established democratic and participatory governance as the preeminent model of political organization. Concepts of human rights and political liberty are now very much a part of the prevailing rhetoric. People live much longer, on the average, than ever before. Also, the different regions of the globe are now more closely linked than they have ever been. This is so not only in the fields of trade, commerce and communication, but also in terms of interactive ideas and ideals.

And yet we also live in a world with remarkable deprivation, destitution and oppression. There are many new problems as well as old ones, including persistence of poverty and unfulfilled elementary needs, occurrence of famines and widespread hunger, violation of elementary political freedoms as well as of basic liberties, extensive neglect of the interests and agency of women, and worsening threats to our environment and to the sustainability of our economic and social lives. Many of these deprivations can be observed, in one form or another, in rich countries as well as poor ones.

Overcoming these problems is a central part of the exercise of development. We have to recognize, it is argued here, the role of freedoms of different kinds in countering these afflictions. Indeed, individual agency is, ultimately, central to addressing these deprivations. On the other hand, the freedom of agency that we individually have is inescapably qualified and constrained by the social, political and economic opportunities that are available to us. There is a deep complementarity between individual agency and social arrangements. It is important to give simultaneous recognition to the centrality of individual freedom *and* to the force of social influences on the extent and reach of individual freedom. To counter the problems that we face, we have to see individual freedom as a social commitment. This is the basic approach that this work tries to explore and examine.

Expansion of freedom is viewed, in this approach, both as the primary end and as the principal means of development. Development consists of the removal of various types of unfreedoms that leave people with little choice and little opportunity of exercising their reasoned agency. The removal of substantial unfreedoms, it is argued here, is *constitutive* of development. However, for a fuller understanding of the connection between development and freedom we have to go beyond that basic recognition (crucial as it is). The intrinsic importance of human freedom, in general, as the preeminent objective of development is strongly supplemented by the instrumental effectiveness of freedoms of particular kinds to promote freedoms of other kinds. The linkages between different types of freedoms are empirical and causal, rather than constitutive and compositional. For example, there is strong evidence that economic and political freedoms help to reinforce one another, rather than being hostile to one another (as they are sometimes taken to be). Similarly, social opportunities of education and health care, which may require public action, complement individual opportunities of economic and political participation and also help to foster our own initiatives in overcoming our respective deprivations. If the point of departure of the approach lies in the identification of freedom as the main object of development, the reach of the policy analysis lies in establishing the empirical linkages that make the viewpoint of freedom coherent and cogent as the guiding perspective of the process of development.

This work outlines the need for an integrated analysis of economic, social and political activities, involving a variety of institutions and many interactive agencies. It concentrates particularly on the roles and interconnections between certain crucial instrumental freedoms, including *economic opportunities, political freedoms, social facilities, transparency guarantees,* and *protective security.* Societal arrangements, involving many institutions (the state, the market, the legal system, political parties, the media, public interest groups and public discussion forums, among others) are investigated in terms of their contribution to enhancing and guaranteeing the substantive freedoms of individuals, seen as active agents of change, rather than as passive recipients of dispensed benefits.

The book is based on five lectures I gave as a Presidential Fellow at the World Bank during the fall of 1996. There was also one follow-up lecture in November 1997 dealing with the overall approach and its implications. I appreciated the opportunity and the challenge involved in this task, and I was particularly happy that this happened at the invitation of President James Wolfensohn, whose vision, skill and humanity I much admire. I was privileged to work closely with him earlier as a Trustee of the Institute for Advanced Study at Princeton, and more recently, I have also watched with great interest the constructive impact of Wolfensohn's leadership on the Bank.

The World Bank has not invariably been my favorite organization. The power to do good goes almost always with the possibility to do the opposite, and as a professional economist, I have had occasions in the past to wonder whether the Bank could not have done very much better. These reservations and criticisms are in print, so I need not make a "confession" of harboring skeptical thoughts. All this made it particularly welcome to have the opportunity to present at the Bank my own views on development and on the making of public policy.

This book, however, is not intended primarily for people working at or for the Bank, or other international organizations. Nor is it just for policy makers and planners of national governments. Rather, it is a general work on development and the practical reasons underlying it, aimed particularly at public discussion. I have rearranged the six lectures into twelve chapters, both for clarity and to make the written version more accessible to nonspecialist readers. Indeed, I have tried to make the discussion as nontechnical as possible, and have referred to the more formal literature—for those inclined in that direction—only in endnotes. I have also commented on recent economic experiences that occurred after my lectures were given (in 1996), such as the Asian economic crisis (which confirmed some of the worst fears I had expressed in those lectures).

In line with the importance I attach to the role of public discussion as a vehicle of social change and economic progress (as the text will make clear), this work is presented mainly for open deliberation and critical scrutiny. I have, throughout my life, avoided giving advice to the "authorities." Indeed, I have never counseled any government, preferring to place my suggestions and critiques—for what they are worth—in the public domain. Since I have been fortunate in living in three democracies with largely unimpeded media (India, Britain, and the United States), I have not had reason to complain about any lack of opportunity of public presentation. If my arguments arouse any interest, and lead to more public discussion of these vital issues, I would have reason to feel well rewarded.

# ACKNOWLEDGMENTS

▼

In doing the research on which this book draws, I had support from John D. and Catherine T. MacArthur Foundation, in a joint project with Angus Deaton. That investigation followed some work I had done earlier for the Helsinki-based World Institute of Development Economics Research, directed then by Lal Jayawardena. It also links closely with my advisory role for the *Human Development Reports* of the United Nations Development Programme, under the remarkable stewardship of Mahbub ul Haq of Pakistan (a close friend from my undergraduate days whose sudden death in 1998 is a blow from which I have not yet fully recovered). Harvard University, where I taught until early 1998, has been marvelously supportive of my research work for many years. I have also drawn on logistic support respectively from the Harvard Institute of International Development, the Harvard Center for Population and Development Studies, and the Centre for History and Economics at King's College, Cambridge University.

I have been very fortunate in having wonderful collaborators. I have had the great opportunity of working for many years with Jean Drèze and of publishing several books jointly with him, which have influenced the present work (collaboration with Jean has the agreeable feature that he does most of the work while making sure that you get most of the credit). It was also wonderful for me to have the chance to do joint work with Sudhir Anand, on subjects closely related to this book. I have also had very fruitful working relations with Angus Deaton, Meghnad Desai, James Foster and Siddiq Osmani. My collaboration with Martha Nussbaum during 1987–89 was of great importance in investigating the concepts of capability and quality of life, used extensively in this book.

In helping with *Human Development Reports*, I have fruitfully interacted with, in addition to Mahbub ul Haq, Sakiko Fukuda-Parr, Selim Jahan, Meghnad Desai and Paul Streeten, and later on with Richard Jolly, who succeeded Mahbub. Other collaborators, advisors and critics on whose help I have relied include Tony Atkinson (on whose ideas I have often drawn), and also Kaushik Basu, Alok Bhargava, David Bloom, Anne Case, Lincoln Chen, Martha Chen, Stanley Fischer, Caren Grown, S. Guhan, Stephan Klasen, A. K. Shiva Kumar, Robert Nozick, Christina Paxson, Ben Polak, Jeffrey Sachs, Tim (Thomas) Scanlon, Joe Stiglitz, Kotaro Suzumura and Jong-il You. I have received helpful comments on the basic ideas and on various versions of the manuscript from Sudhir Anand, Amiya Bagchi, Pranab Bardhan, Ashim Dasgupta, Angus Deaton, Peter Dimock, Jean Drèze, James Foster, Siddiq Osmani, Ingrid Robeyns and Adele Simmons.

I have also benefited from very efficient research assistance from Arun Abraham over a long period, and also from Ingrid Robeyns and Tanni Mukhopadhyay, more recently. Anna Marie Svedrofsky has played a most helpful coordinating role with the logistic arrangements.

As mentioned in the Preface, these lectures were given at the invitation of James Wolfensohn, President of the World Bank, and I have greatly benefited from many discussions with him. The lectures at the Bank were chaired respectively by James Wolfensohn, Caio Kochweser, Ismail Serageldin, Callisto Madavo and Sven Sandstrom, and they each made significant observations on the problems I tried to address. I was, furthermore, very stimulated by the questions that were asked and the remarks that were made in the discussions following my lectures. I also benefited from the opportunity to interact with the staff of the Bank, arranged with impeccable efficiency by Tariq Hussain, who was generally in charge of those lectures.

Finally, my wife, Emma Rothschild, has had to read different versions of disparate arguments at various times, and her advice has always been extremely valuable. Her own work on Adam Smith has been a good source of ideas, since this book draws a great deal on Smith's analyses. I had a close relationship with Adam Smith even before I knew Emma (as those familiar with my earlier writings will know). Under her influence, the plot has thickened. This has been important for the work.

# DEVELOPMENT AS FREEDOM

# DEVELOPMENT AS FREEDOM

Development can be seen, it is argued here, as a process of expanding the real freedoms that people enjoy. Focusing on human freedoms contrasts with narrower views of development, such as identifying development with the growth of gross national product, or with the rise in personal incomes, or with industrialization, or with technological advance, or with social modernization. Growth of GNP or of individual incomes can, of course, be very important as *means* to expanding the freedoms enjoyed by the members of the society. But freedoms depend also on other determinants, such as social and economic arrangements (for example, facilities for education and health care) as well as political and civil rights (for example, the liberty to participate in public discussion and scrutiny). Similarly, industrialization or technological progress or social modernization can substantially contribute to expanding human freedom, but freedom depends on other influences as well. If freedom is what development advances, then there is a major argument for concentrating on that overarching objective, rather than on some particular means, or some specially chosen list of instruments. Viewing development in terms of expanding substantive freedoms directs attention to the ends that make development important, rather than merely to some of the means that, inter alia, play a prominent part in the process.

Development requires the removal of major sources of unfreedom: poverty as well as tyranny, poor economic opportunities as well as systematic social deprivation, neglect of public facilities as well as intolerance or overactivity of repressive states. Despite unprecedented increases in overall opulence, the contemporary world denies elementary freedoms to vast numbers—perhaps even the majority—of people. Sometimes the lack of substantive freedoms relates directly to economic poverty, which robs people of the freedom to satisfy hunger, or to achieve sufficient nutrition, or to obtain remedies for treatable illnesses, or the opportunity to be adequately clothed or sheltered, or to enjoy clean water or sanitary facilities. In other cases, the unfreedom links closely to the lack of public facilities and social care, such as the absence of epidemiological programs, or of organized arrangements for health care or educational facilities, or of effective institutions for the maintenance of local peace and order. In still other cases, the violation of freedom results directly from a denial of political and civil liberties by authoritarian regimes and from imposed restrictions on the freedom to participate in the social, political and economic life of the community.

## EFFECTIVENESS AND INTERCONNECTIONS

Freedom is central to the process of development for two distinct reasons.

1) *The evaluative reason:* assessment of progress has to be done primarily in terms of whether the freedoms that people have are enhanced;

2) *The effectiveness reason:* achievement of development is thoroughly dependent on the free agency of people.

I have already signaled the first motivation: the evaluative reason for concentrating on freedom. In pursuing the second, that of effectiveness, we have to look at the relevant empirical connections, in particular at the mutually reinforcing connections between freedoms of different kinds. It is because of these interconnections, which are explored in some detail in this book, that free and sustainable agency emerges as a major engine of development. Not only is free agency itself a "constitutive" part of development, it also contributes to the strengthening of free agencies of other kinds. The empirical connections that are extensively explored in this study link the two aspects of the idea of "development as freedom."

The relation between individual freedom and the achievement of social development goes well beyond the constitutive connection—

important as it is. What people can positively achieve is influenced by economic opportunities, political liberties, social powers, and the enabling conditions of good health, basic education, and the encouragement and cultivation of initiatives. The institutional arrangements for these opportunities are also influenced by the exercise of people's freedoms, through the liberty to participate in social choice and in the making of public decisions that impel the progress of these opportunities. These interconnections are also investigated here.

## SOME ILLUSTRATIONS: POLITICAL
## FREEDOM AND QUALITY OF LIFE

The difference that is made by seeing freedom as the principal ends of development can be illustrated with a few simple examples. Even though the full reach of this perspective can only emerge from a much more extensive analysis (attempted in the chapters to follow), the radical nature of the idea of "development as freedom" can easily be illustrated with some elementary examples.

First, in the context of the narrower views of development in terms of GNP growth or industrialization, it is often asked whether certain political or social freedoms, such as the liberty of political participation and dissent, or opportunities to receive basic education, are or are not "conducive to development." In the light of the more foundational view of development as freedom, this way of posing the question tends to miss the important understanding that these substantive freedoms (that is, the liberty of political participation or the opportunity to receive basic education or health care) are among the *constituent components* of development. Their relevance for development does not have to be freshly established through their indirect contribution to the growth of GNP or to the promotion of industrialization. As it happens, these freedoms and rights are *also* very effective in contributing to economic progress; this connection will receive extensive attention in this book. But while the causal relation is indeed significant, the vindication of freedoms and rights provided by this causal linkage is over and above the directly constitutive role of these freedoms in development.

A second illustration relates to the dissonance between income per head (even after correction for price variations) and the freedom of individuals to live long and live well. For example, the citizens of

Gabon or South Africa or Namibia or Brazil may be much richer in terms of per capita GNP than the citizens of Sri Lanka or China or the state of Kerala in India, but the latter have very substantially higher life expectancies than do the former.

To take a different type of example, the point is often made that African Americans in the United States are relatively poor compared with American whites, though much richer than people in the third world. It is, however, important to recognize that African Americans have an *absolutely* lower chance of reaching mature ages than do people of many third world societies, such as China, or Sri Lanka, or parts of India (with different arrangements of health care, education, and community relations). If development analysis is relevant even for richer countries (it is argued in this work that this is indeed so), the presence of such intergroup contrasts within the richer countries can be seen to be an important aspect of the understanding of development and underdevelopment.

## TRANSACTIONS, MARKETS AND ECONOMIC UNFREEDOM

A third illustration relates to the role of markets as part of the process of development. The ability of the market mechanism to contribute to high economic growth and to overall economic progress has been widely—and rightly—acknowledged in the contemporary development literature. But it would be a mistake to understand the place of the market mechanism only in derivative terms. As Adam Smith noted, freedom of exchange and transaction is itself part and parcel of the basic liberties that people have reason to value.

To be *generically against* markets would be almost as odd as being generically against conversations between people (even though some conversations are clearly foul and cause problems for others—or even for the conversationalists themselves). The freedom to exchange words, or goods, or gifts does not need defensive justification in terms of their favorable but distant effects; they are part of the way human beings in society live and interact with each other (unless stopped by regulation or fiat). The contribution of the market mechanism to economic growth is, of course, important, but this comes only after the direct significance of the freedom to interchange—words, goods, gifts—has been acknowledged.

As it happens, the rejection of the freedom to participate in the labor market is one of the ways of keeping people in bondage and captivity, and the battle against the unfreedom of bound labor is important in many third world countries today for some of the same reasons the American Civil War was momentous. The freedom to enter markets can itself be a significant contribution to development, quite aside from whatever the market mechanism may or may not do to promote economic growth or industrialization. In fact, the praise of capitalism by Karl Marx (not a great admirer of capitalism in general) and his characterization (in *Das Kapital*) of the American Civil War as "the one great event of contemporary history" related directly to the importance of the freedom of labor contract as opposed to slavery and the enforced exclusion from the labor market. As will be discussed, the crucial challenges of development in many developing countries today include the need for the freeing of labor from explicit or implicit bondage that denies access to the open labor market. Similarly, the denial of access to product markets is often among the deprivations from which many small cultivators and struggling producers suffer under traditional arrangements and restrictions. The freedom to participate in economic interchange has a basic role in social living.

To point to this often neglected consideration is not to deny the importance of judging the market mechanism comprehensively in terms of all its roles and effects, including those in generating economic growth and, under many circumstances, even economic equity. We must also examine, on the other side, the persistence of deprivations among segments of the community that happen to remain excluded from the benefits of the market-oriented society, and the general judgments, including criticisms, that people may have of lifestyles and values associated with the culture of markets. In seeing development as freedom, the arguments on different sides have to be appropriately considered and assessed. It is hard to think that any process of substantial development can do without very extensive use of markets, but that does not preclude the role of social support, public regulation, or statecraft when they can enrich—rather than impoverish—human lives. The approach used here provides a broader and more inclusive perspective on markets than is frequently invoked in *either* defending *or* chastising the market mechanism.

I end this list of illustrations with another that draws directly on a personal recollection from my own childhood. I was playing one afternoon—I must have been around ten or so—in the garden in our family home in the city of Dhaka, now the capital of Bangladesh, when a man came through the gate screaming pitifully and bleeding profusely; he had been knifed in the back. Those were the days of communal riots (with Hindus and Muslims killing each other), which preceded the independence and partitioning of India and Pakistan. The knifed man, called Kader Mia, was a Muslim daily laborer who had come for work in a neighboring house—for a tiny reward—and had been knifed on the street by some communal thugs in our largely Hindu area. As I gave him water while also crying for help from adults in the house, and moments later, as he was rushed to the hospital by my father, Kader Mia went on telling us that his wife had told him not to go into a hostile area in such troubled times. But Kader Mia had to go out in search of work and a bit of earning because his family had nothing to eat. The penalty of his economic unfreedom turned out to be death, which occurred later on in the hospital.

The experience was devastating for me. It made me reflect, later on, on the terrible burden of narrowly defined identities, including those firmly based on communities and groups (I shall have occasion to discuss that issue in this book). But more immediately, it also pointed to the remarkable fact that economic unfreedom, in the form of extreme poverty, can make a person a helpless prey in the violation of other kinds of freedom. Kader Mia need not have come to a hostile area in search of a little income in those terrible times had his family been able to survive without it. Economic unfreedom can breed social unfreedom, just as social or political unfreedom can also foster economic unfreedom.

## ORGANIZATIONS AND VALUES

Many other examples can be given to illustrate the pivotal difference that is made by pursuing a view of development as an integrated process of expansion of substantive freedoms that connect with one another. It is this view that is presented, scrutinized and utilized in this book to investigate the development process in inclusive terms that integrate economic, social and political considerations.

A broad approach of this kind permits simultaneous appreciation of the vital roles, in the process of development, of many different institutions, including markets and market-related organizations, governments and local authorities, political parties and other civic institutions, educational arrangements and opportunities of open dialogue and debate (including the role of the media and other means of communication).

Such an approach also allows us to acknowledge the role of social values and prevailing mores, which can influence the freedoms that people enjoy and have reason to treasure. Shared norms can influence social features such as gender equity, the nature of child care, family size and fertility patterns, the treatment of the environment and many other arrangements and outcomes. Prevailing values and social mores also affect the presence or absence of corruption, and the role of trust in economic or social or political relationships. The exercise of freedom is mediated by values, but the values in turn are influenced by public discussions and social interactions, which are themselves influenced by participatory freedoms. Each of these connections deserves careful scrutiny.

The fact that the freedom of economic transactions tends to be typically a great engine of economic growth has been widely acknowledged, even though forceful detractors remain. It is important not only to give the markets their due, but also to appreciate the role of other economic, social, and political freedoms in enhancing and enriching the lives that people are able to lead. This has a clear bearing even on such controversial matters as the so-called population problem. The role of freedom in moderating excessively high fertility rates is a subject on which contrary views have been held for a long time. While that great eighteenth-century French rationalist Condorcet expected that fertility rates would come down with "the progress of reason," so that greater security, more education and more freedom of reflected decisions would restrain population growth, his contemporary Thomas Robert Malthus differed radically with this position. Indeed, Malthus argued that "there is no reason whatever to suppose that anything beside the difficulty of procuring in adequate plenty the necessaries of life should either indispose this greater number of persons to marry early, or disable them from rearing in health the largest families." The comparative merits of the two different positions—relying respectively on reasoned freedom and economic compulsion—will be investigated later on in this study (the balance of evidence, I shall argue, is certainly more on Condorcet's side). But it is especially important to recognize that this particular controversy is just one example of the debate between profreedom and antifreedom approaches to development that has gone on for many centuries. That debate is still very active in many different forms.

## INSTITUTIONS AND INSTRUMENTAL FREEDOMS

Five distinct types of freedom, seen in an "instrumental" perspective, are particularly investigated in the empirical studies that follow. These include (1) *political freedoms,* (2) *economic facilities,* (3) *social opportunities,* (4) *transparency guarantees* and (5) *protective security.* Each of these distinct types of rights and opportunities helps to advance the general capability of a person. They may also serve to complement each other. Public policy to foster human capabilities and substantive freedoms in general can work through the promotion of these distinct but interrelated instrumental freedoms. In the chapters that follow, each of these different types of freedom—and the institutions involved—will be explored, and their interconnections discussed. There will be an opportunity also to investigate their respective roles in the promotion of overall freedoms of people to lead the kind of lives they have reason to value. In the view of "development as freedom," the instrumental freedoms link with each other and with the ends of enhancement of human freedom in general.

While development analysis must, on the one hand, be concerned with objectives and aims that make these instrumental freedoms consequentially important, it must also take note of the empirical linkages that tie the distinct types of freedom *together,* strengthening their joint importance. Indeed, these connections are central to a fuller understanding of the instrumental role of freedom.

## A CONCLUDING REMARK

Freedoms are not only the primary ends of development, they are also among its principal means. In addition to acknowledging, foundationally, the evaluative importance of freedom, we also have to understand the remarkable empirical connection that links freedoms of different kinds with one another. Political freedoms (in the form of free speech and elections) help to promote economic security. Social opportunities (in the form of education and health facilities) facilitate economic participation. Economic facilities (in the form of opportunities for participation in trade and production) can help to generate personal abundance as well as public resources for social facilities. Freedoms of different kinds can strengthen one another.

These empirical connections reinforce the valuational priorities. In terms of the medieval distinction between "the patient" and "the agent," this freedom-centered understanding of economics and of the process of development is very much an agent-oriented view. With adequate social opportunities, individuals can effectively shape their own destiny and help each other. They need not be seen primarily as passive recipients of the benefits of cunning development programs. There is indeed a strong rationale for recognizing the positive role of free and sustainable agency—and even of constructive impatience.

# CHAPTER I

# THE PERSPECTIVE OF FREEDOM

It is not unusual for couples to discuss the possibility of earning more money, but a conversation on this subject from around the eighth century B.C. is of some special interest. As that conversation is recounted in the Sanskrit text *Brihadaranyaka Upanishad,* a woman named Maitreyee and her husband, Yajnavalkya, proceed rapidly to a bigger issue than the ways and means of becoming more wealthy: *How far would wealth go to help them get what they want?*[1] Maitreyee wonders whether it could be the case that if "the whole earth, full of wealth" were to belong just to her, she could achieve immortality through it. "No," responds Yajnavalkya, "like the life of rich people will be your life. But there is no hope of immortality by wealth." Maitreyee remarks, "What should I do with that by which I do not become immortal?"

Maitreyee's rhetorical question has been cited again and again in Indian religious philosophy to illustrate both the nature of the human predicament and the limitations of the material world. I have too much skepticism of otherworldly matters to be led there by Maitreyee's worldly frustration, but there is another aspect of this exchange that is of rather immediate interest to economics and to understanding the nature of development. This concerns the relation between incomes and achievements, between commodities and capabilities, between our economic wealth and our ability to live as we would like. While there is a connection between opulence and achievements, the linkage may or may not be very strong and may well be extremely contingent on other circumstances. The issue is not the ability to live forever on which Maitreyee—bless her soul—

happened to concentrate, but the capability to live really long (without being cut off in one's prime) and to have a good life while alive (rather than a life of misery and unfreedom)—things that would be strongly valued and desired by nearly all of us. The gap between the two perspectives (that is, between an exclusive concentration on economic wealth and a broader focus on the lives we can lead) is a major issue in conceptualizing development. As Aristotle noted at the very beginning of the *Nicomachean Ethics* (resonating well with the conversation between Maitreyee and Yajnavalkya three thousand miles away), "wealth is evidently not the good we are seeking; for it is merely useful and for the sake of something else."[2]

If we have reasons to want more wealth, we have to ask: What precisely are these reasons, how do they work, on what are they contingent and what are the things we can "do" with more wealth? In fact, we generally have excellent reasons for wanting more income or wealth. This is not because income and wealth are desirable for their own sake, but because, typically, they are admirable general-purpose means for having more freedom to lead the kind of lives we have reason to value.

The usefulness of wealth lies in the things that it allows us to do—the substantive freedoms it helps us to achieve. But this relation is neither exclusive (since there are significant influences on our lives other than wealth) nor uniform (since the impact of wealth on our lives varies with other influences). It is as important to recognize the crucial role of wealth in determining living conditions and the quality of life as it is to understand the qualified and contingent nature of this relationship. An adequate conception of development must go much beyond the accumulation of wealth and the growth of gross national product and other income-related variables. Without ignoring the importance of economic growth, we must look well beyond it.

The ends and means of development require examination and scrutiny for a fuller understanding of the development process; it is simply not adequate to take as our basic objective just the maximization of income or wealth, which is, as Aristotle noted, "merely useful and for the sake of something else." For the same reason, economic growth cannot sensibly be treated as an end in itself. Development has to be more concerned with enhancing the lives we lead and the freedoms we enjoy. Expanding the freedoms that we have reason to value not only makes our lives richer and more unfettered, but also allows us to be fuller social persons, exercising our own volitions and interacting with—and influencing—the world in which we live. In chapter 3 this general approach is more fully proposed and scrutinized, and is evaluatively compared with other approaches that compete for attention.[3]

## FORMS OF UNFREEDOM

Very many people across the world suffer from varieties of unfreedom. Famines continue to occur in particular regions, denying to millions the basic freedom to survive. Even in those countries which are no longer sporadically devastated by famines, undernutrition may affect very large numbers of vulnerable human beings. Also, a great many people have little access to health care, to sanitary arrangements or to clean water, and spend their lives fighting unnecessary morbidity, often succumbing to premature mortality. The richer countries too often have deeply disadvantaged people, who lack basic opportunities of health care, or functional education, or gainful employment, or economic and social security. Even within very rich countries, sometimes the longevity of substantial groups is no higher than that in much poorer economies of the so-called third world. Further, inequality between women and men afflicts—and sometime prematurely ends—the lives of millions of women, and, in different ways, severely restricts the substantive freedoms that women enjoy.

Moving to other deprivations of freedom, a great many people in different countries of the world are systematically denied political liberty and basic civil rights. It is sometimes claimed that the denial of these rights helps to stimulate economic growth and is "good" for rapid economic development. Some have even championed harsher political systems—with denial of basic civil and political rights—for their alleged advantage in promoting economic development. This thesis (often called "the Lee thesis," attributed in some form to the former prime minister of Singapore, Lee Kuan Yew) is sometimes backed by some fairly rudimentary empirical evidence. In fact, more comprehensive intercountry comparisons have not provided any confirmation of this thesis, and there is little evidence that authoritarian politics actually helps economic growth. Indeed, the empirical evidence very strongly suggests that economic growth is more a matter of a friendlier economic climate than of a harsher political system. This issue will receive examination in chapter 6.

Furthermore, economic development has other dimensions, including economic security. Quite often economic insecurity can relate to the lack of democratic rights and liberties. Indeed, the working of democracy and of political rights can even help to prevent famines and other economic disasters. Authoritarian rulers, who are themselves rarely affected by famines (or other such economic calamities), tend to lack the incentive to take timely preventive measures. Democratic governments, in contrast, have to win elections and face public criticism, and have strong incentives to undertake measures to avert famines and other such catastrophes. It is not surprising that no famine has ever taken place in the history of the world in a functioning democracy—be it economically rich (as in contemporary Western Europe or North America) or relatively poor (as in postindependence India, or Botswana, or Zimbabwe). Famines have tended to occur in colonial territories governed by rulers from elsewhere (as in British India or in an Ireland administered by alienated English rulers), or in one-party states (as in the Ukraine in the 1930s, or China during 1958–1961, or Cambodia in the 1970s), or in military dictatorships (as in Ethiopia, or Somalia, or some of the Sahel countries in the near past). Indeed, as this book goes to press, the two countries that seem to be leading the "famine league" in the world are North Korea and Sudan—both eminent examples of dictatorial rule. While the prevention of famine illustrates the incentive advantages with great clarity and force, the advantages of democratic pluralism do, in fact, have a much wider reach.

But—most fundamentally—political liberty and civil freedoms are directly important on their own, and do not have to be justified indirectly in terms of their effects on the economy. Even when people without political liberty or civil rights do not lack adequate economic security (and happen to enjoy favorable economic circumstances), they are deprived of important freedoms in leading their lives and denied the opportunity to take part in crucial decisions regarding public affairs. These deprivations restrict social and political lives, and must be seen as repressive even without their leading to other afflictions (such as economic disasters). Since political and civil freedoms are constitutive elements of human freedom, their denial is a handicap in itself. In examining the role of human rights in development, we have to take note of the constitutive as well as the instrumental importance of civil rights and political freedoms. These issues are examined in chapter 6.

## PROCESSES AND OPPORTUNITIES

It should be clear from the preceding discussion that the view of freedom that is being taken here involves both the *processes* that allow freedom of actions and decisions, and the actual *opportunities* that people have, given their personal and social circumstances. Unfreedom can arise either through inadequate processes (such as the violation of voting privileges or other political or civil rights) or through inadequate opportunities that some people have for achieving what they minimally would like to achieve (including the absence of such elementary opportunities as the capability to escape premature mortality or preventable morbidity or involuntary starvation).

The distinction between the *process aspect* and the *opportunity aspect* of freedom involves quite a substantial contrast. It can be pursued at different levels. I have discussed elsewhere the respective roles and requirements of (as well as mutual connections between) the process aspect and the opportunity aspect of freedom.[4] While this may not be the occasion to go into the complex and subtle issues that relate to this distinction, it is very important to see freedom in a sufficiently broad way. It is necessary to avoid confining attention only to appropriate procedures (as so-called libertarians sometimes do, without worrying at all about whether some disadvantaged people suffer from systematic deprivation of substantive opportunities), or, alternatively, only to adequate opportunities (as so-called consequentialists sometimes do, without worrying about the nature of the processes that bring the opportunities about or the freedom of choice that people have). Both processes and opportunities have importance of their own, and each aspect relates to seeing development as freedom.

## TWO ROLES OF FREEDOM

The analysis of development presented in this book treats the freedoms of individuals as the basic building blocks. Attention is thus paid particularly to the expansion of the "capabilities" of persons to lead the kind of lives they value—and have reason to value. These capabilities can be enhanced by public policy, but also, on the other side, the direction of public policy can be influenced by the effective use of participatory capabilities by the public. The *two-way relationship* is central to the analysis presented here.

There are two distinct reasons for the crucial importance of individual freedom in the concept of development, related respectively to *evaluation* and *effectiveness*.[5] First, in the normative approach used here, substantive individual freedoms are taken to be critical. The success of a society is to be evaluated, in this view, primarily by the substantive freedoms that the members of that society enjoy. This evaluative position differs from the informational focus of more traditional normative approaches, which focus on other variables, such as utility, or procedural liberty, or real income.

Having greater freedom to do the things one has reason to value is (1) significant in itself for the person's overall freedom, and (2) important in fostering the person's opportunity to have valuable outcomes.[6] Both are relevant to the evaluation of freedom of the members of the society and thus crucial to the assessment of the society's development. The reasons for this normative focus (and in particular for seeing justice in terms of individual freedoms and its social correlates) is more fully examined in chapter 3.

The second reason for taking substantive freedom to be so crucial is that freedom is not only the basis of the evaluation of success and failure, but it is also a principal determinant of individual initiative and social effectiveness. Greater freedom enhances the ability of people to help themselves and also to influence the world, and these matters are central to the process of development. The concern here relates to what we may call (at the risk of some oversimplification) the "agency aspect" of the individual.

The use of the term "agency" calls for a little clarification. The expression "agent" is sometimes employed in the literature of economics and game theory to denote a person who is acting on someone else's behalf (perhaps being led on by a "principal"), and whose achievements are to be assessed in the light of someone else's (the principal's) goals. I am using the term "agent" not in this sense, but in its older—and "grander"—sense as someone who acts and brings about change, and whose achievements can be judged in terms of her own values and objectives, whether or not we assess them in terms of some external criteria as well. This work is particularly concerned with the agency role of the individual as a member of the public and as a participant in economic, social and political actions (varying from taking part in the market to being involved, directly or indirectly, in individual or joint activities in political and other spheres).

This has a bearing on a great many public policy issues, varying from such strategic matters as the widespread temptation of policy bosses to use fine-tuned "targeting" (for "ideal delivery" to a supposedly inert population), to such fundamental subjects as attempts to dissociate the running of governments from the process of democratic scrutiny and rejection (and the participatory exercise of political and civil rights).[7]

## EVALUATIVE SYSTEMS: INCOMES AND CAPABILITIES

On the evaluative side, the approach used here concentrates on a factual base that differentiates it from more traditional practical ethics and economic policy analysis, such as the "economic" concentration on the primacy of *income and wealth* (rather than on the characteristics of human lives and substantive freedoms), the "utilitarian" focus on *mental satisfaction* (rather than on creative discontent and constructive dissatisfaction), the "libertarian" preoccupation with *procedures* for liberty (with deliberate neglect of consequences that derive from those procedures) and so on. The overarching case for a different factual base, which focuses on substantive freedoms that people have reason to enjoy, is examined in chapter 3.

This is not to deny that deprivation of individual capabilities can have close links with the lowness of income, which connects in both directions: (1) low income can be a major reason for illiteracy and ill health as well as hunger and undernourishment, and (2) conversely, better education and health help in the earning of higher incomes. These connections have to be fully seized. But there are also other influences on the basic capabilities and effective freedoms that individuals enjoy, and there are good reasons to study the nature and reach of these interconnections. Indeed, precisely because income deprivations and capability deprivations often have considerable correlational linkages, it is important to avoid being mesmerized into thinking that taking note of the former would somehow tell us enough about the latter. The connections are not that tight, and the departures are often much more important from a policy point of view than the limited concurrence of the two sets of variables. If our attention is shifted from an exclusive concentration on income poverty to the more inclusive idea of capability deprivation, we can better understand the poverty of human lives and freedoms in terms of a different informational base (involving statistics of a kind that the income perspective tends to crowd out as a reference point for policy analysis). The role of income and wealth—important as it is along with other influences—has to be integrated into a broader and fuller picture of success and deprivation.

## POVERTY AND INEQUALITY

The implications of this informational base for the analysis of poverty and inequality are examined in chapter 4. There are good reasons for seeing poverty as a deprivation of basic capabilities, rather than merely as low income. Deprivation of elementary capabilities can be reflected in premature mortality, significant undernourishment (especially of children), persistent morbidity, widespread illiteracy and other failures. For example, the terrible phenomenon of "missing women" (resulting from unusually higher age-specific mortality rates of women in some societies, particularly in South Asia, West Asia, North Africa, and China) has to be analyzed with demographic, medical and social information, rather than in terms of low incomes, which sometimes tell us rather little about the phenomenon of gender inequality.[8]

The shift in perspective is important in giving us a different—and more directly relevant—view of poverty not only in the *developing* countries, but also in the more *affluent* societies. The presence of massive unemployment in Europe (10 to 12 percent in many of the major European countries) entails deprivations that are not well reflected in income distribution statistics. These deprivations are often downplayed on the grounds that the European system of social security (including unemployment insurance) tends to make up for the loss of income of the unemployed. But unemployment is not merely a deficiency of income that can be made up through transfers by the state (at heavy fiscal cost that can itself be a very serious burden); it is also a source of far-reaching debilitating effects on individual freedom, initiative, and skills. Among its manifold effects, unemployment contributes to the "social exclusion" of some groups, and it leads to losses of self-reliance, self-confidence and psychological and physical health. Indeed, it is hard to escape a sense of manifest incongruity in contemporary European attempts to move to a more "self-help" social climate without devising adequate policies for reducing the massive and intolerable levels of unemployment that make such self-help extremely difficult.

## INCOME AND MORTALITY

Even in terms of the connection between mortality and income (a subject in which Maitreyee was rather overambitious), it is remarkable that the extent of deprivation for particular groups in very rich countries can be comparable to that in the so-called third world. For example, in the United States, African Americans as a group have no higher—indeed have a lower—chance of reaching advanced ages than do people born in the immensely poorer economies of China or the Indian state of Kerala (or in Sri Lanka, Jamaica or Costa Rica).[9]

This is shown in figures 1.1 and 1.2. Even though the per capita income of African Americans in the United States is considerably lower than that of the white population, African Americans are very many times richer in income terms than the people of China or Kerala (even after correcting for cost-of-living differences). In this context, the comparison of survival prospects of African Americans vis-à-vis those of the very much poorer Chinese, or Indians in Kerala, is of particular interest. African Americans tend to do better in terms of survival at low age groups (especially in terms of infant mortality) vis-à-vis the Chinese or the Indians, but the picture changes over the years.

In fact, it turns out that men in China and in Kerala decisively outlive African American men in terms of surviving to older age

FIGURE I.I: *Variations in Male Survival Rates by Region*

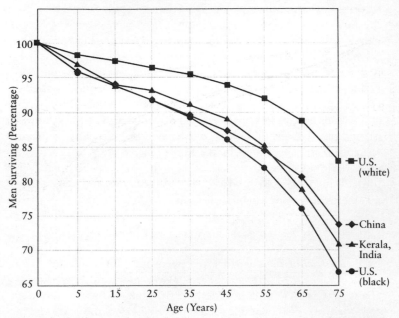

*Sources:* United States, 1991–1993: U.S. Department of Health and Human Services, *Health United States 1995* (Hyattsville, Md.: National Center for Health Statistics, 1996); Kerala, 1991: Government of India, *Sample Registration System: Fertility and Mortality Indicators 1991* (New Delhi: Office of the Registrar General, 1991); China, 1992: World Health Organization, *World Health Statistics Annual 1994* (Geneva: World Health Organization, 1994).

groups. Even African American women end up having a survival pattern for the higher ages similar to that of the much poorer Chinese, and decidedly lower survival rates than the even poorer Indians in Kerala. So it is not only the case that American blacks suffer from *relative* deprivation in terms of income per head vis-à-vis American whites, they also are *absolutely* more deprived than the low-income Indians in Kerala (for both women and men), and the Chinese (in the case of men), in terms of living to ripe old ages. The causal influences on these contrasts (that is, between living standards judged by income per head and those judged by the ability to survive to higher ages) include social arrangements and community relations such as

FIGURE 1.2: *Variations in Female Survival Rates by Region*

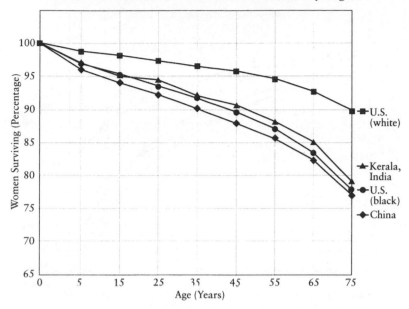

*Sources:* United States, 1991–1993: U.S. Department of Health and Human Services, *Health United States 1995* (Hyattsville, Md.: National Center for Health Statistics, 1996); Kerala, 1991: Government of India, *Sample Registration System: Fertility and Mortality Indicators 1991* (New Delhi: Office of the Registrar General, 1991); China, 1992: World Health Organization, *World Health Statistics Annual 1994* (Geneva: World Health Organization, 1994).

medical coverage, public health care, school education, law and order, prevalence of violence and so on.[10]

It is also worth noting that African Americans in the United States as a whole include a great many internal diversities. Indeed, if we look at the black male populations in particular U.S. cities (such as New York City, San Francisco, St. Louis or Washington, D.C.), we find that they are overtaken in terms of survival by people from China or Kerala at much earlier ages.[11] They are also overtaken by many other third world populations; for example, Bangladeshi men have a better chance of living to ages beyond forty years than African American men from the Harlem district of the prosperous city of New York.[12] All this is in spite of the fact that African Americans in the United States are very many times richer than the people of comparison groups in the third world.

## FREEDOM, CAPABILITY AND THE QUALITY OF LIFE

In the foregoing discussion, I have been concentrating on a very elementary freedom: the ability to survive rather than succumb to premature mortality. This is, obviously, a significant freedom, but there are many others that are also important. Indeed, the range of relevant freedoms can be very wide. The extensive coverage of freedoms is sometimes seen as a problem in getting an "operational" approach to development that is freedom-centered. I think this pessimism is ill-founded, but I shall postpone taking up this issue until chapter 3, when the foundational approaches to valuation will be considered together.

It should, however, be noted here that the freedom-centered perspective has a generic similarity to the common concern with "quality of life," which too concentrates on the way human life goes (perhaps even the choices one has) and not just on the resources or income that a person commands.[13] The focusing on the quality of life and on substantive freedoms, rather than just on income or wealth, may look like something of a departure from the established traditions of economics, and in a sense it is (especially if comparisons are made with some of the more austere income-centered analysis that can be found in contemporary economics). But in fact these broader approaches are in tune with lines of analysis that have been part of professional economics right from the beginning. The Aristotelian connections are obvious enough (Aristotle's focus on "flourishing" and "capacity" clearly relates to the quality of life and to substantive freedoms, as has been discussed by Martha Nussbaum).[14] There are strong connections also with Adam Smith's analysis of "necessities" and conditions of living.[15]

Indeed, the origin of economics was significantly motivated by the need to study the assessment of, and causal influences on, the opportunities that people have for good living. Aside from Aristotle's classic use of this idea, similar notions were much used in the early writings on national accounts and economic prosperity, pioneered by William Petty in the seventeenth century, and followed by Gregory

King, François Quesnay, Antoine-Laurent Lavoisier, Joseph-Louis Lagrange and others. While the national accounts devised by these leaders of economic analysis established the foundations of the modern concept of income, their attention was never confined to this one concept. They also saw the importance of income to be instrumental and circumstantially contingent.[16]

For example, while William Petty had pioneered both "the income method" and "the expenditure method" of estimating national income (the modern methods of estimation directly follow from these early attempts), he was explicitly concerned with "the Common Safety" and "each Man's particular Happiness." Petty's stated objective for undertaking his study related directly to the assessment of people's living conditions. He managed to combine scientific investigation with a significant dose of seventeenth-century politics ("to show" that "the King's subjects are not in so bad a condition as discontented Men would make them"). The impact of commodity consumption on the various functionings of people also received attention from others. For example, Joseph-Louis Lagrange, the great mathematician, was particularly innovative in converting commodities into their function-related characteristics: amounts of wheat and other grains into their nourishment equivalent, amounts of all meat into equivalent units of beef (in terms of their nutritional qualities) and amounts of all beverages into units of wine (remember, Lagrange was French).[17] In concentrating attention on resulting functionings rather than commodities only, we reclaim some of the old heritage of professional economics.

## MARKETS AND FREEDOMS

The role of the market mechanism is another subject that calls for some reclaiming of old heritage. The relation of the market mechanism to freedom and thus to economic development raises questions of at least two quite distinct types, which need to be clearly distinguished. First, a denial of opportunities of transaction, through arbitrary controls, can be a source of unfreedom in itself. People are then prevented from doing what can be taken to be—in the absence of compelling reasons to the contrary—something that is within their right to do. This point does not depend on the efficiency of the market mechanism or on any extensive analysis of the consequences of having or not having a market system; it turns simply on the importance of freedom of exchange and transaction without let or hindrance.

This argument for the market has to be distinguished from a second argument, which is very popular right now: that markets typically work to expand income and wealth and economic opportunities that people have. Arbitrary restrictions of the market mechanism can lead to a reduction of freedoms because of the consequential effects of the absence of markets. Deprivations can result when people are denied the economic opportunities and favorable consequences that markets offer and support.

These two arguments in favor of the market mechanism, both relevant to the perspective of substantive freedoms, have to be separated out. In the contemporary economic literature, it is the latter argument—based on the effective working and favorable results of the market mechanism—that receives virtually all the attention.[18] That argument is certainly strong, in general, and there is plenty of empirical evidence that the market system can be an engine of fast economic growth and expansion of living standards. Policies that restrict market opportunities can have the effect of restraining the expansion of substantive freedoms that would have been generated through the market system, mainly through overall economic prosperity. This is not to deny that markets can sometimes be counterproductive (as Adam Smith himself pointed out, in supporting in particular the need for control in the financial market).[19] There are serious arguments for regulation in some cases. But by and large the positive effects of the market system are now much more widely recognized than they were even a few decades ago.

However, this case for the use of markets is altogether different from the argument that people have the right to undertake transactions and exchange. Even if such rights are not accepted as being inviolable—and entirely independent of their consequences—it can still be argued that there is some social loss involved in denying people the right to interact economically with each other. If it so happens that the effects of such transactions are so bad for others that this prima facie presumption in favor of allowing people to transact as they like may be sensibly restricted, there is still something directly lost in imposing this restriction (even if it is outweighed by the alternative loss of the indirect effects of these transactions on *others*).

The discipline of economics has tended to move away from focusing on the value of freedoms to that of utilities, incomes and wealth. This narrowing of focus leads to an underappreciation of the full role of the market mechanism, even though economics as a profession can hardly be accused of not praising the markets enough. The issue, however, is not the amount of praise, but the reasons for it.

Take for example the well-known argument in economics that a competitive market mechanism can achieve a type of efficiency that a centralized system cannot plausibly achieve both because of the economy of information (each person acting in the market does not have to know very much) and the compatibility of incentives (each person's canny actions can merge nicely with those of others). Consider now, contrary to what is generally assumed, a case in which the same economic result is brought about by a fully centralized system with all the decisions of everyone regarding production and allocation being made by a dictator. Would that have been just as good an achievement?

It is not hard to argue that something would be missing in such a scenario, to wit, the freedom of people to act as they like in deciding on where to work, what to produce, what to consume and so on. Even if in both the scenarios (involving, respectively, free choice and compliance to dictatorial order) a person produces the same commodities in the same way and ends up with the same income and buys the same goods, she may still have very good reason to prefer the scenario of free choice over that of submission to order. There is a distinction between "culmination outcomes" (that is, only final outcomes without taking any note of the process of getting there, including the exercise of freedom) and "comprehensive outcomes" (taking note of the processes through which the culmination outcomes come about)—a distinction the central relevance of which I have tried to analyze more fully elsewhere.[20] The merit of the market system does not lie only in its capacity to generate more efficient culmination outcomes.

The shift in the focus of attention of pro-market economics from freedom to utility has been achieved at some cost: the neglect of the central value of freedom itself. John Hicks, one of the leading economists of this century, who himself was far more utility-oriented than freedom-oriented, did put the issue with admirable clarity in a passage on this subject:

> The liberal, or non-interference, principles of the classical (Smithian or Ricardian) economists were not, in the first place, economic principles; they were an application to economics of principles that were thought to apply to a much wider field. The contention that economic freedom made for economic efficiency was no more than a secondary support. . . . What I do question is whether we are justified in forgetting, as completely as most of us have done, the other side of the argument.[21]

This point may look somewhat esoteric in the context of economic development in view of the priority that the development literature tends to give to generating high incomes, a bigger basket of consumer goods and other culmination results. But it is far from esoteric. One of the biggest changes in the process of development in many economies involves the replacement of bonded labor and forced work, which characterize parts of many traditional agricultures, with a system of free labor contract and unrestrained physical movement. A freedom-based perspective on development picks up this issue immediately in a way that an evaluative system that focuses only on culmination outcomes may not.

The point can be illustrated with the debates surrounding the nature of slave labor in the southern United States before its abolition. The classic study on this subject by Robert Fogel and Stanley Engerman (*Time on the Cross: The Economics of American Negro Slavery*) includes a remarkable finding about the relatively high "pecuniary incomes" of the slaves. (Controversies on some issues covered in this book did not seriously undermine this finding.) The commodity baskets of consumption of slaves compared favorably— certainly not unfavorably—with the incomes of free agricultural laborers. And the slaves' life expectancy too was, relatively speaking, not especially low—"nearly identical with the life expectation of countries as advanced as France and Holland," and "much longer

[than] life expectations [of] free urban industrial workers in both the United States and Europe."[22] And yet slaves did run away, and there were excellent reasons for presuming that the interest of the slaves was not well served by the system of slavery. In fact, even the attempts, after the abolition of slavery, to get the slaves back, to make them work like slaves (particularly in the form of "gang work"), but at high wages, were not successful.

> After the slaves were freed many planters attempted to reconstruct their work gangs on the basis of wage payments. But such attempts generally foundered, despite the fact that the wages offered to freedmen exceeded the incomes they had received as slaves by more than 100 percent. Even at this premium planters found it impossible to maintain the gang system once they were deprived of the right to apply force.[23]

The importance of freedom of employment and that in working practice is crucial to understanding the valuations involved.[24]

In fact, Karl Marx's favorable remarks on capitalism as against the unfreedom of precapitalist labor arrangements related exactly to this question, which also produced Marx's characterization of the American Civil War as "the one great event of contemporary history."[25] Indeed, this issue of market-based freedom is quite central to the analysis of bonded labor—common in many developing countries—and the transition to free-contract labor arrangements. This, in fact, is one of the cases in which Marxian analysis has tended to have an affinity with libertarian concentration on freedom as opposed to utility.

For example, in his major study of transition from bonded labor to wage labor in India, V. K. Ramachandran provides an illuminating picture of the empirical importance of this question in the contemporary agrarian situation in southern India:

> Marx distinguishes between (to use the term used by Jon Elster) the *formal freedom* of the worker under capitalism and the *real unfreedom* of workers in pre-capitalist systems: "the freedom of workers to change employers makes him free in a way not found in earlier modes of production." The study of

the development of wage labour in agriculture is important from another perspective as well. The extension of the freedom of workers in a society to sell their labour power is an enhancement of their positive freedom, which is, in turn, an important measure of how well that society is doing.[26]

The linked presence of labor bondage with indebtedness yields a particularly tenacious form of unfreedom in many precapitalist agricultures.[27] Seeing development as freedom permits a direct approach to this issue that is not parasitic on having to show that labor markets also raise productivity of agriculture—a serious issue on its own but quite different from the question of freedom of contract and employment.

Some of the debates surrounding the terrible issue of child labor also relate to this question of freedom of choice. The worst violations of the norm against child labor come typically from the virtual slavery of children in disadvantaged families and from their being forced into exploitative employment (as opposed to being free and possibly going to school).[28] This direct issue of freedom is an integral part of this vexed question.

## VALUES AND THE PROCESS OF VALUATION

I return now to *evaluation*. Since our freedoms are diverse, there is room for explicit valuation in determining the relative weights of different types of freedoms in assessing individual advantages and social progress. Valuations are, of course, involved in all such approaches (including utilitarianism, libertarianism, and other approaches, to be discussed in chapter 3), even though they are often made implicitly. Those who prefer a mechanical index, without the need to be explicit about what values are being used and why, have a tendency to grumble that the freedom-based approach requires that valuations be explicitly made. Such complaints have frequently been aired. But explicitness, I shall argue, is an important asset for a valuational exercise, especially for it to be open to public scrutiny and criticism. Indeed, one of the strongest arguments in favor of political freedom lies precisely in the opportunity it gives citizens to discuss and debate—and to participate in the selection of—values in the choice of priorities (to be discussed in chapters 6 through 11).

Individual freedom is quintessentially a social product, and there is a two-way relation between (1) social arrangements to expand individual freedoms and (2) the use of individual freedoms not only to improve the respective lives but also to make the social arrangements more appropriate and effective. Also, individual conceptions of justice and propriety, which influence the specific uses that individuals make of their freedoms, depend on social associations—particularly on the interactive formation of public perceptions and on collaborative comprehension of problems and remedies. The analysis and assessment of public policies have to be sensitive to these diverse connections.

## TRADITION, CULTURE AND DEMOCRACY

The issue of participation is also central to some of the foundational questions that have plagued the force and reach of development theory. For example, it has been argued by some that economic development as we know it may actually be harmful for a nation, since it may lead to the elimination of its traditions and cultural heritage.[29] Objections of this kind are often quickly dismissed on the ground that it is better to be rich and happy than to be impoverished and traditional. This may be a persuasive slogan, but it is scarcely an adequate response to the critique under discussion. Nor does it reflect a serious engagement with the critical valuational issue that is being raised by development skeptics.

The more serious issue, rather, concerns the source of authority and legitimacy. There is an inescapable valuational problem involved in deciding what to choose if and when it turns out that some parts of tradition cannot be maintained along with economic or social changes that may be needed for other reasons. It is a choice that the people involved have to face and assess. The choice is neither closed (as many development apologists seem to suggest), nor is it one for the elite "guardians" of tradition to settle (as many development skeptics seem to presume). If a traditional way of life has to be sacrificed to escape grinding poverty or minuscule longevity (as many traditional societies have had for thousands of years), then it is the people directly involved who must have the opportunity to participate in deciding what should be chosen. The real conflict is between

1)  the basic value that the people must be allowed to decide freely what traditions they wish or not wish to follow; and

2)  the insistence that established traditions be followed (no matter what), or, alternatively, people must obey the decisions by religious or secular authorities who enforce traditions—real or imagined.

The force of the former precept lies in the basic importance of human freedom, and once that is accepted there are strong implications on what can or cannot be done in the name of tradition. The approach of "development as freedom" emphasizes this precept.

Indeed, in the freedom-oriented perspective the liberty of all to participate in deciding what traditions to observe cannot be ruled out by the national or local "guardians"—neither by the ayatollahs (or other religious authorities), nor by political rulers (or governmental dictators), nor by cultural "experts" (domestic or foreign). The pointer to any real conflict between the preservation of tradition and the advantages of modernity calls for a participatory resolution, not for a unilateral rejection of modernity in favor of tradition by political rulers, or religious authorities, or anthropological admirers of the legacy of the past. The question is not only not closed, it must be wide open for people in the society to address and join in deciding. An attempt to choke off participatory freedom on grounds of traditional values (such as religious fundamentalism, or political custom, or the so-called Asian values) simply misses the issue of legitimacy and the need for the people affected to participate in deciding what they want and what they have reason to accept.

This basic recognition has remarkable reach and powerful implications. A pointer to tradition does not provide ground for any general suppression of media freedom, or of the rights of communication between one citizen and another. Even if the oddly distorted view of how authoritarian Confucius really was is accepted as being historically correct (a critique of that interpretation will be taken up in chapter 10), this still does not give anyone an adequate ground for practicing authoritarianism through censorship or political restriction, since the legitimacy of adhering today to the views enunciated in the sixth century B.C. has to be decided by those who live today.

Also, since participation requires knowledge and basic educational skills, denying the opportunity of schooling to any group—

say, female children—is immediately contrary to the basic conditions of participatory freedom. While these rights have often been disputed (one of the severest onslaughts coming recently from the leadership of the Taliban in Afghanistan), that elementary requirement cannot be escaped in a freedom-oriented perspective. The approach of development as freedom has far-reaching implications not only for the ultimate objectives of development, but also for processes and procedures that have to be respected.

## CONCLUDING REMARKS

Seeing development in terms of the substantive freedoms of people has far-reaching implications for our understanding of the process of development and also for the ways and means of promoting it. On the evaluative side, this involves the need to assess the requirements of development in terms of removing the unfreedoms from which the members of the society may suffer. The process of development, in this view, is not essentially different from the history of overcoming these unfreedoms. While this history is not by any means unrelated to the process of economic growth and accumulation of physical and human capital, its reach and coverage go much beyond these variables.

In focusing on freedoms in evaluating development, it is not being suggested that there is some unique and precise "criterion" of development in terms of which the different development experiences can always be compared and ranked. Given the heterogeneity of distinct components of freedom as well as the need to take note of different persons' diverse freedoms, there will often be arguments that go in contrary directions. The motivation underlying the approach of "development as freedom" is not so much to order all states—or all alternative scenarios—into one "complete ordering," but to draw attention to important aspects of the process of development, each of which deserves attention. Even after such attention is paid, there will no doubt remain differences in possible overall rankings, but their presence is not embarrassing to the purpose at hand.

What would be damaging would be the neglect—often to be seen in the development literature—of centrally relevant concerns because of a lack of interest in the freedoms of the people involved. An adequately broad view of development is sought in order to focus the evaluative scrutiny on things that really matter, and in particular to avoid the neglect of crucially important subjects. While it may be nice to think that considering the relevant variables will automatically take different people to exactly the same conclusions on how to rank alternative scenarios, the approach requires no such unanimity. Indeed, debates on such matters, which can lead to important political arguments, can be part of the process of democratic participation that characterizes development. There will be occasion, later on in this book, to examine the substantial issue of participation as a part of the process of development.

# CHAPTER 2

# THE ENDS AND THE MEANS
# OF DEVELOPMENT

▼

Let me start off with a distinction between two general attitudes to the process of development that can be found both in professional economic analysis and in public discussions and debates.[1] One view sees development as a "fierce" process, with much "blood, sweat and tears"—a world in which wisdom demands toughness. In particular, it demands calculated neglect of various concerns that are seen as "soft-headed" (even if the critics are often too polite to call them that). Depending on what the author's favorite poison is, the temptations to be *resisted* can include having social safety nets that protect the very poor, providing social services for the population at large, departing from rugged institutional guidelines in response to identified hardship, and favoring—"much too early"—political and civil rights and the "luxury" of democracy. These things, it is argued in this austere attitudinal mode, could be supported later on, when the development process has borne enough fruit: what is needed here and now is "toughness and discipline." The different theories that share this general outlook diverge from one another in pointing to distinct areas of softness that are particularly to be avoided, varying from financial softness to political relaxation, from plentiful social expenditures to complaisant poverty relief.

This hard-knocks attitude contrasts with an alternative outlook that sees development as essentially a "friendly" process. Depending on the particular version of this attitude, the congeniality of the process is seen as exemplified by such things as mutually beneficial exchanges (of which Adam Smith spoke eloquently), or by the working of social safety nets, or of political liberties, or of social development—or some combination or other of these supportive activities.

## CONSTITUTIVE AND INSTRUMENTAL ROLES OF FREEDOM

The approach of this book is much more compatible with the latter approach than with the former.[2] It is mainly an attempt to see development as a process of expanding the real freedoms that people enjoy. In this approach, expansion of freedom is viewed as both (1) the *primary end* and (2) the *principal means* of development. They can be called respectively the "constitutive role" and the "instrumental role" of freedom in development. The constitutive role of freedom relates to the importance of substantive freedom in enriching human life. The substantive freedoms include elementary capabilities like being able to avoid such deprivations as starvation, undernourishment, escapable morbidity and premature mortality, as well as the freedoms that are associated with being literate and numerate, enjoying political participation and uncensored speech and so on. In this constitutive perspective, development involves expansion of these and other basic freedoms. Development, in this view, is the process of expanding human freedoms, and the assessment of development has to be informed by this consideration.

Let me refer here to an example that was briefly discussed in the introduction (and which involves an often raised question in the development literature) in order to illustrate how the recognition of the "constitutive" role of freedom can alter developmental analysis. Within the narrower views of development (in terms of, say, GNP growth or industrialization) it is often asked whether the freedom of political participation and dissent is or is not "conducive to development." In the light of the foundational view of development as freedom, this question would seem to be defectively formulated, since it misses the crucial understanding that political participation and dissent are *constitutive* parts of development itself. Even a very rich person who is prevented from speaking freely, or from participating in public debates and decisions, is *deprived* of something that she has reason to value. The process of development, when judged by the enhancement of human freedom, has to include the removal of this person's deprivation. Even if she had no immediate interest in exercising the freedom to speak or to participate, it would still be a deprivation of her freedoms if she were to be left with no choice on these matters. Development seen as enhancement of freedom cannot but address such deprivations. The relevance of the deprivation of basic political freedoms or civil rights, for an adequate understanding of development, does not have to be established through their indirect contribution to *other* features of development (such as the growth of GNP or the promotion of industrialization). These freedoms are part and parcel of enriching the process of development.

This fundamental point is distinct from the "instrumental" argument that these freedoms and rights may *also* be very effective in contributing to economic progress. That instrumental connection is important as well (and will be discussed particularly in chapters 5 and 6), but the significance of the instrumental role of political freedom as *means* to development does not in any way reduce the evaluative importance of freedom as an *end* of development.

The *intrinsic* importance of human freedom as the preeminent objective of development has to be distinguished from the *instrumental* effectiveness of freedom of different kinds to promote human freedom. Since the focus of the last chapter was mainly on the intrinsic importance of freedom, I shall now concentrate more on the effectiveness of freedom as *means*—not just as end. The instrumental role of freedom concerns the way different kinds of rights, opportunities, and entitlements contribute to the expansion of human freedom in general, and thus to promoting development. This relates not merely to the obvious connection that expansion of freedom of each kind must contribute to development since development itself can be seen as a process of enlargement of human freedom in general. There is much more in the instrumental connection than this constitutive linkage. The effectiveness of freedom as an instrument lies in the fact that different kinds of freedom interrelate with one another, and freedom of one type may greatly help in advancing freedom of other types. The two roles are thus linked by empirical connections, relating freedom of one kind to freedom of other kinds.

## INSTRUMENTAL FREEDOMS

In presenting empirical studies in this work, I shall have the occasion to discuss a number of instrumental freedoms that contribute, directly or indirectly, to the overall freedom people have to live the way they would like to live. The diversities of the instruments involved are quite extensive. However, it may be convenient to identify five distinct types of freedom that may be particularly worth emphasizing in this instrumental perspective. This is by no means an exhaustive list, but it may help to focus on some particular policy issues that demand special attention at this time.

In particular, I shall consider the following types of instrumental freedoms: (1) *political freedoms*, (2) *economic facilities*, (3) *social opportunities*, (4) *transparency guarantees* and (5) *protective security*. These instrumental freedoms tend to contribute to the general capability of a person to live more freely, but they also serve to complement one another. While development analysis must, on the one hand, be concerned with the objectives and aims that make these instrumental freedoms consequentially important, it must also take note of the empirical linkages that tie the distinct types of freedom *together*, strengthening their joint importance. Indeed, these connections are central to a fuller understanding of the instrumental role of freedom. The claim that freedom is not only the primary object of development but also its principal means relates particularly to these linkages.

Let me comment a little on each of these instrumental freedoms. *Political freedoms,* broadly conceived (including what are called civil rights), refer to the opportunities that people have to determine who should govern and on what principles, and also include the possibility to scrutinize and criticize authorities, to have freedom of political expression and an uncensored press, to enjoy the freedom to choose between different political parties, and so on. They include the political entitlements associated with democracies in the broadest sense (encompassing opportunities of political dialogue, dissent and critique as well as voting rights and participatory selection of legislators and executives).

*Economic facilities* refer to the opportunities that individuals respectively enjoy to utilize economic resources for the purpose of consumption, or production, or exchange. The economic entitlements that a person has will depend on the resources owned or available for use as well as on conditions of exchange, such as relative prices and the working of the markets. Insofar as the process of economic development increases the income and wealth of a country, they are reflected in corresponding enhancement of economic entitlements of the population. It should be obvious that in the relation between national income and wealth, on the one hand, and the economic entitlements of individuals (or families), on the other, distributional considerations are important, in addition to aggregative ones. How the additional incomes generated are distributed will clearly make a difference.

The availability and access to finance can be a crucial influence on the economic entitlements that economic agents are practically able to secure. This applies all the way from large enterprises (in which hundreds of thousands of people may work) to tiny establishments that are run on micro credit. A credit crunch, for example, can severely affect the economic entitlements that rely on such credit.

*Social opportunities* refer to the arrangements that society makes for education, health care and so on, which influence the individual's substantive freedom to live better. These facilities are important not only for the conduct of private lives (such as living a healthy life and avoiding preventable morbidity and premature mortality), but also for more effective participation in economic and political activities. For example, illiteracy can be a major barrier to participation in economic activities that require production according to specification or demand strict quality control (as globalized trade increasingly does). Similarly, political participation may be hindered by the inability to read newspapers or to communicate in writing with others involved in political activities.

I turn now to the fourth category. In social interactions, individuals deal with one another on the basis of some presumption of what they are being offered and what they can expect to get. In this sense, the society operates on some basic presumption of trust. *Transparency guarantees* deal with the need for openness that people can expect: the freedom to deal with one another under guarantees of disclosure and lucidity. When that trust is seriously violated, the lives of many people—both direct parties and third parties—may be adversely affected by the lack of openness. Transparency guarantees (including the right to disclosure) can thus be an important category of instrumental freedom. These guarantees have a clear instrumental role in preventing corruption, financial irresponsibility and underhand dealings.

Finally, no matter how well an economic system operates, some people can be typically on the verge of vulnerability and can actually succumb to great deprivation as a result of material changes that adversely affect their lives. *Protective security* is needed to provide a social safety net for preventing the affected population from being reduced to abject misery, and in some cases even starvation and death. The domain of protective security includes *fixed* institutional arrangements such as unemployment benefits and statutory income supplements to the indigent as well as ad hoc arrangements such as famine relief or emergency public employment to generate income for destitutes.

## INTERCONNECTIONS AND COMPLEMENTARITY

These instrumental freedoms directly enhance the capabilities of people, but they also supplement one another, and can furthermore reinforce one another. These interlinkages are particularly important to seize in considering development policies.

The fact that the entitlement to economic transactions tends to be typically a great engine of economic growth has been widely accepted. But many other connections remain underrecognized, and they have to be seized more fully in policy analysis. Economic growth can help not only in raising private incomes but also in making it possible for the state to finance social insurance and active public intervention. Thus the contribution of economic growth has to be judged not merely by the increase in private incomes, but also by the expansion of social services (including, in many cases, social safety nets) that economic growth may make possible.[3]

Similarly, the creation of social opportunities, through such services as public education, health care, and the development of a free and energetic press, can contribute both to economic development and to significant reductions in mortality rates. Reduction of mortality rates, in turn, can help to reduce birth rates, reinforcing the influence of basic education—especially female literacy and schooling—on fertility behavior.

The pioneering example of enhancing economic growth through social opportunity, especially in basic education, is of course Japan. It is sometimes forgotten that Japan had a higher rate of literacy than Europe had even at the time of the Meiji restoration in the mid-nineteenth century, when industrialization had not yet occurred there but had gone on for many decades in Europe. Japan's economic development was clearly much helped by the human resource development related to the social opportunities that were generated. The so-called East Asian miracle involving other countries in East Asia was, to a great extent, based on similar causal connections.[4]

This approach goes against—and to a great extent undermines—the belief that has been so dominant in many policy circles that "human development" (as the process of expanding education, health care and other conditions of human life is often called) is really a kind of luxury that only richer countries can afford. Perhaps the most important impact of the type of success that the East Asian economies, beginning with Japan, have had is the total undermining of that implicit prejudice. These economies went comparatively early for massive expansion of education, and later also of health care, and this they did, in many cases, *before* they broke the restraints of general poverty. And they have reaped as they have sown. Indeed, as Hiromitsu Ishi has pointed out, the priority to human resource development applies particularly to the early history of Japanese economic development, beginning with the Meiji era (1868–1911), and that focus has not intensified with economic affluence as Japan has grown richer and much more opulent.[5]

## DIFFERENT ASPECTS OF CHINA-INDIA CONTRAST

The central role of individual freedoms in the process of development makes it particularly important to examine their determinants. Substantial attention has to be paid to the social influences, including state actions, that help to determine the nature and reach of individual freedoms. Social arrangements may be decisively important in securing and expanding the freedom of the individual. Individual freedoms are influenced, on one side, by the social safeguarding of liberties, tolerance, and the possibility of exchange and transactions. They are also influenced, on the other side, by substantive public support in the provision of those facilities (such as basic health care or essential education) that are crucial for the formation and use of human capabilities. There is need to pay attention to both types of determinants of individual freedoms.

The contrast between India and China has some illustrative importance in this context. The governments of both China and India have been making efforts for some time now (China from 1979 and India from 1991) to move toward a more open, internationally active, market-oriented economy. While Indian efforts have slowly met with some success, the kind of massive results that China has seen has failed to occur in India. An important factor in this contrast lies in the fact that from the standpoint of social preparedness, China is a great deal ahead of India in being able to make use of the market economy.[6] While pre-reform China was deeply skeptical of markets, it was not skeptical of basic education and widely shared health care. When China turned to marketization in 1979, it already had a highly literate people, especially the young, with good schooling facilities across the bulk of the country. In this respect, China was not very far from the basic educational situation in South Korea or Taiwan, where too an educated population had played a major role in seizing the economic opportunities offered by a supportive market system. In contrast, India had a half-illiterate adult population when it turned to marketization in 1991, and the situation is not much improved today.

The health conditions in China were also much better than in India because of the social commitment of the pre-reform regime to health care as well as education. Oddly enough, that commitment, while totally unrelated to its helpful role in market-oriented economic growth, created social opportunities that could be brought into dynamic use after the country moved toward marketization. The social backwardness of India, with its elitist concentration on higher education and massive negligence of school education, and its substantial neglect of basic health care, left that country poorly prepared for a widely shared economic expansion. The contrast between India and China does, of course, have many other aspects (including the differences in their respective political systems, and the much greater variation *within* India of social opportunities such as literacy and health care); these issues will be addressed later. But the relevance of the radically different levels of social preparedness in China and India for widespread market-oriented development is worth noting even at this preliminary stage of the analysis.

It must, however, also be noted that there are real handicaps that China experiences compared with India because it lacks democratic freedoms. This is particularly so when it comes to flexibility of economic policy and the responsiveness of public action to social crisis and unforeseen disasters. The most prominent contrast lies perhaps in the fact that China has had what is almost certainly the largest recorded famine in history (when thirty million people died in the famine that followed the failure of the Great Leap Forward in 1958–1961), whereas India has not had a famine since independence in 1947. When things go well, the protective power of democracy may be less missed, but dangers can lie round the corner (as indeed the recent experiences of some of the East Asian and Southeast Asian economies bring out). This issue too will have to be discussed more fully later on in this book.

There are very many different interconnections between distinct instrumental freedoms. Their respective roles and their specific influences on one another are important aspects of the process of development. In the chapters to follow, there will be opportunities to discuss a number of these interconnections and their extensive reach. However, to illustrate how these interconnections work, let me here go a little into the diverse influences on longevity and life expectancy at birth—capabilities that people value almost universally.

## GROWTH-MEDIATED SOCIAL ARRANGEMENTS

The impact of social arrangements on the freedom to survive can be very strong and may be influenced by quite different instrumental connections. The point is sometimes made that this is not a separate consideration from economic growth (in the form of raising the level of per capita income) since there is a close relation between income per head and longevity. Indeed, it has been argued that it is a mistake to worry about the discord between income achievements and survival chances, since—in general—the statistical connection between them is observed to be quite close. As a point about intercountry statistical connections, seen in isolation, this is indeed correct, but this statistical relation needs further scrutiny before it can be seen as a convincing ground for dismissing the relevance of social arrangements (going beyond income-based opulence).

It is interesting, in this context, to refer to some statistical analyses that have recently been presented by Sudhir Anand and Martin Ravallion.[7] On the basis of intercountry comparisons, they find that life expectancy does indeed have a significantly positive correlation with GNP per head, but that this relationship works mainly through the impact of GNP on (1) the incomes specifically of the poor and (2) public expenditure particularly in health care. In fact, once these two variables are included on their own in the statistical exercise, little *extra* explanation can be obtained from including GNP per head as an additional causal influence. Indeed, with poverty and public expenditure on health as explanatory variables on their own, the connection between GNP per head and life expectancy appears (in the Anand-Ravallion analysis) to vanish altogether.

It is important to emphasize that this result, if vindicated by other empirical studies as well, would not show that life expectancy is not enhanced by the growth of GNP per head, but it would indicate that the connection tends to work particularly *through* public expenditure on health care, and *through* the success of poverty removal. The basic point is that the impact of economic growth depends much on how the *fruits* of economic growth are used. This also helps to explain why some economies, such as South Korea and Taiwan, have been able to raise life expectancy so rapidly through economic growth.

The achievements of the East Asian economies have come under critical scrutiny—and some fire—in recent years, partly because of the nature and severity of what is called "the Asian economic crisis." That crisis is indeed serious, and points to particular failures of economies that were earlier seen—mistakenly—as being comprehensively successful. I shall have the opportunity of considering the special problems and specific failures involved in the Asian economic crisis (particularly in chapters 6 and 7). But it would be an error not to see the great achievements of the East Asian and Southeast Asian economies over several decades, which have transformed the lives and longevities of people in the countries involved. The problems that these countries now face (and have potentially harbored for a long time), which demand attention (including the overall need for political freedoms and open participation as well as for protective security), should not induce us to ignore these countries' achievements in the fields in which they have done remarkably well.

For a variety of historical reasons, including a focus on basic education and basic health care, and early completion of effective land reforms, widespread economic participation was easier to achieve in many of the East Asian and Southeast Asian economies in a way it has not been possible in, say, Brazil or India or Pakistan, where the creation of social opportunities has been much slower and that slowness has acted as a barrier to economic development.[8] The expansion of social opportunities has served to facilitate high-employment economic development and has also created favorable circumstances for reduction of mortality rates and for expansion of life expectancy. The contrast is sharp with some other high-growth countries—such as Brazil—which have had almost comparable growth of GNP per head, but also have quite a history of severe social inequality, unemployment and neglect of public health care. The longevity achievements of these other high-growth economies have moved more slowly.

There are two interesting—and interrelated—contrasts here:

1) for *high economic growth economies,* the contrast between:
    1.1) those *with* great success in raising the length and quality of life (such as South Korea and Taiwan), and
    1.2) those *without* comparable success in these other fields (such as Brazil);
2) for *economies with high success in raising the length and quality of life,* the contrast between:
    2.1) those *with* great success in high economic growth (such as South Korea and Taiwan), and
    2.2) those *without* much success in achieving high economic growth (such as Sri Lanka, *pre-reform* China, the Indian state of Kerala).

I have already commented on the first contrast (between, say, South Korea and Brazil), but the second contrast too deserves policy attention. In our book *Hunger and Public Action,* Jean Drèze and I have distinguished between two types of success in the rapid reduction of mortality, which we called respectively "growth-mediated" and "support-led" processes.[9] The former process works *through* fast economic growth, and its success depends on the growth process being wide-based and economically broad (strong employment orientation has much to do with this), and also on utilization of the enhanced economic prosperity to expand the relevant social services, including health care, education and social security. In contrast with the growth-mediated mechanism, the support-led process does not operate through fast economic growth, but works through a program of skillful social support of health care, education and other relevant social arrangements. This process is well exemplified by the experiences of economies such as Sri Lanka, pre-reform China, Costa Rica or Kerala, which have had very rapid reductions in mortality rates and enhancement of living conditions, without much economic growth.

## PUBLIC PROVISIONING, LOW INCOMES AND RELATIVE COSTS

The support-led process does not wait for dramatic increases in per capita levels of real income, and it works through priority being given to providing social services (particularly health care and basic education) that reduce mortality and enhance the quality of life. Some examples of this relationship are shown in figure 2.1, which presents the GNP per head and life expectancy at birth of six countries (China, Sri Lanka, Namibia, Brazil, South Africa and Gabon) and one sizable state (Kerala) with thirty million people, within a country (India).[10] Despite their very low levels of income, the people of Kerala, or China, or Sri Lanka enjoy enormously higher levels of life expectancy than do much richer populations of Brazil, South Africa and Namibia, not to mention Gabon. Even the *direction* of the inequality points opposite when we compare Kerala, China and Sri Lanka, on one side, with Brazil, South Africa, Namibia and Gabon, on the other. Since life expectancy variations relate to a variety of social opportunities that are central to development (including epidemiological policies, health care, educational facilities and so on), an

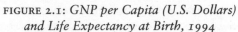

FIGURE 2.1: *GNP per Capita (U.S. Dollars)
and Life Expectancy at Birth, 1994*

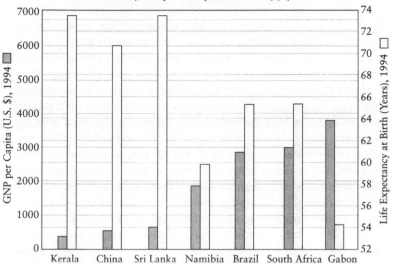

*Sources:* Country data, 1994, World Bank, *World Development Report 1996;* Kerala data, Life expectancy, 1989–1993, Sample Registration System cited in Government of India (1997), Department of Education, *Women in India: A Statistical Profile;* Domestic product per capita, 1992–1993, Government of India (1997), Ministry of Finance, *Economic Survey 1996–1997.*

income-centered view is in serious need of supplementation, in order to have a fuller understanding of the process of development.[11] These contrasts are of considerable policy relevance, and bring out the importance of the support-led process.[12]

Surprise may well be expressed about the possibility of financing support-led processes in poor countries, since resources are surely needed to expand public services, including health care and education. In fact, the need for resources is frequently presented as an argument for *postponing* socially important investments until a country is already richer. Where (as the famous rhetorical question goes) are the poor countries going to find the means for "supporting" these services? This is indeed a good question, but it also has a good answer, which lies very considerably in the economics of relative costs. The viability of this support-led process is dependent on the fact that the relevant social services (such as health care and basic education) are very *labor intensive,* and thus are relatively inexpensive in poor— and low-wage—economies. A poor economy may *have* less money to spend on health care and education, but it also *needs* less money to spend to provide the same services, which would cost much more in the richer countries. Relative prices and costs are important parameters in determining what a country can afford. Given an appropriate social commitment, the need to take note of the variability of relative costs is particularly important for social services in health and education.[13]

It is obvious that the growth-mediated process has an advantage over its support-led alternative; it may, ultimately, offer more, since there are more deprivations—*other than* premature mortality, or high morbidity, or illiteracy—that are very directly connected with the lowness of incomes (such as being inadequately clothed and sheltered). It is clearly better to have high income *as well as* high longevity (and other standard indicators of quality of life), rather than only the latter. This is a point worth emphasizing, since there is some danger of being "overconvinced" by the statistics of life expectancy and other such basic indicators of quality of life.

For example, the fact that the Indian state of Kerala has achieved impressively high life expectancy, low fertility, high literacy and so on despite its low income level per head is certainly an achievement worth celebrating and learning from. And yet the question remains as to why Kerala has not been able to build on its successes in human development to raise its income levels as well, which would have made its success more complete; it can scarcely serve as a "model" case, as some have tried to claim. From a policy point of view, this requires a critical scrutiny of Kerala's economic policies regarding incentives and investments ("economic facilities," in general), despite its unusual success in raising life expectancy and the quality of life.[14] Support-led success does, in this sense, remain shorter in achievement than growth-mediated success, where the increase in economic opulence and the enhancement of quality of life tend to move together.

On the other hand, the success of the support-led process as a route does indicate that a country need not wait until it is much richer (through what may be a long period of economic growth) before embarking on rapid expansion of basic education and health care. The quality of life can be vastly raised, despite low incomes, through an adequate program of social services. The fact that education and health care are also productive in raising economic growth adds to the argument for putting major emphasis on these social arrangements in poor economies, *without* having to wait for "getting rich" *first*.[15] The support-led process is a recipe for rapid achievement of higher quality of life, and this has great policy importance, but there remains an excellent case for moving on from there to broader achievements that include economic growth as well as the raising of the standard features of quality of life.

## MORTALITY REDUCTION IN TWENTIETH-CENTURY BRITAIN

In this context, it is also instructive to reexamine the time pattern of mortality reduction and of the increase in life expectancy in the advanced industrial economies. The role of public provision of health care and nutrition, and generally of social arrangements, in mortality reduction in Europe and the United States over the last few centuries has been well analyzed by Robert Fogel, Samuel Preston and others.[16] The time pattern of the expansion of life expectancy in this century itself is of particular interest, bearing in mind that at the turn of the last century, even Britain—then the leading capitalist market economy—still had a life expectancy at birth that was lower than the average life expectancy for low-income countries today. However, longevity in Britain did rise rapidly over the century, influenced partly by strategies of social programs, and the time pattern of this increase is of some interest.

The expansion of programs of support for nutrition, health care and so on in Britain was not uniformly fast over the decades. There were two periods of remarkably fast expansion of support-oriented policies in this century; they occurred during the two world wars. Each war situation produced much greater sharing of means of survival, including sharing of health care and the limited food supply (through rationing and subsidized nutrition). During the First World War, there were remarkable developments in social attitudes about "sharing" and public policies aimed at achieving that sharing, as has

FIGURE 2.2: *Improvements in Life Expectancy in England and Wales, 1901–1960*

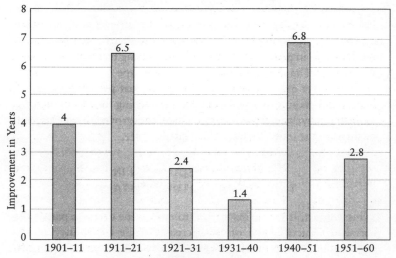

*Sources:* S. Preston, N. Keyfitz, and R. Schoen, *Causes of Death: Life Tables for National Population* (New York: Seminar Press, 1992).

been well analyzed by Jay Winter.[17] During the Second World War also, unusually supportive and shared social arrangements developed, related to the psychology of sharing in beleaguered Britain, which made these radical public arrangements for the distribution of food and health care acceptable and effective.[18] Even the National Health Service was born during those war years.

Did this make any real difference to health and survival? Was there, in fact, a correspondingly faster mortality reduction in these periods of support-led policies in Britain? It is, in fact, confirmed by detailed nutritional studies that during the Second World War, even though the per capita availability of food fell significantly in Britain, cases of undernourishment also *declined* sharply, and extreme undernourishment almost entirely disappeared.[19] Mortality rates also went down sharply (except of course for war mortality itself). A similar thing had happened during the First World War.[20]

Indeed, it is remarkable that interdecade comparisons, based on decadal censuses, show that by a very wide margin the most speedy expansion of life expectancy occurred precisely during those two "war decades" (as shown in figure 2.2, which presents the increase in life expectancy in years during each of the first six decades of this century).[21] While in the other decades life expectancy rose rather moderately (between one year and four years), in each of the two war decades it jumped up by nearly seven years.

We must also ask whether the much sharper increase in life expectancy during the war decades can be explained alternatively, by faster economic growth over those decades. The answer seems to be in the negative. In fact, the decades of fast expansion of life expectancy happened to be periods of *slow* growth of gross domestic product per head, as shown in figure 2.3. It is, of course, possible to hypothesize that the GDP growth had its effects on life expectancy with a time lag of a decade, and while this is not contradicted by figure 2.3 itself, it does not stand up much to other scrutiny, including the analysis of possible causal processes. A much more plausible explanation of the rapid increase in British life expectancy is provided by the changes in the extent of social sharing during the war decades, and the sharp increases in public support for social services (including nutritional support and health care) that went with this. Much light is thrown on these contrasts by studies of health and other living conditions of the population through the war periods, and their connection with social attitudes and public arrangements.[22]

## DEMOCRACY AND POLITICAL INCENTIVES

Illustrations of linkages can come from a great many other connections. Let me briefly comment on one more: that between political liberty and civil rights, on the one hand, and the freedom to avoid economic disasters, on the other. The most elementary vindication of this connection can be seen in the fact, on which I commented earlier (in chapter 1, and indirectly—in discussing the China-India contrast—in the present chapter) that famines do not occur in democracies. Indeed, no substantial famine has ever occurred in a democratic country—no matter how poor.[23] This is because famines are extremely easy to prevent if the government tries to prevent them, and a government in a multiparty democracy with elections and free

FIGURE 2.3: *Growth of GDP (U.K.) and Decadal Increases in Life Expectancy at Birth (England and Wales), 1901–1960*

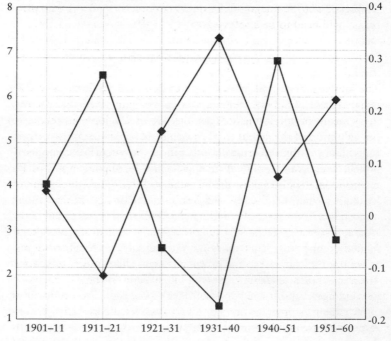

■─Decadal Improvement in Life Expectancy, England and Wales (Left Scale)

◆─Percentage Decadal Growth of GDP per Capita in U.K., 1901–1960 (Right Scale)

*Sources:* A. Madison, *Phases of Capitalist Development* (New York: Oxford University Press, 1982); S. Preston et al., *Causes of Death* (New York: Seminar Press, 1972).

media has strong political incentives to undertake famine prevention. This would indicate that political freedom in the form of democratic arrangements helps to safeguard economic freedom (especially freedom from extreme starvation) and the freedom to survive (against famine mortality).

The security provided by democracy may not be much missed when a country is lucky enough to be facing no serious calamity, when everything is running along smoothly. But the danger of insecurity, arising from changes in the economic or other circumstances or from uncorrected mistakes of policy, can lurk behind what looks like a healthy state. When this connection is discussed more fully (in chapters 6 and 7), the political aspects of the recent "Asian economic crisis" will need to be addressed.

## A CONCLUDING REMARK

The analysis presented in this chapter develops the basic idea that enhancement of human freedom is both the main object and the primary means of development. The objective of development relates to the valuation of the actual freedoms enjoyed by the people involved. Individual capabilities crucially depend on, among other things, economic, social, and political arrangements. In making appropriate institutional arrangements, the instrumental roles of distinct types of freedom have to be considered, going well beyond the foundational importance of the overall freedom of individuals.

The instrumental roles of freedom include several distinct but interrelated components, such as economic facilities, political freedoms, social opportunities, transparency guarantees and protective security. These instrumental rights, opportunities and entitlements have strong interlinkages, which can go in different directions. The process of development is crucially influenced by these interconnections. Corresponding to multiple interconnected freedoms, there is a need to develop and support a plurality of institutions, including democratic systems, legal mechanisms, market structures, educational and health provisions, media and other communication facilities and so on. The institutions can incorporate private initiatives as well as public arrangements and also more mixed structures, such as nongovernmental organizations and cooperative entities.

The ends and means of development call for placing the perspective of freedom at the center of the stage. The people have to be seen, in this perspective, as being actively involved—given the opportunity—in shaping their own destiny, and not just as passive recipients of the fruits of cunning development programs. The state and the society have extensive roles in strengthening and safeguarding human capabilities. This is a supporting role, rather than one of ready-made delivery. The freedom-centered perspective on the ends and the means of development has some claim to our attention.

# CHAPTER 3

# FREEDOM AND THE FOUNDATIONS OF JUSTICE

▼

Let me begin with a parable. Annapurna wants someone to clear up the garden, which has suffered from past neglect, and three unemployed laborers—Dinu, Bishanno and Rogini—all very much want the job. She can hire any one of them, but the work is indivisible and she cannot distribute it among the three. Annapurna would get much the same work done for much the same payment from any of them, but being a reflective person, she wonders who would be the right person to employ.

She gathers that while all of them are poor, Dinu is the poorest of the three; everyone agrees on that fact. This makes Annapurna rather inclined to hire him ("What can be more important," she asks herself, "than helping the poorest?").

However, she also gathers that Bishanno has recently been impoverished and is psychologically most depressed about his predicament. Dinu and Rogini are, in contrast, experienced in being poor and are used to it. Everyone agrees that Bishanno is the unhappiest of the three and would certainly gain more in happiness than the other two. This makes Annapurna rather favorable to the idea of giving the job to Bishanno ("Surely removing unhappiness has to be," she tells herself, "the first priority").

But Annapurna is also told that Rogini is debilitated from a chronic ailment—borne stoically—and could use the money to be earned to rid herself of that terrible disease. It is not denied that Rogini is less poor than the others (though certainly poor) and also not the unhappiest since she bears her deprivation rather cheerfully, used—as she has been—to being deprived all her life (coming from a poor family, and having been trained to reconcile herself to the general belief that, as a young woman, she must neither grumble nor entertain much ambition). Annapurna wonders whether, nevertheless, it might not be right to give the job to Rogini ("It would make the biggest difference," she surmises, "to the quality of life and freedom from illness").

Annapurna wonders what she really should do. She recognizes that if she knew only the fact that Dinu is the poorest (and knew nothing else), she would have definitely opted for giving the work to Dinu. She also reflects that had she known only the fact that Bishanno is the unhappiest and would get the most pleasure from the opportunity (and knew nothing else), she would have had excellent reasons to hire Bishanno. And she can also see that if she was apprised only of the fact that Rogini's debilitating ailment could be cured with the money she would earn (and knew nothing else), she would have had a simple and definitive reason for giving the job to her. But she knows all the three relevant facts, and has to choose among the three arguments, each of which has some pertinence.

There are a number of interesting issues of practical reason in this simple example, but the point I want to emphasize here is that the differences in the principles involved relate to the particular information that is taken to be decisive. If all the three facts are known, the decision rests on which information is given the most weight. The principles thus can best be seen in terms of their respective "informational bases." Dinu's income-egalitarian case focuses on income-poverty; Bishanno's classical utilitarian case concentrates on the metric of pleasure and happiness; Rogini's quality-of-life case centers on the kinds of life the three respectively can lead. The first two arguments are among the most discussed and most used in the economic and ethical literatures. I shall present some arguments for the third. But for the moment my intention is very modest: only to illustrate the critical importance of the informational bases of competing principles.

In the discussion that follows, I comment on both (1) the general question of the importance of the informational base for evaluative judgments and (2) the particular issues of the adequacy of the respective informational bases of some standard theories of social ethics and justice, in particular utilitarianism, libertarianism and Rawlsian theory of justice. While there is clearly much to be learned from the way the informational issue is dealt with in these major approaches in political philosophy, it is also argued that each of the informational bases respectively used—explicitly or implicity—by utilitarianism, libertarianism and Rawlsian justice has serious flaws, if substantive individual freedoms are taken to be important. This diagnosis motivates the discussion of an alternative approach to evaluation that focuses directly on freedom, seen in the form of individual capabilities to do things that a person has reason to value.

It is this last, constructive part of the analysis that is extensively utilized in the rest of the book. If the reader is not much interested in the critiques of other approaches (and the respective advantages and difficulties of utilitarianism, libertarianism or Rawlsian justice), there would be no particular problem in skipping these critical discussions and proceeding directly to the latter part of the chapter.

## INCLUDED AND EXCLUDED INFORMATION

Each evaluative approach can, to a great extent, be characterized by its informational basis: the information that is needed for making judgments using that approach and—no less important—the information that is "excluded" from a direct evaluative role in that approach.[1] Informational *exclusions* are important constituents of an evaluative approach. The excluded information is not permitted to have any direct influence on evaluative judgments, and while this is usually done in an implicit way, the character of the approach may be strongly influenced by insensitivity to the excluded information.

For example, utilitarian principles rest ultimately on utilities only, and even though much instrumental account may be taken of incentives, it is utility information that is seen, eventually, as the only proper basis for evaluation of states of affairs, or for the assessment of actions or rules. In utilitarianism's classical form, as developed particularly by Jeremy Bentham, utility is defined as pleasure, or happiness, or satisfaction, and everything thus turns on these mental achievements.[2] Such potentially momentous matters as individual freedom, the fulfillment or violation of recognized rights, aspects of quality of life not adequately reflected in the statistics of pleasure, cannot directly swing a normative evaluation in this utilitarian structure. They can have an indirect role only *through* their effects on utility numbers (that is, only to the extent that they may have an impact on mental satisfaction, pleasure or happiness). Furthermore, the aggregative framework of utilitarianism has no interest in—or sensitivity to—the actual *distribution* of utilities, since the concentration is entirely on the *total* utility of everyone taken together. All this produces a very limited informational base, and this pervasive insensitivity is a significant limitation of utilitarian ethics.[3]

In modern forms of utilitarianism, the content of "utility" is often seen differently: not as pleasure, satisfaction or happiness, but as the fulfillment of desire, or as some kind of representation of a person's choice behavior.[4] I shall consider these distinctions presently, but it is not hard to see that this redefinition of utility does not in itself eliminate the indifference to freedoms, rights and liberties that is a characteristic feature of utilitarianism in general.

Turning now to libertarianism, it has, in contrast with utilitarian theory, no direct interest either in happiness or in desire fulfillment, and its informational base consists entirely of liberties and rights of various kinds. Even without going into the exact formulas that are used by utilitarianism or by libertarianism respectively to characterize justice, it is clear from the mere contrast of their informational bases that they must take very different—and typically incompatible— views of justice.

In fact, the real "bite" of a theory of justice can, to a great extent, be understood from its informational base: what information is—or is not—taken to be directly relevant.[5] For example, classical utilitarianism tries to make use of the information of different persons' respective happiness or pleasures (seen in a comparative framework), whereas libertarianism demands compliance with certain rules of liberty and propriety, assessing the situation through information on this compliance. They go in different directions, largely driven by what information they respectively take as being central to judging the justice or acceptability of different social scenarios. The informational basis of normative theories in general, and of theories of justice in particular, is of decisive significance, and can be the crucial point of focus in many debates on practical policies (as will be seen in arguments to be taken up later).

In the next few pages, the informational bases of some distinguished approaches to justice will be examined, beginning with utilitarianism. The merits and limitations of each approach can, to a great extent, be understood by examining the reach and limits of its informational base. On the basis of the problems encountered in the different approaches that are commonly used in the context of evaluation and policy making, an alternative approach to justice will be briefly outlined. It concentrates on the informational base of individual freedoms (not utilities), but incorporates sensitivity to consequences which, I would argue, is an appreciable asset of the utilitarian perspective. I shall examine this "capability approach" to justice more fully later on in the present chapter and in the next one.

## UTILITY AS AN INFORMATIONAL BASE

The informational base of standard utilitarianism is the utility sum total in the states of affairs. In the classical, Benthamite form of utilitarianism, the "utility" of a person stands for some measure of his or her pleasure or happiness. The idea is to pay attention to each person's well-being, and in particular to see well-being as essentially a mental characteristic, viz., the pleasure or happiness generated. Interpersonal comparisons of happiness cannot, of course, be done very precisely, nor through standard scientific methods.[6] Nevertheless, most of us do not find it absurd (or "meaningless") to identify some people as being decidedly less happy and more miserable than others.

Utilitarianism has been the dominant ethical theory—and, inter alia, the most influential theory of justice—for much over a century. The traditional economics of welfare and of public policy was for a very long time dominated by this approach, initiated in its modern form by Jeremy Bentham, and pursued by such economists as John Stuart Mill, William Stanley Jevons, Henry Sidgwick, Francis Edgeworth, Alfred Marshall and A. C. Pigou.[7]

The requirements of utilitarian evaluation can be split into three distinct components. The first component is "consequentialism" (not a prepossessing word), and it stands for the claim that all choices (of actions, rules, institutions, and so on) must be judged by their consequences, that is, by the results they generate. This focus on the consequent state of affairs denies particularly the tendency of some normative theories to regard some principles to be right *irrespec-*

*tive* of their results. In fact, it goes further than demanding only consequence-sensitivity, since it rules out that anything other than consequences can ultimately matter. How much of a restriction is imposed by consequentialism has to be judged further, but it is worth mentioning here that this must partly depend on what is or is not included in the list of consequences (for example, whether an action performed can be seen as one of the "consequences" of that action, which—in an obvious sense—it clearly is).

The second component of utilitarianism is "welfarism," which restricts the judgments of state of affairs to the utilities in the respective states (paying no direct attention to such things as the fulfillment or violation of rights, duties, and so on). When welfarism is combined with consequentialism, we get the requirement that every choice must be judged by the respective utilities it generates. For example, any action is judged by the consequent state of affairs (because of consequentialism), and the consequent state of affairs is judged by utilities in that state (because of welfarism).

The third component is "sum-ranking," which requires that the utilities of different people be simply summed together to get their aggregate merit, without paying attention to the distribution of that total over the individuals (that is, the utility sum is to be maximized irrespective of the extent of inequality in the distribution of utilities). The three components together yield the classic utilitarian formula of judging every choice by the sum total of utilities generated through that choice.[8]

In this utilitarian view, *injustice* consists in aggregate loss of utility compared with what could have been achieved. An unjust society, in this view, is one in which people are significantly less happy, taken together, than they need be. The concentration on happiness or pleasure has been removed in some modern forms of utilitarianism. In one variation, utility is defined as desire fulfillment. In this view, what is relevant is the strength of the desire that is being fulfilled, and not the intensity of the happiness that is generated.

Since neither happiness nor desire is very easy to measure, utility is often defined in modern economic analysis as some numerical representation of a person's observable *choices*. There are some technical issues in representability, which need not detain us here. The basic formula is this: if a person would choose an alternative $x$ over another, $y$, then and only then that person has more utility from $x$ than from $y$. The "scaling" of utility has to follow this rule, among others, and in this framework it is not substantively different to affirm that a person has more utility from $x$ than from $y$ than to say that she would choose $x$ given the choice between the two.[9]

## MERITS OF THE UTILITARIAN APPROACH

The procedure of choice-based accounting has some general merits as well as demerits. In the context of utilitarian calculus, its major demerit is that it does not lead immediately to any way of making interpersonal comparisons, since it concentrates on each individual's choice seen separately. This is obviously inadequate for utilitarianism, since it cannot accommodate sum-ranking, which does require interpersonal comparability. As a matter of fact, the choice-based view of utility has been used mainly in the context of approaches that invoke welfarism and consequentialism only. It is a kind of utility-based approach without being utilitarianism proper.

While the merits of the utilitarian approach can be subjected to some debate, it does make insightful points, in particular:

1) the importance of taking account of the *results* of social arrangements in judging them (the case for consequence-sensitivity may be very plausible even when full consequentialism seems too extreme);

2) the need to pay attention to the *well-being* of the people involved when judging social arrangements and their results (the interest in people's well-being has obvious attractions, even if we disagree on the utility-centered mental-metric way of judging well-being).

To illustrate the relevance of results, consider the fact that many social arrangements are advocated because of the attractions of their constitutive features, without any note being taken of their consequential outcomes. Take property rights. Some have found it to be constitutive of individual independence and have gone on to ask that no restriction be placed on the ownership, inheritance and use of property, rejecting even the idea of taxing property or income. Others, on the opposite side of the political divide, have been repelled by the idea of inequalities of ownership—some having so much while others have so little—and they have gone on to demand the abolition of private property.

One can indeed entertain different views on the intrinsic attractions or repulsive features of private property. The consequentialist approach suggests that we must not be swayed only by these features, and must examine the consequences of having—or not having—property rights. Indeed, the more influential defenses of private property tend to come from pointers to its positive consequences. It is pointed out that private property has proved to be, in terms of results, quite a powerful engine of economic expansion and general prosperity. In the consequentialist perspective that fact must occupy a central position in assessing the merits of private property. On the other side, once again in terms of results, there is also much evidence to suggest that unconstrained use of private property—without restrictions and taxes—can contribute to entrenched poverty and make it difficult to have social support for those who fall behind for reasons beyond their control (including disability, age, illness and economic and social misfortune). It can also be defective in ensuring environmental preservation, and in the development of social infrastructure.[10]

Thus, neither of the purist approaches emerges unscathed in terms of analysis by results, suggesting that arrangements regarding property may have to be judged, at least partly, by their likely consequences. This conclusion is in line with the utilitarian spirit, even though full utilitarianism would insist on a very specific way of judging consequences and their relevance. The general case for taking full note of results in judging policies and institutions is a momentous and plausible requirement, which has gained much from the advocacy of utilitarian ethics.

Similar arguments can be presented in favor of taking note of human well-being in judging results, rather than looking only at some abstract and alienated characteristics of states of affairs. The focusing on consequences and on well-being, thus, have points in their favor, and this endorsement—it is only a partial endorsement—of the utilitarian approach to justice relates directly to its informational base.

## LIMITATIONS OF THE UTILITARIAN PERSPECTIVE

The handicaps of the utilitarian approach can also be traced to its informational base. Indeed, it is not hard to find fault with the utilitarian conception of justice.[11] To mention just a few, the following would appear to be among the deficiencies that a fully utilitarian approach yields.

1) *Distributional indifference:* The utilitarian calculus tends to ignore inequalities in the distribution of happiness (only the sum total matters—no matter how unequally distributed). We may be interested in general happiness, and yet want to pay attention not just to "aggregate" magnitudes, but also to extents of inequalities in happiness.

2) *Neglect of rights, freedoms and other non-utility concerns:* The utilitarian approach attaches no intrinsic importance to claims of rights and freedoms (they are valued only indirectly and only to the extent they influence utilities). It is sensible enough to take note of happiness, but we do not necessarily want to be happy slaves or delirious vassals.

3) *Adaptation and mental conditioning:* Even the view the utilitarian approach takes of individual well-being is not very robust, since it can be easily swayed by mental conditioning and adaptive attitudes.

The first two criticisms are rather more immediate than the third, and perhaps I should comment a little only on the third—the issue of mental conditioning and its effect on the utilitarian calculus. Concentrating exclusively on mental characteristics (such as pleasure, happiness or desires) can be particularly restrictive when making *interpersonal* comparisons of well-being and deprivation. Our desires and pleasure-taking abilities adjust to circumstances, especially to make life bearable in adverse situations. The utility calculus can be deeply unfair to those who are persistently deprived: for example, the usual underdogs in stratified societies, perennially oppressed minorities in intolerant communities, traditionally precarious sharecroppers living in a world of uncertainty, routinely overworked sweatshop employees in exploitative economic arrangements, hopelessly sub-dued housewives in severely sexist cultures. The deprived people tend to come to terms with their deprivation because of the sheer necessity of survival, and they may, as a result, lack the courage to demand any radical change, and may even adjust their desires and expectations to what they unambitiously see as feasible.[12] The mental metric of plea-sure or desire is just too malleable to be a firm guide to deprivation and disadvantage.

It is thus important not only to take note of the fact that in the scale of utilities the deprivation of the persistently deprived may look muffled and muted, but also to favor the creation of conditions in which people have real opportunities of judging the kind of lives they would like to lead. Social and economic factors such as basic educa-tion, elementary health care, and secure employment are important not only on their own, but also for the role they can play in giving people the opportunity to approach the world with courage and free-dom. These considerations require a broader informational base, focusing particularly on people's capability to choose the lives they have reason to value.

## JOHN RAWLS AND THE PRIORITY OF LIBERTY

I turn now to the most influential—and in many ways the most important—of contemporary theories of justice, that of John Rawls.[13] His theory has many components, but I start with a particular requirement that John Rawls has called "the priority of liberty." Rawls's own formulation of this priority is comparatively moderate, but that priority takes a particularly sharp form in modern liber-tarian theory, which in some formulations (for example, in the ele-gantly uncompromising construction presented by Robert Nozick) puts extensive classes of rights—varying from personal liberties to property rights—as having nearly complete political precedence over the pursuit of social goals (including the removal of deprivation and destitution).[14] These rights take the form of "side constraints," which simply must not be violated. The procedures that are devised to guar-antee rights, which are to be accepted no matter what consequences follow from them, are simply not on the same plane (so the argument goes) as the things that we may judge to be desirable (utilities, well-being, equity of outcomes or opportunities, and so on). The issue, then, in this formulation, is not the *comparative importance* of rights, but their *absolute priority.*

In less demanding formulations of "priority of liberty" presented in liberal theories (most notably, in the writings of John Rawls), the rights that receive precedence are much less extensive, and essentially consist of various personal liberties, including some basic political and civil rights.[15] But the precedence that these more limited rights receive is meant to be quite complete, and while these rights are much more confined in coverage than those in libertarian theory, they too cannot be in any way compromised by the force of economic needs.

The case for such a complete priority can be disputed by demonstrating the force of other considerations, including that of economic needs. Why should the status of intense economic needs, which can be matters of life and death, be lower than that of personal liberties? This issue was forcefully raised in a general form by Herbert Hart a long time ago (in a famous article in 1973). John Rawls has acknowledged the force of this argument in his later book *Political Liberalism* and suggested ways of accommodating it within the structure of his theory of justice.[16]

If the "priority of liberty" is to be made plausible even in the context of countries that are intensely poor, the content of that priority would have to be, I would argue, considerably qualified. This does not, however, amount to saying that liberty should not have priority, but rather that the form of that demand should not have the effect of making economic needs be easily overlooked. It is, in fact, possible to distinguish between (1) Rawls's strict proposal that liberty should receive overwhelming *precedence* in the case of a conflict, and (2) his general procedure of separating out personal liberty from other types of advantages for *special treatment.* The more general second claim concerns the need to assess and evaluate liberties differently from individual advantages of other kinds.

The critical issue, I would submit, is not complete precedence, but whether a person's liberty should get just the same kind of importance *(no more)* that other types of personal advantages—incomes, utilities and so on—have. In particular, the question is whether the significance of liberty for the society is adequately reflected by the weight that the person herself would tend to give to it in judging her own *overall* advantage. The claim of preeminence of liberty (including basic political liberties and civil rights) disputes that it is adequate to judge liberty simply as an advantage—like an extra unit of income—that the person herself receives from that liberty.

In order to prevent a misunderstanding, I should explain that the contrast is *not* with the value that citizens attach—and have reason to attach—to liberty and rights in their *political* judgments. Quite the contrary: the safeguarding of liberty has to be ultimately related to the general political acceptability of its importance. The contrast, rather, is with the extent to which having more liberty or rights increases an individual's own *personal* advantage, which is only a *part* of what is involved. The claim here is that the political significance of rights can far exceed the extent to which the personal advantage of the holders of these rights is enhanced by having these rights. The interests of others are also involved (since liberties of different people are interlinked), and also the violation of liberty is a procedural transgression that we may have reason to resist as a bad thing in itself. There is, thus, an asymmetry with other sources of individual advantage, for example incomes, which would be valued largely on the basis of how much they contribute to the respective personal advantages. The safeguarding of liberty and basic political rights would have the procedural priority that follows from this asymmetric prominence.

This issue is particularly important in the context of the constitutive role of liberty and political and civil rights in making it possible to have public discourse and communicative emergence of agreed norms and social values. I shall examine this difficult issue more fully in chapters 6 and 10.

## ROBERT NOZICK AND LIBERTARIANISM

I return now to the issue of complete priority of rights, including property rights, in the more demanding versions of libertarian theory. For example, in Nozick's theory (as presented in *Anarchy, State and Utopia*), the "entitlements" that people have through the exercise of these rights cannot, in general, be outweighed because of their results—no matter how nasty those results may be. A very exceptional exemption is given by Nozick to what he calls "catastrophic moral horrors," but this exemption is not very well integrated with the rest of Nozick's approach, nor is this exemption matched with a proper justification (it remains quite ad hoc). The uncompromising priority of libertarian rights can be particularly problematic since the actual consequences of the operation of these entitlements can, quite possibly, include rather terrible results. It can, in particular, lead to the violation of the substantive freedom of individuals to achieve those things to which they have reason to attach great importance, including escaping avoidable mortality, being well nourished and healthy, being able to read, write and count and so on. The importance of these freedoms cannot be ignored on grounds of the "priority of liberty."

For example, as is shown in my *Poverty and Famines,* even gigantic famines can result without anyone's libertarian rights (including property rights) being violated.[17] The destitutes such as the unemployed or the impoverished may starve precisely because their "entitlements"—legitimate as they are—do not give them enough food. This might look like a special case of a "catastrophic moral horror," but horrors of *any* degree of seriousness—all the way from gigantic famines to regular undernourishment and endemic but nonextreme hunger—can be shown to be consistent with a system in which no one's libertarian rights are violated. Similarly, deprivation of other types (for example, the lack of medical care for curable illnesses) can coexist with all libertarian rights (including rights of property ownership) being fully satisfied.

The proposal of a consequence-independent theory of political priority is afflicted by considerable indifference to the substantive freedoms that people end up having—or not having. We can scarcely agree to accept simple procedural rules *irrespective* of consequences—no matter how dreadful and totally unacceptable these consequences might be for the lives of the people involved. Consequential reasoning, in contrast, can attach great importance to the fulfillment or violation of individual liberties (and may even give it a specially favored treatment) without ignoring other considerations, including the actual impact of the respective procedures on the substantive freedoms that people actually have.[18] To ignore consequences in general, including the freedoms that people get—or do not get—to exercise, can hardly be an adequate basis for an acceptable evaluative system.

In terms of its informational basis, libertarianism as an approach is just too limited. Not only does it ignore those variables to which utilitarian and welfarist theories attach great importance, but it also neglects the most basic freedoms that we have reason to treasure and demand. Even if liberty is given a special status, it is highly implausible to claim that it would have as absolute and relentless a priority as libertarian theories insist it must have. We need a broader informational basis of justice.

## UTILITY, REAL INCOME AND INTERPERSONAL COMPARISONS

In traditional utilitarian ethics, "utility" is defined simply as happiness or pleasure, and sometimes as the fulfillment of desires. These ways of seeing utility in terms of mental metrics (of happiness or of desire) have been used not only by such pioneering philosophers as Jeremy Bentham, but also by utilitarian economists such as Francis Edgeworth, Alfred Marshall, A. C. Pigou and Dennis Robertson. As was discussed earlier in this chapter, this mental metric is subject to distortions brought about by psychological adjustment to persistent deprivation. This is indeed a major limitation of the reliance on the subjectivism of mental metrics such as pleasures or desires. Can utilitarianism be rescued from this limitation?

In modern use of "utility" in contemporary choice theory, its identification with pleasure or desire-fulfillment has been largely abandoned in favor of seeing utility simply as the numerical representation of a person's choice. I should explain that this change has occurred not really in response to the problem of mental adjustment, but mainly in reaction to the criticisms made by Lionel Robbins and other methodological positivists that interpersonal comparisons of different people's minds were "meaningless" from the scientific point of view. Robbins argued that there are "no means whereby such comparisons can be accomplished." He even cited—and agreed with—the doubts first expressed by W. S. Jevons, the utilitarian guru, himself: "Every mind is inscrutable to every other mind and no common denominator of feelings is possible."[19] As economists convinced themselves that there was indeed something methodologically wrong in using interpersonal comparison of utilities, the fuller version of the utilitarian tradition soon gave way to various compromises. The particular compromise that is extensively used now is to take utility to be nothing other than the representation of a person's preference. As was mentioned earlier, in this version of utility theory, to say that a person has more utility in state $x$ than in state $y$ is not essentially different from saying that she would choose to be in state $x$ rather than in state $y$.

This approach has the advantage of not requiring that we undertake the difficult exercise of comparing different persons' mental conditions (such as pleasures or desires), but correspondingly, it closes the door *altogether* to the possibility of direct interpersonal comparisons of utilities (utility is each individual's separately scaled representation of her preferences). Since a person does not really have the option of becoming someone else, interpersonal comparisons of choice-based utility cannot be "read off" from the actual choices.[20]

If different persons have different preferences (reflected in, say, different demand functions), there is obviously no way of getting interpersonal comparisons from these diverse preferences. But what if they *shared* the same preference and made the same choices in similar circumstances? Admittedly, this would be a very special case (indeed, as Horace noted, "there are as many preferences as there are people"), but it is still interesting to ask whether interpersonal comparisons can be made under this very special assumption. Indeed, the assumption of common preference and choice behavior is quite often made in applied welfare economics, and this is frequently used to justify the assumption that everyone has the same utility function. This is stylized interpersonal utility comparison with a vengeance. Is that presumption legitimate for the interpretation of utility as a numerical representation of preference?

The answer, unfortunately, is in the negative. It is certainly true that the assumption that everyone has the same utility function would yield the same preferences and choice behavior for all, but so would many other assumptions. For example, if a person gets exactly *half* (or one-third, or one-hundredth, or one-millionth) of the utility from every commodity bundle that another person gets, both will have the same choice behavior and identical demand function, but clearly—by construction—not the same level of utility from any commodity bundle. More mathematically, the numerical representation of choice behavior is not unique; each choice behavior can be represented by a wide set of possible utility functions.[21] The coincidence of choice behavior need not entail any congruence of utilities.[22]

This is not just a "fussy" difficulty in pure theory; it can make a very big difference in practice as well. For example, *even if* a person who is depressed or disabled or ill happens to have the same demand function over commodity bundles as another who is not disadvantaged in this way, it would be quite absurd to insist that she is having the same utility (or well-being, or quality of life) from a given commodity bundle as the other can get from it. For example, a poor person with a parasitic stomach ailment may prefer two kilos of rice over one, in much the same way that another person—equally poor but with no ailment—may, but it would be hard to argue that both do equally well with, say, one kilo of rice. Thus, the assumption of the same choice behavior and same demand function (not a particularly realistic presumption, anyway) would provide no reason to expect the same utility function. Interpersonal comparisons are quite a distinct matter from explaining choice behavior, and the two can be identified only through a conceptual confusion.

These difficulties are often ignored in what are taken to be *utility comparisons* based on choice behavior, but which amount, at best, to comparisons of "real incomes" only—or of the *commodity basis* of utility. Even real-income comparisons are not easy when different persons have diverse demand functions, and this limits the rationale of such comparisons (even of the commodity basis of utility, not to mention utilities themselves). The limitations of treating real-income comparisons as putative utility comparisons are quite severe, partly because of the complete arbitrariness (even when demand functions of different persons are congruent) of the assumption that the same commodity bundle must yield the same level of utility to different persons, and also because of the difficulties in indexing even the commodity basis of utility (when demand functions are divergent).[23]

At the practical level, perhaps the biggest difficulty in the real-income approach to well-being lies in the diversity of human beings. Differences in age, gender, special talents, disability, proneness to illness, and so on can make two different persons have quite divergent opportunities of quality of life *even when* they share exactly the same commodity bundle. Human diversity is among the difficulties that limit the usefulness of real-income comparisons for judging different persons' respective advantages. The different difficulties are briefly considered in the next section, before I proceed to consider an alternative approach to interpersonal comparison of advantages.

## WELL-BEING: DIVERSITIES AND HETEROGENEITIES

We use incomes and commodities as the material basis of our well-being. But what use we can respectively make of a given bundle of commodities, or more generally of a given level of income, depends crucially on a number of contingent circumstances, both personal and social.[24] It is easy to identify at least five distinct sources of variation between our real incomes and the advantages—the well-being and freedom—we get out of them.

1) *Personal heterogeneities:* People have disparate physical characteristics connected with disability, illness, age or gender, and these make their needs diverse. For example, an ill person may need more income to fight her illness—income that a person without such an illness would not need; and even with medical treatment the ill person may not enjoy the same quality of life that a given level of income would yield for the other person. A disabled person may need some prosthesis, an older person more support and help, a pregnant woman more nutritional intake, and so on. The "compensation" needed for disadvantages will vary, and furthermore some disadvantages may not be fully "correctable" even with income transfer.

2) *Environmental diversities:* Variations in environmental conditions, such as climatic circumstances (temperature ranges, rainfall, flooding and so on), can influence what a person gets out of a given level of income. Heating and clothing requirements of the poor in colder climates cause problems that may not be shared by equally poor people in warmer lands. The presence of infectious diseases in a region (from malaria and cholera to AIDS) alters the quality of life that inhabitants of that region may enjoy. So do pollution and other environmental handicaps.

3) *Variations in social climate:* The conversion of personal incomes and resources into the quality of life is influenced also by social conditions, including public educational arrangements, and

the prevalence or absence of crime and violence in the particular location. Issues of epidemiology and pollution are both environmental and socially influenced. Aside from public facilities, the nature of community relationships can be very important, as the recent literature on "social capital" has tended to emphasize.[25]

4) *Differences in relational perspectives:* The commodity requirements of established patterns of behavior may vary between communities, depending on conventions and customs. For example, being *relatively* poor in a rich community can prevent a person from achieving some elementary "functionings" (such as taking part in the life of the community) even though her income, in absolute terms, may be much higher than the level of income at which members of poorer communities can function with great ease and success. For example, to be able to "appear in public without shame" may require higher standards of clothing and other visible consumption in a richer society than in a poorer one (as Adam Smith noted more than two centuries ago).[26] The same parametric variability may apply to the personal resources needed for the fulfillment of self-respect. This is primarily an intersocietal variation, rather than an interindividual variation within a given society, but the two issues are frequently interlinked.

5) *Distribution within the family:* Incomes earned by one or more members of a family are shared by all—nonearners as well as earners. The family is thus the basic unit for consideration of incomes from the standpoint of their use. The well-being or freedom of individuals in a family will depend on how the family income is used in furtherance of the interests and objectives of different members of the family. Thus, intrafamily distribution of incomes is quite a crucial parametric variable in linking individual achievements and opportunities with the overall level of family income. Distributional rules followed within the family (for example, related to gender or age or perceived needs) can make a major difference to the attainments and predicaments of individual members.[27]

These different sources of variation in the relation between income and well-being make opulence—in the sense of high real income—a limited guide to welfare and the quality of life. I shall come back to these variations and their impact later on in this book (particularly in chapter 4), but there must be some attempt before that to address the question: What is the alternative? That is the question I take up next.

## INCOMES, RESOURCES AND FREEDOMS

The view that poverty is simply shortage of income is fairly well established in the literature on the subject. It is not a silly view, since income—properly defined—has an enormous influence on what we can or cannot do. The inadequacy of income is often the major cause of deprivations that we standardly associate with poverty, including starvation and famines. In studying poverty, there is an excellent argument for *beginning* with whatever information we have on the distribution of incomes, particularly low real incomes.[28]

There is, however, an equally good case for not *ending* with income analysis only. John Rawls's classic analysis of "primary goods" provides a broader picture of resources that people need no matter what their respective ends are; this includes income but also other general-purpose "means." Primary goods are general-purpose means that help anyone to promote his or her ends, and include "rights, liberties and opportunities, income and wealth, and the social bases of self-respect."[29] The concentration on primary goods in the Rawlsian framework relates to his view of individual advantage in terms of the opportunities the individuals enjoy to pursue their respective objectives. Rawls saw these objectives as the pursuit of individual "conceptions of the good," which would vary from person to person. If, despite having the same basket of primary goods as another (or even having a larger basket), a person ends up being less happy than the other person (for example, because of having expensive tastes), then no injustice need be involved in this inequality in the utility space. A person, Rawls argued, has to take responsibility for his or her own preferences.[30]

The broadening of the informational focus from incomes to primary goods is not, however, adequate to deal with all the relevant variations in the relationship between income and resources, on the one hand, and well-being and freedom, on the other. Indeed, primary goods themselves are mainly various types of general resources, and the use of these resources to generate the ability to do valuable things is subject to much the same list of variations we considered in the last section in the context of reviewing the relationship between income and well-being: personal heterogeneities, environmental diversities, variations in social climate, differences in relational perspectives and distribution within the family.[31] Personal health and the capability to be healthy can, for example, depend on a great variety of influences.[32]

An alternative to focusing on means of good living is to concentrate on the *actual living* that people manage to achieve (or going beyond that, on the *freedom* to achieve actual livings that one can have reason to value). There have, in fact, been many attempts in contemporary economics to be concerned directly with "levels of living" and its constituent elements, and with the fulfillment of basic needs, at least from A. C. Pigou onward.[33] Beginning in 1990, under the pioneering leadership of Mahbub ul Haq (the great Pakistani economist, who died suddenly in 1998), the United Nations Development Programme (UNDP) has been publishing annual reports on "human development" that have thrown systematic light on the actual lives lived by people, especially by the relatively deprived.[34]

Taking an interest in the lives that people actually lead is not new in economics (as was pointed out in chapter 1). Indeed, the Aristotelian account of the human good (as Martha Nussbaum discusses) was explicitly linked to the necessity to "first ascertain the function of man" and then proceeded to explore "life in the sense of activity" as the basic block of normative analysis.[35] Interest in living conditions is also strongly reflected (discussed earlier) in the writings on national accounts and economic prosperity by pioneering economic analysts, such as William Petty, Gregory King, François Quesnay, Antoine-Laurent Lavoisier and Joseph-Louis Lagrange.

It is also an approach that much engaged Adam Smith. As mentioned earlier, he was concerned with such capability to function as "the ability to appear in public without shame" (rather than only with real income or the commodity bundle possessed).[36] What counts as "necessity" in a society is to be determined, in Smithian analysis, by its need to generate some minimally required freedoms, such as the ability to appear in public without shame, or to take part in the life of the community. Adam Smith put the issue thus:

> By necessaries I understand not only the commodities which are indispensably necessary for the support of life, but what ever the customs of the country renders it indecent for creditable

people, even the lowest order to be without. A linen shirt, for example, is, strictly speaking, not a necessary of life. The Greeks and Romans lived, I suppose, very comfortably though they had no linen. But in the present times, through the greater part of Europe, a creditable day-labourer would be ashamed to appear in public without a linen shirt, the want of which would be supposed to denote that disgraceful degree of poverty which, it is presumed, nobody can well fall into without extreme bad conduct. Custom, in the same manner, has rendered leather shoes a necessary of life in England. The poorest creditable person of either sex would be ashamed to appear in public without them.[37]

In the same way, a family in contemporary America or Western Europe may find it hard to take part in the life of the community without possessing some specific commodities (such as a telephone, a television or an automobile) that are not necessary for community life in poorer societies. The focus has to be, in this analysis, on the freedoms generated by commodities, rather than on the commodities seen on their own.

## WELL-BEING, FREEDOM AND CAPABILITY

I have tried to argue for some time now that for many evaluative purposes, the appropriate "space" is neither that of utilities (as claimed by welfarists), nor that of primary goods (as demanded by Rawls), but that of the substantive freedoms—the capabilities—to choose a life one has reason to value.[38] If the object is to concentrate on the individual's real opportunity to pursue her objectives (as Rawls explicitly recommends), then account would have to be taken not only of the primary goods the persons respectively hold, but also of the relevant personal characteristics that govern the *conversion* of primary goods into the person's ability to promote her ends. For example, a person who is disabled may have a larger basket of primary goods and yet have less chance to lead a normal life (or to pursue her objectives) than an able-bodied person with a smaller basket of primary goods. Similarly, an older person or a person more prone to illness can be more disadvantaged in a generally accepted sense even with a larger bundle of primary goods.[39]

The concept of "functionings," which has distinctly Aristotelian roots, reflects the various things a person may value doing or being.⁴⁰ The valued functionings may vary from elementary ones, such as being adequately nourished and being free from avoidable disease,⁴¹ to very complex activities or personal states, such as being able to take part in the life of the community and having self-respect.

A person's "capability" refers to the alternative combinations of functionings that are feasible for her to achieve. Capability is thus a kind of freedom: the substantive freedom to achieve alternative functioning combinations (or, less formally put, the freedom to achieve various lifestyles). For example, an affluent person who fasts may have the same functioning achievement in terms of eating or nourishment as a destitute person who is forced to starve, but the first person does have a different "capability set" than the second (the first *can* choose to eat well and be well nourished in a way the second cannot).

There can be substantial debates on the particular functionings that should be included in the list of important achievements and the corresponding capabilities.⁴² This valuational issue is inescapable in an evaluative exercise of this kind, and one of the main merits of the approach is the need to address these judgmental questions in an explicit way, rather than hiding them in some implicit framework.

This is not the occasion to go much into the technicalities of representation and analysis of functionings and capabilities. The amount or the extent of each functioning enjoyed by a person may be represented by a real number, and when this is done, a person's actual achievement can be seen as a *functioning vector*. The "capability set" would consist of the alternative functioning vectors that she can choose from.⁴³ While the combination of a person's functionings reflects her actual *achievements*, the capability set represents the *freedom* to achieve: the alternative functioning combinations from which this person can choose.⁴⁴

The evaluative focus of this "capability approach" can be either on the *realized* functionings (what a person is actually able to do) or on the *capability set* of alternatives she has (her real opportunities). The two give different types of information—the former about the things a person does and the latter about the things a person is substantively free to do. Both versions of the capability approach have been used in the literature, and sometimes they have been combined.⁴⁵

According to a well-established tradition in economics, the real value of a set of options lies in the best use that can be made of them, and—given maximizing behavior and the absence of uncertainty—the use that is *actually* made. The use value of the opportunity, then, lies derivatively on the value of one element of it (to wit, the best option or the actually chosen option).[46] In this case, the focusing on a *chosen functioning vector* coincides with concentration on the *capability set,* since the latter is judged, ultimately, by the former.

The freedom reflected in the capability set can be used in other ways as well, since the value of a set need not invariably be identified with the value of the best—or the chosen—element of it. It is possible to attach importance to having opportunities that are *not* taken up. This is a natural direction to go if the *process* through which outcomes are generated has significance of its own.[47] Indeed, "choosing" itself can be seen as a valuable functioning, and having an $x$ when there is no alternative may be sensibly distinguished from choosing $x$ when substantial alternatives exist.[48] Fasting is not the same thing as being forced to starve. Having the option of eating makes fasting what it is, to wit, choosing not to eat when one could have eaten.

## WEIGHTS, VALUATIONS AND SOCIAL CHOICE

Individual functionings can lend themselves to easier interpersonal comparison than comparisons of utilities (or happiness, pleasures or desires). Also, many of the relevant functionings—typically the non-mental characteristics—can be seen distinctly from their mental assessment (not subsumed in "mental adjustment"). The variability in the conversion of means into ends (or into freedom to pursue ends) is already reflected in the extents of those achievements and freedoms that may figure in the list of ends. These are advantages in using the capability perspective for evaluation and assessment.

However, interpersonal comparisons of *overall* advantages also require "aggregation" over heterogeneous components. The capability perspective is inescapably pluralist. First, there are different functionings, some more important than others. Second, there is the issue of what weight to attach to substantive freedom (the capability set) vis-à-vis the actual achievement (the chosen functioning vector).

Finally, since it is not claimed that the capability perspective exhausts all relevant concerns for evaluative purposes (we might, for example, attach importance to rules and procedures and not just to freedoms and outcomes), there is the underlying issue of how much weight should be placed on the capabilities, compared with any other relevant consideration.[49]

Is this plurality an embarrassment for advocacy of the capability perspective for evaluative purposes? Quite the contrary. To insist that there should be only one homogeneous magnitude that we value is to reduce drastically the range of our evaluative reasoning. It is not, for example, to the credit of classical utilitarianism that it values only pleasure, without taking any direct interest in freedom, rights, creativity or actual living conditions. To insist on the mechanical comfort of having just one homogeneous "good thing" would be to deny our humanity as reasoning creatures. It is like seeking to make the life of the chef easier by finding something which—and which *alone*—we all like (such as smoked salmon, or perhaps even french fries), or some one quality which we must all try to maximize (such as the saltiness of the food).

Heterogeneity of factors that influence individual advantage is a pervasive feature of actual evaluation. While we can decide to close our eyes to this issue by simply *assuming* that there is some one homogeneous thing (such as "income" or "utility") in terms of which everyone's overall advantage can be judged and interpersonally compared (and that variations of needs, personal circumstances and so on can be assumed away), this does not resolve the problem but only evades it. Preference fulfillment may have some obvious attraction in dealing with one person's individual needs, but (as was discussed earlier) it does little, on its own, for interpersonal comparisons, central to any social evaluation. Even when each person's preference is taken to be the ultimate arbiter of the well-being for that person, even when everything other than well-being (such as freedom) is ignored, and even when—to take a very special case—everyone has the *same* demand function or preference map, the comparison of market valuations of commodity bundles (or their relative placement on a shared system-of-indifference map in the commodity space) tells us little about interpersonal comparisons.

In evaluative traditions involving fuller specification, considerable heterogeneity is explicitly admitted. For example, in Rawlsian analysis primary goods are taken to be constitutively diverse (including "rights, liberties and opportunities, income and wealth, and the social basis of self-respect"), and Rawls deals with them through an overall "index" of primary goods holdings.[50] While a similar exercise of judging over a space with heterogeneity is involved both in the Rawlsian approach and in the use of functionings, the former is informationally poorer, for reasons discussed already, because of the parametric variation of resources and primary goods vis-à-vis the opportunity to achieve high quality of living.

The problem of valuation is not, however, one of an all-or-nothing kind. Some judgments, with incomplete reach, follow immediately from the specification of a focal space. When some functionings are selected as significant, such a focal space is specified, and the relation of dominance itself leads to a "partial ordering" over the alternative states of affairs. If person $i$ has more of a significant functioning than person $j$, and at least as much of all such functionings, then $i$ clearly has a higher valued functioning vector than $j$ has. This partial ordering can be "extended" by further specifying the possible weights. A unique set of weights will, of course, be *sufficient* to generate a *complete* order, but it is typically not necessary. Given a "range" of weights on which there is agreement (that is, when it is agreed that the weights are to be chosen from a specified range, even without any agreement as to the exact point on that range), there will be a partial ordering based on the intersection of rankings. This partial ordering will get systematically extended as the range is made more and more narrow. Somewhere in the process of narrowing the range—possibly well before the weights are unique—the partial ordering will become complete.[51]

It is of course crucial to ask, in any evaluative exercise of this kind, how the weights are to be selected. This judgmental exercise can be resolved only through reasoned evaluation. For a particular person, who is making his or her own judgments, the selection of weights will require reflection, rather than any interpersonal agreement (or consensus). However, in arriving at an "agreed" range for *social evaluation* (for example, in social studies of poverty), there has to be some kind of a reasoned "consensus" on weights, or at least on a range of weights. This is a "social choice" exercise, and it requires public discussion and a democratic understanding and acceptance.[52] It is not a special problem that is associated only with the use of the functioning space.

There is an interesting choice here between "technocracy" and "democracy" in the selection of weights, which may be worth discussing a little. A choice procedure that relies on a democratic search for agreement or a consensus can be extremely messy, and many technocrats are sufficiently disgusted by its messiness to pine for some wonderful formula that would simply give us ready-made weights that are "just right." However, no such magic formula does, of course, exist, since the issue of weighting is one of valuation and judgment, and not one of some impersonal technology.

We are not prevented, by any means, from proposing that some particular formula—rather than any alternative formula—be used for aggregation, but in this inescapably social-choice exercise its status must depend on its acceptability to others. There is nevertheless a hankering after some "obviously correct" formula to which reasonable people cannot object. A good example comes from T. N. Srinivasan's forceful critique of the capability approach (and its partial use in UNDP's *Human Development Reports*), where he worries about the "varying importance of different capabilities" and proposes the rejection of this approach in favor of the advantage of "the real-income framework" which "includes an operational metric for weighting commodities—the metric of exchange value."[53] How convincing is this critique? There is certainly some metric in market valuation, but what does it tell us?

As was already discussed, the "operational metric" of exchange value does not give us interpersonal comparisons of utility levels, since such comparisons cannot be deduced from choice behavior. There has been some confusion on this subject because of misreading the tradition of consumption theory—sensible within its context—of taking utility to be simply the numerical representation of a given person's choice. That is a useful way to define utility for the analysis of consumption behavior of each person taken separately, but it does not, on its own, offer any procedure whatever for substantive interpersonal comparison. Paul Samuelson's elementary point that it was "not necessary to make interpersonal comparisons of utility in describing exchange,"[54] is the other side of the same coin: nothing about interpersonal comparison of utility is learned from observing "the metric of exchange value."

As noted earlier, this difficulty is present even when everyone has the same demand function. It is intensified when the individual demand functions differ, in which case even comparisons of the commodity basis of utility are problematic. There is nothing in the methodology of demand analysis, including the theory of revealed preference, that permits any reading of interpersonal comparisons of utilities or welfares from observed choices of commodity holdings, and thus from real-income comparisons.

In fact, given interpersonal diversity, related to such factors as age, gender, inborn talents, disabilities and illnesses, the commodity holdings can actually tell us rather little about the nature of the lives that the respective people can lead. Real incomes can, thus, be rather poor indicators of important components of well-being and quality of life that people have reason to value. More generally, the need for *evaluative* judgments is inescapable in comparing individual well-being, or quality of life. Furthermore, anyone who values public scrutiny must be under some obligation to make clear that a judgment *is* being made in using real incomes for this purpose and that the weights implicitly used must be subjected to evaluative scrutiny. In this context, the fact that market-price-based evaluation of utility from commodity bundles gives the misleading impression—at least to some—that an already available "operational metric" has been *preselected for evaluative use* is a limitation rather than an asset. If informed scrutiny by the public is central to any such social evaluation (as I believe is the case), the implicit values have to be made more explicit, rather than being shielded from scrutiny on the spurious ground that they are part of an "already available" metric that the society can immediately use without further ado.

Since the preference for market-price-based evaluation is quite strong among many economists, it is also important to point out that all variables other than commodity holdings (important matters such as mortality, morbidity, education, liberties and recognized rights) get—implicitly—a zero direct weight in evaluations based exclusively on the real-income approach. They can get some *indirect* weight only if—and only to the extent that—they enlarge real incomes and commodity holdings. The confounding of welfare comparison with real-income comparison exacts a heavy price.

There is thus a strong methodological case for emphasizing the need to assign explicitly evaluative weights to different components of quality of life (or of well-being) and then to place the chosen weights for open public discussion and critical scrutiny. In any choice of criteria for evaluative purposes, there would not only be use of value judgments, but also, quite often, use of some judgments on which full agreement would not exist. This is inescapable in a social-choice exercise of this kind.[55] The real issue is whether we can use some criteria that would have greater public support, for evaluative purposes, than the crude indicators often recommended on allegedly technological grounds, such as real-income measures. This is central for the evaluative basis of public policy.

## CAPABILITY INFORMATION: ALTERNATIVE USES

The capability perspective can be used in rather distinct ways. The question as to which practical *strategy* to use for evaluating public policy has to be distinguished from the *foundational* issue as to how individual advantages are best judged and interpersonal comparisons most sensibly made. At the foundational level, the capability perspective has some obvious merits (for reasons already discussed) compared with concentrating on such instrumental variables as income. This does not, however, entail that the most fruitful focus of *practical* attention would invariably be measures of capabilities.

Some capabilities are harder to measure than others, and attempts at putting them on a "metric" may sometimes hide more than they reveal. Quite often income levels—with possible corrections for price differences and variations of individual or group circumstances—can be a very useful way of getting started in practical appraisal. The need for pragmatism is quite strong in using the motivation underlying the capability perspective for the use of available data for practical evaluation and policy analysis.

Three alternative practical approaches may be considered in giving practical shape to the foundational concern.[56]

1) *The direct approach:* This general approach takes the form of directly examining what can be said about respective advantages by examining and comparing vectors of functionings or capabilities. In many ways, this is the most immediate and full-blooded way of

going about incorporating capability considerations in evaluation. It can, however, be used in different forms. The variants include the following:

1.1) "total comparison," involving the ranking of all such vectors vis-à-vis each other in terms of poverty or inequality (or whatever the subject matter is);

1.2) "partial ranking," involving the ranking of some vectors vis-à-vis others, but not demanding completeness of the evaluative ranking;

1.3) "distinguished capability comparison," involving the comparison of some particular capability chosen as the focus, without looking for completeness of coverage.

Obviously, "total comparison" is the most ambitious of the three—often much too ambitious. We can go in that direction—maybe quite far—by not insisting on a complete ranking of all the alternatives. Examples of "distinguished capability comparison" can be seen in concentrated attention being paid to some particular capability variable, such as employment, or longevity, or literacy, or nutrition.

It is possible, of course, to go from a set of separate comparisons of distinguished capabilities to an aggregated ranking of the sets of capabilities. This is where the crucial role of weights would come in, bridging the gap between "distinguished capability comparisons" and "partial rankings" (or even "total comparisons").[57] But it is important to emphasize that despite the incomplete coverage that distinguished capability comparisons provide, such comparisons can be quite illuminating, even on their own, in evaluative exercises. There will be an opportunity to illustrate this issue in the next chapter.

2) *The supplementary approach:* A second approach is relatively nonradical, and involves continued use of traditional procedures of interpersonal comparisons in income spaces, but supplements them by capability considerations (often in rather informal ways). For practical purposes, some broadening of the informational base can be achieved through this route. The supplementation may focus either on direct comparisons of functionings themselves, or on instrumental variables other than income that are expected to influence the determination of capabilities. Such factors as the availability and reach of health care, evidence of gender bias in family allocation, and the prevalence and magnitude of joblessness can add to the par-

tial illumination provided by the traditional measures in the income space. Such extensions can enrich the overall understanding of problems of inequality and poverty by *adding to* what gets known through measures of income inequality and income poverty. Essentially, this involves using "distinguished capability comparison" as a supplementary device.[58]

3) *The indirect approach:* A third line of approach is more ambitious than the supplementary approach but remains focused on the familiar space of incomes, appropriately *adjusted.* Information on determinants of capabilities *other than income* can be used to calculate "adjusted incomes." For example, family income levels may be adjusted downward by illiteracy and upward by high levels of education, and so on, to make them equivalent in terms of capability achievement. This procedure relates to the general literature on "equivalence scales." It also connects with the research on analyzing family expenditure patterns for indirectly assessing causal influences that may not be observed directly (such as the presence or absence of certain types of sex bias within the family).[59]

The advantage of this approach lies in the fact that income is a familiar concept and often allows stricter measurement (than, say, overall "indices" of capabilities). This may permit more articulation and perhaps easier interpretation. The motivation for choosing the "metric" of income in this case is similar to A. B. Atkinson's choice of the income space to measure the effects of income inequality (in his calculation of "equally distributed equivalent income"), rather than the utility space, as was originally proposed by Hugh Dalton.[60] Inequality can be seen in Dalton's approach in terms of utility loss from disparity, and the shift that Atkinson brought in involved assessing the loss from inequality in terms of "equivalent income."

The "metric" issue is not negligible, and the indirect approach does have some advantages. It is, however, necessary to recognize that it is not any "simpler" than direct assessment. First, in assessing the values of equivalent income, we have to consider how income influences the relevant capabilities, since the conversion rates have to be parasitic on the underlying motivation of capability evaluation. Furthermore, all the issues of trade-offs between different capabilities (and those of relative weights) have to be faced in the indirect approach just as much as in the direct approach, since all that is essentially altered is the unit of expression. In this sense the indirect approach is not basically different from the direct approach in terms of the judgments that have to be made to get appropriate measures in the space of equivalent incomes.

Second, it is important to distinguish between income as a *unit* in which to *measure* inequality and income as the *vehicle* of inequality reduction. Even if inequality in capabilities is well measured in terms of equivalent incomes, it does not follow that transferring income would be the best way to counteract the observed inequality. The policy question of compensation or redress raises other issues (effectiveness in altering capability disparities, the respective force of incentive effects and so on), and the easy "reading" of income gaps must not be taken as a suggestion that corresponding income transfers would remedy the disparities most effectually. There is, of course, no need to fall into this mistaken reading of equivalent incomes, but the clarity and immediacy of the income space may pose that temptation, which has to be explicitly resisted.

Third, even though the income space has greater measurability and articulation, the actual magnitudes can be very misleading in terms of the values involved. Consider, for example, the possibility that as the level of income is reduced and a person starts to starve, there may be a sharp drop at some point in the person's chances of survival. Even though the "distance" in the space of incomes between two alternative values may be rather little (measured entirely in terms of income), if the consequence of such a shift is a dramatic change in the chances of survival, then the impact of that small income change can be very large in the space of what really matters (in this case the capability to survive). It may thus be deceptive to think of the difference as being really "little" because the income difference is small. Indeed, since income remains only instrumentally important, we cannot know how significant the income gaps are without actually considering the *consequences* of the income gaps in the space that is ultimately important. If a battle is lost for want of a nail (through a chain of causal connections that the old verse outlines), then that nail made a *big* difference, no matter how trivial it may be in the space of incomes or expenditures.

Each of these approaches has contingent merit that may vary depending on the nature of the exercise, the availability of information, and the urgency of the decisions that have to be taken. Since the capability perspective is sometimes interpreted in terribly exacting terms (total comparisons under the direct approach), it is important to emphasize the catholicity that the approach has. The foundational affirmation of the importance of capabilities can go with various strategies of actual evaluation involving practical compromises. The pragmatic nature of practical reason demands this.

## CONCLUDING REMARKS

Euclid is supposed to have told Ptolemy: "There is no 'royal road' to geometry." It is not clear that there is any royal road to evaluation of economic or social policies either. A variety of considerations that call for attention are involved, and evaluations have to be done with sensitivity to these concerns. Much of the debate on the alternative approaches to evaluation relates to the priorities in deciding on what should be at the core of our normative concern.

It has been argued here that the priorities that are accepted, often implicitly, in the different approaches to ethics, welfare economics, and political philosophy can be brought out and analyzed through identifying the information on which the evaluative judgments rely in the respective approaches. This chapter was concerned particularly with showing how these "informational bases" work, and how the different ethical and evaluative systems use quite different informational bases.

From that general issue, the analysis presented in this chapter moved to specific evaluative approaches, in particular utilitarianism, libertarianism and Rawlsian justice. In line with the view that there are indeed no royal roads to evaluation, it emerged that there are distinct merits in each of these well-established strategies, but that each also suffers from significant limitations.

The constructive part of this chapter proceeded to examine the implications of focusing directly on the substantive freedoms of the individuals involved, and identified a general approach that concentrates on the capabilities of people to do things—and the freedom to lead lives—that they have reason to value. I have discussed this approach elsewhere as well,[61] as have others, and its advantages and limitations are also reasonably clear. It does appear that not only is this approach able to take direct note of the importance of freedom, it can also pay substantial attention to the underlying motivations that contribute to the relevance of the other approaches. In particular, the freedom-based perspective can take note of, inter alia, utilitarianism's interest in human well-being, libertarianism's involvement with processes of choice and the freedom to act and Rawlsian theory's focus on individual liberty and on the resources needed for substantive freedoms. In this sense the capability approach has a breadth and sensitivity that give it a very extensive reach, allowing evaluative attention to be paid to a variety of important concerns, some of which are ignored, one way or another, in the alternative approaches. This extensive reach is possible because the freedoms of persons can be judged through explicit reference to outcomes and processes that they have reason to value and seek.[62]

Different ways of using this freedom-based perspective were also discussed, resisting in particular the idea that the use must take an all-or-none form. In many practical problems, the possibility of using an explicitly freedom-based approach may be relatively limited. Yet even there it is possible to make use of the insights and informational interests involved in a freedom-based approach—without insisting on ignoring other procedures when they can be, within particular contexts, sensibly utilized. The analysis that follows builds on these understandings, in an attempt to throw light on underdevelopment (seen broadly in the form of unfreedom) and development (seen as a process of removing unfreedoms and of extending the substantive freedoms of different types that people have reason to value). A general approach can be used in many different ways, depending on the context and on the information that is available. It is this combination of foundational analysis and pragmatic use that gives the capability approach its extensive reach.

# CHAPTER 4

# POVERTY AS CAPABILITY DEPRIVATION

▼

It was argued in the last chapter that, in analyzing social justice, there is a strong case for judging individual advantage in terms of the capabilities that a person has, that is, the substantive freedoms he or she enjoys to lead the kind of life he or she has reason to value. In this perspective, poverty must be seen as the deprivation of basic capabilities rather than merely as lowness of incomes, which is the standard criterion of identification of poverty.[1] The perspective of capability-poverty does not involve any denial of the sensible view that low income is clearly one of the major causes of poverty, since lack of income can be a principal reason for a person's capability deprivation.

Indeed, inadequate income is a strong predisposing condition for an impoverished life. If this is accepted, what then is all this fuss about, in seeing poverty in the capability perspective (as opposed to seeing it in terms of the standard income-based poverty assessment)? The claims in favor of the capability approach to poverty are, I believe, the following.

1)   Poverty can be sensibly identified in terms of capability deprivation; the approach concentrates on deprivations that are *intrinsically* important (unlike low income, which is only *instrumentally* significant).

2)   There are influences on capability deprivation—and thus on real poverty—*other* than lowness of income (income is not the only instrument in generating capabilities).

3)   The instrumental relation between low income and low capability is *variable* between different communities and even between different families and different individuals (the impact of income on capabilities is contingent and conditional).[2]

The third issue is particularly important in considering and evaluating public action aimed at reducing inequality or poverty. Various reasons for conditional variations have been discussed in the literature (and in chapter 3, earlier), and it is useful to emphasize some of them specifically in the context of practical policy making.

First, the relationship between income and capability would be strongly affected by the age of the person (e.g., by the specific needs of the old and the very young), by gender and social roles (e.g., through special responsibilities of maternity and also custom-determined family obligations), by location (e.g., by proneness to flooding or drought, or by insecurity and violence in some inner-city living), by epidemiological atmosphere (e.g., through diseases endemic in a region) and by other variations over which a person may have no—or only limited—control.[3] In making contrasts of population groups classified according to age, gender, location and so on, these parametric variations are particularly important.

Second, there can be some "coupling" of disadvantages between (1) income deprivation and (2) adversity in converting income into functionings.[4] Handicaps, such as age or disability or illness, reduce one's ability to earn an income.[5] But they also make it harder to convert income into capability, since an older, or more disabled, or more seriously ill person may need more income (for assistance, for prosthesis, for treatment) to achieve the same functionings (even when that achievement is at all possible).[6] This entails that "real poverty" (in terms of capability deprivation) may be, in a significant sense, more intense than what appears in the income space. This can be a crucial concern in assessing public action to assist the elderly and other groups with "conversion" difficulties in addition to lowness of income.

Third, distribution within the family raises further complications with the income approach to poverty. If the family income is used disproportionately in the interest of some family members and not others (for example, if there is a systematic "boy preference" in the family allocation of resources), then the extent of the deprivation of the neglected members (girls in the example considered) may not be adequately reflected in terms of family income. This is a substantial issue in many contexts; sex bias does appear to be a major factor in the family allocation in many countries in Asia and North Africa. The deprivation of girls is more readily checked by looking at capability deprivation (in terms of greater mortality, morbidity, undernourishment, medical neglect, and so on) than can be found on the basis of income analysis.[7]

This issue is clearly not as central in the context of inequality and poverty in Europe or North America, but the presumption—often implicitly made—that the issue of gender inequality does not apply at the basic level to the "Western" countries can be, to some extent, misleading. For example, Italy has one of the highest ratios of "unrecognized" labor by women vis-à-vis recognized labor included in the standard national accounts.[8] The accounting of effort and time expended, and the related reduction of freedom, has some bearing in the analysis of poverty even in Europe and North America. There are also other ways in which intrafamily divisions are important to include among the considerations relevant for public policy in most parts of the world.

Fourth, *relative* deprivation in terms of *incomes* can yield *absolute* deprivation in terms of *capabilities*. Being relatively poor in a rich country can be a great capability handicap, even when one's absolute income is high in terms of world standards. In a generally opulent country, more income is needed to buy enough commodities to achieve the *same social functioning*. This consideration—pioneeringly outlined by Adam Smith in *The Wealth of Nations* (1776)—is quite central to sociological understandings of poverty, and it has been analyzed by W. G. Runciman, Peter Townsend and others.[9]

For example, the difficulties that some groups of people experience in "taking part in the life of the community" can be crucial for any study of "social exclusion." The need to take part in the life of a community may induce demands for modern equipment (televisions, videocassette recorders, automobiles and so on) in a country where such facilities are more or less universal (unlike what would be needed in less affluent countries), and this imposes a strain on a relatively poor person in a rich country even when that person is at a much higher level of income compared with people in less opulent countries.[10] Indeed, the paradoxical phenomenon of hunger in rich countries—even in the United States—has something to do with the competing demands of these expenses.[11]

What the capability perspective does in poverty analysis is to enhance the understanding of the nature and causes of poverty and deprivation by shifting primary attention away from *means* (and one particular means that is usually given exclusive attention, viz., income) to *ends* that people have reason to pursue, and, correspondingly, to the *freedoms* to be able to satisfy these ends. The examples briefly considered here illustrate the additional discernment that results from this basic extension. The deprivations are seen at a more fundamental level—one closer to the informational demands of social justice. Hence the relevance of the perspective of capability-poverty.

## INCOME POVERTY AND CAPABILITY POVERTY

While it is important to distinguish conceptually the notion of poverty as capability inadequacy from that of poverty as lowness of income, the two perspectives cannot but be related, since income is such an important means to capabilities. And since enhanced capabilities in leading a life would tend, typically, to expand a person's ability to be more productive and earn a higher income, we would also expect a connection going from capability improvement to greater earning power and not only the other way around.

The latter connection can be particularly important for the removal of income poverty. It is not only the case that, say, better basic education and health care improve the quality of life directly; they also increase a person's ability to earn an income and be free of income-poverty as well. The more inclusive the reach of basic education and health care, the more likely it is that even the potentially poor would have a better chance of overcoming penury.

The importance of this connection was a crucial point of focus of my recent work on India, done jointly with Jean Drèze, dealing with economic reforms.[12] In many ways, the economic reforms have opened up for the Indian people economic opportunities that were suppressed by overuse of control and by the limitations of what had been called the "license Raj."[13] And yet the opportunity to make use of the new possibilities is not independent of the social preparation that different sections of the Indian community have. While the reforms were overdue, they could be much more productive if the social facilities were there to support the economic opportunities for all sections of the community. Indeed, many Asian economies—first Japan, and then South Korea, Taiwan, Hong Kong, and Singapore, and later post-reform China and Thailand and other countries in East Asia and Southeast Asia—have done remarkably well in spreading the economic opportunities through an adequately supportive social background, including high levels of literacy, numeracy, and basic education; good general health care; completed land reforms; and so on. The lesson of opening of the economy and the importance of trade has been more easily learned in India than the rest of the message from the same direction of the rising sun.[14]

India is, of course, highly diverse in terms of human development, with some regions (most notably, Kerala) having much higher levels of education, health care and land reform than others (most notably, Bihar, Uttar Pradesh, Rajasthan and Madhya Pradesh). The limitations have taken different forms in the different states. It can be argued that Kerala has suffered from what were until recently fairly anti-market policies, with deep suspicion of market-based economic expansion without control. So its human resources have not been as well used in spreading economic growth as they could have been with a more complementary economic strategy, which is now being attempted. On the other hand, some of the northern states have suffered from low levels of social development, with varying degrees of control and market-based opportunities. The need for seizing the relevance of complementarity is very strong in remedying the diverse drawbacks.

It is, however, interesting that despite the rather moderate record in economic growth, Kerala seems to have had a faster rate of reduction in income poverty than any other state in India.[15] While some states have reduced income poverty through high economic growth (Punjab is the most notable example of that), Kerala has relied a great deal on expansion of basic education, health care and equitable land distribution for its success in reducing penury.

While these connections between income poverty and capability poverty are worth emphasizing, it is also important not to lose sight of the basic fact that the reduction of income poverty alone cannot possibly be the ultimate motivation of antipoverty policy. There is a danger in seeing poverty in the narrow terms of income deprivation, and then justifying investment in education, health care and so forth on the ground that they are good means to the end of reducing income poverty. That would be a confounding of ends and means. The basic foundational issues force us, for reasons already discussed, toward understanding poverty and deprivation in terms of lives people can actually lead and the freedoms they do actually have. The expansion of human capabilities fits directly into these basic considerations. It so happens that the enhancement of human capabilities also tends to go with an expansion of productivities and earning power. That connection establishes an important indirect linkage through which capability improvement helps both directly and indirectly in enriching human lives and in making human deprivations more rare and less acute. The instrumental connections, important as they are, cannot replace the need for a basic understanding of the nature and characteristics of poverty.

## INEQUALITY OF WHAT?

The treatment of inequality in economic and social evaluation involves many dilemmas. Substantial inequalities are often hard to defend in terms of models of "fairness." Adam Smith's concern with the interests of the poor (and his outrage at the tendency for those interests to be neglected) related naturally to his use of the imaginative device of what it would look like to an "impartial spectator"— an inquiry that offers far-reaching insights on the requirements of fairness in social judgment.[16] Similarly, John Rawls's idea of "justice as fairness" in terms of what can be expected to be chosen in a hypothetical "original position" in which people do not yet know who they are going to be provides a rich understanding of the demands of equity, and yields the anti-inequality features that are characteristic of his "principles of justice."[17] Patent inequalities in social arrangements can also be difficult to justify in terms of reasonableness to actual members of the society (for example, the case for these inequalities being one that others "cannot reasonably reject": a criterion that Thomas Scanlon has proposed—and powerfully used—for ethical evaluation).[18] Certainly, severe inequalities are not socially attractive, and momentous inequalities can be, some would argue, downright barbaric. Furthermore, the sense of inequality may also erode social cohesion, and some types of inequalities can make it difficult to achieve even efficiency.

And yet attempts to eradicate inequality can, in many circumstances, lead to loss for most—sometimes even for all. This kind of conflict can arise in mild or severe form depending on the exact circumstances. Models of justice—involving the "impartial spectator," or the "original position," or not-reasonable-rejection—have to take note of these diverse considerations.

Not surprisingly, the conflict between aggregative and distributive considerations has received a remarkable amount of professional attention among economists. This is appropriate since it is an important issue.[19] Many compromise formulas have been suggested for evaluating social achievements by taking note simultaneously of aggregative and distributive considerations. A good example is A. B. Atkinson's "equally distributed equivalent income," a concept that adjusts the aggregate income by reducing its accounted value according to the extent of inequality in income distribution, with the trade-off between aggregative and distributive concerns being given by the choice of a parameter that reflects our ethical judgment.[20]

There is, however, a different class of conflicts that relates to the choice of "space"—or of the focal variable in terms of which inequality is to be assessed and scrutinized—and this relates to the subject matter of the previous chapter. Inequality of incomes can differ substantially from inequality in several other "spaces" (that is, in terms of other relevant variables), such as well-being, freedom and different aspects of the quality of life (including health and longevity). And even aggregative achievements would take different forms depending on the space in which the composition—or the "totaling"—is done (for example, ranking societies in terms of average income may differ from ranking them according to average health conditions).

The contrast between the different perspectives of income and capability has a direct bearing on the space in which inequality and efficiency are to be examined. For example, a person with high income but no opportunity of political participation is not "poor" in the usual sense, but is clearly poor in terms of an important freedom. Someone who is richer than most others but suffers from an ailment that is very expensive to treat is obviously deprived in an important way, even though she would not be classified as poor in the usual statistics of income distribution. A person who is denied the opportunity of employment but given a handout from the state as an "unemployment benefit" may look a lot less deprived in the space of incomes than in terms of the valuable—and valued—opportunity of having a fulfilling occupation. Since the issue of unemployment is particularly important in some parts of the world (including contemporary Europe), this is another area where there is a strong need to seize the contrast between income and capability perspectives in the context of inequality assessment.

## UNEMPLOYMENT
## AND CAPABILITY DEPRIVATION

That the judgments of inequality in the space of incomes can be quite different from those related to important capabilities can easily be illustrated with examples of some practical importance. In the European context, this contrast is particularly significant because of the wide prevalence of unemployment in contemporary Europe.[21] The loss of income caused by unemployment can, to a considerable extent, be compensated by income support (including unemployment benefits), as it typically is in Western Europe. If income loss were all that were involved in unemployment, then that loss could be to a great extent erased—for the individuals involved—by income support (there is, of course, the further issue of social costs of fiscal burden and incentive effects involved in this compensation). If, however, unemployment has other serious effects on the lives of the individuals, causing deprivation of other kinds, then the amelioration through income support would be to that extent limited. There is plenty of evidence that unemployment has many far-reaching effects other than loss of income, including psychological harm, loss of work motivation, skill and self-confidence, increase in ailments and morbidity (and even mortality rates), disruption of family relations and social life, hardening of social exclusion and accentuation of racial tensions and gender asymmetries.[22]

Given the massive scale of unemployment in contemporary European economies, the concentration on income inequality only can be particularly deceptive. Indeed, it can be argued that at this time the massive level of European unemployment constitutes at least as important an issue of inequality, in its own right, as income distribution itself. An exclusive focus on income inequality tends to give the impression that Western Europe has done very much better than the United States in keeping inequality down and in avoiding the kind of increase in income inequality that the United States has experienced. In the space of incomes, Europe does indeed have a clearly better record both in terms of levels and trends of inequality, as is brought out by the careful investigation reported in the OECD (Organization for Economic Cooperation and Development) study prepared by A. B. Atkinson, Lee Rainwater and Timothy Smeeding.[23] Not only are the usual measures of income inequality higher in the United States than is the case, by and large, on the European side of the Atlantic, but also the U.S. income inequality has gone up in a way that has not happened in most countries in Western Europe.

And yet if we shift our gaze from income to unemployment, the picture is very different. Unemployment has risen dramatically in much of Western Europe, whereas there has been no such trend in the United States. For example, in the period 1965–1973, the unemployment rate was 4.5 percent in the United States, while Italy had 5.8 percent, France 2.3 percent, and West Germany below 1 percent. By now all three—Italy, France, and Germany—have unemployment rates that hover around 10 to 12 percent, whereas the U.S. unemployment rate is still between 4 and 5 percent. If unemployment batters lives, then that must somehow be taken into account in the analysis of economic inequality. The comparative trends in *income* inequality give Europe an excuse to be smug, but that complacency can be deeply misleading if a broader view is taken of inequality.[24]

The contrast between Western Europe and the United States raises another interesting—and in some ways a more general—question. American social ethics seems to find it possible to be very non-supportive of the indigent and the impoverished, in a way that a typical Western European, reared in a welfare state, finds hard to accept. But the same American social ethics would find the double-digit levels of unemployment, common in Europe, to be quite intolerable.

Europe has continued to accept worklessness—and its increase—with remarkable equanimity. Underlying this contrast is a difference in attitudes toward social and individual responsibilities, to which I shall return.

## HEALTH CARE AND MORTALITY: AMERICAN
## AND EUROPEAN SOCIAL ATTITUDES

The inequality between different racial groups in the United States has received considerable attention recently. For example, in the space of incomes African Americans are decidedly poorer than American whites. This is very often seen as an example of *relative* deprivation of African Americans within the nation, but not compared with poorer people in the rest of the world. Indeed, in comparison with the population of third world countries, African Americans may well be a great many times richer in terms of incomes, even after taking note of price differences. Seen this way, the deprivation of the American blacks seems to pale to insignificance in the international perspective.

But is income the right space in which to make such comparisons? What about the basic capability to live to a mature age, without succumbing to premature mortality? As was discussed in chapter 1, in terms of that criterion the African American men fall well behind the immensely poorer men of China, or the Indian state of Kerala (see figure 1.1, page 22)—and also of Sri Lanka, Costa Rica, Jamaica and many other poor economies. It is sometimes presumed that the remarkably high death rates of African Americans apply only to men, and again only to younger men, because of the prevalence of violence. Death from violence is indeed high among young black men, but this is by no means the whole story. Indeed, as figure 1.2 (page 23) shows, black women too fall not only behind white women in the United States but also behind Indian women in Kerala, and come very close to falling behind Chinese women as well. It may also be noticed in figure 1.1 that American black *men* continue to lose ground vis-à-vis the Chinese and the Indians over the years—well past the younger ages when death from violence is common. More explanation is needed than violent deaths can provide.

Indeed, even if we take higher age groups (say, that between

FIGURE 4.1: *Mortality Rate Ratios of Blacks to Whites (Aged 35–54) Actual and Adjusted for Family Income*

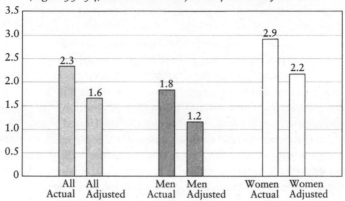

*Source:* M. W. Owen, S. M. Teutsch, D. F. Williamson and J. S. Marks, "The Effects of Known Risk Factors on the Excess Mortality of Black Adults in the United States," *Journal of the American Medical Association* 263, no. 6 (February 9, 1990).

thirty-five and sixty-four years), there is evidence of enormously greater mortality for black men vis-à-vis white men, and black women vis-à-vis white women. And these differentials are not wiped out by adjustment for income differences. In fact, one of the more careful medical studies related to the 1980s shows that the black-white mortality differential remains remarkably large for women even after adjustment for income differentials. Figure 4.1 presents the ratios of the mortality rates of blacks and whites for the country as a whole (based on a sample survey).[25] While U.S. black men have 1.8 times the mortality rate of white men, black women have nearly three times the mortality of white women in this survey. And adjusted for differences in family income, while the mortality rate is 1.2 times higher for black men, it is as much as 2.2 times higher for black women. It, thus, appears that even after full note is taken of income levels, black women die young in very much larger proportions than white women in the contemporary United States.

The broadening of the informational base from income to the basic capabilities enriches our understanding of inequality and poverty in quite radical ways. When we focused on the ability to be employed and to have the associated advantages of employment, the European picture looked quite dismal, and as we turn our attention to the ability to survive, the picture of American inequality is remarkably intense. Underlying these differences and the respective policy priorities associated with them, there may be an important contrast in the attitudes to social and individual responsibilities on the two sides of the Atlantic. In American official priorities, there is little commitment to providing basic health care for all, and it appears that many millions of people (in fact more than 40 million) are without any kind of medical coverage or insurance in the United States. While a considerable proportion of these uninsured people may have volitional reasons for not taking such insurance, the bulk of the uninsured do, in fact, lack the ability to have medical insurance because of economic circumstances, and in some cases because of preexisting medical conditions that private insurers shun. A comparable situation in Europe, where medical coverage is seen as a basic right of the citizen irrespective of means and independent of preexisting conditions, would very likely be politically intolerable. The limits on governmental support for the ill and the poor are too severe in the United States to be at all acceptable in Europe, and so are the social commitments toward public facilities varying from health care to educational arrangements, which the European welfare state takes for granted.

On the other hand, the double-digit unemployment rates that are currently tolerated in Europe would very likely be (as was argued earlier) political dynamite in America, since unemployment rates of that magnitude would make a mockery of people's ability to help themselves. I believe no U.S. government could emerge unscathed from the doubling of the present level of unemployment, which incidentally would still keep the U.S. unemployment ratio below what it currently is in Italy or France or Germany. The nature of the respective political commitments—and lack thereof—would seem to differ fundamentally between Europe and America, and the differences relate closely to seeing inequality in terms of particular failures of basic capabilities.

## POVERTY AND DEPRIVATION IN
## INDIA AND SUB-SAHARAN AFRICA

Extreme poverty is now heavily concentrated in two particular regions of the world: South Asia and sub-Saharan Africa. They have among the lowest levels of per capita income among all the regions, but that perspective does not give us an adequate idea of the nature and content of their respective deprivations, nor of their comparative poverty. If poverty is seen, instead, as the deprivation of basic capabilities, then a more illuminating picture can be obtained from information on aspects of life in these parts of the world.[26] A brief analysis is attempted below, based on a joint study with Jean Drèze, and on two follow-up works of this author.[27]

Around 1991 there were fifty-two countries where the expectation of life at birth was below sixty years, and those countries had a combined population of 1.69 billion.[28] Forty-six of these countries are in South Asia and sub-Saharan Africa—only six are outside these two regions (viz. Afghanistan, Cambodia, Haiti, Laos, Papua New Guinea and Yemen), and the combined population of these six is only 3.5 percent of the total population (1.69 billion) of the fifty-two low-life-expectancy countries. The *whole* of South Asia except Sri Lanka (i.e., India, Pakistan, Bangladesh, Nepal and Bhutan) and the *whole* of sub-Saharan Africa except South Africa, Zimbabwe, Lesotho, Botswana, and a collection of tiny islands (e.g., Mauritius and the Seychelles) belong to the group of the other forty-six low-life-expectancy countries. Of course, there are variations *within* each country. Well-placed sections of the population of South Asia and sub-Saharan Africa enjoy high longevity, and as was discussed earlier, parts of the population of countries even with very high average life expectancy (such as the United States) may have survival problems that compare with conditions in the third world. (For example, American black men in U.S. cities such as New York, San Francisco, St. Louis, or Washington, D.C., have life expectancies well below our cut-off point of sixty years.[29]) But in terms of country averages, South Asia and sub-Saharan Africa do indeed stand out as the regions where short and precarious lives are concentrated in the contemporary world.

TABLE 4.1: *India and Sub-Saharan Africa: Selected Comparisons (1991)*

| | Infant mortality rate comparisons | | |
|---|---|---|---|
| | Region | Population (millions) | Infant mortality rate (per 1,000 live births) |
| INDIA | India | 846.3 | 80 |
| "Worst" three Indian states | Orissa | 31.7 | 124 |
| | Madhya Pradesh | 66.2 | 117 |
| | Uttar Pradesh | 139.1 | 97 |
| "Worst" district of each of the "worst" Indian states | Ganjam (Orissa) | 3.2 | 164 |
| | Tikamgarh (Madhya Pradesh) | 0.9 | 152 |
| | Hardoi (Uttar Pradesh) | 2.7 | 129 |
| "Worst" three countries of sub-Saharan Africa | Mali | 8.7 | 161 |
| | Mozambique | 16.1 | 149 |
| | Guinea-Bissau | 1.0 | 148 |
| SUB-SAHARAN AFRICA | Sub-Saharan Africa | 488.9 | 104 |

*Note:* The age cutoff is 15 years for African figures, and 7 years for Indian figures. Note that in India, the 7+ literacy rate is usually higher than the 15+ literacy rate (e.g., the all-India 7+ literacy rate in 1981 was 43.6%, compared with 40.8% for the 15+ literacy rate).

Indeed, India alone accounts for more than half of the combined population of these fifty-two deprived countries. It is not by any means the worst performer on average (in fact, average life expectancy in India is very close to sixty years and according to latest statistics has just risen above it), but there are large regional variations in living conditions *within* India. Some regions of India (with populations as large as—or larger than—most countries in the world) do as badly as any country in the world. India may do significantly better on average than, say, the worst performers (such as Ethiopia or Zaire, now renamed the Democratic Republic of Congo) in terms of life expectancy and other indicators, but there are large areas within India where life expectancy and other basic living conditions are not very different from those prevailing in these most-deprived countries.[30]

| Adult literacy rate comparisons | | |
|---|---|---|
| Region | Population (millions) | Adult literacy rate* (female/male) |
| India | 846.3 | 39/64 |
| Rajasthan | 44.0 | 20/55 |
| Bihar | 86.4 | 23/52 |
| Uttar Pradesh | 139.1 | 25/56 |
| Barmer (Rajasthan) | 1.4 | 8/37 |
| Kishanganj (Bihar) | 1.0 | 10/33 |
| Bahraich (Uttar Pradesh) | 2.8 | 11/36 |
| Burkina Faso | 9.2 | 10/31 |
| Sierra Leone | 4.3 | 12/35 |
| Benin | 4.8 | 17/35 |
| Sub-Saharan Africa | 488.9 | 40/63 |

*Source:* J. Drèze and A. Sen, *India: Economic Development and Social Opportunity* (Delhi: Oxford University Press, 1995), table 3.1.

Table 4.1 compares the levels of *infant mortality* and *adult literacy* in the least-developed regions of sub-Saharan Africa and India.[31] The table presents the 1991 estimates of these two variables not only for India and sub-Saharan Africa as a whole (first and last rows), but also for the three worst-performing countries of sub-Saharan Africa, the three worst-performing Indian states, and the worst-performing districts of each of these three states. It is remarkable that there is no country in sub-Saharan Africa—or indeed in the world—where estimated infant mortality rates are as high as in the district of Ganjam in Orissa, or where the adult female literacy rate is as low as in the district of Barmer in Rajasthan. Each of these two districts, incidentally, has a larger population than Botswana or Namibia, and the combined population of the two is larger than that of Sierra Leone, Nicaragua or Ireland. Indeed, even entire states such as Uttar Pradesh (which has a population as large as that of Brazil or Russia) do not do much better than the worst-off among the sub-Saharan countries in terms of these basic indicators of living quality.[32]

It is interesting that if we take India and sub-Saharan Africa as a whole, we find that the two regions are not very different in terms of either adult literacy or infant mortality. They do differ in terms of life expectancy, though. The expectation of life in India around 1991 was about sixty years, while it was much below that figure in sub-Saharan Africa (averaging about fifty-two years).[33] On the other hand, there is considerable evidence that the extent of undernourishment is much greater in India than in sub-Saharan Africa.[34]

There is thus an interesting pattern of contrast between India and sub-Saharan Africa in terms of the different criteria of (1) mortality and (2) nutrition. The survival advantage in favor of India can be brought out not only by comparisons of life expectancy, but also by contrasts of other mortality statistics. For example, the median age at death in India was about thirty-seven years around 1991; this compares with a weighted average (of median age at death) for sub-Saharan Africa of a mere five years.[35] Indeed, in as many as five African countries, the median age at death was observed to be three years or below. Seen in this perspective, the problem of premature mortality is enormously sharper in Africa than in India.

But we get a very different balance of disadvantages if we look at the prevalence of *undernourishment* in India via-à-vis Africa. Calculations of general undernourishment are much higher in India than in sub-Saharan Africa on the average.[36] This is so despite the fact that it is India, rather than sub-Saharan Africa, that is self-sufficient in food. Indian "self-sufficiency" is based on the fulfillment of market demand, which can be, in normal years, easily met by domestically produced supply. But the market demand (based on purchasing power) understates the food needs. Actual undernourishment seems to be much higher in India than in sub-Saharan Africa. Judged in terms of the usual standards of retardation in weight for age, the proportion of undernourished children in Africa is 20 to 40 percent, whereas the proportion of undernourished children in India is a gigantic 40 to 60 percent.[37] About half of all Indian children are, it appears, chronically undernourished. While Indians live longer than sub-Saharan Africans, and have a median age at death much higher than Africans have, nevertheless there are many more undernourished children in

India than sub-Saharan Africa—not just in absolute terms but also as a proportion of all children.[38] If we add to it the fact that gender bias at death is a substantial problem in India, but not so in sub-Saharan Africa, we see a picture that is much less favorable to India than to Africa.[39]

There are important policy issues related to the nature and complexity of the respective patterns of deprivation in the two most acute regions of poverty in the world. India's advantage over sub-Saharan Africa in survival relates to a variety of factors that have made Africans especially prone to premature mortality. Since independence, India has been relatively free of the problems of famine and also of large-scale and persistent warfare, which has periodically ravaged a large number of African countries. India's health services—inadequate as they are—have been less overwhelmed by political and military turmoil. Furthermore, many countries of sub-Saharan Africa have had specific experiences of economic *decline*—partly related to wars, unrest and political disorder—which make it particularly hard to improve living standards. A comparative assessment of the achievements and failures of the two regions would have to take note of these and other aspects of their respective development experiences.[40]

One should also note that one problem that India and sub-Saharan Africa have in common is the persistence of endemic illiteracy—a feature that, like low life expectancy, sets South Asia and sub-Saharan Africa apart from most of the rest of the world. As table 4.1 indicates, literacy rates are very similar in the two regions. Both in India and in sub-Saharan Africa, every other adult is illiterate.

The three focal features of deprivation of basic capabilities on which I have concentrated in comparing and contrasting the nature of deprivation in India and in sub-Saharan Africa (viz., *premature mortality, undernourishment* and *illiteracy*) do not, of course, provide a comprehensive picture of capability-poverty in these regions. However, they bring out some striking failures and some crucial policy issues that demand immediate attention. I have also not attempted to produce an "aggregate" measure of deprivation, based on "weighting" the different aspects of capability deprivation.[41] A constructed aggregate may often be far less interesting for policy analysis than the substantive pattern of diverse performances.

FIGURE 4.2: *Female-Male Ratios in Total Population in Selected Communities*

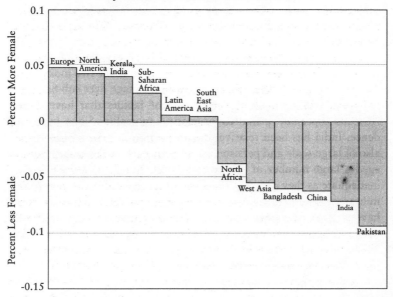

*Source:* Calculated from UN Population Statistics.

## GENDER INEQUALITY AND MISSING WOMEN

I turn now to a specific aspect of a general inequality that has drawn much attention lately; this section draws on my article "Missing Women" published in the *British Medical Journal* in 1992.[42] I refer to the terrible phenomenon of excess mortality and artificially lower survival rates of women in many parts of the world. This is a crude and sharply visible aspect of gender inequality, which often manifests itself in more subtle and less gruesome forms. But despite its crudeness, the artificially higher female mortality rates reflect a very important capability deprivation of women.

In Europe and North America, women tend, generally, to outnumber men by substantial numbers. For example, in the United Kingdom, France and the United States, the ratio of women to men exceeds 1.05. The situation is quite different in many countries in the third world, especially in Asia and North Africa, where the female-male ratio can be as low as 0.95 (Egypt), 0.94 (Bangladesh, China, West Asia), 0.93 (India), or even 0.90 (Pakistan). The significance of these differences is of interest in analyzing female-male inequalities across the world.[43] Figure 4.2 presents this comparative information.

In fact, more boys than girls are born everywhere (typically about 5 percent more). But there is much evidence that women are "hardier" than men and, given symmetrical care, survive better. (Indeed, it appears that even female fetuses have a higher survival rate than do the male fetuses; the proportion of male fetuses in conception is even higher than that in birth.[44]) It is through the lower mortality rates of females that the high female-male ratio of the "West" comes about. There are also other causes for this preponderance of women. There is some remaining impact of deaths of males in past wars. There has been, in general, a greater incidence of smoking among men and also greater proneness toward violent death. But it seems clear that even when these other effects are taken out, women would tend to outnumber men, given symmetrical care.

The low female-male ratios in countries in Asia and North Africa indicate the influence of social factors. It is easily calculated that if these countries had the female-male ratio that obtains in Europe and the United States, there would have been millions more women in these countries (given the number of men).[45] In China alone the number of "missing women," calculated on the basis of the European or American ratio, would be more than 50 million, and on that basis, for these countries taken together, many more than 100 million women may be seen as "missing."

It may not, however, be appropriate to use the European or American ratio, not just because of such special features as wartime deaths. Because of lower mortality rates of females in Europe and America, the female-male ratio rises gradually with age. A lower ratio would be expected in Asia or North Africa partly because of the lower general life expectancy and higher fertility rate. One way of dealing with this issue is to take as the basis of comparison not the female-male ratio in Europe or America, but that in sub-Saharan Africa, where there is little female disadvantage in terms of relative mortality rates, but where life expectancy is no higher and fertility rates are no lower (quite the contrary). Taking the sub-Saharan female-male ratio of 1.022 as the benchmark (used in my earlier studies and in those with Jean Drèze) yields an estimate of 44 million missing women in China, 37 million in India, and a total for these countries still in excess of 100 million.[46]

Another way of dealing with this problem is to calculate what the expected number of females would be had there been no female disadvantage in survival, given the actual life expectancy and the actual fertility rates in these respective countries. It is not easy to calculate that directly, but illuminating estimates have been made by Ansley Coale, through using model population tables based on the historical experience of "Western" countries. This procedure yields 29 million "missing women" in China, 23 million in India, and a total for these countries of around 60 million.[47] While these are lower numbers, they too are fiercely large. More recent estimates, based on the use of more scrutinized historical data, have tended to yield rather larger numbers of missing women (about 90 million, as estimated by Stephan Klasen).[48]

Why are overall mortality rates for females higher than for males in these countries? Consider India, where the age-specific mortality rate for females consistently exceeds that for males until the late thirties. While the excess mortality in the childbearing age may be partly the result of maternal mortality (death during or just after childbirth), obviously no such explanation is possible for female disadvantage in survival in infancy and childhood. Despite occasional distressing accounts of female infanticide in India, that phenomenon, even if present, cannot do anything to explain the magnitude of extra mortality, nor its age distribution. The main culprit would seem to be the comparative neglect of female health and nutrition, especially— but not exclusively—during childhood. There is indeed considerable direct evidence that female children are neglected in terms of health care, hospitalization and even feeding.[49]

Even though the Indian case has been studied more extensively than others (there are more researchers working on this issue in India than in any other country), similar evidence of relative neglect of the health and nutrition of female children can be found in the other countries as well. In China there is even some evidence that the extent of neglect may have increased sharply in recent years, particularly since the compulsory family restrictions (such as the one-child policy in some parts of the country) were introduced, along with other reforms, around 1979. There are also some new, ominous signs in China, such as a radical increase in the reported ratio of male births to female births—quite out of line with the rest of the world. It can, quite possibly, indicate "hiding" of newborn female children (to avoid the rigors of compulsory family restriction), but it can, no less plausibly, also reflect a higher female infant mortality—whether or not induced (with new births and new deaths both going unreported). However, recently, the brunt of the antifemale bias in family composition seems to be in sex-selective abortion, which has become quite widespread in China with the progress of technology.

## CONCLUDING REMARKS

Economists are sometimes criticized for concentrating too much on efficiency and too little on equity. There may be some ground for complaint here, but it must also be noted that inequality has received attention from economists throughout the history of this discipline. Adam Smith, who is often thought of as "the Father of Modern Economics," was deeply concerned with the gulf between the rich and the poor (more on this later, in chapters 5 and 11). Some of the social scientists and philosophers who are responsible for making inequality such a central subject of public attention (such as Karl Marx, John Stuart Mill, B. S. Rowntree and Hugh Dalton, to take writers belonging to very different general traditions) were, in terms of substantive involvement, devoted economists, no matter what else they might also have been. In recent years, economics of inequality as a subject has flourished, with major leadership coming from such writers as A. B. Atkinson.[50] This is not to deny that the focus on efficiency to the exclusion of other considerations is very evident in some works in economics, but economists as a group cannot be accused of neglecting inequality as a subject.

If there is a reason to grumble, it rests more on the relative importance that is attached, in much of economics, to inequality in a very narrow domain, viz., *income inequality*. This narrowness has the effect of contributing to the neglect of other ways of seeing inequality and equity, which has far-reaching bearing on the making of economic policy. Policy debates have indeed been distorted by over-emphasis on income poverty and income inequality, to the neglect of deprivations that relate to other variables, such as unemployment, ill health, lack of education, and social exclusion. Unfortunately, the identification of economic inequality with income inequality is fairly common in economics, and the two are often seen as effectively synonymous. If you tell someone that you are working on economic inequality, it is quite standardly assumed that you are studying income distribution.

To some extent, this implicit identification can be found in the philosophical literature as well. For example, in his interesting and important paper "Equality as a Moral Ideal," Harry Frankfurt, the distinguished philosopher, provides a closely reasoned and powerful critique of what he calls "economic egalitarianism," defining it as "the doctrine that there should be no inequalities in the distribution of money."[51]

The distinction, however, between income inequality and economic inequality is important.[52] Many of the criticisms of economic egalitarianism as a value or a goal apply much more readily to the narrow concept of income inequality than they do to the broader notions of economic inequality. For example, giving a larger share of income to a person with more needs—say, due to a disability—can be seen as militating against the principle of equalizing *incomes*, but it does not go against the broader precepts of economic equality, since the greater need for economic resources due to the disability must be taken into account in judging the requirements of economic equality.

Empirically, the relationship between income inequality and inequality in other relevant spaces can be rather distant and contingent because of various economic influences other than income that affect inequalities in individual advantages and substantive freedoms. For example, in the higher mortality rates of African Americans vis-à-vis the much poorer Chinese, or Indians in Kerala, we see the influence of factors that run in the opposite direction to income inequality, and that involve public policy issues with strong economic components: the financing of health care and insurance, provision of public education, arrangements for local security and so on.

Mortality differences can, in fact, serve as an indicator of very deep inequities that divide races, classes and genders, as the various illustrations in this chapter bring out. For example, the estimations of "missing women" show the remarkable reach of female disadvantage in many parts of the contemporary world, in a way that other statistics may not adequately reflect. Also, since the incomes earned by family members are shared by others in the family, we cannot analyze gender inequality primarily in terms of income differences. We need much more information than is usually available on the division of resource use within the family to get a clearer idea of inequalities in economic affluence. However, statistics on mortality rates as well as other deprivations (such as undernourishment or illiteracy) can directly present a picture of inequality and poverty in some crucial dimensions. This information can also be used to relate the extent of relative deprivation of women to the existing inequalities in opportunities (in earning outside income, in being enrolled in schools and so on). Thus, both descriptive and policy issues can be addressed through this broader perspective on inequality and poverty in terms of capability deprivation.

Despite the crucial role of incomes in the advantages enjoyed by different persons, the relationship between income (and other resources), on the one hand, and individual achievements and freedoms, on the other, is neither constant nor in any sense automatic and irresistible. Different types of contingencies lead to systematic variations in the "conversion" of incomes into the distinct "functionings" we can achieve, and that affects the lifestyles we can enjoy. I have tried to illustrate in this chapter the different ways in which there can be systematic variations in the relationship between incomes earned and substantive freedoms (in the form of capability to lead lives that people have reason to value). The respective roles of personal heterogeneities, environmental diversities, variations in social climate, differences in relational perspectives and distributions within the family have to receive the serious attention they deserve for the making of public policy.

The argument is sometimes made that income is a homogeneous magnitude, whereas capabilities are diverse. This sharp contrast is not entirely correct, in the sense that any income evaluation hides internal diversities with some special—and often heroic—assumptions.[53] Also (as was discussed in chapter 3), interpersonal comparisons of real income give us no basis for interpersonal comparisons even of utility (though that hiatus is often ignored in applied welfare economics through the imposition of wholly arbitrary assumptions). To get from the comparison of the means in the form of income differences to something that can be claimed to be valuable in itself (such as well-being or freedom), we have to take note of circumstantial variations that affect the conversion rates. The presumption that the approach of income comparison is a more "practical" way of getting at interpersonal differences in advantages is hard to sustain.

Furthermore, the need to discuss the valuation of diverse capabilities in terms of public priorities is, I have argued, an asset, forcing us to make clear what the value judgments are in a field where value judgments cannot be—and should not be—avoided. Indeed, public participation in these valuational debates—in explicit or implicit forms—is a crucial part of the exercise of democracy and responsible social choice. In matters of public judgment, there is no real escape from the evaluative need for public discussion. The work of public valuation cannot be replaced by some cunningly clever assumption. Some assumptions that give the appearance of working very nicely and smoothly operate through concealing the choice of values and weights in cultivated opaqueness. For example, the assumption—often implicitly made—that two persons with the same demand function must have the same relation between commodity bundles and well-being (no matter whether one is ill and the other not, one disabled and the other not, and so on) is basically a way of evading the need to consider many significant influences on well-being (as was discussed in chapter 3). That evasion becomes transparent, as I have tried to illustrate, when we supplement income and commodity data with information of other types (including matters of life and death).

The issue of public discussion and social participation is thus central to the making of policy in a democratic framework. The use of democratic prerogatives—both political liberties and civil rights—is a crucial part of the exercise of economic policy making itself, in addition to other roles it may have. In a freedom-oriented approach, the participatory freedoms cannot but be central to public policy analysis.

CHAPTER 5

# MARKETS, STATE AND
# SOCIAL OPPORTUNITY

▼

"It is the customary fate of new truths," says T. H. Huxley in *Science and Culture,* "to begin as heresies and to end as superstitions." Something very like this seems to have happened about the truth of the importance of markets in economic life. There was a time—not very long ago—when every young economist "knew" in what respect the market systems had serious limitations: all the textbooks repeated the same list of "defects." The intellectual rejection of the market mechanism often led to radical proposals for altogether different methods of organizing the world (sometimes involving a powerful bureaucracy and unimagined fiscal burdens), without serious examination of the possibility that the proposed alternatives might involve even bigger failures than the markets were expected to produce. There was, often enough, rather little interest in the new and additional problems that the alternative arrangements may create.

The intellectual climate has changed quite dramatically over the last few decades, and the tables are now turned. The virtues of the market mechanism are now standardly assumed to be so pervasive that qualifications seem unimportant. Any pointer to the defects of the market mechanism appears to be, in the present mood, strangely old-fashioned and contrary to contemporary culture (like playing an old 78 rpm record with music from the 1920s). One set of prejudices has given way to another—opposite—set of preconceptions. Yesterday's unexamined faith has become today's heresy, and yesterday's heresy is now the new superstition.

The need for critical scrutiny of standard preconceptions and political-economic attitudes has never been stronger.[1] Today's prejudices (in favor of the pure market mechanism) certainly need to be carefully investigated and, I would argue, partly rejected. But we have to avoid resurrecting yesterday's follies that refused to see the merits of—indeed even the inescapable need for—markets. We have to scrutinize and decide what parts make sense in the respective perspectives. My illustrious countryman Gautama Buddha may have been too predisposed to see the universal need for "the middle path" (though he did not get around to discussing the market mechanism in particular), but there is something to be learned from his speeches on nonextremism delivered 2,500 years ago.

## MARKETS, LIBERTY AND LABOR

Even though the merits of the market mechanism are now very widely acknowledged, the *reasons* for wanting markets are often not fully appreciated. This issue was discussed in the introduction and in the first chapter of this book, but I must return to it briefly in examining the institutional aspects of development. In recent discussions, the focus in assessing the market mechanism has tended to be on the *results* it ultimately generates, such as the incomes or the utilities yielded by the markets. This is not a negligible issue, and I shall come to it presently. But the more immediate case for the freedom of market transaction lies in the basic importance of that freedom itself. We have good reasons to buy and sell, to exchange, and to seek lives that can flourish on the basis of transactions. To deny that freedom in general would be in itself a major failing of a society. This fundamental recognition is *prior* to any theorem we may or may not be able to prove (on which more presently) in showing what the culmination outcomes of markets are in terms of incomes, utilities and so on.[2]

The ubiquitous role of transactions in modern living is often overlooked precisely because we take them for granted. There is an analogy here with the rather underrecognized—and often unnoticed—role of certain behavioral rules (such as basic business ethics) in developed capitalist economies (with attention being focused only on aberrations when they occur). But when these values are not yet developed, their general presence or absence can make a crucial difference. In the analysis of development, the role of elementary business ethics thus has to be moved out of its obscure presence to a manifest recognition. Similarly, the absence of the freedom to transact can be a major issue in itself in many contexts.[3]

This is, of course, particularly so when the freedom of labor markets is denied by laws, regulations or convention. Even though African American slaves in the pre–Civil War South may have had pecuniary incomes as large as (or even larger than) those of wage laborers elsewhere and may even have lived longer than the urban workers in the North,[4] there was still a fundamental deprivation in the fact of slavery itself (no matter what incomes or utilities it might or might not have generated). The loss of freedom in the absence of employment choice and in the tyrannical form of work can itself be a major deprivation.

The development of free markets in general and of free seeking of employment in particular is a much appreciated fact in historical studies. Even that great critic of capitalism Karl Marx saw the emergence of freedom of employment as momentous progress (as was discussed in chapter 1). But this issue concerns not just history but the present as well, since this freedom is critically important right now in many parts of the world. Let me illustrate this point with four quite different examples.

First, various forms of labor bondage can be found in many countries in Asia and Africa, and there are persistent denials of basic freedom to seek wage employment away from one's traditional bosses. When the Indian newspapers report that the upper-caste landowners in one of the most backward parts of India (viz., Bihar) are terrorizing— through selective murder and rape—the families of laborers "tied" to their lands, there is, of course, an issue of criminality involved, which is why such incidents receive media attention (and which may be ultimately the reason why things may have to change even in these terrible communities). But underlying the criminal activities, the basic economic situation involves a battle for the freedom of employment as well as the ownership of land on which the "tied" laborers are forced to work; these arrangements continue despite their illegality (as a result of postindependence legislation that has been only partly implemented). The situation has been more studied in India than elsewhere (as discussed in chapter 1), but there is enough evidence that similar problems are present in several other countries as well.

Second (to turn now to a very different illustration), the failure of bureaucratic socialism in Eastern Europe and the Soviet Union cannot be fully grasped merely in terms of the economic problems in generating incomes or other results, such as life expectancies. Indeed, in terms of life expectancies, the communist countries often did quite well, relatively speaking (as is readily checked from the demographic statistics of the Soviet Union, pre-reform China, Vietnam and Cuba, among others). In fact, several of the ex-communist countries now are in a significantly *worse* position than they were under communist rule—perhaps nowhere more so than in Russia itself (where the life expectancy at birth of Russian men has dropped now to about fifty-eight years—considerably below those in India or Pakistan).[5] And yet the population is unwilling to vote to return to the previous arrangements, as election results indicate, and even the new successor parties drawing from that old political quarter do not propose such a return (and only demand rather less radical restitutions).

In assessing what happened, the economic inefficiency of the communist system must, of course, be recognized. But there is also the more immediate issue of the denial of freedom in a system where markets were simply ruled out in many fields. Also, people could be disallowed from using the markets even when they existed. For example, they could be barred from seeking employment in an ongoing recruitment process (including some unfavored persons being sent to work where the bosses wanted them to work). In this sense, Friedrich Hayek's chastising description of the communist economies as "the road to serfdom" was indeed a fitting, if severe, rhetoric.[6] In a different—but not unrelated—context, Michal Kalecki (the great Polish economist who returned to Poland with great enthusiasm as the communist rule got established there) noted, in answer to a journalist's question on Poland's progress from capitalism to socialism: "Yes, we have successfully abolished capitalism; all we have to do now is to abolish feudalism."

Third, as was noted in chapter 1, in the distressing subject of child labor (as prevalent, for example, in Pakistan, or India, or Bangladesh), there is an embedded issue of slavery and bondage, since many of the children working in exacting tasks are forced to perform them. The roots of such servitude may go back to the economic deprivation of the families from which they come—sometimes the parents are themselves under some kind of bondage vis-à-vis the employers—and on top of the nasty issue of laboring children, there is also the barbarity of children being *forced* to do things. The freedom to go to school, in particular, is hampered not only by the weakness of primary educational programs in these regions, but in some cases also by the lack of any choice that the children (and often their parents) have in deciding what they want to do.

The issue of child labor tends to divide South Asian economists. Some have argued that merely abolishing child labor without doing anything to enhance the economic circumstances of the families involved may not serve the interest of the children themselves. There is certainly a debatable issue here, but the frequent congruence of child labor with what effectively is slavery does make it, in those cases, a simpler choice. The starkness of slavery yields a forceful case for more vigorous enforcement of antislavery as well as anti-child-labor legislation. The system of child labor—bad enough on its own—is made much beastlier still through its congruence with bondage and effective slavery.

Fourth, the freedom of women to seek employment outside the family is a major issue in many third world countries. This freedom is systematically denied in many cultures, and this in itself is a serious violation of women's liberty and gender equity. The absence of this freedom militates against the economic empowerment of women, and also has many other consequences. Aside from the direct effects of market employment in adding to the economic independence of women, outside work is also causally important in making women have a better "deal" in intrahousehold distributions.[7] Needless to say, women's work at home can be backbreaking, but it is rarely honored or even recognized (and certainly not remunerated), and the denial of the right to work outside the home is a rather momentous violation of women's liberty.[8]

The prohibition of outside employment for women can sometimes be brutally executed in an explicit and fierce way (as, for example, in contemporary Afghanistan). In other cases, the prohibition may work more implicitly through the power of convention and conformity. Sometimes there may not even be, in any clear sense, a ban on women's seeking employment, and yet women reared with traditional values may be quite afraid to break with the tradition and to shock others. The prevailing perceptions of "normality" and "appropriateness" are quite central to this question.

This issue relates to other important concerns of this work, in particular, the need for open discussion of social issues and the advantage of group activities in bringing about substantial social changes. Women's organizations have begun to play a very important part in this transformation in many countries in the world. For example, Self-employed Women's Association (SEWA) has been most effective in bringing about a changed climate of thought, not just more employment for women, in one part of India. So have participatory credit and cooperative organizations, such as the Grameen Bank and Bangladesh Rural Advancement Committee (BRAC) in Bangladesh. While emphasizing the significance of transaction and the right of economic participation (including the right to seek employment freely), and the direct importance of market-related liberties, we must not lose sight of the complementarity of these liberties with the freedoms that come from the operation of other (nonmarket) institutions.[9] This complementarity between different institutions—in particular between nonmarket organizations and the market—is also a central theme of this book.

## MARKETS AND EFFICIENCY

The labor market can be a liberator in many different contexts, and the basic freedom of transaction can be of central importance, quite aside from whatever the market mechanism may or may not achieve in terms of incomes or utilities or other results. But it is important also to examine those consequential results, and I turn now to that—rather different—issue.

In assessing the market mechanism, it is important to take note of the forms of the markets: whether they are competitive or monopolistic (or otherwise uncompetitive), whether some markets may be missing (in ways that are not easily remediable) and so on. Also, the nature of factual circumstances (such as the availability or absence of particular kinds of information, the presence or absence of economies of large scale) may influence the actual possibilities and impose real limitations on what can be achieved through various institutional forms of the market mechanism.[10]

In the absence of such imperfections (including the nonmarketability of some goods and services), classical models of general equilibrium have been used to demonstrate the merits of the market mechanism in achieving economic efficiency. This is standardly defined in terms of what economists call "Pareto optimality": a situation in which the utility (or welfare) of no one can be raised without reducing the utility (or welfare) of someone else. This efficiency achievement—the so-called Arrow-Debreu theorem (after the original authors of the results, Kenneth Arrow and Gerard Debreu[11])—is of real importance despite the simplifying assumptions.[12]

The Arrow-Debreu results show, inter alia, that—given some preconditions—the results of the market mechanism are not improvable in ways that would enhance everyone's utility (or enhance the utility of some without reducing the utility of anyone else).[13]

It is possible, however, to question whether the efficiency sought should not be accounted in terms of *individual freedoms,* rather than *utilities.* This is an especially legitimate question here, since the information focus of this work has been on individual freedoms (not utilities). I have, in fact, demonstrated elsewhere that in terms of some plausible characterizations of substantive individual freedoms, an important part of the Arrow-Debreu efficiency result readily translates from the "space" of utilities to that of individual freedoms, both in terms of freedom to choose *commodity baskets* and in terms of *capabilities to function.*[14] In demonstrating the viability of this extension, similar assumptions are employed as are needed for the original Arrow-Debreu results (such as the absence of nonmarketability). With these presumptions, it turns out that for a cogent characterization of individual freedoms, a competitive market equilibrium guarantees that no one's freedom can be increased any further while maintaining the freedom of everyone else.

For this connection to be established, the importance of substantive freedom has to be judged not just in terms of the *number* of options one has, but with adequate sensitivity to the *attractiveness* of the available options. Freedom has different aspects; personal liberties as well as the liberty to transact have already been discussed earlier. However, for the *freedom to achieve* in line with what one wants to achieve, we have to take note of the merits of the available options.[15] In explaining this freedom-efficiency result (without going into technicalities), it can be pointed out that given canny choice by individuals, efficiency in terms of individual utilities has to be, to a great extent, parasitic on offering the individuals adequate opportunities from which they can choose. These opportunities are not only relevant for what people choose (and the utility they achieve), but also for what useful options they have (and the substantive freedoms they enjoy).

One particular issue may be worth clarifying here, concerning the role of self-interest maximization in achieving the efficiency results of the market mechanism. In the classic (Arrow-Debreu) framework, it is assumed that everyone must be pursuing her self-interest as her exclusive motivation. This behavioral assumption is necessitated by the attempt to establish the result that the market outcome will be "Pareto optimal" (which is defined in terms of individual interests), so that no one's interest could be further enhanced without damaging the interests of others.[16]

The presumption of ubiquitous selfishness is hard to defend empirically. Also, there are circumstances more complex than those presumed in the Arrow-Debreu model (involving more direct interdependences between the interests of different persons) in which self-interested behavior may be far from effective in generating efficient outcomes. Thus, if it were really necessary to assume universal selfishness to establish the efficiency results in the Arrow-Debreu model, then it could be seen as a serious limitation of that approach. However, this limitation can be substantially avoided by examining the demands of efficiency in terms of individual freedoms, rather than just utilities.

The restriction of having to assume self-interested behavior can be removed if our primary concern is with substantive freedoms that people enjoy (no matter for what purpose they use these freedoms), not the extent to which their self-interests are fulfilled (through their own self-interested behavior). No assumption need be made, in this case, about what motivates the individuals' choices, since the point at issue is no longer the achievement of interest fulfillment, but the availability of freedom (no matter whether the freedom is aimed at self-interest or at some other objective). The basic analytical results of the Arrow-Debreu theorem are thus quite independent of the motivations that lie behind the individual preferences, and can be left unaddressed if the object is to show efficiency in preference fulfillment, or efficiency in substantive individual freedoms (irrespective of motivation).[17]

## COUPLING OF DISADVANTAGES
## AND INEQUALITY OF FREEDOMS

The basic result about market efficiency can, in this sense, be extended to the perspective of substantive freedoms. But these efficiency results do not say anything about the equity of outcomes, or about the equity in the distribution of freedoms. A situation can be efficient in the sense that no one's utility or substantive freedom can be enhanced without cutting into the utility or freedom of someone else, and yet there could be enormous inequalities in the distribution of utilities and of freedoms.

The problem of inequality, in fact, gets magnified as the attention is shifted from income inequality to the inequality in the *distribution of substantive freedoms and capabilities*. This is mainly because of the possibility of some "coupling" of income inequality, on the one hand, with unequal advantages in converting incomes into capabilities, on the other. The latter tends to intensify the inequality problem already reflected in income inequality. For example, a person who is disabled, or ill, or old, or otherwise handicapped may, on the one hand, have problems in *earning* a decent income, and on the other, also face greater difficulties in *converting* income into capabilities and into living well. The very factors that may make a person unable to find a good job and a good income (such as a disability) may put the person at a disadvantage in achieving a good quality of life even with the same job and with the same income.[18] This relationship between income-*earning* ability and income-*using* ability is a well-known empirical phenomenon in poverty studies.[19] The interpersonal income inequality in the market outcomes may tend to be magnified by this "coupling" of low incomes with handicaps in the conversion of incomes into capabilities.

The freedom-efficiency of the market mechanism, on the one hand, and the seriousness of freedom-inequality problems, on the other hand, are worth considering *simultaneously*. The equity problems have to be addressed, especially in dealing with serious deprivations and poverty, and in that context, social intervention including governmental support may well have an important role. To a great extent, this is exactly what the social security systems in welfare states try to achieve, through a variety of programs including social provision of health care, public support of the unemployed and the indigent and so on. But the need to pay attention *simultaneously* to efficiency and equity aspects of the problem remains, since equity-motivated interference with the working of the market mechanism can weaken efficiency achievements even as it promotes equity. It is important to be clear about the need for simultaneity in considering the different aspects of social evaluation and justice.

The need for synchronous consideration of distinct goals has already been faced in this work in several other contexts. For example, it was considered in chapter 4 in contrasting the greater social commitment in Europe (more than in the United States) in guaranteeing minimal incomes and health care, with a greater social commitment in the United States (more than in Europe) in maintaining high levels of employment. The two types of commitments may be, to a considerable extent, combinable, but they may also be, at least partly, in conflict with each other. To the extent that there is a conflict, the need for simultaneity in considering the two issues *together* would be important in arriving at *overall* social priorities, paying attention to both efficiency and equity.

## MARKETS AND INTEREST GROUPS

The role that markets play must depend not only on what they can do, but also on what they are allowed to do. There are many people whose interests are well served by the smooth functioning of markets, but there are also groups whose established interests may be hurt by such functioning. If the latter groups are politically more powerful and influential, then they can try to see that markets are not given adequate room in the economy. This can be a particularly serious problem when monopolistic production units flourish—despite inefficiency and various types of ineptitude—thanks to insulation from competition, domestic or foreign. The high product-prices or the low product-qualities that are involved in such artificially propped-up production may impose significant sacrifice on the population at large, but an organized and politically influential group of "industrialists" can make sure that their profits are well protected.

Adam Smith's complaint about the limited use of markets in eighteenth-century Britain was concerned not only with pointing to the social advantages of well-functioning markets, but also with identifying the influence of vested interests in guaranteeing the insulation of their inflated profits from the threatening effects of competition. Indeed, Adam Smith saw the need to understand the working of markets, to a great extent, as an antidote to the arguments standardly used by vested interests against giving competition an adequate role. Smith's intellectual arguments were partly aimed at countering the power and effectiveness of advocacy from entrenched interests.

The market restrictions against which Smith was particularly vocal can be seen, in a broad sense, as "precapitalist" constraints. They differ from public intervention for, say, welfare programs or social safety nets, of which only rudimentary expressions could be found, at his time, in arrangements such as the Poor Laws.[20] They also differ from the functioning of the state in providing such services as public education, of which Smith was very supportive (more on this presently).

As it happens, many of the restrictions that bedevil the functioning of economies in developing countries today—or even allegedly socialist countries of yesterday—are also, broadly, of this "precapitalist" type. Whether we consider the prohibition of some types of domestic trade or international exchange, or the preservation of antiquated techniques and production methods in businesses owned and operated by "protected bourgeoisie," there is a generic similarity between the sweeping advocacy of restricted competition and the flourishing of precapitalist values and habits of thought. The "radicals" of yesterday, such as Adam Smith (whose ideas inspired many of the activists in the French Revolution), or David Ricardo (who resisted Malthus's defense of the productive contribution of torpid landlords), or Karl Marx (who saw competitive capitalism as a major force for progressive change in the world), had little sympathy for the generally anti-market arguments of precapitalist leaders of thought.

It is one of the ironies of the history of ideas that some who advocate radical politics today often fall for old economic positions that were so unequivocally rejected by Smith, Ricardo and Marx. Michal Kalecki's bitter grumble about restriction-ridden Poland ("we have successfully abolished capitalism; all we have to do now is to abolish feudalism"), which I quoted earlier, can be well appreciated in this light. It is not surprising that the protected bourgeoisie often do their best to encourage and support the illusion of radicalism and modernity in dusting up generically anti-market positions from the distant past.

It is important to join these arguments through open-minded criticisms of the claims made in favor of general restriction of competition. This is not to deny that attention must also be paid to the political power of those groups that obtain substantial material benefits from restricting trade and exchange. Many authors have pointed out, with good reason, that the advocacies involved must be judged by identifying the vested interests involved, and by taking note of the influence of "rent-seeking activities" implicit in keeping competition away. As Vilfredo Pareto pointed out, in a famous passage, if "a certain measure A is the case of the loss of one franc to each of a thousand persons, and of a thousand franc gain to one individual, the latter will expend a great deal of energy, whereas the former will resist weakly; and it is likely that, in the end, the person who is attempting to secure the thousand francs via A will be successful."[21] Political influence in search of economic gain is a very real phenomenon in the world in which we live.[22]

Confronting such influences has to occur not merely through resisting—and perhaps even "exposing" (to use an old-fashioned word)—the seekers of profit from captive markets, but also from taking on their intellectual arguments as proper subjects of scrutiny. Economics does have a long tradition in that critical direction, going back at least to Adam Smith himself, who simultaneously pointed his accusing finger at the perpetrators, and went on to debunk their claims in favor of the thesis of social benefits from disallowing competition. Smith argued that the vested interests tend to win because of their "better knowledge of their own interest" (not "their knowledge of publick interest"). He wrote:

The interest of the dealers, however, in any particular branch of trade or manufactures, is always in some respects different from, and even opposite to that of the publick. To widen the market and to narrow the competition, is always the interest of the dealers. To widen the market may frequently be agreeable enough to the interest of the publick; but to narrow the competition must always be against it, and can serve only to enable the dealers, by raising their profits above what they naturally would be, to levy for their own benefit, an absurd tax upon the rest of their fellow-citizens. The proposal of any new law or regulation of commerce which comes from this order, ought always to be listened to with great precaution, and ought never to be adopted till after having been long and carefully examined, not only with the most scrupulous, but with the most suspicious attention.[23]

There is no reason why vested interests must win if open arguments are permitted and promoted. Even as Pareto's famous argument illustrates, there may be a thousand people whose interests are a little hurt by the policy that heavily feeds the interest of one businessman, and once the picture is seized with clarity, there may be no dearth of a majority in opposition to such special pleading. This is an ideal field for more public discussion of the claims and counterclaims on the different sides, and in the test of open democracy, public interest may well have excellent prospects of winning against the spirited advocacy of the small coterie of vested interests. Here too, as in many other areas already examined in this book, the remedy has to lie in more freedom—including that of public discussion and participatory political decisions. Once again, freedom of one kind (in this case, political freedom) can be seen as helping the realization of freedom of other kinds (particularly, that of economic openness).

## NEED FOR CRITICAL SCRUTINY
## OF THE ROLE OF MARKETS

Indeed, critical public discussion is an inescapably important requirement of good public policy since the appropriate role and reach of markets cannot be predetermined on the basis of some grand, general formula—or some all-encompassing attitude—either in favor of placing everything under the market, or of denying everything to the market. Even Adam Smith, while firmly advocating the use of markets where it could work well (and denying the merits of any *general* rejection of trade and exchange), did not hesitate to investigate economic circumstances in which particular restrictions may be sensibly proposed, or economic fields in which nonmarket institutions would be badly needed to supplement what the markets can do.[24]

It must not be presumed that Smith's critique of the market mechanism was always gentle, or, for that matter, that he got his critical points invariably right. Consider, for example, his advocacy of legal restrictions on usury.[25] Smith was, of course, opposed to any kind of general ban on charging interest on loans (as some anti-market thinkers had advocated).[26] However, he wanted to have legal restrictions imposed by the state on the maximum rates of interest that could be charged:

> In countries where interest is permitted, the law, in order to prevent the extortion of usury, generally fixes the highest rate which can be taken without incurring a penalty. . . .
>
> The legal rate, it is to be observed, though it ought to be somewhat above, ought not to be much above the lowest market rate. If the legal rate of interest in Great Britain, for example, was fixed so high as eight or ten per cent, the greater part of the money which was to be lent, would be lent to prodigals and projectors, who alone would be willing to give this high interest. Sober people, who will give for the use of money no more than a part of what they are likely to make by the use of it, would not venture into the competition. A great part of the capital of the country would thus be kept out of the hands which were most likely to make a profitable and advantageous use of it, and thrown into those which were most likely to waste and destroy it.[27]

In Smith's interventionist logic the underlying argument is that market signals can be misleading, and the consequences of the free market may be much waste of capital, resulting from private pursuit of misguided or myopic enterprises, or private waste of social resources. As it happens, Jeremy Bentham took Adam Smith to task in a long letter he wrote to Smith in March 1787, arguing for leaving the market alone.[28] This is a rather remarkable episode in the history of economic thought, with the principal utilitarian interventionist lecturing the pioneering guru of market economics on the virtues of market allocation.[29]

The issue of a legally imposed maximum interest rate is not of much current interest in contemporary debates (in this respect Bentham has clearly won over Smith), but it is important to see why Smith took such a negative view of the impact of "prodigals and projectors" on the economy. He was deeply concerned with the problem of social waste and the loss of productive capital. And he discussed in some detail how this could come about (*Wealth of Nations*, book 2, chapter 3). Regarding "prodigals," Smith saw in them a great potential for social waste, driven as they are "with the passion for present enjoyment." So it is that "every prodigal appears to be a publick enemy." Regarding "projectors," Smith's worries related again to social waste:

> The effects of misconduct are often the same as those of prodigality. Every injudicious and unsuccessful project in agriculture, mines, fisheries, trade, or manufactures, tends in the same manner to diminish the funds destined for the maintenance of productive labour. In every such project, . . . there must always be some diminution in what would otherwise have been the productive funds of the society.[30]

It is not particularly important to assess these specific arguments of Smith, but it is important to see what his general concerns are. What he is considering is the possibility of social loss in the narrowly motivated pursuit of private gains. This is the opposite case to the more famous remark of Smith: "It is not from the benevolence of the butcher, the brewer, or the baker that we expect our dinner, but from their regard to their own interest. We address ourselves, not to their humanity but to their self-love. . . ."[31] If the butcher-brewer-baker example draws our attention to the mutually beneficial role of trade based on self-interest, the prodigal-projector argument points to the possibility that under certain circumstances private profit motives may indeed run counter to social interests. It is this general concern that remains relevant today (not just the particular example of prodigals and projectors).[32] This is very much the central apprehension in considering the social loss involved, for example, in environmentally wasteful or polluting private productions, which fit well with Smith's description of the possibility of "some diminution in what would otherwise have been the productive funds of the society."

The lesson to draw from Smith's analysis of the market mechanism is not any massive strategy of jumping to policy conclusions from some general "pro" or "anti" attitude to markets. After acknowledging the role of trade and exchange in human living, we still have to examine what the other consequences of market transactions actually are. We have to evaluate the actual possibilities critically, with adequate attention being paid to the contingent circumstances that may be relevant in assessing all the results of encouraging markets, or of restraining their operation. If the butcher-brewer-baker example points to a very common circumstance in which our complementary interests are mutually promoted by exchange, the prodigal-projector example illustrates the possibility that this may not work in quite that way in every case. There is no escape from the necessity of critical scrutiny.

## NEED FOR A MANY-SIDED APPROACH

The case for taking a broad and many-sided approach to development has become clearer in recent years, partly as a result of the difficulties faced as well as successes achieved by different countries over the recent decades.[33] These issues relate closely to the need for balancing the role of the government—and of other political and social institutions—with the functioning of markets.

They also suggest the relevance of a "comprehensive development framework" of the kind discussed by James Wolfensohn, the president of the World Bank.[34] This type of framework involves rejecting a compartmentalized view of the process of development (for example, going just for "liberalization" or some other single, overarching process). The search for a single all-purpose remedy (such as "open the markets" or "get the prices right") has had much hold on professional thinking in the past, not least in the World Bank itself. Instead, an integrated and multifaceted approach is needed, with the object of making simultaneous progress on different fronts, including different institutions, which reinforce each other.[35]

Broader approaches are often harder to "sell" than narrowly focused reforms that try to achieve "one thing at a time." This may help to explain why the powerful intellectual leadership of Manmohan Singh in bringing about the needed economic reforms in India in 1991 was so concentrated on "liberalization" only, without a corresponding focus on the much-needed broadening of social opportunities. There is, however, quite a deep complementarity between reducing, on the one hand, the overactivity of the state in running a "license Raj," and, on the other, removing the underactivity of the state in the continuing neglect of elementary education and other social opportunities (with close to half the adult Indians still illiterate and quite unable to participate in an increasingly globalized economy).[36] In the event, Manmohan Singh did initiate some essential reforms, and this is a rightly admired success.[37] And yet that success could have been even greater if the reforms were combined with a commitment to expand the development of social opportunities that had been neglected so persistently in India.

Combining extensive use of markets with the development of social opportunities must be seen as a part of a still broader comprehensive approach that also emphasizes freedoms of other kinds (democratic rights, security guarantees, opportunities of cooperation and so on). In this book, the identification of different instrumental freedoms (such as economic entitlements, democratic freedoms, social opportunities, transparency guarantees and protective security) is based on the recognition of their respective roles as well as their complementarities. Depending on the country considered, the focus of a critique may vary, in light of the particular experience in that country. For example, in India the neglect of social opportunities may be a focus of criticism in a way it may not be in China, whereas the absence of democratic liberties may be more appropriately a focus of a critique of China than it could be of India.

## INTERDEPENDENCE AND PUBLIC GOODS

Those who have tended to take the market mechanism to be the best solution of every economic problem may want to inquire what the limits of that mechanism may be. I have already commented on issues of equity and the need to go beyond efficiency considerations, and in that context, I have tried to discuss why this may call for supplementing the market mechanism by other institutional activities. But even in achieving efficiency, the market mechanism may sometimes be less than effective, particularly in the presence of what are called "public goods."

One of the assumptions standardly made to show the efficiency of the market mechanism is that every commodity—and more generally everything on which our welfares depend—can be bought and sold in the market. It can all be marketed (if we want to place it there), and there is no "nonmarketable" but significant influence on our welfare. In fact, however, some of the most important contributors to human capability may be hard to sell exclusively to one person at a time. This is especially so when we consider the so-called public goods, which people consume *together* rather than separately.[38]

This applies particularly in such fields as environmental preservation, and also epidemiology and public health care. I may be willing to pay my share in a social program of malaria eradication, but I cannot buy my part of that protection in the form of "private good" (like an apple or a shirt). It is a "public good"—malaria-free surroundings—which we have to consume together. Indeed, if I do manage somehow to organize a malaria-free environment where I live, my neighbor too will have that malaria-free environment, without having to "buy" it from anywhere.[39]

The rationale of the market mechanism is geared to private goods (like apples and shirts), rather than to public goods (like the malaria-free environment), and it can be shown that there may be a good case for the provisioning of public goods, going beyond what the private markets would foster.[40] Exactly similar arguments regarding the limited reach of the market mechanism apply to several other important fields as well, where too the provision involved may take the form of a public good. Defense, policing and environmental protection are some of the fields in which this kind of reasoning applies.

There are also rather mixed cases. For example, given the shared communal benefits of basic education, which may transcend the gains of the person being educated, basic education may have a public-good component as well (and can be seen as a semipublic good). The persons receiving education do, of course, benefit from it, but in addition a general expansion of education and literacy in a region can facilitate social change (even the reduction of fertility and mortality, as will be discussed more fully in chapters 8 and 9) and also help to enhance economic progress from which others too benefit. The effective reach of these services may require cooperative activities and provisioning by the state or the local authorities. Indeed, the state has typically played a major role in the expansion of basic education across the world. The rapid spread of literacy in the past history of the rich countries of today (both in the West and in Japan and the rest of East Asia) has drawn on the low cost of public education combined with its shared public benefits.

It is in this context rather remarkable that some market enthusiasts recommend now to the developing countries that they should rely fully on the free market even for basic education—thereby withholding from them the very process of educational expansion that was crucial in rapidly spreading literacy in Europe, North America, Japan, and East Asia in the past. The alleged followers of Adam Smith can learn something from his writings on this subject, including his frustration at the parsimony of public expenditure in the field of education:

> For a very small expence the publick can facilitate, can encourage, and can even impose upon almost the whole body of the people, the necessity of acquiring those most essential parts of education.[41]

The "public goods" argument for going beyond the market mechanism supplements the case for social provisioning that arises from the need of basic capabilities, such as elementary health care and basic educational opportunities. Efficiency considerations thus supplement the argument for equity in supporting public assistance in providing basic education, health facilities and other public (or semipublic) goods.

## PUBLIC PROVISIONING AND INCENTIVES

While these considerations provide good grounds for public expenditure in the areas crucial for economic development and social change, there are contrary arguments that must also be considered in the same context. One issue is that of the fiscal burden of public expenditure, which can be quite large, depending on how much is planned to be done. The fear of budget deficits and inflation (and generally of "macroeconomic instability") tends to haunt contemporary discussions of economic policy, and this is indeed a momentous issue. Another issue is that of incentives, and the effects that a system of public support may have in discouraging initiative and distorting individual efforts. Both these issues—the need for fiscal prudence and the importance of incentives—deserve serious attention. I begin with the latter, and will come back thereafter to fiscal burden and its consequences.[42]

Any pure transfer—the redistribution of income or the free provision of a public service—can potentially have an effect on the incentive system of the economy. For example, it has been argued particularly strongly that generous unemployment insurance can weaken the resolve of the jobless to find employment, and that it has actually done so in Europe. Given the obvious equity argument for such insurance, there may be a difficult issue here if the potential conflict proves to be real and quantitatively substantial. However, since employment is sought for various reasons—not just to receive an income—the partial replacement of the lost wage by public support may not, in fact, be as much of a disincentive against seeking employment as it is sometimes presumed. Indeed, the reach and magnitude of the disincentive effects of unemployment insurance are far from clear. Nevertheless, it is a matter for empirical examination to ascertain how strong the adverse incentive effects may actually be, in order to facilitate informed public discussion of these important matters of public policy, including the choice of an appropriate balance between equity and efficiency.

In most of the developing countries there are few provisions for unemployment insurance in general. But the incentive problem is not absent for that reason. Even for free medical care and health services, or free educational facilities, questions can be raised regarding (1) the extent of the need for these services by the recipients and (2) the extent to which the person could have afforded to pay for these services himself (and might have done so in the absence of free public provisioning). Those who see entitlement to these basic social provisions (medical attention, education and so on) as an inalienable right of citizens would tend to see this kind of questioning as wrongheaded and even perhaps as a distressing denial of the normative principles of a contemporary "society." That position is certainly defendable up to a point, but given the limitation of economic resources, there are serious choices involved here, which cannot be altogether neglected on grounds of some pre-economic "social" principle. At any rate, the incentive issue has to be addressed if only because the *extent* of social support that a society would be able to provide must depend in part on costs and incentives.

## INCENTIVES, CAPABILITIES AND FUNCTIONINGS

The basic problem of incentives is hard to overcome completely. It is, in general, quite hopeless to look for some indicators that are both relevant for identifying deprivation and—when used as the basis of public support—would not lead to any incentive effects. However, the extent of the incentive effects can vary with the nature and form of the criteria used.

The informational focus of poverty analysis in this work has involved a shift in attention from low income to deprivation of basic capabilities. The central argument for this shift is fundamental rather than strategic. I have argued that capability deprivation is more important as a criterion of disadvantage than is the lowness of income, since income is only instrumentally important and its deriva-tive value is contingent on many social and economic circumstances. That argument can now be supplemented by the suggestion that focusing on capability deprivation has some advantage in preventing incentive distortions compared with working with lowness of income as a criterion for transfer and subsidy. This instrumental argument only adds to the fundamental reason for focusing on capabilities.

The assessment of capabilities has to proceed primarily on the basis of observing a person's actual functionings, to be supplemented by other information. There is a jump here (from functionings to capabilities), but it need not be a big jump, if only because the valu-ation of actual functionings is one way of assessing how a person val-ues the options she has. If a person dies prematurely or suffers from a painful and threatening disease, it would be, in most cases, legiti-mate to conclude that she did have a capability problem.

Of course, in some cases, this will not be true. For example, a person may commit suicide. Or she may starve not out of necessity, but because of a decision to fast. But these are relatively rare occurrences, and can be analyzed on the basis of supplementary information, which would relate, in the case of fasting, to religious practices, or political strategies, or such other reasons for fasting. In principle, it is right to go beyond chosen functionings to assess a person's capability, but how far one would be able to go would depend on circumstances. Public policy, like politics, is the art of the possible, and this is important to bear in mind in combining theoretical insights with realistic readings of practical feasibility. What is, however, important to emphasize is that even with the informational focus confined to functionings (longevity, health status, literacy and so on), we get a more instructive measure of deprivation than we can from income statistics alone.

There are, of course, problems even in observing functioning achievements of some kinds. But some of the more basic and elementary ones are more amenable to direct observation, and frequently enough provide useful informational bases for antideprivation policies. The informational bases for seeing the need for literacy campaigns, hospital services and nutritional supplementation need not be particularly obscure.[43] Furthermore, these needs and handicaps may be less open to strategic distortion than the handicap of low income, since income is often easy to hide, especially in most developing countries. If governmental grants were to be given to people on the ground of their poverty alone (leaving them to pay for medical care, educational facilities and so on out of their own incomes), there is likely to be considerable information manipulation. The focus on functionings and capabilities (extensively used in this work) tends to reduce the difficulties of incentive compatibility. Why so?

First, people may typically be reluctant to refuse education, foster illnesses or cultivate undernourishment on purely tactical grounds. The priorities of reasoning and choice tend to militate against deliberately promoting these elementary deprivations. There are, of course, exceptions. Among the most distressing accounts of famine relief experiences are occasional reports of some parents keeping one child in the family thoroughly famished so that the family qualifies to get nutritional support (e.g., in the form of take-home food rations)—

treating the child, as it were, as a meal ticket.[44] But in general such incentive effects in keeping people undernourished, or untreated, or illiterate are relatively rare, for reasons that are not altogether astonishing.

Second, the causal factors underlying some functional deprivations can go much deeper than income deprivation and may be very hard to adjust for purely tactical reasons. For example, physical disabilities, old age, gender characteristics and the like are particularly serious sources of capability handicap because they are beyond the control of the persons involved. And for much the same reason, they are not open to incentive distortions in the way that adjustable features are. This limits the incentive distortions of subsidies targeted on these features.

Third, there is also the somewhat larger issue that the recipients themselves tend to pay more attention to functionings and capabilities achieved (and the quality of life that goes with them) than to just earning more money, and in this way public policy assessment that is done in terms of variables closer to the decisional concerns of individuals may be able to use personal decisions as selection devices. This question relates to the use of self-selection in providing public assistance, with requirement of work and effort, as is frequently practiced in providing famine relief. Only those who are destitute and need money strongly enough to be willing to work reasonably hard for it will volunteer to take up the open opportunities of employment (often at a somewhat low wage), which constitute a widely used form of public relief.[45] This type of targeting has been used very successfully in providing famine prevention, and can have a wider role in enhancing the economic opportunities of the able-bodied deprived population.[46] The rationale of this approach lies in the fact that the potential recipients' choices are governed by considerations that are broader than maximization of income earned. Since the individuals involved focus more on overall opportunities (including the human cost of effort as well as the benefit from extra income), public policy making can make intelligent use of this broader concern.

Fourth, the refocusing of attention from low personal incomes to capability handicaps also points directly to the case for greater emphasis on direct public provisioning of such facilities as health services and educational programs.[47] These services are typically nonshiftable and nonsalable, and of not much use to a person unless he or she actually happens to need them. There is some "built-in matching" in such provisioning.[48] And this feature of capability-directed provisioning makes targeting easier by reducing the scope for incentive distortions.

## TARGETING AND MEANS-TESTING

However, despite these advantages, the decision to target capability handicaps rather than low income does not, in itself, eliminate the need to judge the economic poverty of the potential recipients, since there is also the further issue of *how* the public provisions should be distributed. There is, in particular, the issue of charging for the public services according to the ability to pay, which would bring back the need for ascertaining the income of the potential recipient.

The provisioning of public services has increasingly moved in the direction of means-testing, across the world. The case for this is easy to understand, at least in principle. It reduces the fiscal burden, and the same amount of public funds can be stretched much further in covering the economically needy if the relatively affluent can be made to pay for the benefits they receive (or induced to make a significant contribution to the costs involved). What is more difficult to ensure is that the means be effectively tested with acceptable accuracy, without leading to other, adverse effects.

We must distinguish clearly between two different incentive problems in providing health care or education on the basis of means-testing, related respectively to the information regarding (1) a person's capability handicap (for example, her physical illness) and (2) her economic circumstances (and her ability to pay). As far as the first problem is concerned, the form and fungibility of the help provided can make a significant difference. As was discussed earlier, when social support is given on the basis of direct diagnosis of a specific need (for example, after checking that a person is suffering from some particular illness) and when it is provided free in the form of specific and nontransferable services (such as being medically treated for that ailment), the possibility of informational distortion of the first kind would be substantially reduced. There is a contrast here with providing fungible money for financing medical treatment, which would require more indirect scrutiny. On this score, the direct-service programs such as health care and school education are less open to abuse.

But the second issue is quite different. If the intention is to provide free service for the poor but not for those who can afford to pay, there is the further issue of checking the person's economic circumstances. This can be particularly problematic especially in countries where information on income and wealth is hard to elicit. The European formula of targeting the capability handicap without means-testing, in providing medical coverage, has tended to take the form of a general national health service—open to all who need those medical services. This makes the informational task easier, but does not address the rich-poor division. The American formula of Medicaid targets both (at a more modest level), and has to cope with both the informational challenges.

Since the potential beneficiaries are also agents of action, the art of "targeting" is far less simple than some advocates of means-testing tend to assume. It is important to take note of the problems involved in fine-tuned targeting in general and means-testing in particular, especially since the case for such targeting is, in principle, quite strong and cogent. The possible distortions that may result from attempts at ambitious targeting include the following:[49]

1) *Information distortion:* Any policing system that tries to catch the "cheats" who understate their financial circumstances would make mistakes from time to time and disqualify some bona fide cases. No less important, it would discourage some who are genuinely qualified (to receive the intended benefits) from applying for the benefits to which they are entitled. Given the asymmetry of information, it is not possible to eliminate cheating without putting some of the honest beneficiaries at considerable risk.[50] In trying to eliminate the "type 1" error of including the non-needy among the needy, serious "type 2" errors of not including some really needy people among the listed needy would very likely be committed.

2) *Incentive distortion:* Informational distortion cooks the books, but does not, on its own, alter the underlying real economic situation. But targeted support can *also* affect people's economic behavior. For example, the prospect of losing the support if one were to earn too much can be a deterrent for economic activities. It would be

natural to expect that there would be *some* significant distorting shifts if the qualification for the support is based on a variable (such as income) that is freely adjustable through changing one's economic behavior. The *social* costs of behavioral shifts must include, among other things, the loss of the fruits of economic activities forgone.

3) *Disutility and stigma:* A system of support that requires a person to be identified as poor (and is seen as a special benefaction for those who cannot fully fend for themselves) would tend to have some effects on one's self-respect as well as on respect by others. This may distort the seeking of help, but also there are direct costs and losses involved in feeling—and being—stigmatized. Since the matter of self-respect is often taken by policy leaders to be of rather marginal interest (and considered to be a rather "genteel" concern), I take the liberty of referring to John Rawls's argument that self-respect is "perhaps the most important primary good" on which a theory of justice as fairness has to concentrate.[51]

4) *Administrative costs, invasive loss and corruption:* The procedure of targeting can involve substantial administrative costs—in the form of both resource expenditures and bureaucratic delays—and also losses of individual privacy and autonomy involved in the need for extensive disclosure and the associated program of investigation and policing. There are, furthermore, social costs of asymmetrical power that the potentates of bureaucracy enjoy vis-à-vis the supplicating applicants. And, it should be added, there is greater possibility of corruption here since the potentates acquire, in a targeting system, the power to bestow benefits for which the beneficiaries may be willing to make a facilitating payment.

5) *Political sustainability and quality:* The beneficiaries of targeted social support are often quite weak politically and may lack the clout to sustain the programs in political jostling, or to maintain the quality of the services offered. In the United States, this consideration has been the basis of some well-known arguments for having "universal" programs, which would receive wider support, rather than heavily targeted ones confined only to the poorest.[52] Something of this argument cannot but relate to the poorer countries as well.

The point of outlining these difficulties is not to suggest that targeting must be pointless or always problematic, but only to note that there are considerations that run counter to the simple argument for maximal targeting. Targeting is, in fact, an *attempt*—not a *result*. Even when *successfully* targeted outcomes would be just right, it does not necessarily follow that attempts in the form of targeted programs would produce those outcomes. Since the case for means-testing and for heavy targeting has gained so much ground recently in public circles (based on rather elementary reasoning), the messiness and the disincentive effects of the proposed policy are also worth emphasizing.

## AGENCY AND INFORMATIONAL BASIS

It would be rather hopeless to try to get a case for a universal endorsement or a universal rejection of means-testing on the basis of very general arguments, and the relevance of the preceding discussion lies mainly in pointing to the contrary arguments that exist side by side with the arguments in favor of fine-tuned means-testing. In practice, in this field (as in many others already considered), compromises would have to be made. In a general work of this kind, it would be a mistake to look for some particular "formula" for an optimum compromise. The right approach would have to be sensitive to the circumstances involved—both the nature of the public services to be offered and the characteristics of the society to which they are to be offered. The latter must include the hold of behavioral values of different kinds, which influence individual choices and incentives.

However, the basic issues confronted here are of some general interest for the main approach of this book, and involve both the importance of agency (seeing people as agents rather than as patients) and the informational focus on capability deprivation (rather than only on income poverty). The first question relates to the need, emphasized throughout this work, to see people—even beneficiaries—as agents rather than as motionless patients. The objects of "targeting" are active themselves, and their activities can make the targeting-achievements quite different from targeting-attempts (for reasons already discussed).

The second question relates to the informational aspects of targeting; these include the identifiability of the characteristics relevant for the chosen system of allocation. Here the shift in attention from just income poverty to the deprivation of capabilities helps the task of identifiability. While means-testing still requires that incomes and the ability to pay be identified, nevertheless the other part of the exercise is helped by the direct diagnosis of capability handicap (such as being ill or illiterate). This is a part—an important part—of the information task of public provisioning.

## FINANCIAL PRUDENCE AND NEED FOR INTEGRATION

I turn now to the problem of financial prudence, which has become a major concern across the world in recent decades. The demands for conservatism in finance are very strong now, since the disruptive effects of excessive inflation and instability have come to be widely studied and discussed. Indeed, finance is a subject in which conservatism has some evident merit, and prudence in this field can easily take a conservative form. But we have to be clear as to what financial conservatism demands and why.

The point of financial conservatism is not so much the apparently conspicuous merit of "living within one's means," even though that rhetoric has much appeal. As Mr. Micawber put it rather eloquently in Charles Dickens's *David Copperfield*: "Annual income twenty pounds, annual expenditure nineteen six, result happiness. Annual income twenty pounds, annual expenditure twenty pounds ought six, result misery." The analogy with personal solvency has been powerfully used by many financial conservatives, perhaps most eloquently by Margaret Thatcher. This argument does not, however, provide a clear rule for state policy. Unlike Mr. Micawber, a state *can* continue to spend more than it earns, through borrowing and other means. In fact, nearly every state does so nearly all the time.

The real issue is not whether this can be done (it certainly can be), but what the *effects* of financial overspending might be. The basic issue to be faced, therefore, is the consequential importance of what is sometimes called "macroeconomic stability," in particular the absence of serious inflationary pressure. The case for financial conservatism lies, to a great extent, in the recognition that price stability is important and that it can be deeply threatened by fiscal indulgence and irresponsibility.

What evidence do we have about the pernicious effects of inflation? In a powerful critical survey of international experiences in this area, Michael Bruno notes that "several recorded episodes of moderate inflation (20–40 percent [price rise per year]) and most instances of higher rates of inflation (of which there have been a substantial number) suggest that high inflation goes together with significant negative growth effects." And, "conversely, the cumulative evidence suggests that sharp stabilization from high inflation brings very strong positive growth effects over even the short to medium run."[53]

The policy conclusion to be drawn here requires some subtlety. Bruno also finds that "the growth effects of inflation are at best obscure at low rates of inflation (less than 15–20 percent annually)." He goes on to ask the question: "why worry about low rates of inflation, especially if the costs of *anticipated* inflation can be avoided (by indexation) and those of *unanticipated* inflation seem to be low?"[54] Bruno also points out that "while the root of all high inflations is a financial deficit (and often, though not always, the monetary finance of it), this in turn can be consistent with multiple inflationary equilibria."

The real problem lies in the fact that "inflation is an inherently persistent process and, moreover, the degree of persistence tends to increase with the rate of inflation." Bruno presents a clear picture of how such acceleration of inflation takes place, and makes the lesson graphic with an analogy: "chronic inflation tends to resemble smoking: once you [are] beyond a minimal number it is very difficult to escape a worsening addiction." In fact, "when shocks occur (e.g. a personal crisis for a smoker, a price crisis for an economy) there is great chance that the severity of the habit . . . will jump to a new, higher level that persists even after the shock has abated," and this process can repeat itself.[55]

This is a quintessentially conservative argument, and a very persuasive one it is, based as it is on a rich set of international comparisons. I have no difficulty in endorsing both the analysis and the conclusions drawn by Michael Bruno. What is, however, important to do is to keep track of exactly what has been established and also to see what the demand of financial conservatism really is. It is, in particular, *not* a demand for what I would call the anti-inflationary radicalism that is often confused with financial conservatism. The case made is not for eliminating inflation altogether—irrespective of what has to be sacrificed for that end. Rather, the lesson is to keep in view the likely costs of tolerating inflation against the costs of reducing it, or of eliminating it altogether. The critical issue is to avoid the "dynamic instability" that even seemingly stable chronic inflation tends to have, if it is above a low figure. The policy lesson that Bruno draws is: "The combination of costly stabilization at low rates of inflation and the upward bias of inflationary persistence provide a growth-cost related argument for keeping inflation low even though the large growth costs seem to be directly observed only at higher inflations."[56] The thing to avoid, in this argument, is not just *high* inflation, but—because of dynamic instability—even *moderate* inflation.

However, radicalism in the cause of zero inflation does not emerge here either as particularly wise, or even as the appropriate reading of the demands of financial conservatism. The "clouding" of distinct issues is seen clearly enough in the ongoing fixation with balancing the budget in the United States, which resulted not long ago in partial shutdowns of the U.S. government (and threats of more extensive closures). This has led to an uneasy compromise between the White House and the Congress—a compromise the success of which is rather contingent on the short-run performance of the U.S. economy. *Anti-deficit radicalism* has to be distinguished from genuine *financial conservatism.* There is indeed a strong case for reducing the large budget deficits that are seen in many countries in the world (often made worse by huge burdens of national debt and high rates of its escalation). But this argument must not be confused with the extremism of trying to eliminate budget deficits *altogether* with great rapidity (no matter what the social cost of this might be).

Europe has much more reason to be concerned about budget deficits than the United States has. For one thing, the U.S. budget deficits have been, for many years now, moderate enough to be below the "norms" set up by the Maastricht Agreement for the European Monetary Union (a budget deficit of no more than 3 percent of gross domestic product). There seems to be no deficit at all, at this time. In contrast, most of the European countries had—and still have—rather substantial deficits. It is appropriate that several of these countries are currently making determined attempts to cut the levels of these large deficits (Italy has provided an impressive example of this in recent years).

If there is a question to be raised still, this concerns the overall priorities of European policies—an issue that was discussed earlier, in chapter 4. The point at issue is whether it makes sense to give absolute priority to one objective only, viz., the avoidance of inflation (a priority formalized by many central banks in Western Europe), while tolerating remarkably high rates of unemployment. If the analysis presented in this book is right, the making of public policy in Europe has to give real priority to eliminating the capability deprivation that severe unemployment entails.

Financial conservatism has good rationale and imposes strong requirements, but its demands must be interpreted in the light of the overall objectives of public policy. The role of public expenditure in generating and guaranteeing many basic capabilities calls for attention; it must be considered along with the instrumental need for macroeconomic stability. Indeed, the latter need must be assessed *within* a broad framework of social objectives.

Depending on the particular context, different public policy issues may end up being critically important. In Europe, it could be the nastiness of massive unemployment (close to 12 percent for several major countries). In the United States, a crucial challenge is presented by the absence of any kind of medical insurance or secure coverage for very large numbers of people (the United States is alone among the rich countries in having this problem, and furthermore, the medically uninsured number more than forty million). In India, there is a massive failure of public policy in the extreme neglect of literacy (half the adult population—and two-thirds of adult women—are still illiterate). In East Asia and Southeast Asia, it looks increasingly as if the financial system requires extensive regularization, and there also seems to be a need for a preventive system that can counteract sudden losses of confidence in a country's currency or investment opportunities (as is brought out by the recent experiences of these countries, which had to seek gigantic bailout operations by the International Monetary Fund). The problems are different, and given their complexity, each calls for a serious examination of the objectives and instruments of public policy. The need for financial conservatism—important as it is—fits into this diverse and broad picture, and cannot stand on its own—in solitary isolation—as *the* commitment of the government or of the central bank. The need for scrutiny and comparative assessment of alternative fields of public expenditure is altogether crucial.

## CONCLUDING REMARKS

Individuals live and operate in a world of institutions. Our opportunities and prospects depend crucially on what institutions exist and how they function. Not only do institutions contribute to our freedoms, their roles can be sensibly evaluated in the light of their contributions to our freedom. To see development as freedom provides a perspective in which institutional assessment can systematically occur.

Even though different commentators have chosen to focus on particular institutions (such as the market, or the democratic system, or the media, or the public distribution system), we have to view them together, to be able to see what they can or cannot do in combination with other institutions. It is in this integrated perspective that the different institutions can be reasonably assessed and examined.

The market mechanism, which arouses passion in favor as well as against, is a basic arrangement through which people can interact with each other and undertake mutually advantageous activities. In this light, it is very hard indeed to see how any reasonable critic could be against the market mechanism, as such. The problems that arise spring typically from other sources—not from the existence of markets per se—and include such concerns as inadequate preparedness to make use of market transactions, unconstrained concealment of information or unregulated use of activities that allow the powerful to capitalize on their asymmetrical advantage. These have to be dealt with not by suppressing the markets, but by allowing them to function better and with greater fairness, and with adequate supplementation. The overall achievements of the market are deeply contingent on political and social arrangements.

The market mechanism has achieved great success under those conditions in which the opportunities offered by them could be reasonably shared. In making this possible, the provision of basic education, the presence of elementary medical facilities, the availability of resources (such as land) that can be crucial to some economic activities (such as agriculture) call for appropriate public policies (involving schooling, health care, land reform and so on). Even when the need for "economic reform" in favor of allowing more room for markets is paramount, these nonmarket facilities require careful and determined public action.

In this chapter—and in earlier ones—various examples of this complementarity have been considered and examined. The efficiency contributions of the market mechanism can hardly be doubted, and traditional economic results, in which efficiency is judged by prosperity or opulence or utility, can be extended to efficiency in terms of individual freedoms as well. But these efficiency results do not, on their own, guarantee distributional equity. The problem can be particularly large in the context of inequality of substantive freedoms, when there is a coupling of disadvantages (such as the difficulty of a disabled or an untrained person to *earn* an income being reinforced by her difficulty in making *use* of income for the capability to live well). The far-reaching powers of the market mechanism have to be supplemented by the creation of basic social opportunities for social equity and justice.

In the context of developing countries in general, the need for public policy initiatives in creating social opportunities is crucially important. As was discussed earlier, in the past of the rich countries of today we can see quite a remarkable history of public action, dealing respectively with education, health care, land reforms and so on. The wide sharing of these social opportunities made it possible for the bulk of the people to participate directly in the process of economic expansion.

The real problem here is not the need for financial conservatism in itself, but the underlying—and often unargued—belief that has been dominant in some policy circles that human development is really a kind of luxury that only richer countries can afford. Perhaps the most important impact of the type of success that the East Asian economies have recently had (beginning with Japan—decades earlier) is the total undermining of that implicit prejudice. These economies went comparatively early for massive expansion of education, and later also of health care, and this they did, in many cases, *before* they broke the restraints of general poverty.[57] And despite the financial turmoil that some of these economies have recently experienced, their overall achievements over the decades have typically been quite remarkable. As far as human resources are concerned, they have reaped as they have sown. Indeed, the priority to human resource development applies particularly to the *early* history of Japanese economic development, beginning with the Meiji era in the mid-nineteenth century. That priority has not really intensified as Japan has grown richer and much more opulent.[58] Human development is first and foremost an ally of the poor, rather than of the rich and the affluent.

What does human development do? The creation of social opportunities makes a direct contribution to the expansion of human capabilities and the quality of life (as has already been discussed). Expansion of health care, education, social security, etc., contribute directly to the quality of life and to its flourishing. There is every evidence that even with relatively low income, a country that guarantees health care and education to all can actually achieve remarkable results in terms of the length and quality of life of the entire population. The highly labor-intensive nature of health care and basic education—and human development in general—makes them comparatively cheap in the early stages of economic development, when labor costs are low.

The rewards of human development go, as we have seen, well beyond the direct enhancement of quality of life, and include also its impact on people's productive abilities and thus on economic growth on a widely shared basis.[59] Literacy and numeracy help the participation of the masses in the process of economic expansion (well illustrated from Japan to Thailand). To use the opportunities of global trade, "quality control" as well as "production to specification" can be quite crucial, and they are hard for illiterate or innumerate laborers to achieve and maintain. Furthermore, there is considerable evidence that improved health care as well as nutrition also make the workforce more productive and better remunerated.[60]

On a different subject, there is much confirmation, in the contemporary empirical literature, of the impact of education, especially female education, on reducing fertility rates. High fertility rates can be seen, with much justice, as adverse to the quality of life, especially of young women, since recurrent bearing and rearing of children can be very detrimental to the well-being and freedom of the young mother. Indeed, it is precisely this connection that makes the empowerment of women (through more outside employment, more school education and so on) so effective in reducing fertility rates, since young women have a strong reason for moderating birthrates, and their ability to influence family decisions increases with their empowerment. I shall come back to this issue in chapters 8 and 9.

Those who see themselves as financial conservatives sometimes express skepticism about human development. There is, however, little rational basis for that inference. The benefits of human development are manifest, and can be more fully accounted by taking an adequately comprehensive view of its overall impact. Cost consciousness can help to direct human development in channels that are more productive—directly and indirectly—of the quality of life, but it does not threaten its imperative interest.[61]

Indeed, what really should be threatened by financial conservatism is the use of public resources for purposes where the social benefits are very far from clear, such as the massive expenditures that now go into the military in one poor country after another (often many times larger than the public expenditure on basic education or health care).[62] Financial conservatism should be the nightmare of the militarist, not of the schoolteacher or the hospital nurse. It is an indication of the topsy-turvy world in which we live that the schoolteacher or the nurse feels more threatened by financial conservatism than does the army general. The rectification of this anomaly calls not for the chastising of financial conservatism, but for more pragmatic and open-minded scrutiny of rival claims to social funds.

# CHAPTER 6

# THE IMPORTANCE OF DEMOCRACY

▼

Bordering on the Bay of Bengal, at the southern edge of Bangladesh and of West Bengal in India, there is the Sundarban—which means "beautiful forest." That is the natural habitat of the famous Royal Bengal tiger, a magnificent animal with grace, speed, power, and some ferocity. Relatively few of them are left now, but the surviving tigers are protected by a hunting ban. The Sundarban is also famous for the honey it produces in large clusters of natural beehives. The people who live in the region, desperately poor as they are, go into the forests to collect the honey, which fetches quite a handsome price in the urban markets—maybe even the rupee equivalent of fifty U.S. cents per bottle. But the honey collectors also have to escape the tigers. In a good year, only about fifty or so honey gatherers are killed by tigers, but that number can be very much higher when things don't go so well. While the tigers are protected, nothing protects the miserable human beings who try to make a living by working in those woods, which are deep and lovely—and quite perilous.

This is just one illustration of the force of economic needs in many third world countries. It is not hard to feel that this force must outweigh other claims, including those of political liberty and civil rights. If poverty drives human beings to take such terrible risks—and perhaps to die terrible deaths—for a dollar or two of honey, it might well be odd to concentrate on their liberty and political freedoms. Habeas corpus may not seem like a communicable concept in that context. Priority must surely be given, so the argument runs, to fulfilling economic needs, even if it involves compromising political liberties. It is not hard to think that focusing on democracy and political liberty is a luxury that a poor country "cannot afford."

## ECONOMIC NEEDS AND POLITICAL FREEDOMS

Views such as these are presented with much frequency in international discussions. Why bother about the finesse of political freedoms given the overpowering grossness of intense economic needs? That question, and related ones reflecting doubts about the urgency of political liberty and civil rights, loomed large at the Vienna conference on human rights held in the spring of 1993, and delegates from several countries argued against general endorsement of basic political and civil rights across the globe, in particular in the third world. Rather, the focus would have to be, it was argued, on "economic rights" related to important material needs.

This is a well established line of analysis, and it was advocated forcefully in Vienna by the official delegations of a number of developing countries, led by China, Singapore and other East Asian countries, but not opposed by India and the other South Asian and West Asian countries, nor by African governments. There is, in this line of analysis, the often repeated rhetoric: What should come first—removing poverty and misery, or guaranteeing political liberty and civil rights, for which poor people have little use anyway?

## THE PREEMINENCE OF POLITICAL
## FREEDOMS AND DEMOCRACY

Is this a sensible way of approaching the problems of economic needs and political freedoms—in terms of a basic dichotomy that appears to undermine the relevance of political freedoms because the economic needs are so urgent?[1] I would argue, no, this is altogether the wrong way to see the force of economic needs, or to understand the salience of political freedoms. The real issues that have to be addressed lie elsewhere, and they involve taking note of extensive interconnections between political freedoms and the understanding and fulfillment of economic needs. The connections are not only instrumental (political freedoms can have a major role in providing incentives and information in the solution of acute economic needs), but also constructive. Our conceptualization of economic needs depends crucially on open public debates and discussions, the guaranteeing of which requires insistence on basic political liberty and civil rights.

I shall argue that the intensity of economic needs *adds* to—rather than subtracts from—the urgency of political freedoms. There are three different considerations that take us in the direction of a general preeminence of basic political and liberal rights:

1) their *direct* importance in human living associated with basic capabilities (including that of political and social participation);

2) their *instrumental* role in enhancing the hearing that people get in expressing and supporting their claims to political attention (including the claims of economic needs);

3) their *constructive* role in the conceptualization of "needs" (including the understanding of "economic needs" in a social context).

These different considerations will be discussed presently, but first we have to examine the arguments presented by those who see a real conflict between political liberty and democratic rights, on the one hand, and the fulfillment of basic economic needs, on the other.

## ARGUMENTS AGAINST POLITICAL FREEDOMS AND CIVIL RIGHTS

The opposition to democracies and basic civil and political freedoms in developing countries comes from three different directions. First, there is the claim that these freedoms and rights hamper economic growth and development. This belief, called the Lee thesis (after Lee Kuan Yew, the former prime minister of Singapore, who formulated it succinctly) was briefly described in chapter 1.

Second, it has been argued that if poor people are given the choice between having political freedoms and fulfilling economic needs, they will invariably choose the latter. So there is, by this reasoning, a contradiction between the practice of democracy and its justification: to wit, the majority view would tend to reject democracy—given this choice. In a different but closely related variant of this argument, it is claimed that the real issue is not so much what people actually choose, but what they have *reason* to choose. Since people have reason to want to eliminate, first and foremost, economic deprivation and misery, they have reason enough for not insisting on political freedoms, which would get in the way of their real priorities. The presumed existence of a deep conflict between political freedoms and the fulfillment of economic needs provides an important premise in this syllogism, and in this sense, this variant of the second argument is parasitic on the first (that is, on the truth of the Lee thesis).

Third, it has often been argued that the emphasis on political freedom, liberties and democracy is a specifically "Western" priority, which goes, in particular, against "Asian values," which are supposed to be more keen on order and discipline than on liberty and freedom. For example, the censorship of the press may be more acceptable, it is argued, in an Asian society (because of its emphasis on discipline and order) than in the West. In the 1993 Vienna conference, the foreign minister of Singapore warned that "universal recognition of the ideal of human rights can be harmful if universalism is used to deny or mask the reality of *diversity*." The spokesman of the Chinese Foreign Ministry even put on record this proposition, apparently applicable in China and elsewhere in Asia: "Individuals must put the state's rights before their own."[2]

This last argument involves an exercise in cultural interpretation, and I shall reserve it for a later discussion: in chapter 10.[3] I take up the other two arguments now.

## DEMOCRACY AND ECONOMIC GROWTH

Does authoritarianism really work so well? It is certainly true that some relatively authoritarian states (such as South Korea, Lee's own Singapore and post-reform China) have had faster rates of economic growth than many less authoritarian ones (including India, Costa Rica and Jamaica). But the Lee thesis is, in fact, based on very selective and limited information, rather than on any general statistical testing over the wide-ranging data that are available. We cannot really take the high economic growth of China or South Korea in Asia as a definitive proof that authoritarianism does better in promoting economic growth—any more than we can draw the opposite conclusion on the basis of the fact that the fastest-growing African country (and one of the fastest growers in the world), viz., Botswana, has been a oasis of democracy on that troubled continent. Much depends on the precise circumstances.

In fact, there is rather little general evidence that authoritarian governance and the suppression of political and civil rights are really beneficial in encouraging economic development. The statistical picture is much more complex. Systematic empirical studies give no real support to the claim that there is a general conflict between political freedoms and economic performance.[4] The directional linkage seems to depend on many other circumstances, and while some statistical investigations note a weakly negative relation, others find a strongly positive one. On balance, the hypothesis that there is no relation between them in either direction is hard to reject. Since political liberty and freedom have importance of their own, the case for them remains unaffected.

In this context, it is also important to touch on a more basic issue of research methodology. We must not only look at statistical connections but, furthermore, examine and scrutinize the *causal* processes that are involved in economic growth and development. The economic policies and circumstances that led to the economic success of East Asian economies are by now reasonably well understood. While different empirical studies have varied in emphasis, there is by now a fairly agreed general list of "helpful policies" that includes openness to competition, the use of international markets, a high level of literacy and school education, successful land reforms and public provision of incentives for investment, exporting and industrialization. There is nothing whatsoever to indicate that any of these policies is inconsistent with greater democracy and actually had to be sustained by the elements of authoritarianism that happened to be present in South Korea or Singapore or China.[5]

Furthermore, in judging economic development it is not adequate to look only at the growth of GNP or some other indicators of overall economic expansion. We have to look also at the impact of democracy and political freedoms on the lives and capabilities of the citizens. It is particularly important in this context to examine the connection between political and civil rights, on the one hand, and the prevention of major disasters (such as famines), on the other. Political and civil rights give people the opportunity to draw attention forcefully to general needs, and to demand appropriate public action. Governmental response to the acute suffering of people often depends on the pressure that is put on the government, and this is where the exercise of political rights (voting, criticizing, protesting and so on) can make a real difference. This is a part of the "instrumental" role of democracy and political freedoms. I shall have to come back to this important issue again, later on in this chapter.

## DO POOR PEOPLE CARE ABOUT
## DEMOCRACY AND POLITICAL RIGHTS?

I turn now to the second question. Are the citizens of third world countries indifferent to political and democratic rights? This claim, which is often made, is again based on too little empirical evidence (just as the Lee thesis is). The only way of verifying this would be to put the matter to democratic testing in free elections with freedom of opposition and expression—precisely the things that the supporters of authoritarianism do not allow to happen. It is not clear at all how this proposition can be checked when the ordinary citizens are given little political opportunity to express their views on this and even less to dispute the claims made by the authorities in office. The downgrading of these rights and freedoms is certainly part of the value system of the *government leaders* in many third world countries, but to take that to be the view of the people is to beg a very big question.

It is thus of some interest to note that when the Indian government, under Indira Gandhi's leadership, tried out a similar argument in India, to justify the "emergency" she had misguidedly declared in the mid-1970s, an election was called that divided the voters precisely on this issue. In that fateful election, fought largely on the acceptability of the "emergency," the suppression of basic political and civil rights was firmly rejected, and the Indian electorate—one of the poorest in the world—showed itself to be no less keen on protesting against the denial of basic liberties and rights than it was in complaining about economic poverty. To the extent that there has been any testing of the proposition that poor people in general do not care about civil and political rights, the evidence is entirely against that claim. Similar points can be made by observing the struggle for democratic freedoms in South Korea, Thailand, Bangladesh, Pakistan, Burma (or Myanmar) and elsewhere in Asia. Similarly, while political freedom is widely denied in Africa, there have been movements and protests about that fact whenever circumstances have permitted, even though military dictators have given few opportunities in this respect.

What about the other variant of this argument, to wit, that the poor have *reason* to forgo political and democratic rights in favor of economic needs? This argument, as was noted earlier, is parasitic on the Lee thesis. Since that thesis has little empirical support, the syllogism cannot sustain the argument.

## INSTRUMENTAL IMPORTANCE OF POLITICAL FREEDOM

I turn now from the negative criticisms of political rights to their positive value. The importance of political freedom as a part of basic capabilities has already been discussed in the earlier chapters. We have reason to value liberty and freedom of expression and action in our lives, and it is not unreasonable for human beings—the social creatures that we are—to value unrestrained participation in political and social activities. Also, informed and unregimented *formation* of our values requires openness of communication and arguments, and political freedoms and civil rights can be central for this process. Furthermore, to express publicly what we value and to demand that attention be paid to it, we need free speech and democratic choice.

When we move from the direct importance of political freedom to its instrumental role, we have to consider the political incentives that operate on governments and on the persons and groups that are in office. The rulers have the incentive to listen to what people want if they have to face their criticism and seek their support in elections. As was noted earlier, no substantial famine has ever occurred in any independent country with a democratic form of government and a relatively free press.[6] Famines have occurred in ancient kingdoms and contemporary authoritarian societies, in primitive tribal communities and in modern technocratic dictatorships, in colonial economies run by imperialists from the north and in newly independent countries of the south run by despotic national leaders or by intolerant single parties. But they have never materialized in any country that is independent, that goes to elections regularly, that has opposition parties to voice criticisms and that permits newspapers to report freely and question the wisdom of government policies without extensive censorship.[7] The contrast of experiences will be discussed further in the next chapter, which deals specifically with famines and other crises.

## CONSTRUCTIVE ROLE OF POLITICAL FREEDOM

The instrumental roles of political freedoms and civil rights can be very substantial, but the connection between economic needs and political freedoms may have a *constructive* aspect as well. The exercise of basic political rights makes it more likely not only that there would be a policy response to economic needs, but also that the conceptualization—including comprehension—of "economic needs" itself may require the exercise of such rights. It can indeed be argued that a proper understanding of what economic needs are—their content and their force—requires discussion and exchange. Political and civil rights, especially those related to the guaranteeing of open discussion, debate, criticism, and dissent, are central to the processes of generating informed and reflected choices. These processes are crucial to the formation of values and priorities, and we cannot, in general, take preferences as given independently of public discussion, that is, irrespective of whether open debates and interchanges are permitted or not.

The reach and effectiveness of open dialogue are often underestimated in assessing social and political problems. For example, public discussion has an important role to play in reducing the high rates of fertility that characterize many developing countries. There is, in fact, much evidence that the sharp decline in fertility rates that has taken place in the more literate states in India has been much influenced by public discussion of the bad effects of high fertility rates especially on the lives of young women, and also on the community at large. If the view has emerged in, say, Kerala or Tamil Nadu that a happy family in the modern age is a small family, much discussion and debate have gone into the formation of these perspectives. Kerala now has a fertility rate of 1.7 (similar to that in Britain and France, and well below China's 1.9), and this has been achieved with no coercion, but mainly through the emergence of new values—a process in which political and social dialogues have played a major part. The high level of literacy of the Kerala population, especially female literacy, which is higher than that of every province of China, has greatly contributed to making such social and political dialogues possible (more on this in the next chapter).

Miseries and deprivations can be of various kinds—some more amenable to social remedy than others. The totality of the human predicament would be a gross basis for identifying our "needs." For example, there are many things that we might have good reason to value if they were feasible—we could even want immortality, as Maitreyee did. But we don't see them as "needs." Our conception of needs relates to our ideas of the preventable nature of some deprivations, and to our understanding of what can be done about them. In the formation of these understandings and beliefs, public discussions play a crucial role. Political rights, including freedom of expression and discussion, are not only pivotal in inducing social responses to economic needs, they are also central to the conceptualization of economic needs themselves.

## WORKING OF DEMOCRACY

The intrinsic relevance, the protective role and the constructive importance of democracy can indeed be very extensive. However, in presenting these arguments on the advantages of democracies, there is a danger of overselling their effectiveness. As was mentioned earlier, political freedoms and liberties are permissive advantages, and their effectiveness would depend on how they are exercised. Democracy has been especially successful in preventing those disasters that are easy to understand and where sympathy can take a particularly immediate form. Many other problems are not quite so accessible. For example, India's success in eradicating famines is not matched by that in eliminating regular undernutrition, or curing persistent illiteracy, or inequalities in gender relations (as was discussed in chapter 4). While the plight of famine victims is easy to politicize, these other deprivations call for deeper analysis and more effective use of communication and political participation—in short, fuller practice of democracy.

Inadequacy of practice applies also to some failings in more mature democracies as well. For example, the extraordinary deprivations in health care, education, and social environment of African Americans in the United States help to make their mortality rates exceptionally high (as discussed in chapters 1 and 4), and this is evidently not prevented by the working of American democracy. Democracy has to be seen as creating a set of opportunities, and the use of these opportunities calls for analysis of a different kind, dealing with the *practice* of democratic and political rights. In this respect, the low percentage of voting in American elections, especially by African Americans, and other signs of apathy and alienation, cannot be ignored. Democracy does not serve as an automatic remedy of ailments as quinine works to remedy malaria. The opportunity it opens up has to be positively grabbed in order to achieve the desired effect. This is, of course, a basic feature of freedoms in general—much depends on how freedoms are actually exercised.

## THE PRACTICE OF DEMOCRACY AND THE ROLE OF OPPOSITION

The achievements of democracy depend not only on the rules and procedures that are adopted and safeguarded, but also on the way the opportunities are used by the citizens. Fidel Valdez Ramos, the former president of the Philippines, put the point with great clarity in a November 1998 speech at the Australian National University:

> Under dictatorial rule, people need not think—need not choose—need not make up their minds or give their consent. All they need to do is to follow. This has been a bitter lesson learned from Philippine political experience of not so long ago. By contrast, a democracy cannot survive without civic virtue. . . . The political challenge for people around the world today is not just to replace authoritarian regimes by democratic ones. Beyond this, it is to make democracy work for ordinary people.[8]

Democracy does create this opportunity, which relates both to its "instrumental importance" and to its "constructive role." But with what strength such opportunities are seized depends on a variety of factors, including the vigor of multiparty politics as well as the dynamism of moral arguments and of value formation.[9] For example, in India the priority of preventing starvation and famine was already fully grasped at the time of independence (as it had been in Ireland as well, with its own experience of famine under British rule). The activism of political participants was very effective in preventing famines and in sharply condemning governments for allowing open starvation to occur, and the quickness and force of this process made preventing such calamities an inescapable priority of every government. And yet successive opposition parties have been quite docile in not condemning widespread illiteracy, or the prevalence of non-extreme but serious undernourishment (especially among the children), or the failure to implement land reform programs legislated earlier. This docility of opposition has permitted successive governments to get away with unconscionable neglect of these vital matters of public policy.

In fact, the activism of opposition parties is an important force in nondemocratic societies as well as democratic ones. It can, for example, be argued that despite the lack of democratic guarantees, the vigor and persistence of opposition in pre-democratic South Korea and even in Pinochet's Chile (against heavy odds) were indirectly effective in those countries' governance even before democracy was restored. Many of the social programs that served these countries well were at least partly aimed at reducing the appeal of the opposition, and in this way, the opposition had some effectiveness even before coming to office.[10]

Another such area is the persistence of gender inequality, which too requires forceful engagement, involving critique as well as pointers to reform. Indeed, as these neglected issues come into public debates and confrontations, the authorities have to provide some response. In a democracy, people tend to get what they demand, and more crucially, do not typically get what they do not demand. Two of the neglected areas of social opportunity in India—gender equity and elementary education—are now receiving more attention from the opposition parties, and as a result, from the legislative and executive authorities as well. While the final results will emerge only in the future, we cannot ignore the various moves that are already being made (including proposed legislation that would require that at least a third of the members of Indian parliament must be women, and a schooling program that would extend the right to elementary education to a substantially larger group of children).

In fact, it can be argued that the contribution of democracy in India has not, by any means, been confined to the prevention of economic disasters, such as famines. Despite the limits of its practice, democracy has given India some stability and security about which many people were very pessimistic as the country became independent in 1947. India had, then, an untried government, an undigested partition and unclear political alignments, combined with widespread communal violence and social disorder. It was hard to have faith in the future of a united and democratic India. And yet half a century later we find a democracy that has, taking the rough with the smooth, worked fairly well. Political differences have largely been tackled within the constitutional procedures. Governments have risen and fallen according to electoral and parliamentary rules. India, an ungainly, unlikely, inelegant combination of differences, survives and functions remarkably well as a political unit with a democratic system—indeed held together by its working democracy.

India has also survived the tremendous challenge of having a variety of major languages and a spectrum of religions—an extraordinary heterogeneity of religion and culture. Religious and communal differences are, of course, vulnerable to exploitation by sectarian politicians, and have indeed been so used on several occasions (including in recent years), causing much consternation in the country. But the fact that such consternation greets sectarian violence, and that most of the substantial sections of the nation condemn such deeds, provides ultimately the main democratic guarantee against the narrowly factional exploitation of sectarianism. This is essential for the survival and prosperity of a country as remarkably varied as India, which may have a Hindu majority, but which is also the third largest Muslim country in the world, in which millions of Christians, along with most of the world's Sikhs, Parsees, and Jains, live.

## A CONCLUDING REMARK

Developing and strengthening a democratic system is an essential component of the process of development. The significance of democracy lies, I have argued, in three distinct virtues: (1) its *intrinsic importance,* (2) its *instrumental contributions,* and (3) its *constructive role* in the creation of values and norms. No evaluation of the democratic form of governance can be complete without considering each.

Despite their limitations, political freedoms and civil rights are used effectively often enough. Even in those fields in which they have not yet been very effective, the opportunity exists for making them effective. The permissive role of political and civil rights (in allowing—indeed in encouraging—open discussions and debates, participatory politics and unpersecuted opposition) applies over a very wide domain, even though it has been more effective in some areas than in others. Its demonstrated usefulness in preventing economic disasters is itself quite important. When things go fine and everything is routinely good, this role of democracy may not be badly missed. But it comes into its own when things get fouled up, for one reason or another (for example, the recent financial crisis in East and Southeast Asia that disrupted several economies and left many people destitute). The political incentives provided by democratic governance acquire great practical value at that time.

However, while we must acknowledge the importance of democratic institutions, they cannot be viewed as mechanical devices for development. Their use is conditioned by our values and priorities, and by the use we make of the available opportunities of articulation and participation. The role of organized opposition groups is particularly important in this context.

Public debates and discussions, permitted by political freedoms and civil rights, can also play a major part in the formation of values. Indeed, even the identification of needs cannot but be influenced by the nature of public participation and dialogue. Not only is the force of public discussion one of the correlates of democracy, with an extensive reach, but its cultivation can also make democracy itself function better. For example, more informed and less marginalized public discussion of environmental issues may not only be good for the environment; it could also be important to the health and functioning of the democratic system itself.[11]

Just as it is important to emphasize the need for democracy, it is also crucial to safeguard the conditions and circumstances that ensure the range and reach of the democratic process. Valuable as democracy is as a major source of social opportunity (a recognition that may call for vigorous defense), there is also the need to examine ways and means of making it function well, to realize its potentials. The achievement of social justice depends not only on institutional forms (including democratic rules and regulations), but also on effective practice. I have presented reasons for taking the issue of practice to be of central importance in the contributions that can be expected from civil rights and political freedoms. This is a challenge that is faced both by well-established democracies such as the United States (especially with the differential participation of diverse racial groups) and by newer democracies. There are shared problems as well as disparate ones.

# CHAPTER 7

# FAMINES AND OTHER CRISES

We live in a world with widespread hunger and undernourishment and frequent famines. It is often assumed—if only implicitly—that we can do little to remedy these desperate situations. It is also presumed, frequently enough, that these maladies may actually get worse in the long run, especially with the growth of world population. Tacit pessimism often dominates international reactions to these miseries in the world today. This perceived lack of freedom to remedy hunger can itself lead to fatalism and the absence of serious attempts to remedy the miseries that we see.

There is little factual basis for such pessimism, nor are there any cogent grounds for assuming the immutability of hunger and deprivation. Appropriate policies and actions can indeed eradicate the terrible problems of hunger in the modern world. Based on recent economic, political and social analyses, it is, I believe, possible to identify the measures that can bring about the elimination of famines and a radical reduction in chronic undernourishment. What is important at this time is to make policies and programs draw on the lessons that have emerged from analytical investigations and empirical studies.[1]

This chapter is particularly concerned with famines and other transient "crises," which may or may not include open starvation, but do involve a sudden eruption of severe deprivation for a considerable section of the population (for example, in the recent East and Southeast Asian economic crises). Famines and crises of this kind have to be distinguished from problems of endemic hunger and poverty that may lead to persistent suffering but do not include any fresh explosion of extreme deprivation that suddenly engulfs a portion of the people. Even in analyzing endemic undernourishment and persistent, long-run deprivation later on in this study (mainly in chapter 9), I shall draw on some of the concepts that the study of famines will yield (in this chapter).

For the elimination of hunger in the modern world, it is crucial to understand the causation of famines in an adequately broad way, and not just in terms of some mechanical balance between food and population. What is crucial in analyzing hunger is the substantive freedom of the individual and the family to establish ownership over an adequate amount of food, which can be done either by growing the food oneself (as peasants do), or by buying it in the market (as the nongrowers of food do). A person may be forced into starvation even when there is plenty of food around if he loses his ability to buy food in the market, through a loss of income (for example, due to unemployment or the collapse of the market for goods that he produces and sells to earn a living). On the other side, even when food supply falls sharply in a country or a region, everyone can be saved from starvation by a better sharing of the available food (for example, through creating additional employment and income for the potential famine victims). This can be supplemented and made more effective by getting food from abroad, but many threatening famines have been prevented even without that—simply through a more equal sharing of the reduced domestic supply of food. The focus has to be on the economic power and substantive freedom of individuals and families to buy enough food, and not just on the quantum of food in the country in question.

There is need for economic and political analyses here, as there also is for having a fuller understanding of crises and disasters other than famines. A good example is the kind of predicament that some countries in East Asia and Southeast Asia have recently experienced. In these crises, as in famines, some sections of the population have lost their economic entitlements with unexpected suddenness. The speed and sheer intensity of deprivation in these crises (and also, typically, the unexpectedness of the disasters) differ from the more "regular" phenomenon of general poverty, in the same way that famines differ from endemic hunger.

## ENTITLEMENT AND INTERDEPENDENCE

Hunger relates not only to food production and agricultural expansion, but also to the functioning of the entire economy and—even more broadly—the operation of the political and social arrangements that can, directly or indirectly, influence people's ability to acquire food and to achieve health and nourishment. Furthermore, while much can be done through sensible government policy, it is important to integrate the role of the government with the efficient functioning of other economic and social institutions—varying from trade, commerce and the markets to active functioning of political parties, nongovernmental organizations, and institutions that sustain and facilitate informed public discussion, including effective news media.

Undernourishment, starvation and famine are influenced by the working of the entire economy and society—not just food production and agricultural activities. It is crucial to take adequate note of the economic and social interdependences that govern the incidence of hunger in the contemporary world. Food is not distributed in the economy through charity or some system of automatic sharing. The ability to acquire food has to be *earned*. What we have to concentrate on is not the total food supply in the economy but the "entitlement" that each person enjoys: the commodities over which she can establish her ownership and command. People suffer from hunger when they cannot establish their entitlement over an adequate amount of food.[2]

What determines a family's entitlement? It depends on various distinct influences. First, there is the *endowment*: the ownership over productive resources as well as wealth that commands a price in the market. For much of humanity the only endowment that is at all significant is labor power. The majority of the world's people have little resource other than labor power, which may come combined with a variable amount of skill and experience. But in general, labor, land and other resources make up the basket of assets.

Second, an important influence consists of *production possibilities* and their use. This is where technology comes in: available technology determines the production possibilities, which are influenced by available knowledge as well as the ability of the people to marshal that knowledge and to make actual use of it.

In generating entitlements, the endowment in the form of land and labor may be directly used to produce food—as in the case of agriculture. Or, alternatively, a family or an individual may acquire the ability to buy food by getting a wage income. This will depend on employment opportunities and the prevailing wage rates. These too depend on production possibilities—in agriculture, industry and other activities. Most people in the world do not directly produce food, but earn their ability to get food by getting employment in the production of other commodities, which may vary from cash crops, to craft products, to industrial goods, to sundry services, and involve a variety of occupations. These interdependences may be very central to the analysis of famines, since substantial numbers of people may lose the ability to command food because of problems in the production of other goods, rather than food as such.

Third, much would depend on the *exchange conditions:* the ability to sell and buy goods and the determination of relative prices of different products (for example, craft products vis-à-vis staple food). Given the central—indeed unique—importance of labor power as an endowment for much of humanity, it is crucial to pay attention to the operation of the labor markets. Does a job seeker find employment at the prevailing wages? Also, can craftsmen and service providers manage to sell what they try to sell? At what relative prices (vis-à-vis the price of food in the market)?

These exchange conditions can change dramatically in an economic emergency, leading to the threat of a famine. These shifts can occur very rapidly as a result of a variety of influences. There have been famines associated with sharp changes in relative prices of products (or of wage rate vis-à-vis the price of food) due to quite distinct causes, such as a drought, or a flood, or a general shortfall of employment, or an uneven boom that raises the income of some but not of others, or even an exaggerated fear of food shortage that drives the food prices temporarily up, causing havoc.[3]

In an economic crisis, some services may be hit much harder than others. For example, during the 1943 Bengal famine, the exchange rates between food and the products of particular types altered radically. Other than the wage-food-price ratio, there were big shifts in the relative prices of fish vis-à-vis food grains, and Bengali fishermen were among the worst-affected occupational groups in the 1943 famine. Of course fish is food too, but it is high-quality food, and the poor fishermen have to sell fish to be able to buy cheaper calories in staple foods (in Bengal, this mostly takes the form of rice) to be able to get enough calories to survive. The equilibrium of survival is sustained by this exchange, and a sudden fall in the relative price of fish vis-à-vis rice can devastate this equilibrium.[4]

Many other occupations are also acutely vulnerable to shifts in relative prices and sales proceeds. Take a job like haircutting. Barbers are hit by two sets of problems in a period of economic crisis: (1) in situations of distress people find it quite easy to postpone having their hair cut—so that the demand for the product of the barber may fall sharply; and (2) on top of this "quantity" decline, there is also a sharp fall in relative price of haircutting: during the 1943 Bengal famine, the rate of exchange between haircutting and staple food fell in some districts by *70 or 80 percent*. So the barbers—already poor as they are—went to the wall, as did many other occupational groups. All this happened with very little overall decline in food output or aggregate supply. The combination of greater purchasing power of the urban population (who had benefited from the war boom) and fearful speculative withdrawal of food from the markets helped to generate starvation through a sharp distributional change. Understanding the causation of hunger and starvation calls for an analysis of the entire economic mechanism, not just an accounting of food output and supply.[5]

## FAMINE CAUSATION

Entitlement failures that lead to famines can arise from a variety of causes. In attempting to remedy famines, and even more, to prevent them, this diversity of causal antecedence has to be kept in view. Famines reflect a shared predicament, but not necessarily a shared causation.

For those who do not themselves produce food (for example, industrial workers or service providers), or do not own the food they produce (for example, agricultural wage laborers), the ability to acquire food in the market depends on their earnings, the prevailing food prices, and their nonfood necessary expenditures. Their ability to get food depends on economic circumstance: employment and wage rates for wage laborers, production of other commodities and their prices for craftsmen and service-providers, and so on.

Even for those who do produce food themselves, while their entitlements depend on their *individual* food output, there is no similar dependence on the *national* output of food, on which many famine studies standardly concentrate. Also, sometimes people have to sell expensive foods such as animal products to buy cheaper calories from food grains, as poor pastoral people often do: for example, animal-rearing nomads in the Sahel and in the horn of Africa. The exchange-dependence of the African pastoralist in having to sell animal products including meat to buy cheap calories from staple food is rather similar to that of the Bengali fishermen, discussed earlier, in having to sell fish to buy cheaper calories from rice. These fragile exchange equilibria can be ruptured by shifts in exchange rates. A fall in the price of animal products vis-à-vis food grains can spell disaster for these pastoral people. Some African famines with a strong pastoral component have involved a process of this kind. A drought can lead to a fall in the relative price of animal products (even meat) vis-à-vis traditionally cheaper food, since people often shift the pattern of their consumption *against* expensive food (such as meat) and non-necessities (such as leather goods) in a situation of economic distress. This change in relative prices can make it impossible for the pastoralists to buy enough staple food to survive.[6]

Famines can occur even without any decline in food production or availability. A laborer may be reduced to starvation through unemployment, combined with the absence of a social security system of safety nets (such as unemployment insurance). This can easily happen, and indeed even a large famine can actually occur, *despite* a high and undiminished general level of food availability—perhaps even a "peak" level of food availability—in the economy as a whole.

One example of a famine despite peak food availability is the Bangladesh famine of 1974.[7] This occurred in a year of *greater* food availability per head than in any other year between 1971 and 1976 (see figure 7.1). The starvation was initiated by regional unemployment caused by floods, which affected food output many months later when the reduced crop was harvested (mainly, around December), but the famine occurred earlier than that and was over well before the affected crop matured. The floods led to *immediate* income deprivation of rural laborers in the summer of 1974; they lost the wages that they would have earned from the transplanting of rice and related activities, and that would have given them the means to

FIGURE 7.1: *Food Grains Availability in Bangladesh, 1971–1975*

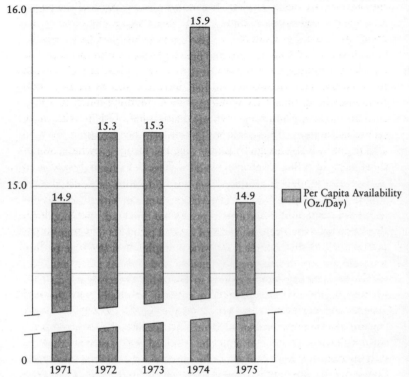

*Source:* Amartya Sen, *Poverty and Famines* (Oxford: Oxford Univeristy Press, 1981), table 9.5. The famine occurred in 1974.

acquire food. The local starvation and panic were followed by more widespread hunger, reinforced by a nervous food market and a steep rise in food prices as a result of exaggerated expectation of future food shortage. The future shortage was overestimated and to some extent manipulated, and the price rise was followed later on by a downward price correction.[8] But by that time the famine had already taken its heavy toll.

Even when a famine *is* associated with a decline in food production (as it clearly was in the case of the Chinese famine of 1958–1961 or in the Irish famines in the 1840s[9]), we still have to go beyond the output statistics to explain why it is that some parts of the population get wiped out, while the rest do just fine. Famines survive by divide-and-rule. For example, a group of peasants may suffer entitlement losses when food output in their territory declines, perhaps due to a local drought, even when there is no general dearth of food in the country. The victims would not have the means to buy food from elsewhere, since they would not have anything much to sell to earn an income, given their own production loss. Others with more secure earnings in other occupations or in other locations may be able to get by well enough by purchasing food from elsewhere. Something very like this happened in the Wollo famine in Ethiopia in 1973, with impoverished residents of the province of Wollo unable to buy food, despite the fact that food prices in Dessie (the capital of Wollo) were no higher than in Addis Ababa and Asmara. Indeed, there is evidence of some food moving *out of* Wollo to the more prosperous regions of Ethiopia, where people had more income to buy food.

Or, to take a different type of case, food prices may shoot up because of the increased purchasing power of some occupational groups, and as a result others who have to buy food may be ruined because the real purchasing power of their money incomes may have shrunk sharply. Such a famine may occur without any decline in food output, resulting as it does from a rise in competing demand rather than a fall in total supply. This is what started off the famine in Bengal in 1943 (discussed earlier), with urban dwellers gaining from the "war boom"—the Japanese army was around the corner and the British and Indian defense expenditures were heavy in urban Bengal, including Calcutta. Once the rice prices started moving up sharply, public panic as well as manipulative speculation played its part in pushing the prices sky high, beyond the reach of a substantial part of the population of rural Bengal.[10] The Devil, then, took the hindmost.[11]

Or, to take yet a different type of case, some workers may find their "occupations gone," as the economy changes and the types and locations of gainful activities shift. This has happened, for example, in sub-Saharan Africa, with changing environmental and climatic conditions. Erstwhile productive workers may then be without work or earnings, and in the absence of social security systems, there would not be anything else to fall back on.

In some other cases, the loss of gainful employment can be a temporary phenomenon, with powerful effects in initiating a famine. For example, in the Bangladesh famine of 1974, the first signs of distress were found among the landless rural laborers, after the summer floods, which disrupted the employment of labor for transplanting rice. These laborers, who led a hand-to-mouth existence, were forced to starve as a result of the loss of wage employment, and this phenomenon occurred much *before* the crop that was adversely affected was to be harvested.[12]

Famines are highly divisive phenomena. Attempts to understand them in terms of *average* food availability per head can be hopelessly misleading. It is rare to find a famine that affected more than 5 or 10 percent of the population. There are, to be sure, alleged accounts of famines in which nearly everyone in a country had to go hungry. But most of these anecdotes do not bear much scrutiny. For example, the authoritative *Encyclopaedia Britannica,* in its vintage eleventh edition, refers to the Indian famine of 1344–1345 as one in which even "the Moghul emperor was unable to obtain the necessaries for his household."[13] But that story runs into some problems. It is sad to have to report that the Moghul empire in India was not established until 1526. Perhaps more important, the Tughlak emperor in power in 1344–1345—Mohammad Bin Tughlak—not only had no great difficulty in securing necessaries for his household, but also had enough means to organize one of the more illustrious programs of famine relief in history.[14] The anecdotes of unified starvation do not tally with the reality of divided fortunes.

## FAMINE PREVENTION

Since famines are associated with the loss of entitlements of one or more occupational groups in particular regions, the resulting starvation can be prevented by systematically re-creating a minimum level of incomes and entitlements for those who are hit by economic changes. The numbers involved, while often absolutely large, are usually small fractions of the total population, and the minimum levels of purchasing power needed to ward off starvation can be quite small. Thus the costs of such public action for famine prevention are typically rather modest even for poor countries, provided they make systematic and efficient arrangements in good time.

Just to get an idea of the magnitudes involved, if potential famine victims constitute, say, 10 percent of the total population of the country (they usually affect a much smaller proportion than that), the share of total income going to these typically poor people would not in normal circumstances exceed, say, about 3 percent of the GNP. Their normal share of food consumption may also, typically, not be greater than 4 or 5 percent of the national food consumption. Thus the resources needed to re-create their *entire* income, or to resupply their entire normal food consumption, starting from zero, do not have to be very large provided the preventive measures are efficiently organized. Of course, famine victims typically have some resources left (so that their entitlements do not have to be re-created from zero), and the *net* resource requirement can thus be even smaller.

Also, a good deal of the mortality associated with famines results from diseases unleashed by debilitation, breakdown of sanitary arrangements, population movements, and infectious spread of diseases endemic in the region.[15] These too can be sharply reduced through sensible public action involving epidemic control and communal health arrangements. In this field too, the returns on small amounts of well-planned public expenditure can be very large indeed.

Famine prevention is very dependent on the political arrangements for entitlement protection. In the richer countries, such protection is provided by antipoverty programs and unemployment insurance. Most developing countries do not have any general system of unemployment insurance, but some of them do provide emergency public employment at times of massive loss of employment caused by natural or non-natural disasters. Compensatory government expenditure in creating employment can help to avert a threatening famine very effectively. Indeed, this is the way potential famines have been prevented from occurring in India since independence—mainly through countervailing employment creation. For example, in 1973 in Maharashtra, to compensate for the loss of employment associated with a severe drought, 5 million temporary jobs were created, which is really a very large number (when account is taken of the workers' family members too). The results were extraordinary: no significant rise in mortality at all, and even no great deterioration of the number of undernourished people, despite a dramatic decline (in many areas 70 percent or more) in food production over a vast region.

## FAMINE AND ALIENATION

The political economy of famine causation and prevention involves institutions and organizations, but it depends, in addition, on perceptions and understandings that accompany the exercise of power and authority. It depends particularly on the alienation of the rulers from those ruled. Even when the immediate causation of a famine is quite different from this, the social or political distance between the governors and the governed can play a crucial role in the nonprevention of the famine.

It is useful, in this context, to consider the famines of the 1840s that devastated Ireland about 150 years ago, killing a higher *proportion* of the population than any other famine anywhere in recorded history.[16] The famine also changed the nature of Ireland in a decisive way. It led to a level of emigration—even under the most terrible conditions of voyage—that has hardly been seen anywhere else in the world.[17] The Irish population even today is very substantially smaller than it was in 1845 when the famine began.

What did cause this calamity, then? In George Bernard Shaw's *Man and Superman*, Mr. Malone, a rich Irish American, refuses to describe the Irish famines of the 1840s as "famine." He tells his English daughter-in-law, Violet, that his father "died of starvation in the black 47." When Violet asks, "The famine?" Malone replies: "No, the starvation. When a country is full of food and exporting it, there can be no famine."

There are several things wrong with Malone's spiked statement. It is certainly true that food was being exported from famished Ireland to prosperous England, but it is not true that Ireland was full of food (indeed, the coexistence of hunger and food exports is a common phenomenon in many famines). Also, while the expressions "starve" and "starvation" can certainly be taken in their old, proactive sense—now largely defunct—of *making* people go without food, in particular *causing* their death from hunger, it is hard to deny that there *was* a famine (as the term is commonly understood) in Ireland at that time.

Malone was making a different—and rather profound—point, admittedly with some literary license. The focal issue concerns the role of human agency in causing and sustaining famines. If the Irish famines were entirely preventable, and in particular, if those in public authority could have prevented them, then the charge of "starving" the Irish would have perspicuity enough. The accusing finger cannot but point to the role of public policy in preventing or not preventing famines, and to the political, social, and cultural influences that determine public policy. The policy issues to be examined concern acts of *omission* as well as of *commission*. Since famines have continued to occur in different countries even in the modern world of unprecedented overall prosperity, questions of public policies and their effectiveness remain as relevant today as they were 150 years ago.

Turning first to the more immediate reasons for the Irish famines, there clearly was, in this case, a reduction in the food output in Ireland, mainly because of a potato blight. However, the role of overall food supply in generating that famine can be assessed in different ways depending on the coverage of our food statistics. Much depends on the area over which food output is considered. As Cormac O Grada has pointed out, if the food output and supply over the entire United Kingdom are considered, then there were no crises of food output or supply, in contrast with what happened specifically in Ireland.[18] Certainly food could have moved from Britain to Ireland if the Irish could have afforded to purchase it. The fact that this did not happen, and exactly the opposite occurred, relates to the poverty of Ireland and to the economic deprivation of the Irish victims. As Terry Eagleton puts it in his forceful literary treatment of the Irish famines, *Heathcliff and the Great Hunger:* "In this sense it can be reasonably claimed that the Irish did not die simply for lack of food, but because they largely lacked the funds to purchase food which was present in abundance in the kingdom as a whole, but which was not sufficiently available to them."[19]

In analyzing the causation of famines, it is important to study the general prevalence of poverty in the country or region involved. In the case of Ireland, the poverty of the Irish in general and the modest size of their assets made them specially vulnerable to the economic decline that occurred with the blight.[20] In that context, focus has to be placed not only on the endemic poverty of the people involved, but also on the special vulnerability of those whose entitlements are particularly fragile when there are economic changes.[21] It is the general defenselessness of the very poor, combined with additional misfortunes created by economic variations, that produces the victims of drastic starvation. The small Irish growers of potatoes were severely hit by the blight, and through the increase in the price of food, others were too.

As far as food itself is concerned, far from there being a systematic import of food into Ireland to break the famine, there was (as mentioned earlier) the opposite movement: the export of food from Ireland to England (especially of food of a somewhat higher quality). Such a "food countermovement" is not altogether rare in a class of famines—the so-called slump famines—in which there is an overall slump in the economy, which makes the purchasing ability of the consumers go down sharply, and the available food supply (reduced as it is) fetches a better price elsewhere. Such food countermovement happened, for example, in the Wollo famine in Ethiopia in 1973 mentioned earlier. Residents of that province were unable to buy food, despite the fact that food prices there were no higher—often substantially lower—than elsewhere in the country. In fact, it has been shown that food was moving *out of* Wollo to the more prosperous regions of Ethiopia where people had more income and thus had greater ability to buy food.[22]

This did happen on quite a large scale in Ireland in the 1840s, when ship after ship—laden with wheat, oats, cattle, pigs, eggs, and butter—sailed down the Shannon bound for well-fed England from famine-stricken Ireland. The export of food from Ireland to England at the height of the famine has been a subject of great bitterness in Ireland, and even today continues to influence the complex mistrust between England and Ireland.

There is no great economic mystery behind the movement of food from Ireland to England during the Irish famines. The market forces would always encourage movement of food to places where people could afford to pay a higher price for it. The prosperous English could do just that, compared with what the impoverished Irish could do. Similarly, in 1973, the residents of Addis Ababa could buy food that the starving wretches in Wollo could not afford.

One must not jump from this to the conclusion that stopping market transactions would be the right way to halt a famine. In some special cases, such a stoppage can serve a limited goal (it could have helped Irish consumers if the food countermovement to England had been restrained), but in general that would still leave untouched the basic problem of the poverty and destitution of the famine victims. To change that, more positive policies would be needed—not the purely negative one of banning market transactions of certain kinds. Indeed, with positive policies of regenerating the lost incomes of the destitute (for example, through public employment programs), the food countermovement could have automatically been reduced or stopped, since the domestic purchasers could have commanded food more affluently.

We know, of course, that very little help was provided by the government of the United Kingdom to alleviate the destitution and starvation of the Irish through the period of the famine. There have been similar occurrences in the empire, but Ireland was distinguished in being part of the British Isles itself. This is where *cultural alienation,* as opposed to purely political asymmetry, is of some significance (though cultural alienation is "political" as well, in a broad sense).

In this context, it is important to bear in mind the fact that by the 1840s, when the Irish famine occurred, an extensive system of poverty relief was fairly well established in Britain, as far as Britain itself was concerned. England too had its share of the poor, and even the life of the employed English worker was far from prosperous (indeed, the year 1845, when the sequence of Irish famines began, was also the year in which Friedrich Engels's classic indictment of the poverty and economic misery of English workers, *The Conditions of the Working Class in England,* was published). But there was still some political commitment to prevent open starvation within England. A similar commitment did not apply to the empire—not even to Ireland. Even the Poor Laws gave the English destitute substantially more rights than the Irish destitute got from the more anemic Poor Laws that were instituted for Ireland.

Indeed, as Joel Mokyr has noted, "Ireland was considered by Britain as an alien and even hostile nation."[23] This estrangement affected many aspects of Irish-British relations. For one thing, as Mokyr notes, it discouraged British capital investment in Ireland. But most relevantly in the present context, there was a relative indifference to famines and suffering in Ireland and less determination in London to prevent Irish destitution and starvation. Richard Ned Lebow has argued that while poverty in Britain was typically attributed to economic change and fluctuations, poverty in Ireland was viewed as being caused by laziness, indifference and ineptitude, so that "Britain's mission" was seen not as one "to alleviate Irish distress but to civilize her people and to lead them to feel and act like human beings."[24] This may be a somewhat exaggerated view, but it is hard to think that famines like those in Ireland in the 1840s would have been at all allowed to occur in Britain.

In looking behind the social and cultural influences that shape public policy and that in this case allowed the famines to occur, it is important to appreciate the sense of dissociation and superiority that characterized the British attitude toward the Irish. The cultural roots of the Irish famines extend as far back as Edmund Spenser's *The Faerie Queene* (published in 1590), and perhaps even earlier. The tendency to blame the victims, plentiful in *The Faerie Queene* itself, survived through the famines of the 1840s, and the Irish taste for potatoes was added to the list of the calamities that the natives had, in the English view, brought on themselves.

The conviction of cultural superiority merges well with the asymmetry of political power.[25] Winston Churchill's famous remark that the Bengal famine of 1943, which was the last famine in British India (and also the last famine in India altogether), was caused by the tendency of the natives to breed "like rabbits" belongs to this general tradition of blaming the colonial subject; it nicely supplemented Churchill's other belief that Indians were "the beastliest people in the world, next to the Germans."[26] One cannot but sympathize with Winston Churchill's double jeopardy confronted by beastly Germans wanting to topple his government and beastly Indians requesting good governance.

Charles Edward Trevelyan, the head of the Treasury during the Irish famines, who saw not much wrong with British economic policy in Ireland (of which he was in charge), pointed to Irish habits as part of the explanation of the famines. Chief among the habitual failures was the tendency of the Irish poor to eat only potatoes, which made them dependent on one crop. Indeed, Trevelyan's view of the causation of the Irish famines permitted him to link them with his analysis of Irish cooking: "There is scarcely a woman of the peasant class in the West of Ireland whose culinary art exceeds the boiling of a potato."[27] The remark is of interest not just because it is rather rare for an Englishman to find a suitable occasion for making international criticism of culinary art. Rather, the pointing of an accusing finger at the meagerness of the diet of the Irish poor well illustrates the tendency to blame the victim. The victims, in this view, had helped themselves to a disaster, despite the best efforts of the administration in London to prevent it.

Cultural alienation has to be added to the lack of political incentives (discussed in chapter 6) in explaining British nonaction during the Irish famines. Famines are, in fact, so easy to prevent that it is amazing that they are allowed to occur at all.[28] The sense of distance between the ruler and the ruled—between "us" and "them"—is a crucial feature of famines. That distance is as severe in the contemporary famines in Ethiopia, Somalia and Sudan as it was in Ireland and India under foreign domination in the last century.

## PRODUCTION, DIVERSIFICATION AND GROWTH

I return now to the economics of famine prevention. In preventing famines, it helps to have a more opulent and growing economy. Economic expansion typically reduces the need for entitlement protection, and also enhances the resources available for providing that protection. This is a lesson of obvious importance for sub-Saharan Africa, where the lack of overall economic growth has been a major underlying source of deprivation. The proneness to famines is much greater when the population is generally impoverished and when public funds are hard to secure.

Attention has to be paid to the need for incentives to generate the growth of outputs and incomes—including, inter alia, the expansion of food output. This calls for devising sensible price incentives, but also for measures to encourage and enhance technical change, skill formation and productivity—both in agriculture and in other fields.[29]

While growth of food output is important, the main issue concerns overall economic growth, since food is purchasable in the world market. A country can purchase food from abroad if it has the means to do this (based, say, on industrial production). If, for example, we compare food production per head in 1993–1995 with that in 1979–1981 in different countries in Asia and Africa, we find a *decline* of 1.7 percent in South Korea, 12.4 percent in Japan, 33.5 percent in Botswana and 58.0 percent in Singapore. We do not, however, observe any growing hunger in these economies, since they also experienced fast expansion of real income per head through other means (such as industries or mining), and they happen to be richer anyway. The sharing of the increased income made the citizens of these countries more able to secure food than before, despite the falling food output. In contrast, even though there was little or no decline in food production per head in economies such as Sudan (7.7 percent *increase*), or Burkina Faso (29.4 percent *increase*), those economies experienced considerable unfolding of hunger because of their general poverty and the vulnerable economic entitlements of many substantial groups. It is essential to focus on the actual processes through which a person or a family establishes command over food.

It is often pointed out—rightly—that food output per head has been falling in sub-Saharan Africa until recently. This is indeed so and is obviously a matter of concern, and it has implications for many aspects of public policy, varying from agricultural research to population control. But, as was noted earlier, the same fact of falling food output per head applies to many countries in other regions of the world as well.[30] These countries did not experience famines both (1) because they achieved relatively high growth rates in other areas of production, and (2) because the dependence on food output as a source of income is much less in these countries than in the typical sub-Saharan African economy.

The tendency to think of growing more food as the only way of solving a food problem is strong and tempting, and often it does have some rationale. But the picture is more complex than that, related to alternative economic opportunities and the possibilities of international trade. As far as lack of growth is concerned, the major feature of sub-Saharan Africa's problems is not the particular lack of growth in food output as such, but the *general* lack of economic growth altogether (of which the problem of food output is only one part). The need for a more diversified production structure is very strong in sub-Saharan Africa, given the climatic uncertainties, on the one hand, and the possibility of expanding in other fields of productive activity, on the other. The often-advocated strategy of concentrating exclusively on the expansion of agriculture—and specifically food crops—is like putting all the eggs in the same basket, and the perils of such a policy can be great indeed.

It is, of course, unlikely that the dependence of sub-Saharan Africa on food production as a source of income can be dramatically reduced in the short run. But some diversification can be attempted straightaway, and even the reduction of overdependence on a few crops can enhance security of incomes. In the long run, for sub-Saharan Africa to join in the process of economic expansion that has taken place in much of the rest of the world, sources of income and growth outside food production and even outside agriculture would have to be more vigorosly sought and used.

## THE EMPLOYMENT ROUTE AND THE AGENCY ISSUE

Even when the opportunities of international trade are absent, how the total food supply is shared between different groups within the country can be crucially important. Famines can be prevented by re-creating lost incomes of the potential victims (for example, through the temporary creation of wage employment in specially devised public projects), giving them the ability to compete for food in the market, making the available supply more equally shared. In most situations in which famines have occurred, a more equal sharing of food would have prevented starvation (though expanding the food supply would obviously have made things easier). Famine prevention through employment creation, with or without expanding the total food availability, has been well used in many countries, including India, Botswana and Zimbabwe.[31]

The employment route also happens to encourage the processes of trade and commerce, and does not disrupt economic, social and family lives. The people helped can mostly stay on in their own homes, close to their economic activities (like farming), so that these economic operations are not disrupted. The family life too can continue in a normal way, rather than people being herded into emergency camps. There is also more social continuity, and, furthermore, less danger of the spread of infectious diseases, which tend to break out in the overcrowded camps. In general, the approach of relief through employment also allows the potential famine victims to be treated as active agents, rather than as passive recipients of governmental handouts.[32]

Another point to note here (in line with the overall approach of this book) is the combined uses of different social institutions in this process of famine prevention. Public policy here takes the form of drawing on very different institutional arrangements:

1) *state support* in creating income and employment;
2) operation of *private markets* for food and labor;
3) reliance on normal *commerce and business*.

The integration of the respective roles of different social institutions—involving the market as well as nonmarket organizations—is very important for an adequately broad approach to the prevention of famines, as it is, in fact, for economic development in general.

## DEMOCRACY AND FAMINE PREVENTION

Earlier on in this book I referred to the role of democracy in preventing famines. The argument related particularly to the political incentives generated by elections, multiparty politics and investigative journalism. It is certainly true that there has never been a famine in a functioning multiparty democracy.

Is this observed historical association a causal one, or simply an accidental occurrence? The possibility that the connection between democratic political rights and the absence of famines is a "bogus correlation" may seem plausible enough when one considers the fact that the democratic countries are typically also rather rich and thus, perhaps, immune from famines for other reasons. But the absence of famines holds even for those democratic countries that happen to be very poor, such as India, Botswana or Zimbabwe.

Indeed, the democratic poor countries sometimes have had much larger declines in the production and supply of food, and also sharper collapse of the purchasing power of substantial sections of the population, than some nondemocratic countries. But while the dictatorial countries had major famines, the democratic ones managed to avert famines altogether despite the worse food situation. For example, Botswana had a fall in food production of 17 percent and Zimbabwe one of 38 percent between 1979–1981 and 1983–1984, in the same period in which the food production decline amounted to a relatively modest 11 or 12 percent in Sudan and Ethiopia. But while Sudan and Ethiopia, with comparatively smaller declines in food output, had massive famines, Botswana and Zimbabwe had none, and this was largely due to timely and extensive famine prevention policies by these latter countries.[33]

Had the governments in Botswana and Zimbabwe failed to undertake timely action, they would have been under severe criticism and pressure from the opposition and would have gotten plenty of flak from newspapers. In contrast, the Ethiopian and Sudanese governments did not have to reckon with those prospects, and the political incentives provided by democratic institutions were thoroughly absent in those countries. Famines in Sudan and Ethiopia—and in many other countries in sub-Saharan Africa—were fed by the political immunity enjoyed by governmental leaders in authoritarian countries. This would seem to apply to the present situation in North Korea as well.

Indeed, famines are very easy to prevent through regenerating the lost purchasing power of hard-hit groups, and this can be done through various programs, including—as was just discussed—the creation of emergency employment in short-term public projects. Postindependence India has had, on different occasions, very large declines in food production and availability, and also quite gigantic destruction of the economic solvency of large groups of people, and still famines have been prevented through giving the potential famine victims "entitlement" to food, through wage income in employment-oriented projects and other means. It is obvious that getting more food into the famine-stricken region helps to alleviate the famine if the potential famine victims have the economic power to buy the food, for which too creating income for those without any (or with very little) is quite crucial. But even in the absence of any food import into the region, the creation of income for the destitute people itself helps to alleviate hunger through a better sharing of the available food.[34]

In the 1973 drought in Maharashtra in India, food production fell so sharply that the per capita food output was half that in sub-Saharan Africa. And yet there was no famine in Maharashtra (where five million people were employed in rapidly organized public projects), while there were very substantial famines in sub-Saharan Africa.[35] Aside from these intercountry contrasts of experiences in famine prevention, which bring out forcefully the protective role of democracy, there is also some interesting intertemporal evidence relating to a country's *transition* to democracy. For example, India continued to have famines right up to the time of independence in 1947. The last famine—one of the largest—was the Bengal famine in the spring and summer of 1943 (which I had the experience of witnessing, in its full rigor, as a nine-year-old boy); it is estimated that between two million and three million people died in that famine. Since independence and the installation of a multiparty democratic system, there has been no substantial famine, even though severe crop failures and massive loss of purchasing power have occurred often enough (for example, in 1968, 1973, 1979 and 1987).

## INCENTIVES, INFORMATION AND
## THE PREVENTION OF FAMINES

The causal connection between democracy and the nonoccurrence of famines is not hard to seek. Famines kill millions of people in different countries in the world, but they don't kill the rulers. The kings and the presidents, the bureaucrats and the bosses, the military leaders and the commanders never are famine victims. And if there are no elections, no opposition parties, no scope for uncensored public criticism, then those in authority don't have to suffer the political consequences of their failure to prevent famines. Democracy, on the other hand, would spread the penalty of famines to the ruling groups and political leaders as well. This gives them the political incentive to *try* to prevent any threatening famine, and since famines are in fact easy to prevent (the economic argument clicks into the political one at this stage), the approaching famines are firmly prevented.

The second issue concerns *information*. A free press and the practice of democracy contribute greatly to bringing out information that can have an enormous impact on policies for famine prevention (for example, information about the early effects of droughts and floods and about the nature and impact of unemployment). The most elementary source of basic information from distant areas about a threatening famine are enterprising news media, especially when there are incentives—provided by a democratic system—for bringing out facts that may be embarrassing to the government (facts that an authoritarian government would tend to censor out). Indeed, I would argue that a free press and an active political opposition constitute the best early-warning system a country threatened by famines can have.

The connection between political rights and economic needs can be illustrated in the specific context of famine prevention by considering the massive Chinese famines of 1958–1961. Even before the recent economic reforms, China had been much more successful than India in economic development in many significant respects. For example, the average life expectancy went up in China much more than in India, and well before the reforms of 1979 had already come close to the high figures that are quoted now (nearly seventy years at birth). Nevertheless, there was a major failure in China in its inability to prevent famines. The Chinese famines of 1958–1961 killed, it is now estimated, close to thirty million people—ten times more than even the gigantic 1943 famine in British India.[36]

The so-called Great Leap Forward initiated in the late 1950s had been a massive failure, but the Chinese government refused to admit that and continued to pursue dogmatically much the same disastrous policies for three more years. It is hard to imagine that anything like this could have happened in a country that goes to the polls regularly and that has an independent press. During that terrible calamity the government faced no pressure from newspapers, which were controlled, and none from opposition parties, which were absent.

The lack of a free system of news distribution also misled the government itself, fed by its own propaganda and by rosy reports of local party officials competing for credit in Beijing. Indeed, there is evidence that just as the famine was moving toward its peak, the Chinese authorities mistakenly believed that they had 100 million more metric tons of grain than they actually did.[37]

Interestingly enough, even Chairman Mao, whose radical hopes and beliefs had much to do with the initiation of, and official persistence with, the Great Leap Forward, himself identified the *informational* role of democracy, once the failure was belatedly acknowledged. In 1962, just after the famine had killed so many millions, Mao made the following observation, to a gathering of seven thousand cadres:

> Without democracy, you have no understanding of what is happening down below; the situation will be unclear; you will be unable to collect sufficient opinions from all sides; there can be no communication between top and bottom; top-level organs of leadership will depend on one-sided and incorrect material to decide issues, thus you will find it difficult to avoid being subjectivist; it will be impossible to achieve unity of understanding and unity of action, and impossible to achieve true centralism.[38]

Mao's defense of democracy here is quite limited. The focus is exclusively on the informational side—ignoring its incentive role, and also the intrinsic and constitutive importance of democracy.[39] Nevertheless it is extremely interesting that Mao himself acknowledged the extent to which disastrous official policies were caused by the lack of the informational links that a more democratic system can provide in averting disasters of the kind that China experienced.

## PROTECTIVE ROLE OF DEMOCRACY

These issues remain relevant in the contemporary world—even in the economically successful China of today. Since the economic reforms of 1979, official Chinese pronouncements have provided plentiful admission of the importance of *economic* incentives, without making a similar acknowledgment of the role of *political* incentives. When things go reasonably well, this permissive role of democracy might not be greatly missed, but as and when big policy mistakes are made, that lacuna can be quite disastrous. The significance of the democracy movements in contemporary China has to be judged in this light.

Another set of examples comes from sub-Saharan Africa, which has been plagued by persistent famines since the early 1970s. There are many factors underlying the famine-proneness of this region, varying from ecological issues of climatic deterioration—making crops more uncertain—to the firmly negative effects of persistent wars and skirmishes. But the typically authoritarian nature of many of the sub-Saharan Africa polities also has had much to do with causing the frequent famines.[40]

The nationalist movements were all firmly anticolonial, but not always steadfastly pro-democratic, and it is only recently that asserting the value of democracy has achieved some political respectability in many countries of sub-Saharan Africa. And in this political milieu, the cold war in the world did not help at all. The United States and the West were ready to support undemocratic governments if they were sufficiently anticommunist, and the Soviet Union and China would support governments inclined to be on their respective sides no matter how antiegalitarian they might be in their domestic policies. When opposition parties were banned and newspapers suppressed, there were very few international protests.

One must not deny that there were African governments even in some one-party states that were deeply motivated toward averting disasters and famines. There are examples of this varying from the tiny country of Cape Verde to the politically experimental Tanzania. But quite often the absence of opposition and the suppression of free newspapers gave the respective governments an immunity from criticism and political pressure that translated into thoroughly insensitive and callous policies. Famines were often taken for granted, and it was common to put the blame for the disasters on natural causes and on the perfidy of other countries. In various ways, Sudan, Somalia, Ethiopia, several of the Sahel countries and others provide glaring examples of how badly things can go wrong without the discipline of opposition parties and the news media.

This is not to deny that famines in these countries were often associated with crop failures. When a crop fails, it not only affects the food supply, it also destroys the employment and livelihood of a great many people. But the occurrence of crop failure is not independent of public policy (such as governmental fixing of relative prices, or the policy regarding irrigation and agricultural research). Further, even with crop failures, a famine can be averted by a careful redistribution policy (including that of employment creation). Indeed, as was discussed earlier, democratic countries like Botswana, or India, or Zimbabwe, have been entirely successful in preventing famines despite sharp declines in food output and entitlements of large sections of the population, whereas nondemocratic countries have frequently experienced unprevented famines despite much more favorable food situations. It would not be unreasonable to conclude that democracy can be a very positive influence in the prevention of famines in the contemporary world.

## TRANSPARENCY, SECURITY AND ASIAN ECONOMIC CRISES

This preventive role of democracy fits well into the demand for what was called "protective security" in the listing of different types of instrumental freedoms. Democratic governance, including multi-party elections and open media, makes it very likely that some arrangements for basic protective security will be instituted. In fact, the occurrence of famines is only one example of the protective reach of democracy. The positive role of political and civil rights applies to the prevention of economic and social disasters in general.

When things are routinely good and smooth, this instrumental role of democracy may not be particularly missed. But it comes into its own when things get fouled up, for one reason or another. And then the political incentives provided by democratic governance acquire great practical significance. There may be some important economic as well as political lessons here. Many economic technocrats recommend the use of economic incentives (which the market system provides) while ignoring political incentives (which democratic systems could guarantee). But economic incentives, important as they are, are no substitute for political incentives, and the absence of an adequate system of political incentives is a lacuna that cannot be filled by the operation of economic inducement.

This is an important issue because the danger of insecurity, arising from changes in the economic or other circumstances or from uncorrected mistakes of policy, can lurk behind what may look very much like a healthy economy. The recent problems of East Asia and Southeast Asia bring out, among many other things, the penalty of un-democratic governance. This is so in two striking respects, involving the neglect of two instrumental freedoms that were discussed earlier, viz., "protective security" (presently under scrutiny) and "transparency guarantee" (important for the provision of security and for incentives to economic and political agents).

First, the development of the financial crisis in some of these economies has been closely linked with the lack of transparency in business, in particular the lack of public participation in reviewing financial and business arrangements. The absence of an effective democratic forum has been consequential in this failing. The opportunity that would have been provided by democratic processes to challenge the hold of selected families or groups could have made a big difference.

The discipline of financial reform that the International Monetary Fund tried to impose on the economies in default was, to a considerable extent, linked to the lack of openness and disclosure and the involvement of unscrupulous business linkages that were characteristic in parts of these economies. These characteristics connect strongly with a system of nontransparent commercial arrangements. When a depositor places his or her money in a bank there may be some expectation that it will be used, along with other money, in ways that would not involve undue risk and could be openly disclosed. This trust was often violated, which certainly needed changing. I am not commenting here on whether the IMF's management of the crises was exactly right, or whether the insistence on immediate reforms could have been sensibly postponed until financial confidence had returned in these economies.[41] But no matter how these adjustments would have been best done, the role of transparency freedom—or rather its absence—in the development of the Asian crises cannot be easily doubted.

The pattern of risk and improper investments could have been placed under much greater scrutiny if democratic critics were able to demand that in, say, Indonesia or South Korea. But of course neither of these countries had the democratic system that would have allowed such demands to come from outside the government. The unchallenged power of governance was easily translated into an unquestioned acceptance of nonaccountability and nontransparency, often reinforced by strong family links between the government and the financial bosses. In the emergence of the economic crises, the undemocratic nature of the governments played an important part.

Second, once the financial crisis led to a general economic recession, the protective power of democracy—not unlike that which prevents famines in democratic countries—was badly missed. The newly dispossessed did not have the hearing they needed.[42] A fall of total gross national product of, say, even 10 percent may not look like much, if it follows the experience of past economic growth of 5 or 10 percent every year for some decades. And yet that decline can decimate lives and create misery for millions, if the burden of contraction is not shared together but allowed to be heaped on those—the unemployed or those newly made economically redundant—who can least bear it. The vulnerable in Indonesia may not have missed democracy when things went up and up, but that very lacuna kept their voice muffled and ineffective as the unequally shared crisis developed. The protective role of democracy is strongly missed when it is most needed.

## CONCLUDING REMARKS

The challenge of development includes *both* the elimination of persistent, endemic deprivation and the prevention of sudden, severe destitution. However, the respective demands on institutions and policies of the two can be distinct and even dissimilar. Success in one field may not guarantee success in the other. For example, consider the comparative performances of China and India over the last half century. It is clear that China has been much more successful than India in raising life expectancy and reducing mortality. Indeed, its superior performance goes back to well before the economic reforms of 1979. (China's overall progress in enhancing life expectancy has been, in fact, rather slower in the post-reform period than in the pre-reform stretch.) While India is a rather more diverse country than is China, and there are parts of India (such as Kerala) in which life expectancy has risen considerably faster than in China, nevertheless for the two countries as a whole the comparison of general increase in life expectancy is entirely in favor of China. And yet China also had (as was discussed earlier in this chapter) the largest recorded famine in history, when thirty million people perished in the famines that followed the failure of the Great Leap Forward, during 1958–1961. In contrast, India has not had a famine since independence. The prevention of famines and other disastrous crises is a somewhat different discipline from that of overall increase in average life expectancy and other achievements.

Inequality has an important role in the development of famines and other severe crises. Indeed, the absence of democracy is in itself an inequality—in this case of political rights and powers. But more than that, famines and other crises thrive on the basis of severe and sometimes suddenly increased inequality. This is illustrated by the fact that famines can occur even without a large—or any—diminution of total food supply, because some groups may suffer an abrupt loss of market power (through, for example, sudden and massive unemployment), with starvation resulting from this new inequality.[43]

Similar issues arise in understanding the nature of economic crises, such as the recent ones in East and Southeast Asia. Take, for example, the crises in Indonesia, in Thailand, and earlier on, even in South Korea. It may be wondered why should it be so disastrous to have, say, a 5 or 10 percent fall in gross national product in one year when the country in question has been growing at 5 or 10 percent *per year for decades*. Indeed, at the *aggregate* level this is not quintessentially a disastrous situation. And yet, if that 5 or 10 percent decline is not shared evenly by the population, and if it is heaped instead largely on the poorest part of the population, then that group may have very little income left (no matter what the overall growth performance might have been in the past). Such general economic crises, like famines, thrive on the basis of the Devil taking the hindmost. This is partly why arrangement for "protective security" in the form of social safety nets is such an important instrumental freedom (as discussed in chapter 2) and why political freedoms in the form of participatory opportunities as well as civil rights and liberties are ultimately crucial even for economic rights and for survival (as discussed in chapter 6 and earlier in this chapter).

The issue of inequality is, of course, important also in the continuation of endemic poverty. But here too the nature of—and causal influences on—inequality may differ somewhat between the problem of persistent deprivation and that of sudden destitution. For example, the fact that South Korea has had economic growth with relatively egalitarian income distribution has been extensively—and rightly—recognized.[44] This, however, was no guarantee of equitable attention in a crisis situation in the absence of democratic politics. In particular, it did not place in position any regular social safety net, or any rapidly responding system with compensatory protection. The emergence of fresh inequality and unchallenged destitution can co-exist with a previous experience of "growth with equity" (as it was often called).

This chapter has been mainly concerned with the problem of averting famines and preventing calamitous crises. This is one important part of the process of development as freedom, for it involves the enhancement of the security and protection that the citizens enjoy. The connection is both constitutive and instrumental. First, protection against starvation, epidemics, and severe and sudden deprivation is itself an enhancement of the opportunity to live securely and well. The prevention of devastating crises is, in this sense, part and parcel of the freedom that people have reason to value. Second, the process of preventing famines and other crises is significantly helped by the use of instrumental freedoms, such as the opportunity of open discussion, public scrutiny, electoral politics, and uncensored media. For example, the open and oppositional politics of a democratic country tends to force any government in office to take timely and effective steps to prevent famines, in a way that did not happen in the case of famines under nondemocratic arrangements—whether in China, Cambodia, Ethiopia or Somalia (as in the past), or in North Korea or Sudan (as is happening today). Development has many aspects, and they call for adequately differentiated analyses and scrutiny.

CHAPTER 8

# WOMEN'S AGENCY
# AND SOCIAL CHANGE

▼

Mary Wollstonecraft's classic book *A Vindication of the Rights of Woman,* published in 1792, had various distinct claims within the general program of "vindication" that she outlined. The rights she spoke about included not only some that particularly related to the well-being of women (and the entitlements that were directly geared to promote that well-being), but also rights that were aimed mainly at the free agency of women.

Both these features figure in the agenda of women's movements today, but it is, I think, fair to say that the agency aspects are beginning to receive some attention at last, in contrast to the earlier exclusive concentration on well-being aspects. Not long ago, the tasks these movements faced primarily involved working to achieve better treatment for women—a squarer deal. The concentration was mainly on women's *well-being*—and it was a much needed corrective. The objectives have, however, gradually evolved and broadened from this "welfarist" focus to incorporate—and emphasize—the active role of women's *agency*. No longer the passive recipients of welfare-enhancing help, women are increasingly seen, by men as well as women, as active agents of change: the dynamic promoters of social transformations that can alter the lives of *both* women and men.[1]

## AGENCY AND WELL-BEING

The nature of this shift in concentration and emphasis is sometimes missed because of the *overlap* between the two approaches. The active agency of women cannot, in any serious way, ignore the urgency of rectifying many inequalities that blight the well-being of women and subject them to unequal treatment; thus the agency role must be much concerned with women's well-being also. Similarly, coming from the other end, any practical attempt at enhancing the well-being of women cannot but draw on the agency of women themselves in bringing about such a change. So the *well-being aspect* and the *agency aspect* of women's movements inevitably have a substantial intersection. And yet they cannot but be different at a foundational level, since the role of a person as an "agent" is fundamentally distinct from (though not independent of) the role of the same person as a "patient."² The fact that the agent may have to see herself as a patient as well does not alter the additional modalities and responsibilities that are inescapably associated with the agency of a person.

To see individuals as entities that experience and have well-being is an important recognition, but to stop there would amount to a very restricted view of the personhood of women. Understanding the agency role is thus central to recognizing people as responsible persons: not only are we well or ill, but also we act or refuse to act, and can choose to act one way rather than another. And thus we— women *and* men—must take responsibility for doing things or not doing them. It makes a difference, and we have to take note of that difference. This elementary acknowledgment, though simple enough in principle, can be exacting in its implications, both for social analysis and for practical reason and action.

The changing focus of women's movements is, thus, a crucial *addition* to previous concerns; it is not a rejection of those concerns. The old concentration on the well-being of women, or, to be more exact, on the "ill-being" of women, was not, of course, pointless. The relative deprivations in the well-being of women were—and are— certainly present in the world in which we live, and are clearly important for social justice, including justice for women. For example, there is plenty of evidence that identifies the biologically "contrary" (socially generated) "excess mortality" of women in Asia and North Africa, with gigantic numbers of "missing women"—"missing" in the sense of being dead as a result of gender bias in the distribution of health care and other necessities (on this see my essay "Missing Women" in *British Medical Journal*, March 1992).[3] That problem is unquestionably important for the well-being of women, and in understanding the treatment of women as "less than equal." There are also pervasive indications of culturally neglected needs of women across the world. There are excellent reasons for bringing these deprivations to light and keeping the removal of these iniquities very firmly on the agenda.

But it is also the case that the limited role of women's active agency seriously afflicts the lives of *all* people—men as well as women, children as well as adults. While there is every reason not to slacken the concern about women's well-being and ill-being, and to continue to pay attention to the sufferings and deprivations of women, there is also an urgent and basic necessity, particularly at this time, to take an agent-oriented approach to the women's agenda.

Perhaps the most immediate argument for focusing on women's *agency* may be precisely the role that such an agency can play in removing the iniquities that depress the *well-being* of women. Empirical work in recent years has brought out very clearly how the relative respect and regard for women's well-being is strongly influenced by such variables as women's ability to earn an independent income, to find employment outside the home, to have ownership rights and to have literacy and be educated participants in decisions within and outside the family. Indeed, even the survival disadvantage of women compared with men in developing countries seems to go down sharply—and may even get eliminated—as progress is made in these agency aspects.[4]

These different aspects (women's earning power, economic role outside the family, literacy and education, property rights and so on) may at first sight appear to be rather diverse and disparate. But what they all have in common is their positive contribution in adding force to women's voice and agency—through independence and empowerment. For example, working outside the home and earning an independent income tend to have a clear impact on enhancing the social standing of a woman in the household and the society. Her contribution to the prosperity of the family is then more visible, and she also has more voice, because of being less dependent on others. Further, outside employment often has useful "educational" effects, in terms of exposure to the world outside the household, making her agency more effective. Similarly, women's education strengthens women's agency and also tends to make it more informed and skilled. The ownership of property can also make women more powerful in family decisions.

The diverse variables identified in the literature thus have a unified empowering role. This role has to be related to the acknowledgment that women's power—economic independence as well as social emancipation—can have far-reaching impacts on the forces and organizing principles that govern divisions *within* the family and in society as a whole, and can, in particular, influence what are implicitly accepted as women's "entitlements."[5]

## COOPERATIVE CONFLICT

To understand the process, we can start by noting that women and men have both *congruent* and *conflicting* interests that affect family living. Decision making in the family thus tends to take the form of pursuing cooperation, with some agreed solution—usually *implicit*— of the conflicting aspects. Such "cooperative conflict" is a general feature of many group relations, and an analysis of cooperative conflicts can provide a useful way of understanding the influences that operate on the "deal" that women get in family divisions. There are gains to be made by both parties through following implicitly agreed patterns of behavior. But there are many alternative possible agreements—some more favorable to one party than others. The choice of one such cooperative arrangement from the set of alternative possibilities leads to a particular distribution of joint benefits.[6]

Conflicts between the partially disparate interests within family living are typically resolved through implicitly agreed patterns of behavior that may or may not be particularly egalitarian. The very nature of family living—sharing a home and leading joint lives— requires that the elements of conflict must not be explicitly emphasized (dwelling on conflicts will be seen as a sign of a "failed" union), and sometimes the deprived woman cannot even clearly assess the extent of her relative deprivation. Similarly, the perception of who is doing how much "productive" work, or who is "contributing" how much to the family's prosperity, can be very influential, even though the underlying "theory" regarding how "contributions" and "productivity" are to be assessed may rarely be discussed explicitly.

## PERCEPTIONS OF ENTITLEMENT

The perception of individual contributions and appropriate entitlements of women and men plays a major role in the division of a family's joint benefits between men and women.[7] As a result, the circumstances that influence these perceptions of contributions and appropriate entitlements (such as women's ability to earn an independent income, to work outside the home, to be educated, to own property) can have a crucial bearing on these divisions. The impact of greater empowerment and independent agency of women thus includes the correction of the iniquities that blight the lives and well-being of women vis-à-vis men. The lives that women save through more powerful agency will certainly include their own.[8]

That, however, is not the whole story. There are other lives—men's and children's—also involved. Even within the family, the lives affected may be those of the children, since there is considerable evidence that women's empowerment within the family can reduce child mortality significantly. Going well beyond that, women's agency and voice, influenced by education and employment, can in turn influence the nature of the public discussion on a variety of social subjects, including acceptable fertility rates (not just in the family of the particular women themselves) and environmental priorities.

There is also the important issue of *intrafamily* division of food, health care, and other provisions. Much depends on how the family's economic means are used to cater to the interests of different individuals in the household: women and men, girls and boys, children and adults, old and young.[9]

The arrangements for sharing within the family are given, to a great extent, by established conventions, but they are also influenced by such factors as the economic role and empowerment of women and the value systems of the community at large.[10] In the evolution of value systems and conventions of intrafamily division, an important role can be played by female education, female employment and female ownership rights, and these "social" features can be very crucial for the economic fortunes (as well as well-being and freedom) of different members of the family.[11]

In the context of the general theme of this book, this relationship is worth considering a bit more. As has already been discussed, the most useful way of understanding famines is in terms of the loss of entitlement—a sharp decline in the substantive freedom to buy food. This would lead to a collapse in the amount of food the family as a whole can buy and consume. While distributional problems within the family can be serious even in famine situations, they are particularly crucial in determining the general undernourishment and hunger of different members of the family in situations of persistent poverty, which is "normal" in many communities. It is in the continued inequality in the division of food—and (perhaps even more) that of health care—that gender inequality manifests itself most blatantly and persistently in poor societies with strong antifemale bias.

This antifemale bias seems to be influenced by the social standing and economic power of women in general. Men's relative dominance connects with a number of factors, including the position of being the "breadwinner" whose economic power commands respect even within the family.[12] On the other side of the coin, there is considerable evidence that when women can and do earn income outside the household, this tends to enhance the relative position of women even in the distributions within the household.

While women work long hours every day at home, since this work does not produce a remuneration it is often ignored in the accounting of the respective contributions of women and men in the family's joint prosperity.[13] When, however, the work is done outside the home and the employed woman earns a wage, her contribution to the family's prosperity is more visible. She also has more voice, because of being less dependent on others. The higher status of women even affects, it appears, ideas on the female child's "due." So the freedom to seek and hold outside jobs can contribute to the reduction of women's relative—and absolute—deprivation. Freedom in one area (that of being able to work outside the household) seems to help to foster freedom in others (in enhancing freedom from hunger, illness and relative deprivation).

There is also considerable evidence that fertility rates tend to go down with greater empowerment of women. This is not surprising, since the lives that are most battered by the frequent bearing and rearing of children are those of young women, and anything that enhances young women's decisional power and increases the attention that their interests receive tends, in general, to prevent over-frequent childbearing. For example, in a comparative study of nearly three hundred districts within India, it emerges that women's education and women's employment are the two most important influences in reducing fertility rates.[14] The influences that help the emancipation of women (including women's literacy and women's employment) do make a major difference to fertility rates. I shall return to this presently in the context of assessing the nature and severity of the "world population problem." General problems of environmental overcrowding, from which both women and men may suffer, link closely with women's specific freedom from the constant bearing and rearing of children that plagues the lives of young women in many societies in the developing world.

## CHILD SURVIVAL
## AND THE AGENCY OF WOMEN

There is considerable evidence that women's education and literacy tend to reduce the mortality rates of children. The influence works through many channels, but perhaps most immediately, it works through the importance that mothers typically attach to the welfare of the children, and the opportunity the mothers have, when their agency is respected and empowered, to influence family decisions in that direction. Similarly, women's empowerment appears to have a strong influence in reducing the much observed gender bias in survival (particularly against young girls).

Countries with basic gender inequality—India, Pakistan, Bangladesh, China, Iran, those in West Asia, those in North Africa and others—often tend to have higher female mortality of infants and children, in contrast with the situation in Europe or America or sub-Saharan Africa, where female children typically have a substantial survival advantage. In India, male and female death rates in the 0–4 age group are now very similar to each other in terms of the average for the country as a whole, but a heavy disadvantage persists for women in regions where gender inequality is particularly pronounced, including most states of northern India.[15]

One of the most interesting studies of these issues—presented in an important statistical contribution by Mamta Murthi, Anne-Catherine Guio, and Jean Drèze—deals with data from 296 districts in India in the census of India of 1981.[16] There have been follow-up studies by Mamta Murthi and Jean Drèze dealing with later evidence, particularly the 1991 census, which broadly confirm the findings based on the 1981 census.[17]

A set of different—but interrelated—causal relations are examined in the studies. The variables to be explained include fertility rates, child mortality rates, and also female disadvantage in child survival (reflecting the *ratio* of female-to-male mortality in the 0–4 age group) in interdistrict comparisons. These variables are related to a number of other district-level variables with explanatory potential, such as female literacy rates, female labor force participation, incidence of poverty (and levels of income), extent of urbanization, availability of medical facilities and the proportion of socially underprivileged groups (scheduled castes and scheduled tribes) in the population.[18]

What should we expect to be the impact on child survival and mortality of the variables that may link most closely to women's agency—in this case women's participation in the labor force and women's literacy and education? It is natural to expect this connection to be entirely positive as far as women's literacy and education are concerned. This is strongly confirmed (more on this presently).

However, in the case of women's labor force participation, social and economic analyses have tended to identify factors working in different directions. First, involvement in gainful employment has many positive effects on a woman's agency roles, which often include greater emphasis being placed on child care and greater ability to attach more priority to child care in joint family decisions. Second, since men typically show great reluctance to share the domestic chores, this greater desire for more priority on child care may not be easy for the women to execute when they are saddled with the "double burden" of household work and outside employment. Thus the net effect could go in either direction. In the Murthi et al. study, the analysis of Indian district-level data does not yield any statistically significant, definite pattern on the connection between women's outside employment and the survival of children.[19]

Female literacy, in contrast, is found to have an unambiguous and statistically significant reducing impact on under-five mortality, even after controlling for male literacy. This is consistent with growing evidence of a close relationship between female literacy and child survival in many countries in the world, and particularly in intercountry comparisons.[20] In this case, the impact of greater empowerment and agency role of women is not reduced in effectiveness by problems arising from inflexible male participation in child care and household work.

There is also the further issue of *gender bias* in child survival (as opposed to *total* child survival). For this variable, it turns out that the female labor force participation rate and female literacy rate *both* have very strong ameliorating effects on the extent of female disadvantage in child survival, with higher levels of female literacy and labor force participation being strongly associated with lower levels of relative female disadvantage in child survival. By contrast, variables that relate to the *general* level of development and modernization *either* turn out to have no statistically significant effect, *or* suggest that modernization (when not accompanied by empowerment of women) can even *strengthen,* rather than weaken, the gender bias in child survival. This applies to, inter alia, urbanization, male literacy, the availability of medical facilities, and the level of poverty (with higher levels of poverty being associated with *higher* female-male ratios among the poor). In so far as a positive connection does exist in India between the level of development and reduced gender bias in survival, it seems to work mainly *through* variables that are directly related to women's agency, such as female literacy and female labor force participation.

It is worth making a further comment on the impact of enhanced women's agency through greater female education. Murthi, Guio and Drèze's statistical analysis indicates that, in quantitative terms, the effect of female literacy on child mortality is extraordinarily large. It is more powerful an influence in reducing child mortality than the other variables that also work in that general direction. For instance, keeping other variables constant, an increase in the crude female literacy rate from, say, 22 percent (the actual 1981 figure for India) to

75 percent reduces the predicted value of under-five mortality for males and females combined from 156 per thousand (again, the actual 1981 figure) to 110 per thousand.

The powerful effect of female literacy contrasts with the comparatively ineffective roles of, say, male literacy or general poverty reduction as instruments of child mortality reduction. The increase in male literacy over the same range (from 22 to 75 percent) only reduces under-five mortality from 169 per thousand to 141 per thousand. And a 50 percent reduction in the incidence of poverty (from the actual 1981 level) only reduces the predicted value of under-five mortality from 156 per thousand to 153 per thousand.

Here again, the message seems to be that some variables relating to women's agency (in this case, female literacy) often play a much more important role in promoting social well-being (in particular, child survival) than variables relating to the general level of opulence in the society. These findings have important practical implications.[21] Both types of variables can be influenced through public action, but respectively require rather different forms of public intervention.

## AGENCY, EMANCIPATION AND FERTILITY REDUCTION

The agency role of women is also particularly important for the reduction of fertility rates. The adverse effects of high birthrates powerfully include the denial of substantial freedoms—through persistent childbearing and child rearing—routinely imposed on many Asian and African women. There is, as a result, a close connection between women's *well-being* and women's *agency* in bringing about a change in the fertility pattern. Thus it is not surprising that reductions in birthrates have often followed the enhancement of women's status and power.

These connections are indeed reflected in interdistrict variations of the total fertility rate in India. In fact, among all the variables included in the analysis presented by Murthi, Guio and Drèze, the *only* ones that have a statistically significant effect on fertility are female literacy and female labor force participation. Once again, the importance of women's agency emerges forcefully from this analysis, especially in comparison with the weaker effects of variables relating to general economic progress.

The negative linkage between female literacy and fertility appears to be, on the whole, empirically well founded.[22] Such connections have been widely observed in other countries also, and it is not surprising that they should emerge in India. The unwillingness of educated women to be shackled to continuous child rearing clearly plays a role in bringing about this change. Education also makes the horizon of vision wider, and, at a more mundane level, helps to disseminate the knowledge of family planning. And of course educated women tend to have greater freedom to exercise their agency in family decisions, including in matters of fertility and childbirth.

The particular case of the most socially advanced state in India, viz., Kerala, is also worth noting here, because of its particular success in fertility reduction based on women's agency. While the total fertility rate for India as a whole is still higher than 3.0, that rate in Kerala has now fallen well below the "replacement level" (around 2.0, roughly speaking two children per couple) to 1.7, which is also considerably lower than China's fertility rate of 1.9. Kerala's high level of female education has been particularly influential in bringing about a precipitate decline in birthrate. Since female agency and literacy are important also in the reduction of mortality rates, that is another—more indirect—route through which women's agency (including female literacy) may have helped to reduce birthrates, since there is some evidence that a reduction of death rates, especially of children, tends to contribute to the reduction of fertility rates. Kerala has also had other favorable features for women's empowerment and agency, including a greater recognition of women's property rights for a substantial and influential part of the community.[23] There will be an opportunity to further probe these connections, along with other possible causal linkages, in the next chapter.

## WOMEN'S POLITICAL, SOCIAL AND ECONOMIC ROLES

There is plenty of evidence that when women get the opportunities that are typically the preserve of men, they are no less successful in making use of these facilities that men have claimed to be their own over the centuries. The opportunities at the highest political levels happen to have come to women, in many developing countries, only in rather special circumstances—often related to the demise of their more established husbands or fathers—but the chances have been invariably seized with much vigor. While the recent history of the role of women in top leadership positions in Sri Lanka, India, Bangladesh, Pakistan, the Philippines, Burma or Indonesia may be very well recognized, there is a need to pay more attention to the part that women have been able to play—given the opportunity—at diverse levels of political activities and social initiatives.[24]

The impact of women's activities on social life can be similarly extensive. Sometimes the roles are well known and well anticipated or are becoming so (the impact of women's education on the reduction of fertility rates—already discussed—is a good example of that). However, there are also other connections that call for greater investigation and analysis. One of the more interesting hypotheses concerns the relation between men's influence and the prevalence of violent crimes. The fact that most of the violent crimes in the world are committed by men is well recognized, but there are possible causal influences that have not yet received the attention they may deserve.

An interesting statistical finding in India relates to extensive interdistrict contrasts that show a strong—and statistically very significant—relation between the female-male ratio in the population and the scarcity of violent crimes. Indeed, the inverse connection between murder rates and the female-male ratio in the population has been observed by many researchers, and there have been alternative explanations of the causal processes involved.[25] Some have looked for causal explanations running from the incidence of violent crimes leading to a greater preference for sons (taken to be better equipped to encounter a violent society), whereas others have seen it running from a larger presence of women (less inclined toward violence) to a consequently lower rate of crime.[26] There can also be some third factor that relates both to violent crime and to the male dominance of the sex ratio. There are many issues to be sorted out here, but the importance of gender and the influence of women's agency vis-à-vis men's are hard to overlook under any of the alternative explanations.

If we turn now to economic activities, women's participation can also make a big difference. One reason for the relatively low participation of women in day-to-day economic affairs in many countries is a relative lack of access to economic resources. The ownership of land and capital in the developing countries has tended to be very heavily biased in favor of the male members of the family. It is typically much harder for a woman to start a business enterprise, even of a very modest size, given the lack of collateral resources.

And yet there is plenty of evidence that whenever social arrangements depart from the standard practice of male ownership, women can seize business and economic initiative with much success. It is also clear that the result of women's participation is not merely to generate income for women, but also to provide the social benefits that come from women's enhanced status and independence (including the reduction of mortality and fertility rates, just discussed). The economic participation of women is, thus, both a reward on its own (with associated reduction of gender bias in the treatment of women in family decisions), and a major influence for social change in general.

The remarkable success of the Grameen Bank in Bangladesh is a good example of this. That visionary microcredit movement, led by Muhammad Yunus, has consistently aimed at removing the disadvantage from which women suffer, because of discriminatory treatment in the rural credit market, by making a special effort to provide credit to women borrowers. The result has been a very high proportion of women among the customers of the Grameen Bank. The remarkable record of that bank in having a very high rate of repayment (reported to be close to 98 percent) is not unrelated to the way women have responded to the opportunities offered to them and to the prospects of ensuring the continuation of such arrangements.[27] Also in Bangladesh, similar emphasis has been placed on women's participation by BRAC, led by another visionary leader, Fazle Hasan Abed.[28] These and other economic and social movements in Bangladesh have done a lot not merely to raise the "deal" that women get, but also—through the greater agency of women—to bring about other major changes in the society. For example, the sharp decline in fertility rate that has occurred in Bangladesh in recent years seems to have clear connections with the increasingly higher involvement of women in social and economic affairs, in addition to much greater availability of family planning facilities, even in rural Bangladesh.[29]

Another area in which women's involvement in economic affairs varies is that of agricultural activities related to land ownership. There too the economic opportunities that women get can have a decisive influence on the working of the economy and the related social arrangements. Indeed, "a field of one's own" (as Bina Agarwal calls it) can be a major influence on women's initiative and involvement, with far-reaching effects on the balance of economic and social power between women and men.[30] Similar issues arise in understanding women's role in environmental developments, particularly in conserving natural resources (such as trees), with a particular linkage to women's life and work.[31]

Indeed, the empowerment of women is one of the central issues in the process of development for many countries in the world today. The factors involved include women's education, their ownership pattern, their employment opportunities and the workings of the labor market.[32] But going beyond these rather "classic" variables, they include also the nature of the employment arrangements, attitudes of the family and of the society at large toward women's economic activities, and the economic and social circumstances that encourage or resist change in these attitudes.[33] As Naila Kabeer's illuminating study of the work and economic involvement of Bangladeshi women in Dhaka and London brings out, the continuation of, or break from, past arrangements is strongly influenced by the exact economic and social relations that operate in the local environment.[34] The changing agency of women is one of the major mediators of economic and social change, and its determination as well as consequences closely relate to many of the central features of the development process.[35]

## A CONCLUDING REMARK

The focus on the agency role of women has a direct bearing on women's well-being, but its reach goes well beyond that. In this chapter, I have tried to explore the distinction between—and interrelations of—agency and well-being, and then have gone on to illustrate the reach and power of women's agency, particularly in two specific fields: (1) in promoting child survival and (2) in helping to reduce fertility rates. Both these matters have general developmental interest that goes well beyond the pursuit specifically of female well-being, though—as we have seen—female well-being is also directly involved and has a crucial intermediating role in enhancing these general achievements.

The same applies to many other areas of economic, political and social action, varying from rural credit and economic activities, on the one hand, to political agitation and social debates, on the other.[36] The extensive reach of women's agency is one of the more neglected areas of development studies, and most urgently in need of correction. Nothing, arguably, is as important today in the political economy of development as an adequate recognition of political, economic and social participation and leadership of women. This is indeed a crucial aspect of "development as freedom."

# CHAPTER 9

# POPULATION, FOOD AND FREEDOM

▼

The contemporary age is not short of terrible and nasty happenings, but the persistence of extensive hunger in a world of unprecedented prosperity is surely one of the worst. Famines visit many countries with astonishing severity—"fierce as ten furies, terrible as hell" (to borrow John Milton's words). In addition, massive endemic hunger causes great misery in many parts of the world—debilitating hundreds of millions and killing a sizable proportion of them with statistical regularity. What makes this widespread hunger even more of a tragedy is the way we have come to accept and tolerate it as an integral part of the modern world, as if it is a tragedy that is essentially unpreventable (in the way ancient Greek tragedies were).

I have already argued against judging the nature and severity of the problems of hunger, undernourishment, and famine by concentrating on food output only. However, food output must be *one* of the variables that can, inter alia, influence the prevalence of hunger. Even the price at which food can be bought by the consumers will be affected by the size of the food output. Furthermore, when we consider food problems at the global level (rather than at the national or local level), there is obviously no opportunity of getting food from "outside" the economy. For these reasons, the often aired fear that food production per head is falling in the world cannot be dismissed out of hand.

## IS THERE A WORLD FOOD CRISIS?

But is the fear justified? Is the world food output falling behind world population in what is seen as a "race" between the two? The fear that this is precisely what is happening, or that it will soon happen, has had remarkable staying power despite relatively little evidence in its favor. Malthus, for example, anticipated two centuries ago that food production was losing the race and that terrible disasters would result from the consequent imbalance in "the proportion between the natural increase of population and food." He was quite convinced, in his late-eighteenth-century world, that "the period when the number of men surpass their means of subsistence has long since arrived."[1] However, since the time when Malthus first published his famous *Essay on Population* in 1798, the world population has grown nearly six times, and yet food output and consumption per head are very considerably higher now than in Malthus's time, and this has occurred along with an unprecedented increase in general living standards.

However, the fact that Malthus was badly mistaken in his diagnosis of overpopulation at his time (with less than a billion people around) and in his prognosis about the terrible consequences of population growth does not establish that all fears about population growth at all times must be similarly erroneous. But what about the present? Is food production really losing the race with population growth? Table 9.1 presents the indices of food production per head (based on statistics from the Food and Agricultural Organization of the United Nations) for the world as a whole as well as for some of the major regions in terms of three-year averages (to avoid being misled by year-to-year fluctuations), with the average for 1979–1981 serving as the base of the index (100); index values are given up to 1996–1997. (Adding the 1998 figures does not alter the basic picture.) Not only is there no real decline in world food production per head (quite the contrary), but also the largest per capita increases have come in the more densely populated areas of the third world (in particular, China, India and the rest of Asia).

The African food output has, however, declined (on which I have already commented), and the prevalence of poverty in Africa puts it in

TABLE 9.1: *Indices of Food Production per Head by Regions*

| Regions | 1974–1976 | 1979–1981 | 1984–1986 | 1994–1996 | 1996–1997 |
|---------|-----------|-----------|-----------|-----------|-----------|
| World | 97.4 | 100.0 | 104.4 | 108.4 | 111.0 |
| Africa | 104.9 | 100.0 | 95.4 | 98.4 | 96.0 |
| Asia | 94.7 | 100.0 | 111.6 | 138.7 | 144.3 |
| India | 96.5 | 100.0 | 110.7 | 128.7 | 130.5 |
| China | 90.1 | 100.0 | 120.7 | 177.7 | 192.3 |
| Europe | 94.7 | 100.0 | 107.2 | 102.3 | 105.0 |
| North and Central America | 90.1 | 100.0 | 99.1 | 99.4 | 100.0 |
| U.S.A. | 89.8 | 100.0 | 99.3 | 102.5 | 103.9 |
| South America | 94.0 | 100.0 | 102.8 | 114.0 | 117.2 |

*Note:* With the three-year average of 1979–1981 as the base, the three-year averages for the years 1984–1986, 1994–1996 and 1996–1997 are obtained from the United Nations (1995, 1998), table 4. The three-year averages for the earlier years (1974–1976) are based on the United Nations (1984), table 1. There may be slight differences in the relative weights between the two sets of comparisons, so that the series should not be taken to be fully comparable between the two sides of 1979–1981, but the quantitative difference made by this, if any, is likely to be quite small. *Sources:* United Nations, *FAO Quarterly Bulletin of Statistics,* 1995 and 1998, and *FAO Monthly Bulletin of Statistics,* August 1984.

a very vulnerable situation. However, as was argued earlier (in chapter 7) the problems of sub-Saharan Africa are mainly a reflection of a general economic crisis (indeed a crisis with strong social and political as well as economic components)—not specifically of a "food production crisis." The food production story fits into a larger predicament that has to be addressed in broader terms.

There is, in fact, no significant crisis in world food production at this time. The rate of expansion of food production does, of course, vary over time (and in some years of climatic adversity there is even a decline, giving the alarmists a field day for a year or two), but the *trend* is quite clearly upward.

## ECONOMIC INCENTIVES AND FOOD PRODUCTION

It is also important to note that this rise in world food production has taken place despite a sharply declining trend in world food prices in real terms, as table 9.2 indicates. The period covered—more than forty-five years—is from 1950–1952 to 1995–1997. This entails a decline of economic incentives to produce more food in many areas of commercial food production in the world, including North America.

TABLE 9.2: *Food Prices in Constant 1990*
*U.S. Dollars: 1950–1952 to 1995–1997*

| Food | 1950–1952 | 1995–1997 | % change |
|---|---|---|---|
| Wheat | 427.6 | 159.3 | -62.7 |
| Rice | 789.7 | 282.3 | -64.2 |
| Sorghum | 328.7 | 110.9 | -66.2 |
| Maize | 372.0 | 119.1 | -68.0 |

*Note:* The units are constant (1990) U.S. dollars per metric ton, adjusted by the G-5 Manufacturing Unit Value (MUV) index.
*Sources:* World Bank, *Commodity Markets and the Developing Countries,* November 1998, table A1 (Washington, D.C.); World Bank, *Price Prospects for Major Primary Commodities,* vol. 2, tables A5, A10, A15 (Washington, D.C., 1993).

Food prices do, of course, fluctuate in the short run, and panicky statements were often made in response to an increase in the mid-1990s. But this was a small rise compared with the big fall since 1970 (see figure 9.1). Indeed, there is a strongly declining long-term trend, and there is nothing yet to indicate that the long-run downward trend of the relative price of food has been reversed. Last year, during 1998, the world prices for wheat and coarse grain declined again by 20 percent and 14 percent respectively.[2]

In the context of an economic analysis of the present situation, we cannot ignore the disincentive effect that the lowering of world food prices has already had on food production. It is, thus, particularly impressive that the world food output has nevertheless continued to grow, well ahead of population growth. In fact, had more food been produced (without curing the income shortage from which most of

FIGURE 9.1: *Food Prices in Constant 1990 U.S. Dollars*

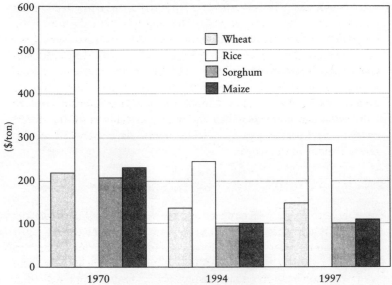

*Note:* The units are constant (1990) U. S. dollars deflated by the G-5 Manufacturing Unit Value (MUV) index.
*Source:* World Bank, *Commodity Markets and Developing Countries* (Washington, D.C.: World Bank, 1998), table A1.

the hungry people in the world suffer), the selling of food would have been even more of a problem than is reflected in the declining food prices. Not surprisingly, the biggest increases have come from regions (such as China and India) where the domestic food markets are relatively insulated from world markets and the declining trend of world food prices.

It is important to see the production of food as a result of human agency, and to understand the incentives that operate on people's decisions and actions. Like other economic activities, commercial production of food is influenced by markets and prices. At this time, the world food production is being kept in check by the lack of demand and falling food prices; this in turn reflects the poverty of some of the neediest people. Technical studies on the opportunity to produce more food (if and when the demand increases) outline very substantial opportunities of making the food production per head grow much faster in per capita terms. Indeed, yield per hectare has continued to rise in every region of the world, and for the world as a whole, it went up on average by about 42.6 kilograms per hectare per year during 1981–1993.[3] In terms of world food production, 94 percent of the rise in cereal production between 1970 and 1990 reflected an increase in yield per unit of land, and only 6 percent was due to area increase.[4] With greater demand for food, the intensification of cultivation can be expected to continue, especially since the differences in yield per hectare are still enormously large between the different regions in the world.

## BEYOND THE TREND OF FOOD OUTPUT PER HEAD

All this does not, however, wipe out the need for slowing down the population growth. Indeed, the environmental challenge is not just that of food production—there are many other issues related to population growth and overcrowding. But it does indicate that there is little reason for any great pessimism that food output will soon start falling behind population growth. In fact, a tendency to concentrate on food production only, neglecting food *entitlement,* can be deeply counterproductive. Policy makers may be misled if insulated from the real situation of hunger—and even threats of famines—by favorable food output situations.

For example, in the Bengal famine of 1943, the administrators were so impressed by the fact that there was no significant food output decline (on which they were right) that they failed to anticipate— and for some months even refused to recognize—the famine as it hit Bengal with stormy severity.[5] Just as "Malthusian pessimism" may be misleading as a predictor of the food situation in the world, what may be called "Malthusian optimism" can kill millions when the administrators get entrapped by the wrong perspective of food-output-per-head and ignore early signs of disaster and famine. A misconceived theory can kill, and the Malthusian perspective of food-to-population ratio has much blood on its hands.

## POPULATION GROWTH AND
## THE ADVOCACY OF COERCION

While the Malthusian long-run fears about food output are baseless, or at least premature, there are good reasons to worry about the rate of growth of world population in general. There is little doubt that the growth rate of world population has speeded up over the last century at a remarkable rate. It took the world population millions of years to reach the first billion, then 123 years to get to the second, followed by 33 years to the third, 14 years to the fourth, and 13 years to the fifth billion, with the promise of a sixth billion to come in another 11 years (according to the projections of the United Nations).[6] The number of people on earth grew by about 923 million (1980–1990 alone), and that increase is close enough to the size of the *total* population of the *entire* world in Malthus's time. The 1990s, when they are done, will not have been significantly less expansionary.

If this were to continue the world certainly would be tremendously overcrowded before the end of the twenty-first century. There are, however, many clear signs that the rate of growth of world population is beginning to slow down, and the question that has to be asked is whether the reasons behind that slowdown are likely to become stronger, and if so, at what rate. No less importantly, it has to be asked whether something should be done through public policy to help the process of slowdown.

This is a highly divisive subject, but there is a strong school of thought that favors, if only implicitly, a coercive solution to this problem. There have also been several practical moves in that direction recently—most famously in China, in a set of policies introduced in 1979. The issue of coercion raises three different questions:

1)  Is coercion at all acceptable in this field?
2)  In the absence of coercion will population growth be unacceptably fast?
3)  Is coercion likely to be effective and work without harmful side effects?

## COERCION AND REPRODUCTIVE RIGHTS

The acceptability of coercion in matters of family decisions raises very deep questions. Opposition to it can come both from those who would give priority to the family to decide how many children to have (it is, in this view, a quintessentially family decision), and from those who argue that this is a matter in which the potential mother in particular must have the deciding voice (especially when it comes to abortion and other matters that directly involve the woman's body). To be sure, the latter position is usually articulated in the context of asserting the right to have an abortion (and to practice birth control in general), but there is clearly a corresponding claim that would leave the woman to decide *not* to abort if that is what she wants (no matter what the state wants). So something substantial does turn on the status and significance of reproductive rights.[7]

The rhetoric of rights is omnipresent in contemporary political debates. There is, however, often an ambiguity in these debates about the sense in which "rights" are invoked, in particular whether the reference is to institutionally sanctioned rights that have juridical force, or whether the appeal is to the prescriptive force of normative rights that can precede legal empowerment. The distinction between the two senses is not entirely clear-cut, but there is a reasonably clear issue as to whether rights can have intrinsic normative importance and not just instrumental relevance in a legal context.

That rights can have intrinsic—and possibly pre-legal—value has been denied by many political philosophers, particularly utilitarians. Jeremy Bentham in particular is on record as having described the idea of natural rights as "nonsense," and the concept of "natural and imprescriptible rights" as "nonsense on stilts," which I take to mean highly mounted nonsense that is made arbitrarily prominent by artificial elevation. Bentham saw rights entirely in instrumental terms and considered their institutional roles in the pursuit of objectives (including the promotion of aggregate utility).

A sharp contrast between two approaches to rights can be seen here. If rights in general, including reproductive rights, were to be seen in Benthamite terms, then whether or not coercion should be acceptable in this field would turn entirely on its consequences, in particular utility consequences, without attaching any indigenous importance whatsoever to the fulfillment or violation of the putative rights themselves. In contrast to this, if rights were to be seen as not only important but also as having priority over any accounting of consequences, then the rights would have to be accepted unconditionally. Indeed, in libertarian theory, this is exactly what happens to the delineated rights, which are seen as appropriate no matter what consequences they yield. These rights would, then, be appropriate parts of social arrangements *irrespective* of their consequences.

I have argued, elsewhere, against the necessity of opting for one or the other approach in this dichotomy, and have presented arguments for a consequential system that incorporates the fulfillment of rights among other goals.[8] It shares with utilitarianism a consequentialist approach (but differs from it in not confining attention to utility consequences only), and it shares with a libertarian system the attachment of intrinsic importance to rights (but differs from it in not giving it complete priority irrespective of other consequences). Such a "goal-rights system" has many attractive properties as well as versatility and reach, which I have tried to discuss elsewhere.[9]

I shall not repeat here the arguments in favor of such a goal-rights approach (though I shall take the opportunity of saying a bit more on this approach in the next chapter). But in making comparison with utilitarianism, it is hard to believe that it can be adequate to explain our support for rights of various kinds (including those of privacy, autonomy and liberty) only—and exclusively—in terms of their utility consequences. The rights of minorities often have to be preserved against the intrusion of a majority's persecution and its grand gains in utility. As John Stuart Mill—a great utilitarian himself—noted, there is sometimes "no parity" between utility generated from different activities, such as (to quote Mill) "the feeling of a person for his own opinion, and the feeling of another who is offended at his holding it."[10] That lack of parity would apply, in the present context, to the importance that the parents attach to the decision on how many children to have compared with the importance that others, *including* the potentates running the government, may place on this subject. In general, the case for seeing intrinsic importance in autonomy and liberty is not easy to escape, and this can easily conflict with no-nonsense maximization of the utility consequences (taking no note of the *process* of generation of utilities).[11]

It is, thus, implausible to confine consequential analysis only to utilities, and in particular to exclude the fulfillment and violation of rights related to liberties and autonomies. But it is also not particularly credible to make these rights completely immune, as in the libertarian formulation, to consequences they have—no matter how terrible the consequences might be. In the context of reproductive rights, the fact that they are taken to be significant does not entail that they are so overarchingly important that they must be fully protected even if they were to generate disasters and massive misery and hunger. In general, the consequences of having and exercising a right must ultimately have some bearing on the overall acceptability of that right.

The consequences of population growth for the food problem and hunger have already been discussed, and there is no real basis for great alarmism here, at this time. But if the process of population explosion were to continue, then the world might well be in a much more difficult situation even in terms of food. There are, in addition, other problems connected with fast population growth, including urban overcrowding and of course the environmental challenges at the local and global levels.[12] It is very important to examine what prospects of a slowdown of population growth can be seen now. This takes us to the second of the three questions.

## MALTHUSIAN ANALYSIS

Even though Malthus is typically credited with having provided the pioneering analysis of the possibility that population may tend to grow too much, the possibility that continued increase in population might conceivably lead to "a continual diminution of happiness" was in fact aired, before Malthus, by Condorcet, the French mathematician and great Enlightenment thinker, who first presented the core of the scenario that underlies the "Malthusian" analysis of the population problem, with "the increase in the number of men surpassing their means of subsistence" resulting in "either a continual diminution of happiness and population, a movement truly retrograde, or, at least, a kind of oscillation between good and evil."[13]

Malthus loved this analysis of Condorcet's, was inspired by it and quoted it with great approval in his famous essay on population. Where the two men disagreed was in their respective views of fertility behavior. Condorcet anticipated a voluntary reduction in fertility rates and predicted the emergence of new norms of smaller family size based on "the progress of reason." He anticipated a time when people "will know that, if they have a duty towards those who are not yet born, that duty is not to give them existence but to give them happiness." This type of reasoning, buttressed by the expansion of education, especially female education (of which Condorcet was one of the earliest and most vocal advocates), would lead people, Condorcet thought, to lower fertility rates and smaller families, which people would choose voluntarily, "rather than foolishly to encumber the world with useless and wretched beings."[14] Having identified the problem, Condorcet noted its likely solution.

Malthus thought all this most unlikely. In general, he saw little chance of solving social problems through reasoned decisions by the persons involved. As far as the effects of population growth were concerned, Malthus was convinced of the inevitability of population outrunning food supply, and in this context, took the limits of food production to be relatively inflexible. And, most relevantly for the topic of this chapter, Malthus was particularly skeptical of voluntary family planning. While he did refer to "moral restraint" as an alternative way of reducing the pressure of population (alternative, that is, to misery and elevated mortality), he saw little real prospect that such restraint would be voluntary.

Over the years, Malthus's views on what can be taken to be inevitable varied somewhat, and he was clearly less certain of his earlier prognosis as the years progressed. There is a tendency in modern Malthus scholarship to emphasize the elements of "shift" in his position, and there is indeed ground for distinguishing between the early Malthus and the late Malthus. But his basic distrust of the power of reason, as opposed to the force of economic compulsion, in making people choose smaller families remained largely unmodified. Indeed, in one of his last works, published in 1830 (he died in 1834), he insisted on his conclusion that:

there is no reason whatever to suppose that anything beside the difficulty of procuring in adequate plenty the necessaries of life should either indispose this greater number of persons to marry early, or disable them from rearing in health the largest families.[15]

It was because of this disbelief in the voluntary route that Malthus identified the need for a *forced* reduction in population growth rates, which he thought would come from the compulsion of nature. The fall in living standards resulting from population growth would not only increase mortality rates dramatically (what Malthus called "positive checks"), but would also force people, through economic penury, to have smaller families. The basic link in the argument is Malthus's conviction—and this is the important point—that population growth rate cannot be effectively pulled down by "anything beside the *difficulty* of procuring in adequate plenty the necessaries of life."[16] Malthus's opposition to the Poor Laws and the support for the indigent related to his belief in this causal connection between poverty and low population growth.

The history of the world since that Malthus-Condorcet debate has not given much comfort to Malthus's point of view. Fertility rates have come down sharply with social and economic development. This has happened in Europe and North America, and is currently happening over much of Asia, and to a considerable extent in Latin America. The fertility rates remain the highest and relatively stationary in the least privileged countries—particularly in sub-Saharan Africa—which are not yet experiencing much economic or social development, and which have continued to remain poor as well as backward in terms of basic education, health care and life expectancy.[17]

The general fall in fertility rates can be explained in rather different ways. The positive association between development and fertility reduction is often summarized by the ungainly slogan "Development is the best contraceptive." While there may be some truth in this rather undifferentiated thought, there are various components of development, which the West has experienced together, including rise in income per head, expansion of education, greater economic independence of women, reduction of mortality rates and spread of family planning opportunities (parts of what may be called social development). We need a discriminating analysis.

## ECONOMIC OR SOCIAL DEVELOPMENT

There are several theories as to what is causing this fertility decline. One influential example is Gary Becker's model of fertility determination. Even though Becker has presented his theory as an "extension" of Malthus's analysis, and even though his analysis shares many features of Malthus's analysis (including the tradition of seeing the family as *one* decision-making unit with no divisions within it— on this more presently), Becker has, in fact, negated Malthus's conclusion that prosperity raises population growth, rather than reducing it. In Becker's analysis, the effects of economic development on investment to improve the "quality" of children (such as investment in education) play an important part.[18]

In contrast with Becker's approach, the *social* theories of fertility decline point to changes in preferences as a result of social development, such as expansion of education in general and female education in particular.[19] This is, of course, one of the connections that Condorcet emphasized. However, we have to distinguish between (1) changes in the number of children desired by a family despite unchanged preferences, because of the influence of changing costs and benefits, and (2) shifts in such preferences as a result of social change, such as modification of acceptable communal norms, and greater weighting of the interests of women in the aggregate objectives of the family. Condorcet focused on the latter, Becker on the former.

There is also the simple issue of availability of birth control facilities and the dissemination of knowledge and technology in this field. Despite some early skepticism on this subject, it is now reasonably clear that knowledge and practical affordability do make a difference to the family's fertility behavior in countries with high birthrate and scarce family control facilities.[20] For example, the sharp fertility decline in Bangladesh has been linked to the family planning movement, and in particular to the greater availability of knowledge and facilities. It is certainly significant that Bangladesh has been able to cut its fertility rate from 6.1 to 3.4 in a mere decade and a half (between 1980 and 1996).[21] This achievement debunks the belief that people will not voluntarily embrace family planning in the less-developed countries. However, Bangladesh still has a long way to go, and while it is going that way (the fertility rate has continued to drop rapidly), to get near the pure replacement level (corresponding to total fertility rates around 2.0 or 2.1) something more than mere availability of birth control facilities would be needed.

## EMPOWERMENT OF YOUNG WOMEN

One line of analysis that has emerged very powerfully in recent years (and which I have already articulated in earlier chapters) gives the empowerment of women a pivotal role in the decisions of families and in the genesis of communal norms. However, so far as historical data are concerned, since these different variables tend to move together, it is not easy to separate out the effects of economic growth from those of social changes (given what statisticians call "multi-collinearity"). I shall presently pursue this distinction further, with the use of cross-section—rather than intertemporal—comparisons. What should be, however, abundantly clear is that some things "beside the difficulty of procuring in adequate plenty the necessaries of life" have made people choose radically smaller families. There is no reason why the high-fertility developing countries cannot follow others that have already reduced their fertility rates through the combined process of economic and social development (no matter which component of that development plays exactly what part).

However, we have to be more clear as to what the critical parameters would be in changing the climate of fertility. There is now quite extensive statistical evidence, based on comparison between different countries and different regions (that is, cross-section studies, as they are called), that link women's education (including literacy) and the lowering of fertility across different countries in the world.[22] Other factors considered include the involvement of women in so-called gainful activities outside the home, the opportunity of women to earn an independent income, the property rights of women and the general status and standing of women in the social culture. I have presented these issues already in the book, but there is a need to link up these discussions.

These connections have been observed in intercountry comparisons, but also in comparisons within a large country—such as between the different districts of India. The most recent—and the most extensive—study of this connection is the important statistical contribution by Mamta Murthi, Anne-Catherine Guio and Jean Drèze, discussed in chapter 8.[23] As was noted, among all the variables included in that analysis, the *only* ones that are seen to have a statistically significant effect on fertility are (1) female literacy and (2) female labor force participation. The importance of women's agency emerges forcefully from this analysis, especially in comparison with the weaker effects of variables relating to economic development.

Going by this analysis, economic development may be far from "the best contraceptive," but social development—especially the women's education and employment—can be very effective indeed. Many of the richest Indian districts in, say, Punjab and Haryana have very much *higher* fertility rates than the southern districts with much lower per capita income but with much higher female literacy and female job opportunities. Indeed, in the comparison between nearly three hundred Indian districts, the level of real income per capita has almost no impact, compared with the sharp and effective difference made by women's education and women's economic independence. While the original Murthi-Guio-Drèze paper drew on the 1981 census, the main conclusions reached there have been confirmed by the analysis of the 1991 census done by Drèze and Murthi (cited earlier).

## EXTERNALITY, VALUES AND COMMUNICATION

The powerful evidence in favor of these statistical relations has to be distinguished from the social and cultural accounting of these influences, including the account—referred to earlier—that both education and outside earning increase a woman's decisional autonomy. There are, in fact, many different ways in which school education may enhance a young woman's decisional power within the family: through its effect on her social standing, her ability to be independent, her power to articulate, her knowledge of the outside world, her skill in influencing group decisions and so on.

I should note that the literature has also produced some arguments contrary to the belief that women's autonomy increases with schooling and that this helps to reduce fertility rates. The contrary evidence has come entirely from some interfamily (as opposed interdistrict) studies.[24] While the informational coverage in these studies is relatively small (a great deal smaller than the massive all-India study of Murthi, Guio and Drèze), nevertheless it would be wrong to dismiss the contrary evidence too readily.

However, it does make a difference as to what we take to be the proper unit of analysis. If it is supposed that women's influence increases with the general level of literacy in a *region* (through informed social discussion and value formation), then examining *interfamily* contrasts would not capture this influence. The *inter-district* comparisons investigated by Murthi, Guio and Drèze incorporate relations that are "external" to the family but "internal" to a region, such as communication among different families in a region.[25] The importance of public discussion and interchange is one of the major general themes of this book.

## HOW EFFECTIVE IS COERCION?

How do these influences compare with what can be achieved through coercive policies of the kind tried in China? Policies such as the "one-child family" have been tried in large parts of China since the reforms of 1979. Also, the government often refuses to offer housing and related benefits to families with too many children, thus penalizing the children as well as the dissident adults. China's total fertility rate (a measure of the average number of children born per woman) is now 1.9, significantly below India's 3.1, and also very much below the weighted average—about 5.0—for low-income countries other than China and India.[26]

The Chinese example appeals to many who are panic-stricken at the thought of the "population bomb" and want a rapid solution. In considering the acceptability of this route, it is important, first of all, to note that the process has involved some cost, including the violation of rights with some intrinsic importance. Sometimes the enforcement of family size restriction has been very severely punitive. A recent article in *The New York Times* reports:

> The villagers of Tongmuchong did not need any convincing on that day when Mrs. Liao, the family-planning official, threatened to blow up their houses. Last year, in the neighboring village of Xiaoxi, a man named Huang Fuqu, along with his

wife and three children, was ordered out of his house. To the horror of all those who watched, the house was then blasted into rubble. On a nearby wall, the government dynamiters painted a warning: "Those who do not obey the family planning police will be those who lose their fortunes."[27]

Human rights groups and women's organizations in particular have been especially concerned with the loss of freedom involved in this process.[28]

Second, aside from the fundamental issue of reproductive and other freedoms, there are other consequences to consider in evaluating compulsory birth control. The social consequences of such compulsion, including the ways in which an unwilling population tends to react when it is coerced, can often be quite terrible. For example, the demands for a "one-child family" can lead to the neglect—or worse—of infants, thereby increasing the infant mortality rate. Also, in a country with a strong preference for male children—a characteristic China shares with India and many other countries in Asia and North Africa—a policy of allowing only one child per family can be particularly detrimental for girls, for example, in the form of fatal neglect of female children. This, it appears, is exactly what has happened on a fairly large scale in China.

Third, any change in reproductive behavior that is brought about by compulsion need not be particularly stable. A spokesman for the State Family Planning Commission in China told some journalists earlier this year:

At present low birth rates are not steady in China. This is because the birth concept of the broad masses has not changed fundamentally.[29]

Fourth, it is not by any means clear how much *additional* reduction in the fertility rate has actually been achieved by China through these coercive methods. It is reasonable to accept that many of China's longstanding social and economic programs have been valuable in reducing fertility, including those programs that have expanded education (for women as well as men), made health care more generally available, provided more job opportunities for women and—more recently—stimulated rapid economic growth. These factors would themselves have tended to help in the reduction in the birthrate, and it is not clear how much *extra* lowering of fertility rates has been achieved in China through compulsion. In fact, even in the absence of compulsion, we would expect the Chinese fertility rate to be much lower than the Indian average, given China's significantly greater achievement in education, health care, female job opportunities and other ingredients of social development.

In order to "take out" the influence of these social variables, as opposed to coercion, we can note the much greater heterogeneity of India than China, and look specifically at those Indian states which are comparatively advanced in these social fields. In particular, the state of Kerala provides an interesting comparison with China, since it too enjoys high levels of basic education, health care and so on, somewhat ahead of the Chinese average.[30] Kerala also has some other favorable features for women's empowerment and agency, including a greater recognition, by legal tradition, of women's property rights for a substantial and influential part of the community.[31]

Kerala's birthrate of 18 per thousand is actually lower than China's 19 per thousand, and this has been achieved without any compulsion by the state. Kerala's fertility rate is 1.7, compared with China's 1.9 for the mid-1990s. This is in line with what we could expect through progress in factors that help voluntary reduction in birthrates.[32]

## SIDE EFFECTS AND SPEED OF
## FERTILITY REDUCTION

It is also worth noting that since Kerala's low fertility has been achieved voluntarily, there is no sign of the adverse effects that were noted in the case of China—for example, heightened female infant mortality and widespread abortion of female fetuses. Kerala's infant mortality rate per thousand live births (16 for girls, 17 for boys) is much lower than China's (33 for girls and 28 for boys), even though both regions had similar infant mortality rates around the time, in 1979, when the one-child policy was initiated in China.[33] There is also no tendency toward sex-selective abortion of female fetuses in Kerala, as there is in China.

It is also necessary to examine the claim in support of compulsory birth control programs that the speed with which fertility rates can be cut down through coercive means is very much higher than for voluntary reductions. But this piece of generalization is not supported by Kerala's experience either. Its birthrate has fallen from 44 per thousand in the 1950s to 18 by 1991—a decline no less fast than that in China.

It could, however, be argued that looking at this very long period does not do justice to the effectiveness of the "one-child family" and other coercive policies that were introduced only in 1979, and that we ought really to compare what has happened between 1979 and now. So let us do just that. In 1979, when the one-child policy was introduced in China, Kerala had a *higher* fertility rate than China: 3.0 as opposed to China's 2.8. By 1991 its fertility rate of 1.8 is as much *below* China's 2.0 as it had been above it in 1979. Despite the added "advantage" of the one-child policy and other coercive measures, the fertility rate seems to have fallen much more slowly in China than in Kerala, even in this period.

Another Indian state, Tamil Nadu, has had no slower a fall of fertility rate, from 3.5 in 1979 to 2.2 in 1991. Tamil Nadu has had an active, but cooperative, family planning program, and it could use for this purpose a comparatively good position in terms of social achievements within India: one of the highest literacy rates among the major Indian states, high female participation in gainful employment, and relatively low infant mortality. Coercion of the type employed in China has not been used either in Tamil Nadu or in Kerala, and both have achieved much faster declines in fertility than China has achieved since it introduced the one-child policy and the related measures.

Within India, contrasts between the records of the different states offer some further insights on this subject. While Kerala and Tamil Nadu have radically reduced fertility rates, other states in the so-called northern heartland (such as Uttar Pradesh, Bihar, Madhya Pradesh, Rajasthan) have much lower levels of education, especially female education, and of general health care. These states all have high fertility rates—between 4.4 and 5.1[34] This is in spite of a persistent tendency in those states to use heavy-handed methods of family planning, including some coercion (in contrast with the more voluntary and collaborative approach used in Kerala and Tamil Nadu).[35]

The regional contrasts within India strongly argue for voluntarism (based, inter alia, on the active and educated participation of women), as opposed to coercion.

## TEMPTATIONS OF DURESS

While India has been much more cautious than China in considering the option of coercive birth control, there is much evidence that the possibility of coercive policies greatly attracts many activists in India. In the mid-1970s, the government of India, under Indira Gandhi's leadership, tried a good deal of compulsion in this field using the legal opportunities that she opened up through her declaration of "emergency" and the collateral suspension of some standard protections of civil and personal rights. The northern states, as was mentioned earlier, have various regulations and conventions that force family control measures, particularly in the irreversible form of sterilization, often of women.[36]

Even when coercion is not part of official policy, the government's firm insistence on "meeting the family-planning targets" often leads administrators and health care personnel at different levels to resort to all kinds of pressure tactics that come close to compulsion.[37] Examples of such tactics, used sporadically in particular regions, include vague but chilling verbal threats, making sterilization a condition of eligibility for antipoverty programs, denying maternity benefits to mothers of more than two children, reserving certain kinds of health care services to persons who have been sterilized, and forbidding persons who have more than two children from contesting elections for local governments (the panchayats).[38]

The last measure, introduced a few years ago in the northern states of Rajasthan and Haryana, has been widely praised in some circles, even though denial of the opportunity to contest elections involves a strong violation of a basic democratic right. Legislation was also proposed (though not passed) in the Indian parliament that would bar anyone from holding national or state office if he or she has more than two children.

It is sometimes argued that in a poor country it would be a mistake to worry too much about the unacceptability of coercion— a luxury that only the rich countries can "afford"—and that poor people are not really bothered by coercion. It is not at all clear on what evidence this argument is based. The people who suffer most from these coercive measures—who are brutally forced to do things they do not want to do—are often among the poorest and least privileged in the society. The regulations and the way they are applied are also particularly punitive with respect to women's exercise of reproductive freedom. For example, even such barbarous practices as trying to assemble poorer women in sterilization camps, through various kinds of pressure, have been used in several rural regions in north India as the deadline for meeting "sterilization targets" approaches.

Indeed, the acceptability of coercion to a poor population cannot be tested except through democratic confrontation, precisely the opportunity that authoritarian governments withhold from their citizens. Such a testing has not occurred in China, but it was indeed attempted in India during the "emergency period" in the 1970s when compulsory birth control was tried by Mrs. Gandhi's government, along with suspending various legal rights and civil liberties. As was mentioned earlier, the policy of coercion in general, including that in reproduction, was overwhelmingly defeated in the general elections that followed. The poverty-stricken electorate of India showed no less interest in voting against coercive violation of political, civil, and reproductive rights than it takes in protesting against economic and social inequality. Interest in liberty and basic rights can also be illustrated from the contemporary political movements in many other countries in Asia and Africa.

There is, in fact, another feature of people's reaction to coercion—that of voting with their feet. As Indian family planning specialists have noted, voluntary birth control programs in India received a severe setback from that brief program of compulsory sterilization, since people had become deeply suspicious of the entire family-planning movement. Aside from having little immediate impact on fertility rates, the coercive measures of the emergency period introduced in some regions in India were, in fact, followed by a long period of *stagnation* in the birthrate, which ended only around 1985.[39]

## A CONCLUDING REMARK

The magnitude of the population problem is often somewhat exaggerated, but nevertheless there are good grounds for looking for ways and means of reducing fertility rates in most developing countries. The approach that seems to deserve particular attention involves a close connection between public policies that enhance gender equity and the freedom of women (particularly education, health care and job opportunities for women) and individual responsibility of the family (though the decisional power of potential parents, particularly the mothers).[40] The effectiveness of this route lies in the close linkage between young women's well-being and their agency.

This general picture applies to developing countries as well, despite their poverty. There is no reason why it should not. While arguments are often presented to suggest that people who are very poor do not value freedom in general and reproductive freedom in particular, the evidence, insofar as it exists, is certainly to the contrary. People do, of course, value—and have reason to value—other things *as well,* including well-being and security, but that does not make them indifferent to their political, civil or reproductive rights.

There is little evidence that coercion works faster than what can be achieved through voluntary social change and development. Coercive family planning can also have seriously unfavorable consequences other than the violation of reproductive freedom, in particular an adverse impact on infant mortality (especially female infant mortality in countries with an entrenched antifemale bias). There is nothing here that gives definite ground for transgressing the basic importance of reproductive rights for the sake of achieving other good consequences.

In terms of policy analysis, there is much evidence now, based on intercountry comparisons as well as interregional contrasts within a large country, that women's empowerment (including female education, female employment opportunities and female property rights) and other social changes (such as mortality reduction) have a very strong effect in reducing fertility rate. Indeed, it is difficult to ignore the policy lessons implicit in these developments. The fact that these developments are highly desired for other reasons as well (including the reduction of gender inequity) makes them central concerns in development analysis. Also, social mores—what is taken to be "standard behavior"—are not independent of the understanding and appreciation of the nature of the problem. Public discussion can make a big difference.

Reducing fertility is important not only because of its consequences for economic prosperity, but also because of the impact of high fertility in diminishing the freedom of people—particularly of young women—to live the kind of lives they have reason to value. In fact, the lives that are most battered by the frequent bearing and rearing of children are those of young women who are reduced to being progeny-generating machines in many countries in the contemporary world. That "equilibrium" persists partly because of the low decisional power of young women in the family and also because of unexamined traditions that make frequent childbearing the uncritically accepted practice (as was the case even in Europe until the last century)—no injustice being seen there. The promotion of female literacy, of female work opportunities and of free, open and informed public discussion can bring about radical changes in the understanding of justice and injustice.

The view of "development as freedom" gets reinforced by these empirical connections, since—it turns out—the solution of the problem of population growth (like the solution of many other social and economic problems) can lie in expanding the freedom of the people whose interests are most directly affected by overfrequent childbearing and child rearing, viz., young women. The solution of the population problem calls for *more* freedom, not less.

# CHAPTER 10

# CULTURE AND HUMAN RIGHTS

The idea of human rights has gained a great deal of ground in recent years, and it has acquired something of an official status in international discourse. Weighty committees meet regularly to talk about the fulfillment and violation of human rights in different countries in the world. Certainly the *rhetoric* of human rights is much more widely accepted today—indeed much more frequently invoked—than it has ever been in the past. At least the language of national and international communication seems to reflect a shift in priorities and emphasis, compared with the prevailing dialectical style even a few decades ago. Human rights have also become an important part of the literature on development.

And yet this apparent victory of the idea and use of human rights coexists with some real skepticism, in critically demanding circles, about the depth and coherence of this approach. The suspicion is that there is something a little simple-minded about the entire conceptual structure that underlies the oratory on human rights.

## THREE CRITIQUES

What, then, appears to be the problem? I think there are three rather distinct concerns that critics tend to have about the intellectual edifice of human rights. There is, first, the worry that human rights confound consequences of legal systems, which give people certain well-defined rights, with pre-legal principles that cannot really give one a justiciable right. This is the issue of the legitimacy of the demands of human rights: How can human rights have any real status except through entitlements that are sanctioned by the state, as the ultimate legal authority? Human beings in nature are, in this view, no more born with human rights than they are born fully clothed; rights would have to be acquired through legislation, just as clothes are acquired through tailoring. There are no pre-tailoring clothes; nor any pre-legislation rights. I shall call this line of attack the *legitimacy critique*.

The second line of attack concerns the *form* that the ethics and politics of human rights takes. Rights are entitlements that require, in this view, correlated duties. If person A has a right to some $x$, then there has to be some agency, say B, that has a duty to provide A with $x$. If no such duty is recognized, then the alleged rights, in this view, cannot but be hollow. This is seen as posing a tremendous problem for taking human rights to be rights at all. It may be all very nice, so the argument runs, to say that every human being has a right to food or to medicine, but so long as no agency-specific duties have been characterized, these rights cannot really "mean" very much. Human rights, in this understanding, are heartwarming sentiments, but they are also, strictly speaking, incoherent. Thus viewed, these claims are best seen not so much as rights, but as lumps in the throat. I shall call this the *coherence critique*.

The third line of skepticism does not take quite such a legal and institutional form, but views human rights as being in the domain of social ethics. The moral authority of human rights, in this view, is conditional on the nature of acceptable ethics. But are such ethics really universal? What if some cultures do not regard rights as particularly valuable, compared to other prepossessing virtues or qualities? The disputation of the reach of human rights has often come from such cultural critiques; perhaps the most prominent of these is based on the idea of the alleged skepticism of Asian values toward human rights. Human rights, to justify that name, demand universality, but there are no such universal values, the critics claim. I shall call this the *cultural critique*.

## THE LEGITIMACY CRITIQUE

The legitimacy critique has a long history. It has been aired, in different forms, by many skeptics of rights-based reasoning about ethical issues. There are interesting similarities as well as differences between different variants of this criticism. There is, on the one hand, Karl Marx's insistence that rights cannot really *precede* (rather than follow) the institution of the state. This is spelled out in his combatively forceful pamphlet "On the Jewish Question." There are, on the other hand, the reasons that Jeremy Bentham gave for describing "natural rights" (as mentioned before) as "nonsense" and the concept of "natural and imprescriptible rights" as "nonsense on stilts." But common to these—and many other—lines of critique is an insistence that rights must be seen in postinstitutional terms as instruments, rather than as a prior ethical entitlement. This militates, in a rather fundamental way, against the basic idea of universal human rights.

Certainly, taken as aspiring legal entities, pre-legal moral claims can hardly be seen as giving justiciable rights in courts and other institutions of enforcement. But to reject human rights on this ground is to miss the point of the exercise. The demand for legality is no more than just that—a demand—which is justified by the ethical importance of acknowledging that certain rights are appropriate entitlements of all human beings. In this sense, human rights may stand for claims, powers and immunities (and other forms of warranty associated with the concept of rights) supported by ethical judgments, which attach intrinsic importance to these warranties.

In fact, human rights may also exceed the domain of *potential,* as opposed to *actual,* legal rights. A human right can be effectively invoked in contexts even where its *legal* enforcement would appear to be most inappropriate. The moral right of a wife to participate fully, as an equal, in serious family decisions—no matter how chauvinist her husband is—may be acknowledged by many who would nevertheless not want this requirement to be legalized and enforced by the police. The "right to respect" is another example in which legalization and attempted enforcement would be problematic, even bewildering.

Indeed, it is best to see human rights as a set of ethical claims, which must not be identified with legislated legal rights. But this normative interpretation need not obliterate the usefulness of the idea of human rights in the kind of context in which they are typically invoked. The freedoms that are associated with particular rights may be the appropriate focal point for debate. We have to judge the plausibility of human rights as a system of ethical reasoning and as the basis of political demands.

## THE COHERENCE CRITIQUE

I turn now to the second critique: whether we can coherently talk about rights without specifying whose duty it is to guarantee the fulfillment of the rights. There is indeed a mainstream approach to rights that takes the view that rights can be sensibly formulated only in combination with correlated duties. A person's right to something must, then, be coupled with another agent's duty to provide the first person with that something. Those who insist on that binary linkage tend to be very critical, in general, of invoking the rhetoric "rights" in "human rights" without exact specification of responsible agents and their duties to bring about the fulfillment of these rights. Demands for human rights are, then, seen just as loose talk.

A question that motivates some of this skepticism is: How can we be sure that rights are realizable unless they are matched by corresponding duties? Indeed, some do not see any sense in a right unless it is balanced by what Immanuel Kant called a "perfect obligation"— a specific duty of a particular agent for the realization of that right.[1]

It is, however, possible to resist the claim that any use of rights except with co-linked perfect obligations must lack cogency. In many legal contexts that claim may indeed have some merit, but in normative discussions rights are often championed as entitlements or powers or immunities that it would be good for people to have. Human rights are seen as rights shared by all—irrespective of citizenship— the benefits of which everyone *should* have. While it is not the specific duty of any given individual to make sure that the person has her rights fulfilled, the claims can be generally addressed to all those who are in a position to help. Indeed, Immanuel Kant himself had characterized such general demands as "imperfect obligations" and had gone on to discuss their relevance for social living. The claims are addressed generally to anyone who can help, even though no particular person or agency may be charged to bring about the fulfillment of the rights involved.

It may of course be the case that rights, thus formulated, sometimes end up unfulfilled. But it is surely possible for us to distinguish between a right that a person has which has not been fulfilled and a right that the person does not have. Ultimately, the ethical assertion of a right goes beyond the value of the corresponding freedom only to the extent that some demands are placed on others that they should try to help. While we may be able to manage well enough with the language of freedom rather than of rights (indeed it is the language of freedom that I have been mainly invoking in *Development as Freedom*), there may sometimes be a good case for suggesting—or demanding—that others help the person to achieve the freedom in question. The language of rights can supplement that of freedom.

## THE CULTURAL CRITIQUE AND ASIAN VALUES

The third line of critique is perhaps more engaging, and has certainly received more attention. Is the idea of human rights really so universal? Are there not ethics, such as in the world of Confucian cultures, that tend to focus on discipline rather than on rights, on loyalty rather than on entitlement? Insofar as human rights include claims to political liberty and civil rights, alleged tensions have been identified particularly by some Asian theorists.

The nature of Asian values has often been invoked in recent years to provide justification for authoritarian political arrangements in Asia. These justifications of authoritarianism have typically come not from independent historians but from the authorities themselves (such as governmental officers or their spokesmen) or those close to people in power, but their views are obviously consequential in governing the states and also in influencing the relation between different countries.

Are Asian values opposed—or indifferent—to basic political rights? Such generalizations are often made, but are they well grounded? In fact, generalizations about Asia are not easy, given its size. Asia is where about 60 percent of the total world population live. What can we take to be the values of so vast a region, with such diversity? There are no quintessential values that apply to this immensely large and heterogeneous population, none that separate them out as a group from people in the rest of the world.

Sometimes the advocates of "Asian values" have tended to look primarily at East Asia as the region of particular applicability. The generalization about the contrast between the West and Asia often concentrates on the land to the east of Thailand, even though there is a more ambitious claim that the rest of Asia is also rather "similar." For example, Lee Kuan Yew outlines "the fundamental difference between Western concepts of society and government and East Asian concepts" by explaining, "when I say East Asians, I mean Korea, Japan, China, Vietnam, as distinct from Southeast Asia, which is a mix between the Sinic and the Indian, though Indian culture itself emphasizes similar values."[2]

In fact, however, even East Asia itself has much diversity, and there are many variations to be found among Japan and China and Korea and other parts of East Asia. Various cultural influences from within and outside the region have affected human lives over the history of this rather large territory. These influences still survive in a variety of ways. To illustrate, my copy of Houghton Mifflin's international *Almanac* describes the religion of the 124 million Japanese in the following way: 112 million Shintoist and 93 million Buddhist.[3] Different cultural influences still color aspects of the identity of the contemporary Japanese, and the same person can be *both* Shintoist and Buddhist.

Cultures and traditions overlap over regions such as East Asia and even within countries such as Japan or China or Korea, and attempts at generalization about "Asian values" (with forceful—and often brutal—implications for masses of people in this region with diverse faiths, convictions and commitments) cannot but be extremely crude. Even the 2.8 million people of Singapore have vast variations of cultural and historical traditions. Indeed, Singapore has an admirable record in fostering intercommunity amity and friendly coexistance.

## THE CONTEMPORARY WEST
## AND CLAIMS TO UNIQUENESS

Authoritarian lines of reasoning in Asia—and more generally in non-Western societies—often receive indirect backing from modes of thought in the West itself. There is clearly a tendency in America and Europe to assume, if only implicitly, the primacy of political freedom and democracy as a fundamental and ancient feature of Western culture—one not to be easily found in Asia. It is, as it were, a contrast between the authoritarianism allegedly implicit in, say, Confucianism vis-à-vis the respect for individual liberty and autonomy allegedly deeply rooted in Western liberal culture. Western promoters of personal and political liberty in the non-Western world often see this as bringing Occidental values to Asia and Africa. The world is invited to join the club of "Western democracy" and to admire and endorse traditional "Western values."

In all this, there is a substantial tendency to extrapolate *backward* from the present. Values that European Enlightenment and other relatively recent developments have made common and widespread cannot really be seen as part of the long-run Western heritage—experienced in the West over millennia.[4] What we do find in the writings by particular Western classical authors (for example, Aristotle) is support for selected *components* of the comprehensive notion that makes up the contemporary idea of political liberty. But support for such components can be found in many writings in Asian traditions as well.

To illustrate this point, consider the idea that personal freedom for all is important for a good society. This claim can be seen as being composed of two distinct components, to wit, (1) *the value of personal freedom:* that personal freedom is important and should be guaranteed for those who "matter" in a good society, and (2) *equality of freedom:* everyone matters and the freedom that is guaranteed for one must be guaranteed for all. The two together entail that personal freedom should be guaranteed, on a shared basis, for all. Aristotle wrote much in support of the former proposition, but in his exclusion of women and slaves did little to defend the latter. Indeed, the championing of equality in this form is of quite recent origin. Even in a society stratified according to class and caste, freedom could be seen to be of great value for the privileged few (such as the Mandarins or the Brahmins), in much the same way freedom is valued for nonslave men in corresponding Greek conceptions of a good society.

Another useful distinction is between (1) *the value of toleration:* that there must be toleration of diverse beliefs, commitments, and actions of different people; and (2) *equality of tolerance:* the toleration that is offered to some must be reasonably offered to all (except when tolerance of some will lead to intolerance for others). Again, arguments for some tolerance can be seen plentifully in earlier Western writings, without that tolerance being supplemented by equality of tolerance. The roots of modern democratic and liberal ideas can be sought in terms of *constitutive* elements, rather than as a whole.

In doing a comparative scrutiny, the question has to be asked whether these constitutive components can be seen in Asian writings in the way they can be found in Western thought. The presence of these components must not be confused with the absence of the opposite, viz., of ideas and doctrines that clearly *do not* emphasize freedom and tolerance. Championing of order and discipline can be found in Western classics as well. Indeed, it is by no means clear to me that Confucius is more authoritarian in this respect than, say, Plato or St. Augustine. The real issue is not whether these nonfreedom perspectives are *present* in Asian traditions, but whether the freedom-oriented perspectives are *absent* there.

This is where the diversity of Asian value systems—which incorporates but transcends regional diversity—becomes quite central. An obvious example is the role of Buddhism as a form of thought. In Buddhist tradition, great importance is attached to freedom, and the part of the earlier Indian theorizing to which Buddhist thoughts relate has much room for volition and free choice. Nobility of conduct has to be achieved in freedom, and even the ideas of liberation (such as *moksha*) have this feature. The presence of these elements in Buddhist thought does not obliterate the importance for Asia of ordered discipline emphasized by Confucianism, but it would be a mistake to take Confucianism to be the only tradition in Asia— indeed even in China. Since so much of the contemporary authoritarian interpretation of Asian values concentrates on Confucianism, this diversity is particularly worth emphasizing.

## INTERPRETATIONS OF CONFUCIUS

Indeed, the reading of Confucianism that is now standard among authoritarian champions of Asian values does less than justice to the variety within Confucius's own teachings.[5] Confucius did not recommend blind allegiance to the state.[6] When Zilu asks him "how to serve a prince," Confucius replies, "Tell him the truth even if it offends him."⁷ Those in charge of censorship in Singapore or Beijing might take a very different view. Confucius is not averse to practical caution and tact, but does not forgo the recommendation to oppose a bad government. "When the [good] way prevails in the state, speak boldly and act boldly. When the state has lost the way, act boldly and speak softly."⁸

Indeed, Confucius provides a clear pointer to the fact that the two pillars of the imagined edifice of Asian values, namely loyalty to family and obedience to the state, can be in severe conflict with each other. Many advocates of the power of "Asian values" see the role of the state as an extension of the role of the family, but as Confucius noted, there can be tension between the two. The Governor of She told Confucius, "Among my people, there is a man of unbending integrity: when his father stole a sheep, he denounced him." To this Confucius replied, "Among my people, men of integrity do things differently: a father covers up for his son, a son covers up for his father—and there is integrity in what they do."⁹

## ASHOKA AND KAUTILYA

Confucius's ideas were altogether more complex and sophisticated than the maxims that are frequently championed in his name. There is also a tendency to neglect other authors in the Chinese culture and to ignore other Asian cultures. If we turn to Indian traditions, we can, in fact, find a variety of views on freedom, tolerance, and equality. In many ways, the most interesting articulation of the need for tolerance on an egalitarian basis can be found in the writings of Emperor Ashoka, who in the third century B.C. commanded a larger Indian empire than any other Indian king (including the Mughals, and even the Raj, if we leave out the native states that the British let be). He turned his attention to public ethics and enlightened politics in a big way after being horrified by the carnage he saw in his own victorious battle against the kingdom of Kalinga (what is now Orissa). He converted to Buddhism, and not only helped to make it a world religion by sending emissaries abroad with the Buddhist message to east and west, but also covered the country with stone inscriptions describing forms of good life and the nature of good government.

The inscriptions give a special importance to tolerance of diversity. For example, the edict (now numbered XII) at Erragudi puts the issue thus:

> ... a man must not do reverence to his own sect or disparage that of another man without reason. Depreciation should be for specific reason only, because the sects of other people all deserve reverence for one reason or another.
>
> By thus acting, a man exalts his own sect, and at the same time does service to the sects of other people. By acting contrariwise, a man hurts his own sect, and does disservice to the sects of other people. For he who does reverence to his own sect while disparaging the sects of others wholly from attachment to his own, with intent to enhance the splendour of his own sect, in reality by such conduct inflicts the severest injury on his own sect.[10]

The importance of tolerance is emphasized in these edicts from the third century B.C., both for public policy by the government and as advice for behavior of citizens to one another.

On the domain and coverage of tolerance, Ashoka was a universalist, and demanded this for all, including those whom he described as "forest people," the tribal population living in preagricultural economic formations. Ashoka's championing of egalitarian and universal tolerance may appear un-Asian to some commentators, but his views are firmly rooted in lines of analysis already in vogue in intellectual circles in India in the preceding centuries.

It is, however, interesting to look in this context at another Indian author whose treatise on governance and political economy was also profoundly influential and important. I refer to Kautilya, the author of *Arthashastra,* which can be translated as "the economic science," though it is at least as much concerned with practical politics as with economics. Kautilya was a contemporary of Aristotle, in the fourth century B.C., and worked as a senior minister of Emperor Chandragupta Maurya, Emperor Ashoka's grandfather, who had established the large Maurya empire across the subcontinent.

Kautilya's writings are often cited as a proof that freedom and tolerance were not valued in the Indian classical tradition. There are two aspects of the impressively detailed account of economics and politics to be found in *Arthashastra* that might tend to suggest such a diagnosis. First, Kautilya is a consequentialist of quite a narrow kind. While the objectives of promoting happiness of the subjects and order in the kingdom are strongly backed up by detailed policy advice, the king is seen as a benevolent autocrat, whose power, admittedly to do good, is to be maximized through good organization. Thus, *Arthashastra,* on the one hand, presents penetrating ideas and suggestions on such practical subjects as famine prevention and administrative effectiveness that remain relevant even today (more than two thousand years later),[11] and yet, on the other hand, its author is ready to advise the king about how to get his way, if necessary, through violating the freedom of his opponents and adversaries.

Second, Kautilya seems to attach little importance to political or economic equality, and his vision of good society is strongly stratified according to lines of class and caste. Even though the objective of promoting happiness, which is given an exalted position in the hierarchy of values, applies to all, the other objectives are clearly inegalitarian in form and content. There is the obligation to provide the less fortunate members of the society the support that they need for escaping misery and enjoying life, and Kautilya specifically identifies as the duty of the king to "provide the orphans, the aged, the infirm, the afflicted, and the helpless with maintenance," along with providing "subsistence to helpless women when they are carrying and also to the [newborn] children they give birth to."[12] But that obligation to support is very far from the valuing of these people's freedom to decide how to live—the tolerance of heterodoxy.

What, then, do we conclude from this? Certainly Kautilya is no democrat, no egalitarian, no general promoter of everyone's freedom. And yet, when it comes to characterizing what the most favored people—the upper classes—should get, freedom figures quite prominently. Denying personal liberty to the upper classes (the so-called Arya) is seen as unacceptable. Indeed, regular penalties, some of which are heavy, are specified for the taking of such adults or children in indenture, even though the slavery of the existing slaves is seen as perfectly acceptable.[13] To be sure, we do not find in Kautilya anything like the clear articulation that Aristotle provides of the importance of free exercise of capability. But the focusing on freedom is clear enough in Kautilya as far as the upper classes are concerned. It contrasts with the governmental duties to the lower orders, which take the paternalistic form of public attention and state assistance for the avoidance of acute deprivation and misery. However, insofar as a view of a good life emerges in all this, it is one that is entirely consistent with a freedom-valuing ethical system. The domain of that concern is, to be sure, confined to the upper groups of society, but this is not radically different from the Greek concern with free men as opposed to slaves or women. In respect to coverage, Kautilya differs from the universalist Ashoka, but not entirely from the particularist Aristotle.

## ISLAMIC TOLERANCE

I have been discussing in some detail the political ideas and practical reason presented by two forceful, but very different, expositions in India respectively in the fourth and the third century B.C., because their ideas in turn have influenced later Indian writings. But we can look at many other authors as well. Among powerful expositors and practitioners of tolerance of diversity in India must of course be counted the great Moghul emperor Akbar, who reigned between 1556 and 1605. Again, we are not dealing with a democrat, but with a powerful king who emphasized the acceptability of diverse forms of social and religious behavior, and who accepted human rights of various kinds, including freedom of worship and religious practice, that would not have been so easily tolerated in parts of Europe in Akbar's time.

For example, as the year 1000 in the Muslim Hejira calendar was reached in 1591–1592, there was some excitement about it in Delhi and Agra (not unlike what is happening right now as the year 2000 in the Christian calendar approaches). Akbar issued various enactments at this juncture of history and these focused, inter alia, on religious tolerance, including the following:

No man should be interfered with on account of religion, and anyone [is] to be allowed to go over to a religion he pleased.
 If a Hindu, when a child or otherwise, had been made a Muslim against his will, he is to be allowed, if he pleased, to go back to the religion of his fathers.[14]

Again, the domain of tolerance, while religion-neutral, was not universal in other respects, including in terms of gender equality, or equality between younger and older people. The enactment went on to argue for the forcible repatriation of a young Hindu woman to her father's family if she had abandoned it in pursuit of a Muslim lover. In the choice between supporting the young lovers and the young woman's Hindu father, old Akbar's sympathies are entirely with the father. Tolerance and equality at one level are combined with intolerance and inequality at another level, but the extent of general tolerance on matters of belief and practice is quite remarkable. It may not be irrelevant to note in this context, especially in the light of the hard sell of "Western liberalism," that while Akbar was making these pronouncements, the Inquisitions were in full bloom in Europe.

Because of the experience of contemporary political battles, especially in the Middle East, Islamic civilization is often portrayed as being fundamentally intolerant and hostile to individual freedom. But the presence of diversity and variety *within* a tradition applies very much to Islam as well. In India, Akbar and most of the other Moghuls provide good examples of both theory and practice of political and religious tolerance. Similar examples can be found in other parts of the Islamic culture. The Turkish emperors were often more tolerant than their European contemporaries. Abundant examples of this can be found also in Cairo and Baghdad. Indeed, even the great Jewish scholar Maimonides, in the twelfth century, had to run away from an intolerant Europe (where he was born) and from its persecution of Jews, to the security of a tolerant and urbane Cairo and the patronage of Sultan Saladin.

Similarly, Alberuni, the Iranian mathematician, who wrote the first general book on India in the early eleventh century (aside from translating Indian mathematical treatises into Arabic), was among the earliest of anthropological theorists in the world. He noted—and protested against—the fact that "depreciation of foreigners . . . is common to all nations towards each other." He devoted much of his life to fostering mutual understanding and tolerance in his eleventh-century world.

It is easy to multiply examples. The point to be seized is that the modern advocates of the authoritarian view of "Asian values" base their reading on very arbitrary interpretations and extremely narrow selections of authors and traditions. The valuing of freedom is not confined to one culture only, and the Western traditions are not the only ones that prepare us for a freedom-based approach to social understanding.

## GLOBALIZATION: ECONOMICS, CULTURE AND RIGHTS

The issue of democracy also has a close bearing on another cultural matter that has received some justified attention recently. This concerns the overwhelming power of Western culture and lifestyle in undermining traditional modes of living and social mores. For anyone concerned about the value of tradition and of indigenous cultural modes this is indeed a serious threat.

The contemporary world is dominated by the West, and even though the imperial authority of the erstwhile rulers of the world has declined, the dominance of the West remains as strong as ever—in some ways stronger than before, especially in cultural matters. The sun does not set on the empire of Coca-Cola or MTV.

The threat to native cultures in the globalizing world of today is, to a considerable extent, inescapable. The one solution that is not available is that of stopping globalization of trade and economies, since the forces of economic exchange and division of labor are hard to resist in a competitive world fueled by massive technological evolution that gives modern technology an economically competitive edge.

This is a problem, but not just a problem, since global trade and commerce can bring with it—as Adam Smith foresaw—greater economic prosperity for each nation. But there can be losers as well as gainers, even if in the net the aggregate figures move up rather than down. In the context of economic disparities, the appropriate response has to include concerted efforts to make the form of globalization less destructive of employment and traditional livelihood, and to achieve gradual transition. For smoothing the process of transition, there also have to be opportunities for retraining and acquiring of new skills (for people who would otherwise be displaced), in addition to providing social safety nets (in the form of social security and other supportive arrangements) for those whose interests are harmed—at least in the short run—by the globalizing changes.

This class of responses will to some extent work for the cultural side as well. Skill in computer use and the harvesting of Internet and similar facilities transform not only economic possibilities, but also the lives of the people influenced by such technical change. Again, this is not necessarily regrettable. There remain, however, two problems—one shared with the world of economics and another quite different.[15]

First, the world of modern communication and interchange requires basic education and training. While some poor countries in the world have made excellent progress in this area (countries in East Asia and Southeast Asia are good examples of that), others (such as those in South Asia and Africa) have tended to lag behind. Equity in cultural as well as economic opportunities can be profoundly important in a globalizing world. This is a shared challenge for the economic and the cultural world.

The second issue is quite different and distances the cultural problem from the economic predicament. When an economic adjustment takes place, few tears are shed for the superseded methods of production and for the overtaken technology. There may be some nostalgia for specialized and elegant objects (such as an ancient steam engine or an old-fashioned clock), but in general old and discarded machinery is not particularly wanted. In the case of culture, however, lost traditions may be greatly missed. The demise of old ways of living can cause anguish, and a deep sense of loss. It is a little like the extinction of older species of animals. The elimination of old species in favor of "fitter" species that are "better" able to cope and multiply can be a source of regret, and the fact that the new species are "better" in the Darwinian system of comparison need not be seen as consolation enough.[16]

This is an issue of some seriousness, but it is up to the society to determine what, if anything, it wants to do to preserve old forms of living, perhaps even at significant economic cost. Ways of life can be preserved if the society decides to do just that, and it is a question of balancing the costs of such preservation with the value that the society attaches to the objects and the lifestyles preserved. There is, of course, no ready formula for this cost-benefit analysis, but what is crucial for a rational assessment of such choices is the ability of the people to participate in public discussions on the subject. We come back again to the perspective of capabilities: that different sections of the society (and not just the socially privileged) should be able to be active in the decisions regarding what to preserve and what to let go. There is no compulsion to preserve every departing lifestyle even at heavy cost, but there is a real need—for social justice—for people to be able to take part in these social decisions, if they so choose.[17] This gives further reason for attaching importance to such elementary capabilities as reading and writing (through basic education), being well informed and well briefed (through free media), and having realistic chances of participating freely (through elections, referendums and the general use of civil rights). Human rights in the broadest sense are involved in this exercise as well.

## CULTURAL INTERCHANGE AND PERVASIVE INTERDEPENDENCE

On top of these basic recognitions, it is also necessary to note the fact that cross-cultural communication and appreciation need not necessarily be matters of shame and disgrace. We do have the capacity to enjoy things that have originated elsewhere, and cultural nationalism or chauvinism can be seriously debilitating as an approach to living. Rabindranath Tagore, the great Bengali poet, commented on this issue rather eloquently:

> Whatever we understand and enjoy in human products instantly becomes ours, wherever they might have their origin. I am proud of my humanity when I can acknowledge the poets and artists of other countries as my own. Let me feel with unalloyed gladness that all the great glories of man are mine.[18]

While there is some danger in ignoring uniqueness of cultures, there is also the possibility of being deceived by the presumption of ubiquitous insularity.

It is indeed possible to argue that there are more interrelations and more cross-cultural influences in the world than is typically acknowledged by those alarmed by the prospect of cultural subversion.[19] The culturally fearful often take a very fragile view of each culture and tend to underestimate our ability to learn from elsewhere without being overwhelmed by that experience. Indeed, the rhetoric of "national tradition" can help to hide the history of outside influences on the different traditions. For example, chili may be a central part of Indian cooking as we understand it (some even see it as something of a "signature tune" of Indian cooking), but it is also a fact that chili was unknown in India until the Portuguese brought it there only a few centuries ago. (Ancient Indian culinary art used pepper, but no chili.) Today's Indian curries are no less "Indian" for this reason.

Nor is there anything particularly shady in the fact that—given the blustering popularity of Indian food in contemporary Britain—the British Tourist Board describes curry as authentic "British fare." A couple of summers ago I even encountered in London a marvelous description of a person's incurable "Englishness": she was, we were informed, "as English as daffodils or chicken tikka masala."

The image of regional self-sufficiency in cultural matters is deeply misleading, and the value of keeping traditions pure and unpolluted is hard to sustain. Sometimes the intellectual influences from abroad may be more roundabout and many-sided. For example, some chauvinists in India have complained about the use of "Western" terminology in school curriculum, for example in modern mathematics. But the interrelations in the world of mathematics make it hard to know what is "Western" and what is not. To illustrate, consider the term "sine" used in trigonometry, which came to India straight through the British, and yet in its genesis there is a remarkable Indian component. Aryabhata, the great Indian mathematician of the fifth century, had discussed the concept of "sine" in his work, and had called it, in Sanskrit, *jya-ardha* ("half-chord"). From there the term moved on in an interesting migratory way, as Howard Eves describes:

> Aryabhata called it *ardha-jya* ("half-chord") and *jya-ardha* ("chord-half"), and then abbreviated the term by simply using *jya* ("chord"). From *jya* the Arabs phonetically derived *jiba*, which, following Arabic practice of omitting vowels, was

written as *jb*. Now *jiba*, aside from its technical significance, is a meaningless word in Arabic. Later writers who came across *jb* as an abbreviation for the meaningless word *jiba* substituted *jaib* instead, which contains the same letters, and is a good Arabic word meaning "cove" or "bay." Still later, Gherardo of Cremona (ca. 1150), when he made his translations from the Arabic, replaced the Arabian *jaib* by its Latin equivalent, *sinus* [meaning a cove or a bay], from whence came our present word *sine*.[20]

My point is not at all to argue against the unique importance of each culture, but rather to plead in favor of the need for some sophistication in understanding cross-cultural influences as well as our basic capability to enjoy products of other cultures and other lands. We must not lose our ability to understand one another and to enjoy the cultural products of different countries in the passionate advocacy of conservation and purity.

## UNIVERSALIST PRESUMPTIONS

Before closing this chapter I must also consider a further issue related to the question of cultural separatism, given the general approach of this book. It will not have escaped the reader that this book is informed by a belief in the ability of different people from different cultures to share many common values and to agree on some common commitments. Indeed, the overriding value of freedom as the organizing principle of this work has this feature of a strong universalist presumption.

The claim that "Asian values" are particularly indifferent to freedom, or that attaching importance to freedom is quintessentially a "Western" value, has been disputed already, earlier on in this chapter. The point, however, is sometimes made that the tolerance of heterodoxy in matters of religion, in particular, is historically a very special "Western" phenomenon. When I published a paper in an American magazine disputing the authoritarian interpretation of "Asian values" ("Human Rights and Asian Values," *The New Republic,* July 14 and 21, 1997), the responses that I got typically included some support for my disputation of the alleged specialness of "Asian values" (as being generally authoritarian), but then they went on to argue that the West, on the other hand, was really quite special—in terms of tolerance.

It was claimed that the tolerance of *religious* skepticism and heterodoxy was a specifically "Western" virtue. One commentator proceeded to outline his understanding that "Western tradition" is absolutely unique in its "acceptance of religious tolerance at a sufficient level that even atheism is permitted as a principled rejection of beliefs." The commentator is certainly right to claim that religious tolerance, including the tolerance of skepticism and atheism, is a central aspect of social freedom (as John Stuart Mill also explained persuasively).[21] The disputant went on to remark: "Where in Asian history, one asks, can Amartya Sen find anything equivalent to this remarkable history of skepticism, atheism and free thought?"[22]

This is indeed a fine question, but the answer is not hard to find. In fact, there is some embarrassment of riches in deciding which part of Asian history to concentrate on, since the answer could come from many different components of that history. For example, in the context of India in particular, one could point to the importance of the atheistic schools of Carvaka and Lokayata, which originated well before the Christian era, and produced a durable, influential and vast atheistic literature.[23] Aside from intellectual documents arguing for atheistic beliefs, heterodox views can be found in many orthodox documents as well. Indeed, even the ancient epic *Ramayana*, which is often cited by Hindu political activists as the holy book of the divine Rama's life, contains sharply dissenting views. For example, the *Ramayana* relates the occasion when Rama is lectured by a worldly pundit called Javali on the folly of religious beliefs: "O Rama, be wise, there exists no world but this, that is certain! Enjoy that which is present and cast behind thee that which is unpleasant."[24]

It is also relevant to reflect on the fact that the only world religion that is firmly agnostic, viz., Buddhism, is Asian in origin. Indeed, it originated in India in the sixth century B.C., around the time when the atheistic writings of the Carvaka and Lokayata schools were particularly active. Even the Upanishads (a significant component of the Hindu scriptures that originated a little earlier—from which I have already quoted in citing Maitreyee's question) discussed, with evident respect, the view that thought and intelligence are the results of material conditions in the body, and "when they are destroyed," that is, "after death," "no intelligence remains."[25] Skeptical schools of thought survived in Indian intellectual circles over the millennia, and even as late as the fourteenth century, Madhava Acarya (himself a good Vaishnavite Hindu), in his classic book called *Sarvadarśana-samgraha* ("Collection of All Philosophies"), devoted the entire first chapter to a serious presentation of the arguments of the Indian athe-istic schools. Religious skepticism and its tolerance are not uniquely Western as a phenomenon.

References were made earlier to tolerance in general in Asian cul-tures (such as the Arabic, the Chinese and the Indian), and religious tolerance is a part of it, as the examples cited bring out. Examples of violations—often *extreme* violations—of tolerance are not hard to find in any culture (from medieval inquisitions to modern concentra-tion camps in the West, and from religious slaughter to the victimiz-ing oppression of the Taliban in the East), but voices have been persistently raised in favor of freedom—in different forms—in dis-tinct and distant cultures. If the universalist presumptions of this book, particularly in valuing the importance of freedom, are to be rejected, the grounds for rejection must lie elsewhere.

## A CONCLUDING REMARK

The case *for* basic freedoms and for the associated formulations in terms of rights rests on:

1) their *intrinsic* importance;
2) their *consequential* role in providing political incentives for economic security;
3) their *constructive* role in the genesis of values and priorities.

The case is no different in Asia than it is anywhere else, and the dismissal of this claim on the ground of the special nature of Asian values does not survive critical scrutiny.[26]

As it happens, the view that Asian values are quintessen-tially authoritarian has tended to come, in Asia, almost exclusively from spokesmen of those in power (sometimes supplemented—and reinforced—by Western statements demanding that people endorse what are seen as specifically "Western liberal values"). But foreign ministers, or government officials, or religious leaders, do not have a monopoly in interpreting local culture and values. It is important to listen to the voices of dissent in each society.[27] Aung San Suu Kyi has no less legitimacy—indeed clearly has rather more—in interpreting what the Burmese want than have the military rulers of Myanmar, whose candidates she had defeated in open elections before being put in jail by the defeated military junta.

The recognition of diversity within different cultures is extremely important in the contemporary world.[28] Our understanding of the presence of diversity tends to be somewhat undermined by constant bombardment with oversimple generalizations about "Western civilization," "Asian values," "African cultures" and so on. Many of these readings of history and civilization are not only intellectually shallow, they also add to the divisiveness of the world in which we live. The fact is that in any culture, people seem to like to argue with one another, and frequently do exactly that—given the chance. The presence of dissidents makes it problematic to take an unambiguous view of the "true nature" of local values. In fact, dissidents tend to exist in every society—often quite plentifully—and they are frequently willing to take very great risks regarding their own security. Indeed, had the dissidents not been so tenaciously present, authoritarian polities would not have had to undertake such repressive measures in practice, to supplement their intolerant beliefs. The presence of dissidents *tempts* the authoritarian ruling groups to take a repressive view of local culture and, at the same time, that presence itself *undermines* the intellectual basis of such univocal interpretation of local beliefs as homogenous thought.[29]

Western discussion of non-Western societies is often too respectful of authority—the governor, the minister, the military junta, the religious leader. This "authoritarian bias" receives support from the fact that Western countries themselves are often represented, in international gatherings, by governmental officials and spokesmen, and they in turn seek the views of their opposite numbers from other countries. An adequate approach of development cannot really be so centered only on those in power. The reach has to be broader, and the need for popular participation is not just sanctimonious rubbish. Indeed, the idea of development cannot be dissociated from it.

As far as the authoritarian claims about "Asian values" are concerned, it has to be recognized that values that have been championed in the past of Asian countries—in East Asia as well as elsewhere in Asia—include an enormous variety.[30] Indeed, in many ways they are similar to substantial variations that are often seen in the history of ideas in the West also. To see Asian history in terms of a narrow category of authoritarian values does little justice to the rich varieties of thought in Asian intellectual traditions. Dubious history does nothing to vindicate dubious politics.

# CHAPTER 11

# SOCIAL CHOICE AND
# INDIVIDUAL BEHAVIOR

The idea of using reason to identify and promote better and more acceptable societies has powerfully moved people in the past and continues to do so now. Aristotle agreed with Agathon that even God could not change the past. But he also thought that the future was ours to make. This could be done by basing our choices on reason.[1] For this we need an appropriate evaluative framework; we also need institutions that work to promote our goals and valuational commitments, and furthermore we need behavioral norms and reasoning that allow us to achieve what we try to achieve.

Before I proceed further along this line, I must also discuss some grounds for skepticism of the possibility of reasoned progress, which can be found in the literature. If these grounds are compelling, then they may indeed be devastating for the approach pursued in this book. It would be silly to build an ambitious structure on the foundations of quicksand.

I would like to identify three distinct lines of skepticism that seem to demand particular attention. First, the point is sometimes made that given the heterogeneity of preferences and values that different people have, even in a given society, it is not possible to have a coherent framework for reasoned social assessment. There can be, in this view, no such thing as a rational and coherent social evaluation. Kenneth Arrow's famous "impossibility theorem" is sometimes invoked in this context to drive the point home.[2] That remarkable theorem is typically interpreted as proving the impossibility of rationally deriving social choice from individual preferences, and it has been taken to be a deeply pessimistic result. The analytical content of the theorem as well as its substantive interpretations would have to be examined. The idea of an "informational base" already explored in chapter 3 will turn out to be crucial in this context.

A second line of critique takes a particularly methodological form, and draws on an argument that questions our ability to have what we *intend* to have, arguing that "unintended consequences" dominate actual history. The importance of unintended consequences has been emphasized in different ways by Adam Smith, Carl Menger and Friedrich Hayek, among others.[3] If most of the important things that happen are not intended (and not brought about through purposive action), then reasoned attempts at pursuing what we want might appear to be rather pointless. We have to examine what precisely the implications are of the insights that emerge from the work in this field that was pioneered by Smith.

A third class of doubts relates to a skepticism, which many people entertain, about the possible *range* of human values and behavioral norms. Can our modes of behavior go at all beyond narrowly defined self-interest? If not, it is argued that while the market mechanism may still work (since it is supposed to invoke nothing other than human selfishness), we cannot have social arrangements that call for anything more "social" or "moral" or "committed." The possibility of reasoned social change, in this view, cannot go beyond the working of the market mechanism (even if it leads to inefficiency, or inequality, or poverty). To ask for more would be, in this perspective, hopelessly utopian.

The primary interest of this chapter is in examining the relevance of values and reasoning in enhancing freedoms and in achieving development. I shall consider the three arguments in turn.

## IMPOSSIBILITY AND INFORMATIONAL BASES

The Arrow theorem does not in fact show what the popular interpretation frequently takes it to show. It establishes, in effect, not the impossibility of rational social choice, but the impossibility that arises when we try to base social choice on a limited class of information. At the risk of oversimplification, let me briefly consider one way of seeing the Arrow theorem.

Take the old example of the "voting paradox," with which eighteenth-century French mathematicians such as Condorcet and Jean-Charles de Borda were much concerned. If person 1 prefers option *x* to option *y* and *y* to *z*, while person 2 prefers *y* to *z* and *z* to *x*, and person 3 prefers *z* to *x* and *x* to *y*, then we do know that the majority rule would lead to inconsistencies. In particular, *x* has a majority over *y*, which has a majority over *z*, which in turn enjoys a majority over *x*. Arrow's theorem shows, among other insights it offers, that not just the majority rule, but *all* mechanisms of decision making that rely on the same informational base (to wit, only individual orderings of the relevant alternatives) would lead to some inconsistency or infelicity, unless we simply go for the dictatorial solution of making one person's preference ranking rule the roost.

This is an extraordinarily impressive and elegant theorem—one of the most beautiful analytical results in the field of social science. But it does not at all rule out decision mechanisms that use more—or different—informational bases than voting rules do. In taking a social decision on economic matters, it would be natural for us to consider other types of information.

Indeed, a majority rule—whether or not consistent—would be a nonstarter as a mechanism for resolving economic disputes. Consider the case of dividing a cake among three persons, called (not very imaginatively) 1, 2, and 3, with the assumption that each person votes to maximize only her own share of the cake. (This assumption simplifies the example, but nothing fundamental depends on it, and it can be replaced by other types of preferences.) Take any division of the cake among the three. We can always bring about a "majority improvement" by taking a part of any one person's share (let us say, person 1's share), and then dividing it between the other two (viz., 2 and 3). This way of "improving" the social outcome would work— given that the social judgment is by majority rule—even if the person thus victimized (viz., 1) happens to be the poorest of the three. Indeed, we can continue taking away more and more of the share of the poorest person and dividing the loot between the richer two—all the time making a majority improvement. This process of "improvement" can go on until the poorest has no cake left to be taken away.

What a wonderful chain, *in the majoritarian perspective,* of social betterment!

Rules of this kind build on an informational base consisting only of the preference rankings of the persons, without any notice being taken of who is poorer than whom, or who gains (and who loses) how much from shifts in income, or any other information (such as how the respective persons happened to earn the particular shares they have). The informational base for this class of rules, of which the majority decision procedure is a prominent example, is thus extremely limited, and it is clearly quite inadequate for making informed judgments about welfare economic problems. This is not primarily because it leads to inconsistency (as generalized in the Arrow theorem), but because we cannot really make social judgments with so little information.

## SOCIAL JUSTICE
## AND RICHER INFORMATION

Acceptable social rules would tend to take notice of a variety of other relevant facts in judging the division of the cake: who is poorer than whom, who gains how much in terms of welfare or of the basic ingredients of living, how is the cake being "earned" or "looted" and so on. The insistence that no other information is needed (and that other information, if available, could not influence the decisions to be taken) makes these rules not very interesting for economic decision making. Given this recognition, the fact that there is *also* a problem of inconsistency—in dividing a cake through votes—may well be seen not so much as a problem, but as a welcome relief from the unswerving consistency of brutal and informationally obtuse procedures.

In terms of the example considered at the beginning of chapter 3, none of the arguments used to make a case for hiring either Dinu or Bishanno or Rogini would be usable in the Arrow informational base. Dinu's case rested on his being the poorest, Bishanno's case on his being the unhappiest and Rogini's case on her being most ill—all of which are external facts outside the informational base of the preference rankings of the three persons (given Arrow's conditions). In fact, in making economic judgments we tend, in general, to use much broader types of information than is permitted in the class of mechanisms compatible with the Arrow framework.

Indeed, the spirit of "impossibility" is not, I believe, the right way of seeing Arrow's "impossibility theorem."[4] Arrow provides a general approach to thinking about social decisions based on individual conditions, and his theorem—and a class of other results established after his pioneering work—show that what is possible and what is not may turn crucially on what information is taken into effective account in making social decisions. Indeed, through informational *broadening*, it is possible to have coherent and consistent criteria for social and economic assessment. The "social choice" literature (as this field of analytical exploration is called), which has resulted from Arrow's pioneering move, is as much a world of possibility as of conditional impossibilities.[5]

## SOCIAL INTERACTION
## AND PARTIAL ACCORD

Another point to note, on a related issue, is that the politics of social consensus calls not only for acting on the basis of *given* individual preferences, but also for sensitivity of social decisions to the *development* of individual preferences and norms. In this context, particular importance has to be attached to the role of public discussion and interactions in the emergence of shared values and commitments.[6] Our ideas of what is just and what is not may respond to the arguments that are presented for public discussion, and we tend to react to one another's views sometimes with a compromise or even a deal, and at other times with relentless inflexibility and stubbornness. Preference formation through social interaction is a major subject of interest in this study, and it will be pursued further later on in this chapter and in the next.

It is also important to recognize that agreed social arrangements and adequate public policies do not require that there be a unique "social ordering" that completely ranks all the alternative social possibilities. Partial agreements still separate out acceptable options (and weed out unacceptable ones), and a workable solution can be based on the contingent acceptance of particular provisions, without demanding complete social unanimity.[7]

It can also be argued that judgments of "social justice" do not really call for a tremendous fine-tuning precision: such as a claim that a tax rate of 39.0 percent is just, whereas 39.5 per cent would not be (or even that the former is "more just than" the latter). Rather, what is needed is a working agreement on some basic matters of identifiably intense injustice or unfairness.

Indeed, the insistence on the completeness of judgments of justice over every possible choice is not only an enemy of practical social action, it may also reflect some misunderstanding of the nature of justice itself. To take an extreme example, in agreeing that the occurrence of a preventable famine is socially unjust, we do not also lay claim to an ability to determine what *exact* allocation of food among all the citizens will be "most just." The recognition of evident injustice in preventable deprivation, such as widespread hunger, unnecessary morbidity, premature mortality, grinding poverty, neglect of female children, subjugation of women, and phenomena of that kind does not have to await the derivation of some complete ordering over choices that involve finer differences and puny infelicities. Indeed, the overuse of the concept of justice reduces the force of the idea when applied to the terrible deprivations and inequities that characterize the world in which we live. Justice is like a cannon, and it need not be fired (as an old Bengali proverb puts it) to kill a mosquito.

## INTENDED CHANGES
## AND UNINTENDED CONSEQUENCES

I turn now to the second of the identified reasons for skepticism of the idea of reasoned progress, to wit, the alleged dominance of "unintended" consequences and the related doubts about the possibility of reasoned and intentional advancement. The idea that unintended consequences of human action are responsible for many of the big changes in the world is not hard to appreciate. Things often do not go as we plan. Sometimes we have excellent reasons for being grateful for this, whether we consider the discovery of penicillin from a leftover dish not intended for that purpose, or the destruction of the Nazi party caused by—but not intended in—Hitler's military overconfidence. One would have to take a very limited view of history to expect that consequences match expectations as a general rule.

There is, however, nothing embarrassing in all this to the rationalistic approach underlying this book. What is needed for such an approach is not any general requirement that there should be no unintended effects, but only that reasoned attempts to bring about social change should, in the relevant circumstances, help us to get better results. There are plenty of examples of success in social and economic reforms guided by motivated programs. Attempts at universal literacy, when seriously undertaken, tend to succeed, as they have in Europe and North America, and also in Japan and elsewhere in East Asia. Epidemics of smallpox and many other illnesses have been eliminated or sharply reduced. The development of national health services in European countries has made health care available to most citizens in a way it was not earlier on. Things are, often enough, exactly as they seem, and indeed more or less what they seemed to people who worked hard to get there. While these success stories have to be supplemented by accounts of failures and deflections, lessons can be learned from what went wrong, in order to do things better next time. Learning by doing is a great ally of the rationalist reformer.

What then do we make of the thesis allegedly championed by Adam Smith and definitely advocated by Carl Menger and Friedrich Hayek that many—perhaps most—good things that happen are typically the unintended results of human action? The "general philosophy" underlying this adulation of unintended consequences deserves serious examination. I shall begin with Adam Smith, both because he was the alleged originator of this theory, and also because this book does have a strongly "Smithian" character.

We have to begin by noting that Smith was deeply skeptical of the morals of the rich—there is no author (not even Karl Marx) who made such strong criticism of the motives of the economically well placed vis-à-vis the interests of the poor. Many rich proprietors, Adam Smith argued in *The Theory of Moral Sentiments*, published in 1759 (seventeen years before *Wealth of Nations*), pursue, "in their natural selfishness and rapacity," only "their vain and insatiable desires."[8] And yet others can, in many circumstances, benefit from their actions since the actions of different people can be productively complementary. Smith was not going to praise the rich for consciously doing any good to others. The thesis of unintended consequences involved the continuation of Smith's skepticism of the rich. The selfish and the rapacious are led, argued Smith, "by an invisible hand," to "advance the interest of the society," and this they achieve "without intending it, without knowing it." With those words—and a little help from Menger and Hayek—"the theory of unintended consequences" was born.

It was also in this general context that Smith outlined his much cited discussion—already quoted earlier—of the merits of economic exchange in *Wealth of Nations*:

> It is not from the benevolence of the butcher, the brewer, or the baker, that we expect our dinner, but from their regard to their own interest. We address ourselves, not to their humanity but to their self-love. . . .[9]

The butcher sells bread to the consumer, not because he intends to promote the consumer's welfare, but because he wants to make money. Similarly, the baker and the brewer pursue their respective self-interests, but end up helping others. The consumer, in her turn, is not trying to promote the interests of the butcher or the baker or the brewer, but to pursue her own interest in buying meat or bread or beer. However, the butcher and the baker and the brewer benefit from the consumer's search for her own satisfaction. The individual, as Smith saw it, is "led by an invisible hand to promote an end which was no part of his intention."[10]

The championing of "unintended consequences" took off from these rather modest beginnings. Carl Menger, in particular, argued that this is a central proposition in economics (though, he thought, Smith did not get it fully right), and later on, Friedrich Hayek developed this theory further, describing it as a "profound insight into the object of all social theory."[11]

How significant a theory is this? Hayek was much taken by the elementary fact that important consequences are often unintended. In itself, this fact can scarcely be surprising. Any action has very many consequences, and only some of them could have been intended by the actors. I go out of the house in the morning to post a letter. You see me. It was no part of my intention to cause that you see me on the street (I was just trying to post a letter), but this was a result of my going out of the house to the mailbox. It is an unintended consequence of my action. To take another example: The presence of a multitude of people in a room causes it to be heated up and this can be quite important in an overheated room in which a party is being held. No one intended to heat up the room, but together they might yield just such a consequence.

Is there great sagacity in recognizing all this? I would argue, perhaps not a great deal. Indeed, it is hard to think that there can be much profundity in the general conclusion that many consequences are entirely unintended.[12] Despite my admiration for Friedrich Hayek and his ideas (he has contributed more than perhaps anyone else to our understanding of constitutionality, the relevance of rights, the importance of social processes, and many other central social and economic concepts), I have to say that this modest recognition can scarcely be seen as a momentous thought. If it is, as Hayek puts it, a "profound insight," then there is something wrong with profundity.

But there is another way of seeing the same issue, and maybe that is what Hayek intended to emphasize. It is not so much that some consequences are unintended, but that causal analysis can make the unintended effects reasonably *predictable*. Indeed, the butcher may predict that exchanging meat for money not only benefits him, but also the consumer (the buyer of meat), so that the relationship can be expected to work on both sides and is thus sustainable. And the brewer, the baker and the consumer may, similarly, also expect these economic relations to be sustainable. An *unintended* consequence need not be *unpredictable,* and much depends on this fact. Indeed, the confidence of each party in the continuation of such market relations rests specifically on such predictions being made or being implicitly presumed.

If this is the way the idea of unintended consequences is understood (in terms of *anticipation* of important but unintended consequences), it is in no way hostile to the possibility of rationalist reform. In fact, quite the contrary. Economic and social reasoning can take note of consequences that may not be intended, but which nevertheless result from institutional arrangements, and the case for particular institutional arrangements can be better evaluated by noting the likelihood of various unintended consequences.

## SOME ILLUSTRATIONS FROM CHINA

Sometimes the consequences that occur were not only not intended but were not anticipated either. Such examples are important not only to underline the fact that human expectations are fallible, but also to provide inputs for learning for future policy making. Perhaps a couple of examples from recent Chinese history will help to illustrate these issues.

There has been much discussion since the 1979 economic reforms of the apparently negative impact of economic reform on a number of important social goals, including the way the rural health care arrangements work. The reformers did not intend these negative social effects, but these effects seem to have occurred. For example, the introduction of the "responsibility system" in Chinese agriculture in the late 1970s, which did away with the earlier cooperative systems (and ushered in a period of unprecedented agricultural expansion), also made the financing of public health care that much more difficult in rural areas. The health care system used to be, to a great extent, financed through the cooperative system on a nonvoluntary basis. It proved, in fact, very difficult to replace that arrangement by a voluntary system of medical insurance to be taken out by the rural population. This possibly did make it harder to maintain the improvements in public health care in the period immediately following the reforms. The effects apparently came as something of a surprise to the reformers, and if that was the case, it can be argued that the results might have been better predicted on the basis of a fuller study of health care financing in China and elsewhere.

To consider a different type of example, coercive family planning measures (including the "one-child family" policy) introduced in China in 1979, to reduce the birthrate, seem to have contributed adversely to the reduction of infant mortality, especially of female babies (as was discussed in chapter 9). To some extent, there has, in fact, been even some accentuation of the neglect and mortality of female infants (if not infanticide), and certainly many more sex-specific abortions, as the families have tried to conform to the governmental norms on the total number of children without giving up their male-child preference. The architects of social reform and obligatory family planning did not intend to produce adverse effects on infant mortality in general and on female infant mortality in particular; nor did they want to encourage sex-specific abortion. They had only intended to reduce fertility. But these adverse consequences did actually follow and deserve attention and remedy.

The central issue, then, is whether these adverse effects were predictable and should have been *anticipated,* even though not intended. The nature of economic and social reforms in China could have benefited from more predictive analysis of causes and effects, including unintended effects. The fact that the adverse effects were *not intended* did not imply that they could not be at all predicted. A clearer understanding of these consequences could have led to a better conception of what was involved in the proposed changes, and possibly could even have led to preventive or corrective policies.

These examples from recent Chinese experience deal with unintended consequences that were unfavorable from a social point of view. The direction of these unintended effects is not similar to the main class of unintended consequences considered by Adam Smith, Carl Menger and Friedrich Hayek, where the consequences considered are typically *favorable.* There is, however, a basic comparability between the working of the two types of cases, even though the nature of the unintended consequences is attractive in one case and unattractive in the other.

In fact, the occurrence of *favorable* unintended consequences (the Smith-Menger-Hayek case) also has some parallels in the field of economic planning in China, though for that we have to look at other parts of recent Chinese history. As the fast economic progress of East Asian and Southeast Asian economies gets more fully analyzed, it is becoming increasingly clear that it is not only the openness of the economies—and greater reliance on domestic and international trade—that led to such rapid economic transition in these economies. The groundwork was laid also by positive social changes, such as land reforms, the spread of education and literacy and better health care. What we are looking at here is not so much the social consequences of economic reforms, but the economic consequences of social reforms. The market economy flourishes on the foundations of such social development. As India has been lately recognizing, lack of social development can quite severely hold up the reach of economic development.[13]

When and how did these social changes occur in China? The main thrust of these social changes was in the pre-reform period, before 1979—indeed a lot of it during the active days of Maoist policy. Was Mao *intending* to build the social foundations of a market economy and capitalist expansion (as he certainly did succeed in doing)? That hypothesis would be hard to entertain. And yet the Maoist policies of land reform, expansion of literacy, enlargement of public health care and so on had a very favorable effect on economic growth in post-reform China. The extent to which *post-reform* China draws on the results achieved in *pre-reform* China needs greater recognition.[14] The positive unintended consequences are important here.

Since Mao did not consider seriously the likelihood that a flourishing market economy would emerge in China, it is not surprising that he did not consider this particular entailment of the social changes that were being brought in under his leadership. And yet there is a general connection here that is quite close to the focus on capability in this work. The social changes under consideration (expansion of literacy, basic health care, and land reform) do enhance human capability to lead worthwhile and less vulnerable lives. But these capabilities are also associated with improving the productivity and employability of the people involved (expanding what is called their "human capital"). The interdependence between human capability in general and human capital in particular could be seen as being reasonably predictable. While it may not have been any part of Mao's intention to make things easier for market-based economic expansion in China, a social analyst should have been well placed—even then—to predict just such a relationship. Anticipation of such social relations and causal connections helps us to reason sensibly about social organization and about possible lines of social change and progress.

Thus, the anticipation of unintended consequences is part of—rather than contrary to—a rationalist approach to organizational reform and social change. The insights developed by Smith, Menger and Hayek draw our attention to the importance of studying unintended effects (as they themselves respectively proceeded to do), and it would be a complete mistake to think that the importance of unintended effects undermines the need for rational assessment of all effects—unintended as well as intended. There is nothing here to undermine the importance of trying to anticipate *all* the likely consequences of alternative policies, nor anything to subvert the need for basing policy decisions on rational assessment of alternative scenarios.

## SOCIAL VALUES AND PUBLIC INTEREST

I turn now to the third argument. What about the claim that human beings are uncompromisingly self-interested? How do we respond to the deep skepticism regarding the possibility of broader social values? Would every freedom that people enjoy be invariably exercised in such a self-centered way that the expectation of reasoned social progress and public action has to be entirely illusory?

I would argue that such skepticism would be quite unjustified. Self-interest is, of course, an extremely important motive, and many works on economic and social organization have suffered from not paying adequate attention to this basic motivation. And yet we also see actions—day in and day out—that reflect values which have clear social components that take us well beyond the narrow confines of purely selfish behavior. The emergence of social norms can be facilitated both by communicative reasoning and by evolutionary selection of behavioral modes. There is, by now, quite a vast literature on this subject, and I shall not dwell on this at great length.[15]

The use of socially responsible reasoning and of ideas of justice relates closely to the centrality of individual freedom. This is not to claim that people invariably invoke their ideas of justice, or utilize their powers of socially sensitive reasoning, in deciding on how to exercise their freedom. But a sense of justice is among the concerns that *can* move people and often *do*. Social values can play—and have played—an important part in the success of various forms of social organization, including the market mechanism, democratic politics, elementary civil and political rights, provision of basic public goods, and institutions for public action and protest.

Different persons may have very different ways of interpreting ethical ideas including those of social justice, and they may even be far from certain about how to organize their thoughts about it. But the basic ideas of justice are not alien to social beings, who worry about their own interests but are also able to think about family members, neighbors, fellow citizens and about other people in the world. The thought experiment involving the "impartial spectator" that Adam Smith beautifully analyzed (beginning with the powerful question: What would an "impartial spectator" make of it?) is a formalization of an informal—and pervasive—idea that occurs to most of us. Space does not have to be artificially created in the human mind for the idea of justice or fairness—through moral bombardment or ethical haranguing. That space already exists, and it is a question of making systematic, cogent and effective use of the general concerns that people do have.

## THE ROLE OF VALUES IN CAPITALISM

While capitalism is often seen as an arrangement that works only on the basis of the greed of everyone, the efficient working of the capitalist economy is, in fact, dependent on powerful systems of values and norms. Indeed, to see capitalism as nothing other than a system based on a conglomeration of greedy behavior is to underestimate vastly the ethics of capitalism, which has richly contributed to its redoubtable achievements.

The use of formal economic models to understand the operation of market mechanisms, as is the standard practice in economic theory, is to some extent a double-edged sword. The models can give insight into the way the real world operates.[16] On the other hand, the structure of the model can conceal some implicit assumptions that produce the regular relations that the models build on. Successful markets operate the way they do not just on the basis of exchanges being "allowed," but also on the solid foundation of institutions (such as effective legal structures that support the rights ensuing from contracts) and behavioral ethics (which makes the negotiated contracts viable without the need for constant litigation to achieve compliance). The development and use of trust in one another's words and promises can be a very important ingredient of market success.

That something other than the unleashing of greed is involved in the emergence and development of the capitalist system was, of course, clear to the early defenders of capitalism. The Manchester liberals did not fight just for the victory of greed and self-love. Their concept of humanity incorporated a broader domain of values. While they may have been overly optimistic about what human beings (when left to themselves) can—and will—do, they were right to see some spontaneity in the feelings that people have for one another, and to entertain the possibility of an enlightened understanding of the need for mutually beneficial behavior (without constant prodding by the state).

The same applies to Adam Smith, who considered a variety of values involved in economic, social and political relations. Even those early commentators (such as Montesquieu and James Stuart) who saw capitalism as a kind of replacement of "passions" by "interest" tended to draw attention to the fact that the pursuit of interest in an intelligent and rational way can be a great moral improvement over being driven by fervor, craving and tyrannical propensities. "Interest," James Stuart thought, was the "most effective bridle" against "the folly of despotism." As Albert Hirschman has beautifully analyzed, the early champions of capitalism saw a great motivational improvement in the emergence of capitalist ethics: "it would activate some benign human proclivities at the expense of some malignant ones."[17]

Despite its effectiveness, capitalist ethics is, in fact, deeply limited in some respects, dealing particularly with issues of economic inequality, environmental protection and the need for cooperation of different kinds that operate outside the market. But within its domain, capitalism works effectively through a system of ethics that provides the vision and the trust needed for successful use of the market mechanism and related institutions.

## BUSINESS ETHICS, TRUST AND CONTRACTS

Successful operation of an exchange economy depends on mutual trust and the use of norms—explicit and implicit.[18] When these behavioral modes are plentiful, it is easy to overlook their role. But when they have to be cultivated, that lacuna can be a major barrier to economic success. There are plenty of examples of the problems faced in precapitalist economies because of the underdevelopment of capitalist virtues. Capitalism's need for motivational structures that are more complex than pure profit maximization has been acknowledged in various forms, over a long time, by many leading social scientists, such as Marx, Weber, Tawney and others.[19] That nonprofit motives have a role in the success of capitalism is not a new point, even though the wealth of historical evidence and conceptual arguments in that direction is often neglected in contemporary professional economics.[20]

A basic code of good business behavior is a bit like oxygen: we take an interest in its presence only when it is absent. Adam Smith had noted this general tendency in an interesting remark in his "History of Astronomy":

> . . . an object with which we are quite familiar, and which we
> see every day, produces, though both great and beautiful, but a
> small effect upon us; because our admiration is not supported
> either by Wonder or by Surprise.[21]

What may not cause wonder or surprise in Zurich or London or Paris may, however, be quite problematic in Cairo or Bombay or Lagos (or Moscow), in their challenging struggle to establish the norms and institutions of a functioning market economy. Even the problem of political and economic corruption in Italy, which has been much discussed in recent years (and has also led to radical changes in the political equilibrium in Italy), relates a good deal to the somewhat dualist nature of the Italian economy, with elements of "underdevelopment" in some parts of the economy and the most dynamic capitalism elsewhere in the same economy.

In the economic difficulties experienced in the former Soviet Union and countries in Eastern Europe, the absence of institutional structures and behavioral codes that are central to successful capitalism has been particularly important. There is need for the development of an alternative system of institutions and codes with its own logic and loyalties that may be quite standard in the evolved capitalist economies, but that are relatively hard to install suddenly as a part of "planned capitalism." Such changes can take quite some time to function—a lesson that is currently being learned rather painfully in the former Soviet Union and in parts of Eastern Europe. The importance of institutions and behavioral experiences was rather eclipsed there in the first flush of enthusiasm about the magic of allegedly automatic market processes.

The need for institutional developments has some clear connection with the role of codes of behavior, since institutions based on interpersonal arrangements and shared understandings operate on the basis of common behavior patterns, mutual trust and confidence in the other party's ethics. The reliance on rules of behavior may typically be implicit rather than explicit—indeed so implicit that its importance can be easily overlooked in situations where such confidence is not problematic. But wherever it *is* problematic, overlooking the need for it can be quite disastrous. The emergence of Mafia-style operations in the former Soviet Union has recently received some attention, but to deal with this issue we have to examine its behavioral antecedents, including Adam Smith's analysis of the far-reaching role of "the established rules of behaviour."

## VARIATIONS OF NORMS AND INSTITUTIONS WITHIN THE MARKET ECONOMY

Behavioral codes vary even among the developed capitalist economies, and so does their effectiveness in promoting economic performance. While capitalism has been very successful in radically enhancing output and raising productivity in the modern world, it is still the case that the experiences of different countries are quite diverse. The successes of East Asian economies (in recent decades), and most notably of Japan (stretching further back), raise important questions about the modeling of capitalism in traditional economic theory. To see capitalism as a system of pure profit maximization based on individual ownership of capital is to leave out much that has made the system so successful in raising output and in generating income.

Japan has frequently been seen as the greatest example of successful capitalism, and despite the longish period of recent recession and financial turmoil, this diagnosis is unlikely to be completely washed away. However, the motivation pattern that dominates Japanese business has much more content than would be provided by pure profit maximization. Different commentators have emphasized distinct motivational features in Japan. Michio Morishima has outlined the special characteristics of the "Japanese ethos" as emerging from particular features of the history of Japan and its tendency toward rule-based behavior patterns.[22] Ronald Dore and Robert Wade have identified the influence of "Confucian ethics."[23] Masahiko Aoki has seen cooperation and behavioral codes in terms that are more responsive to strategic reasoning.[24] Kotaro Suzumura has emphasized the combination of commitment with a competitive atmosphere and reasoned public policy.[25] Eiko Ikegami has stressed the influence of Samurai culture.[26] There are other behavior-based accounts as well.

Indeed, there is some truth even in the apparently puzzling claim made in *The Wall Street Journal* that Japan is "the only communist nation that works."[27] That enigmatic remark points to the nonprofit motivations underlying many economic and business activities in Japan. We have to understand and interpret the peculiar fact that one of the most successful capitalist nations in the world flourishes economically with a motivation structure that departs, in some significant spheres, from the simple pursuit of self-interest, which—we have been told—is the bedrock of capitalism.

Japan does not, by any means, provide the only example of a special business ethics in promoting capitalist success. The merits of selfless work and devotion to enterprise in raising productivity have been seen as important for economic achievements in many countries in the world, and there are many variations in these behavioral codes even among the most developed industrial nations.

## INSTITUTIONS, BEHAVIORAL NORMS AND THE MAFIA

To conclude the discussion of different aspects of the role of values in capitalist success, we must see the system of ethics underlying capitalism as involving a good deal more than sanctifying greed and admiring cupidity. The success of capitalism in transforming the general level of economic prosperity in the world has drawn on morals and codes of behavior that have made market transactions economical and effective. In making use of the opportunities offered by the market mechanism and greater use of trade and exchange, the developing countries have to pay attention not only to the virtues of prudential behavior, but also to the role of complementary values, such as the making and sustaining of trust, avoiding the temptations of pervasive corruption, and making assurance a workable substitute for punitive legal enforcement. In the history of capitalism there have been significant variations within the basic capitalist behavioral codes, with divergent achievements and experiences, and there are things to be learned there as well.

The big challenges that capitalism now faces in the contemporary world include issues of inequality (especially that of grinding poverty in a world of unprecedented prosperity) and of "public goods" (that is, goods that people share together, such as the environment). The solution to these problems will almost certainly call for institutions that take us beyond the capitalist market economy. But the reach of the capitalist market economy itself is, in many ways, extendable by an appropriate development of ethics sensitive to these concerns. The compatibility of the market mechanism with a wide range of values is an important question, and it has to be faced along with exploring the extension of institutional arrangements beyond the limits of the pure market mechanism.

Problems related to behavioral codes that have received most attention in recent deliberations include economic corruption and its links with organized crime. In Italian discussions on this subject, the role of what have been called "deontological codes" has been much invoked in public discussions. The possible use of such codes of honor and of duty in combatting illegal and unfair procedures in influencing public policy has received attention, and this line of remedy has been considered even as a way of reducing the hold of the Mafia on government operations.[28]

There are social functions that an organization like the Mafia can perform in relatively primitive parts of the economy, in supporting mutually beneficial transactions. The functional roles of such organizations depend greatly on the actual behavioral modes in the legal and above-the-counter economy. One example is the part played by such organizations in ensuring the enforcement of contracts and deals, as Stefano Zamagni and others have discussed.[29] The market system requires arrangements for implementation, to stop a contracting party from letting others down. Such enforcement can either come from the law and its implementation, or—alternatively—be based on mutual trust and an implicit sense of obligation.[30] Since the effective reach of the government can be limited and slow in this field, many business transactions proceed on the basis of trust and honor.

When, however, the standards of market ethics are not yet established, and feelings of business trust are not well developed, contracts may be hard to sustain. In such circumstances, an outside organization can deal with the breach and provide a socially valued service in the form of strong-arm enforcement. An organization like the Mafia can play a functional role here and can receive appreciation in precapitalist economies being drawn rapidly into capitalist transactions. Depending on the nature of the interrelations, enforcement of this type may end up being useful for different parties, many of which have no interest at all in corruption or crime. Each contracting party may simply need the "assurance" that the other economic agents are also doing the appropriate thing.[31]

The part played by enforcement organizations to generate such "assurance" depends on the absence of behavioral codes that would reduce the need for such external enforcement. The enforcing function of extralegal organizations would shrink with an increase in trusting and trust-generating behavior. The complementarity between behavioral norms and institutional reform can, thus, be very close indeed.[32] This is a very general issue to consider in dealing with the hold of Mafia-like organizations, especially in some backward economies.

While the Mafia is a detestable organization, we have to understand the economic basis of its influence by supplementing the recognition of the power of guns and bombs with an understanding of some economic activities that make the Mafia a functionally relevant part of the economy. That functional attraction would cease as and when the combined influences of legal enforcement of contracts and behavioral conformity related to mutual trust and normative codes make the Mafia's role in this field quite redundant. There is thus a general connection between the limited emergence of business norms and the hold of organized crime in such economies.

## ENVIRONMENT, REGULATIONS AND VALUES

The need to go beyond market rules has been much discussed recently in the context of environmental protection. There have been some arrangements—and many proposals—of governmental regulations as well as provision of appropriate incentives through taxes and subsidies. But there is also an issue of ethical behavior, related to environment-friendly norms. This question fits right into the type of considerations that Adam Smith discussed extensively in *The Theory of Moral Sentiments,* though the protection of the environment was not a specific problem that had been prominent at that time (nor one to which Smith had paid much explicit attention).

There is also a connection here, as was discussed earlier (in chapter 5), with Smith's deep worry about the wastefulness that results from activities of "prodigals and projectors." He had sought to reduce the influence of wasteful investment through the control of interest rates, since he was afraid of the wasteful investor's greater ability to offer high interest without being able to do much good to the life on this planet.[33] Smith had linked his support for intervention with the need to control usury—a recommendation for which Jeremy Bentham took him to task.[34]

The modern-day "prodigals and projectors" are involved in fouling the air and the waters, and Smith's general analysis has much relevance to understanding the problems and difficulties they generate as well as the different lines of remedy that may exist. The respective roles of regulation and behavioral restraints are important to discuss in this context. The environmental challenge is part of a more general problem related to resource allocation involving "public goods," where the commodity is enjoyed in common rather than separately by one consumer only. For efficient provision of public goods, not only do we have to consider the possibility of state action and social provisioning, we also have to examine the part that can be played by the development of social values and of a sense of responsibility that may reduce the need for forceful state action. For example, the development of environmental ethics can do some of the job that is proposed to be done through compelling regulation.

## PRUDENCE, SYMPATHY AND COMMITMENT

In some of the literature in economics and politics (but less often in philosophy), the term "rational choice" is used, with breathtaking simplicity, for the discipline of systematic choice based exclusively on personal advantage. If personal advantage is narrowly defined, then this type of "rational" modeling would make it hard to expect that considerations of ethics, or justice, or the interest of future generations will have much role in our choices and actions.

Should rationality be so narrowly characterized? If rational behavior includes canny advancement of our objectives, there is no reason why the canny pursuit of sympathy, or canny promotion of justice, cannot be seen as exercises in rational choice. In departing from narrowly self-interested behavior, it is convenient to distinguish between two different routes of departure, viz., "sympathy" and "commitment."[35] First, our conception of self-interest may itself include our concern for others, and sympathy may thus be incorporated within the notion of the person's own well-being, broadly defined. Second, going beyond our broadly defined well-being or self-interest, we may be willing to make sacrifices in pursuit of other values, such as social justice or nationalism or communal welfare (even at some personal cost). This kind of departure, involving *commitment* (rather than just *sympathy*), invokes values other than personal well-being or self-interest (including the self-interest involved in promoting the interests of those with whom we sympathize).

The distinction can be illustrated with an example. If you help a destitute person because his destitution makes you very unhappy, that would be a sympathy-based action. If, however, the presence of the destitute does not make you particularly unhappy, but does fill you with the determination to change a system that you think is unjust (or more generally, your determination is not fully explainable by the unhappiness that the presence of the destitute creates), then this would be a commitment-based action.

There is, in an important sense, no sacrifice of self-interest, or of well-being, involved in being responsive to our sympathies. Helping a destitute may make you better off if you suffer at his suffering. Committed behavior may, however, involve self-sacrifice, since the reason for your attempt to help is your sense of injustice, rather than your desire to relieve your own sympathetic suffering. Nevertheless, there is still an element of one's "self" involved in the pursuit of one's commitments, since the commitments are one's own. More important, even though committed behavior may or may not be conducive to the promotion of one's personal advantage (or well-being), such a pursuit need not involve any denial of the person's rational will.[36]

Adam Smith discussed the need for both kinds of departures. "The most humane actions," he argued, "require no self-denial, no self-command, no great exertion of the sense of propriety," since they follow what our "sympathy would of its own accord prompt us to do."[37] "But it is otherwise with generosity." And so it is with broader values such as justice, which require the person to restrain his self-interest and "make the impartial spectator enter into the principles of his conduct" and may call for "greater exertions of public spirit."[38]

Crucial to Smith's view of "propriety of humanity and justice" is "the concord between the affections of the agent and those of the spectators."[39] Smith's conception of the rational person places this person firmly in the company of others—right in the middle of a society to which he belongs. The person's evaluations as well as actions invoke the presence of others, and the individual is not dissociated from "the public."

In this context it is important to dispute the common description of Adam Smith—the father of modern economics—as the single-minded prophet of self-interest. There is quite a well-established tradition in economics (and indeed in general public discussion) of taking Smith to have seen only self-interest in the rational world (and to have been happy with what he had allegedly seen). This is done by choosing some passages—usually one (the baker-brewer-butcher statement, quoted earlier)—from his vast writings. This has given currency to a very distorted view of Smith, which is summarized by George Stigler (otherwise a fine author and economist) as: "self-interest dominates the majority of men."[40]

It is certainly true that Smith did argue in that particular passage, which has been quoted incredibly often (sometimes quite out of context), that we do not need to invoke "benevolence" to explain why the butcher, the brewer or the baker *wants* to sell his products to us, and why we *want* to buy his products.[41] Smith was clearly right to point out that the *motivation* for mutually beneficial exchange certainly does not need anything more than what Smith called "self-love," and this is decidedly important to note, since exchange is so central to economic analysis. But in dealing with other problems—those of distribution and equity and of rule-following for generating productive efficiency—Smith emphasized broader motivations. In these broader contexts, while prudence remained "of all virtues that which is most helpful to the individual," he explained why "humanity, generosity, and public spirit, are the qualities most useful to others."[42] The variety of motivations that we have reason to accommodate is, in fact, quite central to Smith's remarkably rich analysis of human behavior. This is very distant from George Stigler's Smith, and far from the caricature of Smith as the big guru of self-interest. We can say by twisting Shakespeare a little, that while some men are born small and some achieve smallness, Adam Smith has had much smallness thrust upon him.[43]

What is at issue here is what our great contemporary philosopher John Rawls has called the "moral powers" shared by us: "a capacity for a sense of justice and for a conception of the good." Rawls sees the presumption of these shared powers as central to "the tradition of democratic thought," along with "powers of reason (of judgment, thought, and inference connected with these powers)."[44] In fact, the role of values is extensive in human behavior, and to deny this would amount not only to a departure from the tradition of democratic thought, but also to the limiting of our rationality. It is the power of reason that allows us to consider our obligations and ideals as well as our interests and advantages. To deny this freedom of thought would amount to a severe constraint on the reach of our rationality.

## MOTIVATIONAL CHOICE
## AND EVOLUTIONARY SURVIVAL

In assessing the demands of rational behavior, it is also important to go beyond the immediate choice of isolated objectives to the emergence and endurance of objectives through their effectiveness and survival. Recent works on the formation of preferences, and the role of evolution in that formation, have tended to broaden very substantially the scope and coverage of rational choice theory.[45] Even if *ultimately* no individual has a direct reason to be concerned with justice and ethics, these considerations may be instrumentally important for economic success, and may, through that advantage, survive better than their rivals, in social rules of behavior.

This type of "derived" reasoning can be contrasted with behavioral rules being deliberately chosen by an individual through an ethical examination of how one "should" act (as was famously explored, for example, by Immanuel Kant and Adam Smith).[46] The ethical reasons for a "direct"—rather than derived—concern for justice and altruism have been pursued in different forms in modern ethical writings as well. Practical ethics of behavior incorporate, in addition to purely moral concerns, various influences of a social and psychological nature, including norms and mores of some complexity.[47]

Considerations of justice can be accommodated in our deliberations *both* for "direct" and for "derived" reasons, and they need not necessarily be seen as "alternatives." Even if behavioral norms and concerns emerge on ethical or social or psychological grounds, their long-run survival can scarcely be independent of their consequences and of the evolutionary processes that may come into play. On the other side, in studying evolutionary selection within a broad framework, there is no need to confine the admission of non-self-interested behavior *only* to evolutionary selection, with no independent role of rational deliberation. It is possible to combine deliberative and evolutionary selection of committed behavior within one integrated framework.[48]

The values that influence us may emerge in quite different ways. First, they may come from *reflection and analysis*. The reflections may relate directly with our concerns and responsibilities (as Kant and Smith both emphasized), or indirectly with the effects of good behavior (for example, the advantages of having a good reputation and of encouraging trust).

Second, they may arise from our willingness to *follow convention*, and to think and act in ways that the established mores suggest we do.[49] This type of "concordant behavior" can extend the reach of reasoning beyond the limits of the individual's own critical assessment, since we can emulate what others have found reasons to do.[50]

Third, *public discussion* can have a strong influence on value formation. As Frank Knight—the great Chicago economist—noted, values "are established or validated and recognized through discussion, an activity which is at once social, intellectual, and creative."[51] In the context of public choice, James Buchanan has pointed out: "The definition of democracy as 'government by discussion' implies that individual values can and do change in the process of decision-making."[52]

Fourth, a crucial role may be played by *evolutionary selection*. Behavior patterns can survive and flourish because of their consequential role. Each of these categories of behavioral choice (reflective choice, concordant behavior, public discussion, and evolutionary selection) demands attention, and in conceptualizing human behavior there is a case for treating them jointly as well as severally. The role of values in social behavior fits into this broad network.

## ETHICAL VALUES AND POLICY MAKING

I turn now from the discussion of the ethics and norms of people in general to the values relevant in the making of public policy. Policy makers have two distinct, though interrelated, sets of reasons for taking an interest in the values of social justice. The first—and the more immediate—reason is that justice is a central concept in identifying the aims and objectives of public policy and also in deciding on the instruments that are appropriate in pursuing the chosen ends. Ideas of justice, and in particular the informational bases of particular approaches to justice (discussed in chapter 3), can be particularly crucial for the cogency and reach of public policy.

The second—more indirect—reason is that all public policies are dependent on how individuals and groups in the society behave. These behaviors are influenced, inter alia, by the understanding and interpretation of the demands of social ethics. For the making of public policy it is important not only to assess the demands of justice and the reach of values in choosing the objectives and priorities of public policy, but also to understand the values of the public at large, including their sense of justice.

Since the latter (more indirect) role of juridical concepts is probably more complex (and certainly less often analyzed), it may be useful to illustrate the role that norms and ideas of justice play in the determination of behavior and conduct, and how that can influence the direction of public policy. In discussing the influence of norms of fertility behavior (in chapter 8 and 9), the connection was already illustrated earlier, but I consider now another important example: the prevalence of corruption.

## CORRUPTION, INCENTIVES AND BUSINESS ETHICS

The prevalence of corruption is rightly regarded as one of the major stumbling blocks in the path to successful economic progress, for example in many Asian and African countries. A high level of corruption can make public policies ineffective and can also draw investment and economic activities away from productive pursuits toward the towering rewards of underhanded activities. It can also lead—as was discussed earlier—to the fostering of violent organizations such as the Mafia.

Corruption is not, however, a new phenomenon, nor are proposals for dealing with it. Ancient civilizations provide evidence of widespread illegality and corruption. Some produced considerable literature on ways of reducing corruption, especially of public officials. Indeed, we can get from this historical literature some insight on ways of preventing corruption today.

What, then, *is* "corrupt" behavior? Corruption involves the violation of established rules for personal gain and profit. Obviously it cannot be eradicated by inducing people to be *more* self-interested. Nor would it make sense to try to reduce corruption simply by asking people to be *less* self-interested in general—there has to be a specific reason to sacrifice personal gain.

It is, to some extent, possible to alter the balance of gains and losses from corrupt behavior through organizational reform. First, systems of inspection and penalty have figured prominently, through the ages, in the proposed rules for preventing corruption. For example, the Indian political analyst Kautilya, in the fourth century B.C., carefully distinguished between forty different ways in which a public servant can be tempted to be financially corrupt and described how a system of spot checks followed by penalties and rewards could prevent these activities.[53] Clear systems of rules and penalties, along with rigorous enforcement, can make a difference to behavior patterns.

Second, some regulational regimes encourage corruption by giving discretionary power to the officers who can grant favor to others—businessmen in particular—that may be worth a lot of money to them. The overcontrolled economy (the "license Raj," as the system is called in India) is an ideal breeding ground for corruption, as the experience of South Asia particularly demonstrates. Even if such regimes were not counterproductive in other respects as well (as they frequently are), the social cost of corruption can be reason enough to shun such arrangements.

Third, the temptation to be corrupt is strongest when the officers have a lot of power but are themselves relatively poor. This is the case at lower levels of administration in many overcontrolled economies, and explains why corruption reaches down all the way in the bureaucratic system, encompassing petty officers as well as senior administrators. Partly to deal with this problem, many bureaucrats in ancient China were paid a "corruption-preventing allowance" (called *yang-lien*) to give them incentive to remain clean and law-abiding.[54]

These and other inducements can have effectiveness, but it is hard to make the prevention of corruption turn entirely on financial incentives. Indeed, each of the three lines of attack just outlined has its own limitation. First, systems of catching thieves often do not work, since supervision and inspection are not always effective. There is also the complex issue of providing the right incentives for thief-catchers (so that they are not bought off). Second, any system of governance cannot but give some power to the officers that is worth something to others who may try to offer inducements for corruption. The reach of such power can certainly be reduced, but any substantive executive power can be potentially open to abuse. Third, even rich officers often try to make themselves richer still, and do so at some risk, which may be worth it if the stakes are high. There have been plenty of examples of this in recent years from different countries.

These limitations should not prevent us from doing what can be done to make the organizational changes effective, but an exclusive reliance on incentives based on personal gain cannot fully eliminate corruption. Indeed, in societies in which corrupt behavior of the standard type is quite unusual, the reliance is, to a great extent, on compliance with codes of behavior rather than on financial incentive to be noncorrupt. This forces attention on the norms and modes of behavior that respectively prevail in different societies.

Plato suggested in the *Laws* that a strong sense of duty would help to prevent corruption. But he also noted, wisely, that this would be "no easy task." What is at issue is not just the general sense of dutifulness, but the particular attitude to rules and conformity, which has a direct bearing on corruption. All this comes under the general rubric of what Adam Smith called "propriety." Giving priority to rules of honest and upright behavior can certainly be among the values that a person respects. And there are many societies in which respect for such rules provides a bulwark against corruption. Indeed, intercultural variations in rule-based behavior are among the most striking diversities in the contemporary world, whether we contrast business modes between Western Europe and South or Southeast Asia, or (*within* Western Europe) between Switzerland and parts of Italy.

Modes of behavior are not, however, immutable. How people behave often depends on how they see—and perceive—others as behaving. Much depends, therefore, on the reading of prevailing behavioral norms. A sense of "relative justice" vis-à-vis a comparison group (in particular, others similarly placed) can be an important influence on behavior. Indeed, the argument that "others do the same" was one of the more commonly cited "reasons" for corrupt behavior found in the Italian parliamentary inquiry that looked into the linkage between corruption and the Mafia in 1993.[55]

The importance of imitation—and of following established "conventions"—has been emphasized by those commentators who felt moved to study the bearing of "moral sentiments" on social, political and economic life. Adam Smith noted:

> Many men behave very decently, and through the whole of their lives avoid any considerable degree of blame, who yet, perhaps, never felt the sentiment upon the propriety of which we found our approbation of their conduct, but *acted merely from a regard to what they saw were the established rules of behaviour.*[56]

In the reading of "established rules of behaviour," importance may be particularly attached to the conduct of people in positions of power and authority. This makes the behavior of senior civil servants especially important in installing norms of conduct. Indeed, writing in China in 122 B.C., the authors of *Hui-nan Tzu* put the problem thus:

> If the measuring line is true, then the wood will be straight, not because one makes a special effort, but because that which it is "ruled" by makes it so. In the same way if the ruler is sincere and upright, then honest officials will serve in his government and scoundrels will go into hiding, but if the ruler is not upright, then evil men will have their way and loyal men will retire to seclusion.[57]

There is, I believe, sense in this piece of ancient wisdom. Corrupt behavior in "high places" can have effects far beyond the direct consequences of that behavior, and the insistence on starting at the top does have reasoning behind it.

I am not trying to propose here an "algorithm" for eliminating corruption. There are grounds for paying special attention to the possibility of altering the balance of gains and losses through organizational reforms such as those discussed earlier. But there is also room for addressing the climate of norms and behavioral modes, in which imitation and a sense of "relative justice" can play an important part. Justice among thieves may not look like "justice" to others (just as "honor among thieves" may not seem particularly honorable), but it certainly can have that appearance to the protagonists.

For a fuller understanding of the challenge of corruption, we have to drop the presumption that only personal profits move people, and values and norms simply do not count. They do count, as is well illustrated by the variation of behavioral modes in different societies. There is room for change, and some of it can cumulate as well as disseminate. Just as the presence of corrupt behavior encourages other corrupt behavior, the diminution of the hold of corruption can weaken it further. In trying to alter a climate of conduct, it is encouraging to bear in mind the fact that each vicious circle entails a virtuous circle if the direction is reversed.

## CONCLUDING REMARKS

This chapter began with scrutinizing some arguments for skepticism of the idea of reasoned social progress—an idea that is quite central to the approach presented in this book. One argument questions the possibility of rational social choice, invoking in particular Kenneth Arrow's well-known "impossibility theorem." It turns out, however, that what is at issue is not the possibility of rational social choice, but the use of an adequate informational base for social judgments and decisions. That is an important understanding, but it is not a pessimistic one. Indeed, the critical role of informational bases was discussed in earlier chapters as well (particularly in chapter 3), and the issue of adequacy has to be appropriately assessed in that light.

The second argument expresses skepticism of thinking in terms of intended consequences and focuses instead on the overwhelming importance of "unintended" effects. There is something to be learned from this skepticism as well. However, the main lesson is not the futility of rational assessment of social options, but the need to anticipate the *unintended but predictable* consequences. It is a question of not being overwhelmed by the force of intention, and also of not ignoring the so-called side effects. The empirical illustrations—several of them from the experiences of China—indicate why the failure is not one of causal untractability, but of sticking to a partial vision. Sensible reasoning has to demand more.

The third argument relates to the understanding of motivations. It takes the form of arguing that human beings are uncompromisingly self-centered and self-interested, and given that presumption, the point is sometimes made that the only system that can work effectively is just the capitalist market economy. However, this view of human motivation is not easy to sustain in terms of empirical observations. Nor is it correct to conclude that the success of capitalism as an economic system depends only on self-interested behavior, rather than on a complex and sophisticated value system that has many other ingredients, including reliability, trust, and business honesty (in the face of contrary temptations). Every economic system makes some demands of behavioral ethics, and capitalism is no exception. And values do have very considerable reach in influencing the behavior of individuals.

In emphasizing the possible role of values and norms in individual behavior, it is not my intention to argue that most people are moved more by their sense of justice than by their prudential and material concerns. Far from it. In making predictions of behavior—whether in personal work, private business, or public services—it is important to avoid the error of assuming that people are peculiarly virtuous and desperately keen to be just. Indeed, many well-meant planning exercises in the past have come to grief through overreliance on selfless individual conduct. In recognizing the role of broader values, we must not fail to note the extensive role of intelligent self-seeking, as well as of gross cupidity and greed.

It is a question of having a balance in our behavioral assumptions. We must not fall for the "high-minded sentimentality" of presuming that everyone is intensely moral and value-driven. Nor must we replace that unreal assumption by the equally unreal opposite assumption—what can be called "low-minded sentimentality." This presumption, which some economists seem to prefer, takes the form of assuming that we are not at all influenced by values (only by crude considerations of personal advantage).[58] Whether we deal with "work ethics," or "business morality," or "corruption," or "public responsibility," or "environmental values," or "gender equity," or ideas of "the right family size," we have to take note of variations—and changeability—in priorities and norms. In analyzing issues of efficiency and equity, or the removal of poverty and subjugation, the role of values cannot but be crucial.

The purpose of the empirical discussions involving corruption (and earlier on, fertility behavior) is not merely to examine issues that are important in themselves, but also to illustrate the significance of norms and values in behavior patterns that may be crucial for the making of public policy. The illustrations also serve to outline the role of public interaction in the formation of values and ideas of justice. In the making of public policy the agency of "the public" has to be considered in different perspectives. The empirical connections not only illustrate the reach of concepts of justice and morality that people entertain, but also point to the extent to which value formation is a social process involving public interactions.

It is clear that we have good reason to pay special attention to creating conditions for more informed understanding and enlightened public discussion. This has some strong policy implications; for example, those that relate to the freedom of thought and action of young women, especially through expanding literacy and school education and through the enhancement of women's employment, earning ability and economic empowerment (as discussed in chapters 8 and 9). There is also a big role for freedom of the press and the media, in their ability to take up these issues on an extensive basis.

The crucial function of public discussions is sometimes only partially recognized. In China, despite the control over the press in other respects, issues of family size have been widely discussed, and the emergence of a different set of norms regarding family size has been actively sought by public leaders. But similar considerations apply to many other areas of economic and social change, in which, too, open public discussion can greatly help. The lines of permissibility (and of encouragement) in China reflect the priorities of state policy. There is, in fact, something of a conflict here, which remains unresolved. It is reflected in the oddities of partial success in the chosen areas. For example, a reduction of fertility rates in China has been accompanied by an accentuation of gender bias in infant mortality and a sharp increase in sex-selective abortions. A fertility-rate reduction that is achieved not through coercion but through a greater acceptance of gender justice (including, inter alia, the freedom of women not to be overwhelmed by overfrequent childbearing and -rearing) would suffer from less internal tension.

Public policy has a role not only in attempting to implement the priorities that emerge from social values and affirmations, but also in facilitating and guaranteeing fuller public discussion. The reach and quality of open discussions can be helped by a variety of public policies, such as press freedom and media independence (including the absence of censorship), expansion of basic education and schooling (including female education), enhancement of economic independence (especially through employment, including female employment), and other social and economic changes that help individuals to be participating citizens. Central to this approach is the idea of the public as an active participant in change, rather than as a passive and docile recipient of instructions or of dispensed assistance.

# CHAPTER 12

# INDIVIDUAL FREEDOM AS
# A SOCIAL COMMITMENT

Bertrand Russell, who was a firm atheist, was once asked what he would do if, following his death, he were to encounter God after all. Russell is supposed to have answered, "I will ask him: God Almighty, why did you give so little evidence of your existence?"[1] Certainly the appalling world in which we live does not—at least on the surface—look like one in which an all-powerful benevolence is having its way. It is hard to understand how a compassionate world order can include so many people afflicted by acute misery, persistent hunger and deprived and desperate lives, and why millions of innocent children have to die each year from lack of food or medical attention or social care.

This issue, of course, is not new, and it has been a subject of some discussion among theologians. The argument that God has reasons to want us to deal with these matters ourselves has had considerable intellectual support. As a nonreligious person, I am not in a position to assess the theological merits of this argument. But I can appreciate the force of the claim that people themselves must have responsibility for the development and change of the world in which they live. One does not have to be either devout or nondevout to accept this basic connection. As people who live—in a broad sense—together, we cannot escape the thought that the terrible occurrences that we see around us are quintessentially our problems. They are our responsibility—whether or not they are also anyone else's.

As competent human beings, we cannot shirk the task of judging how things are and what needs to be done. As reflective creatures, we have the ability to contemplate the lives of others. Our sense of responsibility need not relate only to the afflictions that our own behavior may have caused (though that can be very important as well), but can also relate more generally to the miseries that we see around us and that lie within our power to help remedy. That responsibility is not, of course, the only consideration that can claim our attention, but to deny the relevance of that general claim would be to miss something central about our social existence. It is not so much a matter of having exact rules about how precisely we ought to behave, as of recognizing the relevance of our shared humanity in making the choices we face.[2]

## INTERDEPENDENCE BETWEEN FREEDOM AND RESPONSIBILITY

That question of responsibility raises another. Shouldn't a person herself be entirely responsible for what happens to her? Why should others take responsibility for influencing her life? That thought, in one form or another, seems to move many political commentators, and the idea of self-help fits well into the mood of the present times. Going further, some argue that dependence on others is not only ethically problematic, it is also practically defeatist in sapping individual initiative and effort, and even self-respect. Who better to rely on than oneself to look after one's interests and problems?

The concerns that give force to this line of reasoning can indeed be very important. A division of responsibility that places the burden of looking after a person's interest on another person can lead to the loss of many important things in the form of motivation, involvement and self-knowledge that the person herself may be in a unique position to have. Any affirmation of social responsibility that *replaces* individual responsibility cannot but be, to varying extents, counterproductive. There is no substitute for individual responsibility.

The limited reach and plausibility of an exclusive reliance on personal responsibility can best be discussed only after its essential role has first been recognized. However, the substantive freedoms that we respectively enjoy to exercise our responsibilities are extremely contingent on personal, social, and environmental circumstances. A child who is denied the opportunity of elementary schooling is not only deprived as a youngster, but also handicapped all through life (as a person unable to do certain basic things that rely on reading, writing and arithmetic). The adult who lacks the means of having medical treatment for an ailment from which she suffers is not only prey to preventable morbidity and possibly escapable mortality, but may also be denied the freedom to do various things—for herself and for others—that she may wish to do as a responsible human being. The bonded laborer born into semislavery, the subjugated girl child stifled by a repressive society, the helpless landless laborer without substantial means of earning an income are all deprived not only in terms of well-being, but also in terms of the ability to lead responsible lives, which are contingent on having certain basic freedoms. Responsibility *requires* freedom.

The argument for social support in expanding people's freedom can, therefore, be seen as an argument *for* individual responsibility, not against it. The linkage between freedom and responsibility works both ways. Without the substantive freedom and capability to do something, a person cannot be responsible for doing it. But actually having the freedom and capability to do something does impose on the person the duty to consider whether to do it or not, and this does involve individual responsibility. In this sense, freedom is both necessary and sufficient for responsibility.

The alternative to an exclusive reliance on individual responsibility is not, as is sometimes assumed, the so-called nanny state. There is a difference between "nannying" an individual's choices and creating more opportunity for choice and for substantive decisions for individuals who can then act responsibly on that basis. The social commitment to individual freedom need not, of course, operate only through the state, but must also involve other institutions: political and social organizations, community-based arrangements, non-governmental agencies of various kinds, the media and other means of public understanding and communication, and the institutions that allow the functioning of markets and contractual relations. The arbitrarily narrow view of individual responsibility—with the individual standing on an imaginary island unhelped and unhindered by others—has to be broadened not merely by acknowledging the role of the state, but also by recognizing the functions of other institutions and agents.

## JUSTICE, FREEDOM AND RESPONSIBILITY

Central to the challenges we face in the contemporary world is our idea of an acceptable society. Why are some social arrangements hard to cherish? What can we do to make a society more tolerable? Underlying such ideas lie some theories of evaluation and—often implicitly—even some basic understanding of social justice. This is not, of course, the occasion to investigate theories of justice in any detail, which I have tried to do elsewhere.[3] I have, however, used in this work some general evaluative ideas (briefly discussed in chapters 1–3) that make use of notions of justice and their informational requirements. It may be useful to examine the connection of those ideas with what has been discussed in the intermediate chapters.

First, I have argued for the primacy of substantive freedoms in judging individual advantage and in evaluating social achievements and failures. The perspective of freedom need not be merely procedural (though processes do matter, inter alia, in assessing what is going on). The basic concern, I have argued, is with our capability to lead the kind of lives we have reason to value.[4] This approach can give a very different view of development from the usual concentration on GNP or technical progress or industrialization, all of which have contingent and conditional importance without being the defining characteristics of development.[5]

Second, the freedom-oriented perspective can accommodate considerable variations within that general approach. Freedoms are inescapably of different kinds, and in particular there is the important distinction, already discussed, between the "opportunity aspect" and the "process aspect" of freedom (on this see the discussion in chapter 1). While these different constituent components of freedom often go together, sometimes they may not, and much will then depend on the relative weights that are placed on the different items.[6]

Also, a freedom-oriented approach can go with different emphases on the relative claims of efficiency and equity. There can be conflicts between (1) having less inequality of freedoms and (2) getting as much freedom as possible for all, irrespective of inequalities. The shared approach permits the formulation of a class of different theories of justice with the same general orientation. Of course, the conflict between equity-oriented and efficiency-oriented considerations is not "special" to the perspective of freedoms. It arises no matter whether we concentrate on freedoms or on some other way of judging individual advantage (for example by happiness or "utilities," or by "resources" or "primary goods" that the persons respectively have). In standard theories of justice this conflict is addressed by proposing some very specific formula, such as the utilitarian requirement to maximize the sum total of utilities irrespective of distribution, or the Rawlsian Difference Principle that requires maximizing the advantage of the worst off, no matter how this may affect the advantages of all others.[7]

In contrast, I have not argued for a specific formula to "settle" this question, and have concentrated instead on acknowledging the force and legitimacy of both aggregative and distributive concerns. That acknowledgment itself, along with the need to pay substantial attention to each of these concerns, draws our attention forcefully to the relevance of some basic but neglected issues in public policy, dealing with poverty, inequality and social performance *seen in the perspective of freedom*. The relevance of both aggregative and distributive judgments in assessing the process of development is quite central to understanding the challenge of development. But this does not require us to rank all development experiences in one linear order. What is, in contrast, indispensably important is an adequate understanding of the informational basis of evaluation—the kind of information we need to examine in order to assess what is going on and what is being seriously neglected.

In fact, as discussed in chapter 3 (and elsewhere[8]) at the level of the pure theory of justice, it would be a mistake to lock prematurely into one specific system for "weighting" some of these competitive concerns, which would severely restrict the room for democratic decision making in this crucial resolution (and more generally in "social choice," including the variety of processes that relate to participation). Foundational ideas of justice can separate out some basic issues as being inescapably relevant, but they cannot plausibly end up, I have argued, with an exclusive choice of some highly delineated formula of relative weights as being the unique blueprint for "the just society."⁹

For example, a society that allows famines to occur when prevention is possible is unjust in a clearly significant way, but that diagnosis does not have to rest on a belief that some unique pattern of distribution of food, or of income, or of entitlements, among all the people in the country, will be maximally just, trailed by other exact distributions (all completely ordered vis-à-vis one another). The greatest relevance of ideas of justice lies in the identification of *patent injustice,* on which reasoned agreement is possible, rather than in the derivation of some extant formula for how the world should be precisely run.

Third, even as far as patent injustice is concerned, no matter how inescapable it may look in terms of foundational ethical arguments, the emergence of a shared recognition of that "injustice" may be dependent in practice on open discussion of issues and feasibilities. Extreme inequalities in matters of race, gender, and class often survive on the implicit understanding—to use a phrase that Margaret Thatcher made popular (in a different but somewhat related context)—that "there is no alternative." For example, in societies in which antifemale bias has flourished and been taken for granted, the understanding that this is not inevitable may itself require empirical knowledge as well as analytical arguments, and in many cases, this can be a laborious and challenging process.¹⁰ The role of public discussion to debate conventional wisdom on both practicalities and valuations can be central to the acknowledgment of injustice.

Given the role that public debates and discussions must have in the formation and utilization of our social values (dealing with competing claims of different principles and criteria), basic civil rights and political freedoms are indispensable for the emergence of social values. Indeed, the freedom to participate in critical evaluation and in the process of value formation is among the most crucial freedoms of social existence. The choice of social values cannot be settled merely by the pronouncements of those in authority who control the levers of government. As was discussed earlier (in the introduction and chapter 1), we must see a frequently asked question in the development literature to be fundamentally misdirected: Do democracy and basic political and civil rights help to promote the process of development? Rather, the emergence and consolidation of these rights can be seen as being *constitutive* of the process of development.

This point is quite separate from the *instrumental* role of democracy and basic political rights in providing security and protection to vulnerable groups. The exercise of these rights can indeed help in making states more responsive to the predicament of vulnerable people and, thus, contribute to preventing economic disasters such as famines. But going beyond that, the general enhancement of political and civil freedoms is central to the process of development itself. The relevant freedoms include the liberty of acting as citizens who matter and whose voices count, rather than living as well-fed, well-clothed, and well-entertained vassals. The instrumental role of democracy and human rights, important as it undoubtedly is, has to be distinguished from its constitutive importance.

Fourth, an approach to justice and development that concentrates on substantive freedoms inescapably focuses on the agency and judgment of individuals; they cannot be seen merely as patients to whom benefits will be dispensed by the process of development. Responsible adults must be in charge of their own well-being; it is for them to decide how to use their capabilities. But the capabilities that a person does actually have (and not merely theoretically enjoys) depend on the nature of social arrangements, which can be crucial for individual freedoms. And there the state and the society cannot escape responsibility.

It is, for example, a shared responsibility of the society that the system of labor bondage, where prevalent, should end, and that bonded laborers should be free to accept employment elsewhere. It is also a social responsibility that economic policies should be geared to providing widespread employment opportunities on which the economic and social viability of people may crucially depend. But it is, ultimately, an individual responsibility to decide what use to make of the opportunities of employment and what work options to choose. Similarly, the denial of opportunities of basic education to a child, or of essential health care to the ill, is a failure of social responsibility, but the exact utilization of the educational attainments or of health achievements cannot but be a matter for the person herself to determine.

Also, the empowerment of women, through employment opportunities, educational arrangements, property rights and so on, can give women more freedom to influence a variety of matters such as intrafamily division of health care, food and other commodities, and work arrangements as well as fertility rates, but the exercise of that enhanced freedom is ultimately a matter for the person herself. The fact that statistical predictions can often be plausibly made on the ways this freedom is likely to be used (for example, in predicting that female education and female employment opportunity would reduce fertility rates and the frequency of childbearing) does not negate the fact that it is the exercise of the women's enhanced freedom that is being anticipated.

## WHAT DIFFERENCE DOES FREEDOM MAKE?

The perspective of freedom, on which this study has concentrated, must not be seen as being hostile to the large literature on social change that has enriched our understanding of the process for many centuries. While parts of the recent development literature have tended to concentrate very much on some limited indicators of development such as the growth of GNP per head, there is quite a long tradition against being imprisoned in that little box. There have indeed been many broader voices, including that of Aristotle, whose ideas are of course among the sources on which the present analysis draws (with his clear diagnosis in *Nicomachean Ethics*: "wealth is evidently not the good we are seeking; for it is merely useful and for the sake of something else").[11] It applies also to such pioneers of "modern" economics as William Petty, the author of *Political Arithmetick* (1691), who supplemented his innovation of national income accounting with motivating discussions on much broader concerns.[12]

Indeed, the belief that the enhancement of freedom is ultimately an important motivating factor for assessing economic and social change is not at all new. Adam Smith was explicitly concerned with crucial human freedoms.[13] So was Karl Marx, in many of his writings, for example when he emphasized the importance of "replacing the domination of circumstances and chance over individuals by the domination of individuals over chance and circumstances."[14] The protection and enhancement of liberty supplemented John Stuart Mill's utilitarian perspective very substantially, and so did his specific outrage at the denial of substantive freedoms to women.[15] Friedrich Hayek has been emphatic in placing the achievement of economic progress within a very general formulation of liberties and freedoms, arguing: "Economic considerations are merely those by which we reconcile and adjust our different purposes, none of which, in the last resort, are economic (except those of the miser or the man for whom making money has become an end in itself)."[16]

Several development economists have also emphasized the importance of freedom of choice as a criterion of development. For example, Peter Bauer, who has quite a record of "dissent" in development economics (including an insightful book called *Dissent on Development*) has argued powerfully for the following characterization of development:

> I regard the extension of the range of choice, that is, an increase in the range of effective alternatives open to the people, as the principal objective and criterion of economic development; and I judge a measure principally by its probable effects on the range of alternatives open to individuals.[17]

W. A. Lewis also stated, in his famous opus *The Theory of Economic Growth,* that the objective of development is increasing "the range of human choice." However, after making this motivational point, Lewis decided, ultimately, to concentrate his analysis simply on "the growth of output per head," on the ground that this "gives man greater control over his environment and thereby increases his freedom."[18] Certainly, other things given, an increase in output and income would expand the range of human choice—particularly over commodities purchased. But, as was discussed earlier, the range of substantive choice on valuable matters depends also on many other factors.

## WHY THE DIFFERENCE?

It is, in this context, important to ask whether there is really any substantial difference between development analysis that focuses (as Lewis and many others choose to do) on "the growth of output per head" (such as GNP per capita), and a more foundational concentration on expanding human freedom. Since the two are related (as Lewis rightly points out), why are the two approaches to development—inescapably linked as they are—not substantively congruent? What difference can a focal concentration on freedom make?

The differences arise for two rather distinct reasons, related respectively to the "process aspect" and the "opportunity aspect" of freedom. First, since freedom is concerned with *processes of decision making* as well as *opportunities to achieve valued outcomes,* the domain of our interest cannot be confined only to the outcomes in the form of the promotion of high output or income, or the generation of high consumption (or other variables to which the concept of economic growth relates). Such processes as participation in political decisions and social choice cannot be seen as being—at best—among the *means* to development (through, say, their contribution to economic growth), but have to be understood as constitutive parts of the *ends* of development in themselves.

The second reason for the difference between "development as freedom" and the more conventional perspectives on development relates to contrasts within the *opportunity aspect* itself, rather than being related to the process aspect. In pursuing the view of development as freedom, we have to examine—in addition to the freedoms involved in political, social and economic processes—the extent to which people have the opportunity to achieve outcomes that they value and have reason to value. The levels of real income that people enjoy are important in giving them corresponding opportunities to purchase goods and services and to enjoy living standards that go with those purchases. But as some of the empirical investigations presented earlier in this book showed, income levels may often be inadequate guides to such important matters as the freedom to live long, or the ability to escape avoidable morbidity, or the opportunity to have worthwhile employment, or to live in peaceful and crime-free communities. These non-income variables point to opportunities that a person has excellent reasons to value and that are not strictly linked with economic prosperity.

Thus, both the *process* aspect and the *opportunity* aspect of freedom require us to go well beyond the traditional view of development in terms of "the growth of output per head." There is also the fundamental difference in perspective in valuing freedom *only for* the use that is to be made of that freedom, and valuing it *over and above* that. Hayek may have overstated his case (as he often did) when he insisted that "the importance of our being free to do a particular thing has nothing to do with the question of whether we or the majority are ever likely to make use of that possibility."[19] But he was, I would argue, entirely right in distinguishing between (1) the *derivative* importance of freedom (dependent only on its actual use) and (2) the *intrinsic* importance of freedom (in making us free to choose something we may or may not actually choose).

Indeed, sometimes a person may have a very strong reason to have an option precisely for the purpose of rejecting it. For example, when Mahatma Gandhi *fasted* to make a political point against the Raj, he was not merely *starving,* he was rejecting the option of eating (for that is what fasting is). To be able to fast, Mohandas Gandhi had to have the option of eating (precisely to be able to reject it); a famine victim could not have made a similar political point.[20]

While I do not want to go down the purist route that Hayek chooses (in dissociating freedom from actual use altogether), I would emphasize that freedom has many aspects. The *process* aspect of freedom would have to be considered in addition to the *opportunity* aspect, and the opportunity aspect itself has to be viewed in terms of *intrinsic* as well as *derivative* importance. Furthermore, freedom to participate in public discussion and social interaction can also have a *constructive* role in the formation of values and ethics. Focusing on freedom does indeed make a difference.

## HUMAN CAPITAL
## AND HUMAN CAPABILITY

I must also briefly discuss another relation which invites a comment, to wit, the relation between the literature on "human capital" and the focus in this work on "human capability" as an expression of freedom. In contemporary economic analysis the emphasis has, to a considerable extent, shifted from seeing capital accumulation in primarily physical terms to viewing it as a process in which the productive quality of human beings is integrally involved. For example, through education, learning, and skill formation, people can become much more productive over time, and this contributes greatly to the process of economic expansion.[21] In recent studies of economic growth (often influenced by empirical readings of the experiences of Japan and the rest of East Asia as well as Europe and North America), there is a much greater emphasis on "human capital" than used to be the case not long ago.

How does this shift relate to the view of development—development as freedom—presented in this book? More particularly, what, we may ask, is the connection between "human capital" orientation and the emphasis on "human capability" with which this study has been much concerned? Both seem to place humanity at the center of attention, but do they have differences as well as some congruence? At the risk of some oversimplification, it can be said that the literature on human capital tends to concentrate on the agency of human beings in augmenting production possibilities. The perspective of human capability focuses, on the other hand, on the ability—the substantive freedom—of people to lead the lives they have reason to value and to enhance the real choices they have. The two perspectives cannot but be related, since both are concerned with the role of human beings, and in particular with the actual abilities that they achieve and acquire. But the yardstick of assessment concentrates on different achievements.

Given her personal characteristics, social background, economic circumstances and so on, a person has the ability to do (or be) certain things that she has reason to value. The reason for valuation can be *direct* (the functioning involved may directly enrich her life, such as being well-nourished or being healthy), or *indirect* (the functioning involved may contribute to further production, or command a price in the market). The human capital perspective can—in principle—be defined very broadly to cover both types of valuation, but it is typically defined—by convention—primarily in terms of indirect value: human qualities that can be employed as "capital" in *production* (in the way physical capital is). In this sense, the narrower view of the human capital approach fits into the more inclusive perspective of human capability, which can cover both direct and indirect consequences of human abilities.

Consider an example. If education makes a person more efficient in commodity production, then this is clearly an enhancement of human capital. This can add to the value of production in the economy and also to the income of the person who has been educated. But even with the same level of income, a person may benefit from education—in reading, communicating, arguing, in being able to choose in a more informed way, in being taken more seriously by others and so on. The benefits of education, thus, exceed its role as human capital in commodity production. The broader human-capability perspective would note—and value—these additional roles as well. The two perspectives are, thus, closely related but distinct.

The significant transformation that has occurred in recent years in giving greater recognition to the role of "human capital" is helpful for understanding the relevance of the capability perspective. If a person can become more productive in making commodities through better education, better health and so on, it is not unnatural to expect that she can, through these means, also directly achieve more—and have the freedom to achieve more—in leading her life.

The capability perspective involves, to some extent, a return to an integrated approach to economic and social development championed particularly by Adam Smith (both in the *Wealth of Nations* and in *The Theory of Moral Sentiments*). In analyzing the determination of production possibilities, Smith emphasized the role of education as well as division of labor, learning by doing and skill formation. But the development of human capability in leading a worthwhile life (as well as in being more productive) is quite central to Smith's analysis of "the wealth of nations."

Indeed, Adam Smith's belief in the power of education and learning was peculiarly strong. Regarding the debate that continues today on the respective roles of "nature" and "nurture," Smith was an uncompromising—and even a dogmatic—"nurturist." Indeed, this fitted in well with his massive confidence in the improvability of human capabilities:

> The difference of natural talents in different men is, in reality, much less than we are aware of; and the very different genius which appears to distinguish men of different professions, when grown up to maturity, is not upon many occasions so

much the cause, as the effect of division of labour. The difference between the most dissimilar characters, between a philosopher and a common street porter, for example, seems to arise not so much from nature, as from habit, custom, and education. When they came into the world, and for the first six or eight years of their existence, they were, perhaps, very much alike, and neither their parents nor play-fellows could perceive any remarkable difference.[22]

It is not my purpose here to examine whether Smith's emphatically nurturist views are right, but it is useful to see how closely he links *productive* abilities and *lifestyles* to education and training and presumes the improvability of each.[23] That connection is quite central to the reach of the capability perspective.[24]

There is, in fact, a crucial valuational difference between the human-capital focus and the concentration on human capabilities— a difference that relates to some extent to the distinction between means and ends. The acknowledgment of the role of human qualities in promoting and sustaining economic growth—momentous as it is—tells us nothing about *why* economic growth is sought in the first place. If, instead, the focus is, ultimately, on the expansion of human freedom to live the kind of lives that people have reason to value, then the role of economic growth in expanding these opportunities has to be integrated into that more foundational understanding of the process of development as the expansion of human capability to lead more worthwhile and more free lives.[25]

The distinction has a significant practical bearing on public policy. While economic prosperity helps people to have wider options and to lead more fulfilling lives, so do more education, better health care, finer medical attention, and other factors that causally influence the effective freedoms that people actually enjoy. These "social developments" must directly count as "developmental," since they help us to lead longer, freer and more fruitful lives, *in addition* to the role they have in promoting productivity or economic growth or individual incomes.[26] The use of the concept of "human capital," which concentrates only on one part of the picture (an important part, related to broadening the account of "productive resources"), is certainly an enriching move. But it does need supplementation. This is because human beings are not merely means of production, but also the end of the exercise.

Indeed, in arguing with David Hume, Adam Smith had the occasion to emphasize that to see human beings only in terms of their productive use is to slight the nature of humanity:

> . . . it seems impossible that the approbation of virtue should be of the same kind with that by which we approve of a convenient or a well-contrived building, or that we should have no other reason for praising a man than that for which we commend a chest of drawers.[27]

Despite the usefulness of the concept of human capital, it is important to see human beings in a broader perspective (breaking the analogy with "a chest of drawers"). We must go *beyond* the notion of human capital, after acknowledging its relevance and reach. The broadening that is needed is additional and inclusive, rather than, in any sense, an *alternative* to the "human capital" perspective.

It is important to take note also of the instrumental role of capability expansion in bringing about *social* change (going well beyond *economic* change). Indeed, the role of human beings even as instruments of change can go much beyond economic production (to which the perspective of "human capital" standardly points), and include social and political development. For example, as was discussed earlier, expansion of female education may reduce gender inequality in intrafamily distribution and also help to reduce fertility rates as well as child mortality rates. Expansion of basic education may also improve the quality of public debates. These instrumental achievements may be ultimately quite important—taking us well beyond the production of conventionally defined commodities.

In looking for a fuller understanding of the role of human capabilities, we have to take note of:

1) their *direct* relevance to the well-being and freedom of people;

2) their *indirect* role through influencing *social* change; and

3) their *indirect* role through influencing *economic* production.

The relevance of the capability perspective incorporates each of these contributions. In contrast, in the standard literature human capital is seen primarily in terms of the third of the three roles. There is a clear overlap of coverage, and it is indeed an important overlap. But there is also a strong need to go well beyond that rather limited and circumscribed role of human capital in understanding development as freedom.

## A FINAL REMARK

In this book I have tried to present, analyze and defend a particular approach to development, seen as a process of expanding substantive freedoms that people have. The perspective of freedom has been used both in the evaluative analysis for assessing change, and in the descriptive and predictive analysis in seeing freedom as a causally effective factor in generating rapid change.

I have also discussed the implications of this approach for policy analysis as well as for the understanding of general economic, political and social connections. A variety of social institutions—related to the operation of markets, administrations, legislatures, political parties, nongovernmental organizations, the judiciary, the media and the community in general—contribute to the process of development precisely through their effects on enhancing and sustaining individual freedoms. Analysis of development calls for an integrated understanding of the respective roles of these different institutions and their interactions. The formation of values and the emergence and evolution of social ethics are also part of the process of development that needs attention, along with the working of markets and other institutions. This study has been an attempt to understand and investigate this interrelated structure, and to draw lessons for development in that broad perspective.

It is a characteristic of freedom that it has diverse aspects that relate to a variety of activities and institutions. It cannot yield a view of development that translates readily into some simple "formula" of accumulation of capital, or opening up of markets, or having efficient economic planning (though each of these particular features fits into the broader picture). The organizing principle that places all the different bits and pieces into an integrated whole is the overarching concern with the process of enhancing individual freedoms and the social commitment to help to bring that about. That unity is important, but at the same time we cannot lose sight of the fact that freedom is an inherently diverse concept, which involves—as was discussed extensively—considerations of processes as well as substantive opportunities.

This diversity is not, however, a matter of regret. As William Cowper puts it:

> Freedom has a thousand charms to show,
> That slaves, howe'er contented, never know.

Development is indeed a momentous engagement with freedom's possibilities.

▼

## Chapter 1: *The Perspective of Freedom*

1. *Brihadaranyaka Upanishad* 2.4, 2–3.

2. Aristotle, *The Nicomachean Ethics*, translated by D. Ross (Oxford: Oxford University Press, revised edition, 1980), book 1, section 5, p. 7.

3. I have discussed, in earlier publications, different aspects of a freedom-centered view of social evaluation; on this see my "Equality of What?" in *Tanner Lectures on Human Values*, volume 1, edited by S. McMurrin (Cambridge: Cambridge University Press, 1980); *Choice, Welfare and Measurement* (Oxford: Blackwell; Cambridge, Mass.: MIT Press, 1982; republished, Cambridge, Mass.: Harvard University Press, 1997); *Resources, Values and Development* (Cambridge, Mass.: Harvard University Press, 1984); "Well-Being, Agency and Freedom: The Dewey Lectures 1984," *Journal of Philosophy* 82 (April 1985); *Inequality Reexamined* (Oxford: Clarendon Press; Cambridge, Mass.: Harvard University Press, 1992). See also Martha Nussbaum and Amartya Sen, eds., *The Quality of Life* (Oxford: Clarendon Press, 1993).

4. In my Kenneth Arrow Lectures, included in *Freedom, Rationality and Social Choice: Arrow Lectures and Other Essays* (Oxford: Clarendon Press, forthcoming). A number of technical issues in the assessment and evaluation of freedom are also examined in that analysis.

5. The evaluative and the operational reasons have been explored more fully in my "Rights and Agency," *Philosophy and Public Affairs* 11 (1982), reprinted in *Consequentialism and Its Critics*, edited by Samuel Scheffler; "Well-Being, Agency and Freedom"; *On Ethics and Economics* (Oxford: Blackwell, 1987).

6. The components correspond respectively to (1) the process aspect and (2) the opportunity aspect of freedom, which are analyzed in my Kenneth Arrow Lectures, included in *Freedom, Rationality and Social Choice*, cited earlier.

7. I have tried to discuss the issue of "targeting" in "The Political Economy of Targeting," keynote address to the 1992 Annual World Bank Conference on Development Economics, published in *Public Spending and the Poor: Theory and Evidence*, edited by Dominique van de Walle and Kimberly Nead (Baltimore: Johns Hopkins University Press, 1995). The issue of political freedom as a part of development is addressed in my "Freedoms and Needs," *New Republic*, January 10 and 17, 1994.

8. I have discussed this issue in "Missing Women," *British Medical Journal* 304 (1992).

9. These and other such comparisons are presented in my "The Economics of Life and Death," *Scientific American* 266 (April 1993), and "Demography and Welfare Economics," *Empirica* 22 (1995).

10. On this see my "Economics of Life and Death," and also the medical literature cited there. See also Jean Drèze and Amartya Sen, *Hunger and Public Action* (Oxford: Clarendon Press, 1989). On this general issue, see also M. F. Perutz, "Long Live the Queen's Subjects," *Philosophical Transactions of the Royal Society of London* 352 (1997).

11. This can be worked out from the background data used to make life expectancy calculations (for 1990), as presented in C.J.L. Murray, C. M. Michaud, M. T. McKenna and J. S. Marks, *U.S. Patterns of Mortality by County and Race: 1965–1994* (Cambridge, Mass.: Harvard Center for Population and Development Studies, 1998). See especially table 6d.

12. See Colin McCord and Harold P. Freeman, "Excess Mortality in Harlem," *New England Journal of Medicine* 322 (January 18, 1990); see also M. W. Owen, S. M. Teutsch, D. F. Williamson and J. S. Marks, "The Effects of Known Risk Factors on the Excess Mortality of Black Adults in the United States," *Journal of the American Medical Association* 263, no. 6 (February 9, 1990).

13. See Nussbaum and Sen, eds., *The Quality of Life* (1993).

14. See Martha Nussbaum, "Nature, Function and Capability: Aristotle on Political Distribution," *Oxford Studies in Ancient Philosophy* (1988; supplementary volume); see also Nussbaum and Sen, eds., *The Quality of Life* (1993).

15. See Adam Smith, *An Inquiry into the Nature and Causes of the Wealth of Nations* (1776), republished, edited by R. H. Campbell and A. S. Skinner (Oxford: Clarendon Press, 1976), volume 2, book 5, chapter 2 (section on "Taxes upon Consumable Commodities"), pp. 469–71.

16. These issues are discussed in my Tanner Lectures at Cambridge in 1985, published in *The Standard of Living,* edited by Geoffrey Hawthorn (Cambridge: Cambridge University Press, 1987).

17. Lagrange thus presented in the late eighteenth century what was probably the first analysis of what came to be known in our times as "the new view of consumption" (Kevin J. Lancaster, "A New Approach to Consumer Theory," *Journal of Political Economy* 74 [1996], and W. M. Gorman, "A Possible Procedure for Analysing Quality Differentials in the Egg Market," *Review of Economic Studies* 47 [1980]). These and related matters are discussed in my *The Standard of Living* (1987).

18. A distinguished exception is Robert Nozick, *Anarchy, State and Utopia* (New York: Basic Books, 1974).

19. This was mainly in the context of Adam Smith's support for legislation against "usury," and the need to control the turmoil that follows from the overindulgence of speculative investment by those whom Adam Smith called "prodigals and projectors." See Smith, *Wealth of Nations,* volume 1, book 2, chapter 4, paragraphs 14–15, in the edition of Campbell and Skinner (1976), pp. 356–7. The term "projector" is used by Smith not in the neutral sense of "one who forms a project," but in the pejorative sense, apparently common from 1616 (according to *The Shorter Oxford English Dictionary*), meaning, among other things, "a promoter of bubble companies; a speculator; a cheat." Giorgio Basevi has drawn my attention to some

interesting parallels between Smith's criticism and Jonathan Swift's unflattering portrayal of "projectors" in *Gulliver's Travels*, published in 1726, half a century before *Wealth of Nations*.

20. The importance of the distinction between "comprehensive outcomes" and "culmination outcomes," in various different contexts, is discussed in my "Maximization and the Act of Choice," *Econometrica* 65 (July 1997). For the relevance of the distinction in the specific case of the market mechanism and its alternatives, see my "Markets and Freedoms," *Oxford Economic Papers* 45 (1993), and "Markets and the Freedom to Choose," in *The Ethical Foundations of the Market Economy*, edited by Horst Siebert (Tübingen: J.C.B. Mohr, 1994). See also chapter 4 of the present work.

21. J. R. Hicks, *Wealth and Welfare* (Oxford: Basil Blackwell, 1981), p. 138.

22. Robert W. Fogel and Stanley L. Engerman, *Time on the Cross: The Economics of American Negro Slavery* (Boston: Little, Brown, 1974), pp. 125–6.

23. Fogel and Engerman, *Time on the Cross* (1974), pp. 237–8.

24. Different aspects of this momentous issue have been examined in Fernando Henrique Cardoso, *Capitalismo e Escravidão no Brasil Meridionel: O negro na sociadade escravocrata do Rio Grande do Sul* (Rio de Janeiro: Paz e Terra, 1977); Robin Blackburn, *The Overthrow of Colonial Slavery, 1776–1848* (London and New York: Verso, 1988); Tom Brass and Marcel van der Linden, eds., *Free and Unfree Labour* (Berne: European Academic Publishers, 1997); Stanley L. Engerman, ed., *Terms of Labor: Slavery, Serfdom and Free Labor* (Stanford, Calif.: Stanford University Press, 1998).

25. Karl Marx, *Capital*, volume 1 (London: Sonnenschein, 1887), chapter 10, section 3, p. 240. See also his *Grundrisse* (Harmondsworth: Penguin Books, 1973).

26. V. K. Ramachandran, *Wage Labour and Unfreedom in Agriculture: An Indian Case Study* (Oxford: Clarendon Press, 1990), pp. 1–2.

27. An important empirical study of this aspect of bondage and unfreedom, among others, can be found in Sudipto Mundle, *Backwardness and Bondage: Agrarian Relations in a South Bihar District* (New Delhi: Indian Institute of Public Administration, 1979).

28. On this see *Decent Work: The Report of the Director-General of the ILO* (Geneva: ILO, 1999). This is one of the special emphases in the program of the new director-general, Juan Somavia.

29. This point of view is forcefully developed in Stephen M. Marglin and Frederique Appfel Marglin, eds., *Dominating Knowledge* (Oxford: Clarendon Press, 1993). On related anthropological insights, see also Veena Das, *Critical Events: An Anthropological Perspective on Contemporary India* (Delhi: Oxford University Press, 1995).

## Chapter 2: *The Ends and the Means of Development*

1. I have discussed this contrast in an earlier paper, "Development Thinking at the Beginning of the 21st Century," in *Economic and Social Development into the XXI Century*, edited by Louis Emmerij (Washington, D.C.: Inter-American Development Bank, distributed by Johns Hopkins University Press, 1997). See also my "Economic Policy and Equity: An Overview," in *Economic Policy and Equity*, edited by Vito Tanzi, Ke-young Chu and Sanjeev Gupta (Washington, D.C.: International Monetary Fund, 1999).

2. This chapter served as the basis of a keynote address given at the World Bank Symposium on Global Finance and Development in Tokyo, March 1–2, 1999.

3. On this see Jean Drèze and Amartya Sen, *Hunger and Public Action* (Oxford: Clarendon Press, 1989).

4. On this see World Bank, *The East Asian Miracle: Economic Growth and Public Policy* (Oxford: Oxford University Press, 1993). See also Vito Tanzi et al., *Economic Policy and Equity* (1999).

5. See Hiromitsu Ishi, "Trends in the Allocation of Public Expenditure in Light of Human Resource Development—Overview in Japan," mimeographed, Asian Development Bank, Manila, 1995. See also Carol Gluck, *Japan's Modern Myths: Ideology in the Late Meiji Period* (Princeton: Princeton University Press, 1985).

6. On this see Jean Drèze and Amartya Sen, *India: Economic Development and Social Opportunity* (Delhi: Oxford University Press, 1995), and the Probe Team, *Public Report on Basic Education in India* (Delhi: Oxford University Press, 1999).

7. Sudhir Anand and Martin Ravallion, "Human Development in Poor Countries: On the Role of Private Incomes and Public Services," *Journal of Economics Perspectives* 7 (1993).

8. On this issue see my joint book with Jean Drèze, *India: Economic Development and Social Opportunity* (1995).

9. Drèze and Sen, *Hunger and Public Action* (1989); see particularly chapter 10.

10. Even though Kerala is merely a state rather than a country, nevertheless, with its population close to thirty million, it is larger than the majority of countries in the world (including, for example, Canada).

11. On this see my "From Income Inequality to Economic Inequality," Distinguished Guest Lecture to the Southern Economic Association, published in *Southern Economic Journal* 64 (October 1997), and "Mortality as an Indicator of Economic Success and Failure," first Innocenti Lecture to UNICEF (Florence: UNICEF, 1995), also published in *Economic Journal* 108 (January 1998).

12. See also Richard A. Easterlin, "How Beneficent Is the Market? A Look at the Modern History of Mortality," mimeographed, University of Southern California, 1997.

13. This issue is discussed in Drèze and Sen, *Hunger and Public Action* (1989).

14. I shall return to this question later on; see also Drèze and Sen, *India: Economic Development and Social Opportunity* (1995).

15. The need for supplementing and supporting market-friendly policies for economic growth with a rapid expansion of the social infrastructure (such as public health care and basic education) is discussed in some detail, in the context of the Indian economy, in my joint book with Jean Drèze, *India: Economic Development and Social Opportunity* (1995).

16. See Robert W. Fogel, "Nutrition and the Decline in Mortality since 1700: Some Additional Preliminary Findings," working paper 1802, National Bureau of Economic Research, 1986; Samuel H. Preston, "Changing Relations between Mortality and Level of Economic Development," *Population Studies* 29 (1975), and "American Longevity: Past, Present and Future," Policy Brief no. 7, Maxwell School of Citizenship and Public Affairs, Syracuse University, 1996. See also Lincoln C. Chen, Arthur Kleinman and Norma C. Ware, eds., *Advancing Health in Developing Countries* (New York: Auburn House, 1992); Richard G. Wilkinson, *Unhealthy*

*Societies: The Afflictions of Inequality* (New York: Routledge, 1996); Richard A. Easterlin, "How Beneficent Is the Market?" (1997).

17. See J. M. Winter, *The Great War and the British People* (London: Macmillan, 1986).

18. See R. M. Titmuss, *History of the Second World War: Problems of Social Policy* (London: HMSO, 1950).

19. On this see R. J. Hammond, *History of the Second World War: Food* (London: HMSO, 1951). See also Titmuss, *History of the Second World War: Problems of Social Policy* (1950).

20. See Winter, *Great War and the British People* (1986).

21. The data relate to England and Wales, since the aggregate British figures could not be found. However, since England and Wales form such an overwhelmingly big part of the United Kingdom, not a great deal is lost by this restriction of coverage.

22. See the works of R. J. Hammond, R. M. Titmuss, and J. M. Winter, cited earlier, and the other works to which they refer, and also the discussion and the references in Drèze and Sen, *Hunger and Public Action* (1989), chapter 10.

23. I have discussed this in "Development: Which Way Now?" *Economic Journal* 92 (December 1982) and *Resources, Values and Development* (Cambridge, Mass.: Harvard University Press, 1984), and jointly with Jean Drèze in *Hunger and Public Action* (1989).

## Chapter 3: *Freedom and the Foundations of Justice*

1. The role of informational exclusion and inclusion is discussed in my "On Weights and Measures: Informational Constraints in Social Welfare Analysis," *Econometrica* 45 (October 1977), reprinted in *Choice, Welfare and Measurement* (Oxford: Blackwell; Cambridge, Mass.: MIT Press, 1982; republished, Cambridge Mass.: Harvard University Press, 1997), and "Informational Analysis of Moral Principles," in *Rational Action,* edited by Ross Harrison (Cambridge: Cambridge University Press, 1979).

2. See Jeremy Bentham, *An Introduction to the Principles of Morals and Legislation* (London: Payne, 1789; republished, Oxford: Clarendon Press, 1907).

3. An informational critique of utilitarianism can be found in my "Utilitarianism and Welfarism," *Journal of Philosophy* 7 (September 1979), and "Well-Being, Agency and Freedom: The Dewey Lectures 1984," *Journal of Philosophy* 82 (April 1985).

4. On the distinctions, see J.C.B. Gosling, *Pleasure and Desire* (Oxford: Clarendon Press, 1969); John C. Harsanyi, *Essays in Ethics, Social Behaviour, and Scientific Explanation* (Dordrecht: Reidel, 1977).

5. On the methodological issue involved, see my "On Weights and Measures" (1977) and "Informational Analysis of Moral Principles" (1979).

6. Lionel Robbins was particularly influential in arguing that there could be no scientific basis for the possibility of interpersonal comparison of happiness ("Interpersonal Comparisons of Utility," *Economic Journal* 48 [1938]), and his critique had the effect of severely undermining utilitarianism as a mainstream approach in welfare economics.

7. Bentham, *An Introduction to the Principles of Morals and Legislation* (1789); John Stuart Mill, *Utilitarianism* (London, 1861; republished London: Collins/

Fontana, 1962); Henry Sidgwick, *The Method of Ethics* (London: Macmillan, 1874); William Stanley Jevons, *The Theory of Political Economy* (London: Macmillan, 1871; reprinted, 5th edition, 1957); Francis Edgeworth, *Mathematical Psychics: An Essay on the Application of Mathematics to the Moral Sciences* (London: Kegan Paul, 1881); Alfred Marshall, *Principles of Economics* (London: Macmillan, 8th edition, 1920); A. C. Pigou, *The Economics of Welfare* (London: Macmillan, 1920).

8. This is the simplest version of utilitarianism. For some complex and less direct versions, see particularly R. M. Hare, *Moral Thinking: Its Levels, Methods and Point* (Oxford: Clarendon Press, 1981); and James Griffin, *Well-Being: Its Meaning, Measurement, and Moral Importance* (Oxford: Clarendon Press, 1986).

9. The technical issues involved and some limitations of defining utility in the binary framework of choice are discussed in my *Choice, Welfare and Measurement* (1982), and more informally in *On Ethics and Economics* (Oxford: Blackwell, 1987).

10. See, for example, Independent Commission on Population and Quality of Life, *Caring for the Future* (Oxford: Oxford University Press, 1996); see also Mark Sagoff, *The Economy of the Earth* (Cambridge: Cambridge University Press, 1988), and Kjell Arne Brekke, *Economic Growth and the Environment* (Cheltenham, U.K.: Edward Elgar, 1997), among other works.

11. I have presented my reservations about utilitarianism in, among other places, *Collective Choice and Social Welfare* (San Francisco: Holden-Day, 1970; republished, Amsterdam: North-Holland, 1979); *On Economic Inequality* (Oxford: Clarendon Press, 1973); *Inequality Reexamined* (Oxford: Clarendon Press; Cambridge, Mass.: Harvard University Press, 1992). For powerful critiques of the utilitarian tradition, see John Rawls, *A Theory of Justice* (Cambridge, Mass.: Harvard University Press, 1971); Bernard Williams, "A Critique of Utilitarianism," in *Utilitarianism: For and Against*, by J.J.C. Smart and B. Williams (Cambridge: Cambridge University Press, 1973); Robert Nozick, *Anarchy, State and Utopia* (New York: Basic Books, 1974); Ronald Dworkin, *Taking Rights Seriously* (London: Duckworth, 1978); Joseph Raz, *Ethics in the Public Domain* (Oxford: Clarendon Press, 1994; revised edition, 1995); among other contributions.

12. See Sen, *Inequality Reexamined* (1992), and Martha Nussbaum, *Sex and Social Justice* (New York: Oxford University Press, 1999).

13. Rawls, *A Theory of Justice* (1971).

14. Nozick, *Anarchy, State and Utopia* (1974). See, however, Nozick's later—more qualified—position in *The Examined Life* (New York: Simon & Schuster, 1989).

15. Rawls, *A Theory of Justice* (1971); see also his *Political Liberalism* (New York: Columbia University Press, 1993), especially lecture 8.

16. H.L.A. Hart, "Rawls on Liberty and Its Priority," *University of Chicago Law Review* 40 (Spring 1973), reprinted in *Reading Rawls*, edited by Norman Daniels (New York: Basic Books, 1975); and Rawls, *Political Liberalism* (1993), lecture 8.

17. See my *Poverty and Famines: An Essay on Entitlement and Deprivation* (Oxford and New York: Oxford University Press, 1981), and a joint book with Jean Drèze, *Hunger and Public Action* (Oxford and New York: Oxford University Press, 1989). See also Jeffrey L. Coles and Peter J. Hammond, "Walrasian Equilibrium

without Survival: Existence, Efficiency and Remedial Policy," in *Choice, Welfare and Development: A Festschrift in Honour of Amartya K. Sen,* edited by Kaushik Basu, Prasanta Pattanaik and Kotaro Suzumura (Oxford: Clarendon Press, 1995).

18. Particular proposals of broadened consequential systems that incorporate rights can be found in my "Rights and Agency," *Philosophy and Public Affairs* 11 (1982), reprinted in *Consequentialism and Its Critics,* edited by Samuel Scheffler (Oxford: Oxford University Press, 1988); and "Well-Being, Agency and Freedom: The Dewey Lectures 1984," *Journal of Philosophy* 82 (April 1985). See also my *Freedom, Rationality and Social Choice: Arrow Lectures and Other Essays* (Oxford: Clarendon Press, forthcoming).

19. Robbins, "Interpersonal Comparisons of Utility" (1938), p. 636. For critiques of this position (in particular, of the general denial of the scientific status of interpersonal comparisons of utility), see I.M.D. Little, *A Critique of Welfare Economics* (Oxford: Clarendon Press, 1950; 2d edition, 1957); B.M.S. Van Praag, *Individual Welfare Functions and Consumer Behaviour* (Amsterdam: North-Holland, 1968); Amartya Sen, *On Economic Inequality* (Oxford: Clarendon Press, 1973; expanded edition, 1997); Amartya Sen, "Interpersonal Comparisons of Welfare," in *Economics and Human Welfare,* edited by Michael Boskin (New York: Academic Press, 1980), and reprinted in my *Choice, Welfare and Measurement* (1982); and the papers of Donald Davidson and Allan Gibbard in *Foundations of Social Choice Theory,* edited by Jon Elster and A. Hylland (Cambridge: Cambridge University Press, 1986); and Jon Elster and John Roemer, eds., *Interpersonal Comparisons of Well-Being* (Cambridge: Cambridge University Press, 1991).

20. John Harsanyi extends the choice definition of utility to interpersonal comparisons by considering *hypothetical* choices, whereby it is imagined that a person does consider becoming someone else ("Cardinal Welfare, Individualistic Ethics, and Interpersonal Comparison of Utility," *Journal of Political Economy* 63 [1955], reprinted in his *Essays in Ethics, Social Behaviour, and Scientific Explanation* [Dordrecht: Reidel, 1976]). Indeed, Harsanyi's approach to utilitarian welfare economics is based on valuing a social arrangement in terms of having an equal chance of being anyone in the society. This is an extremely useful thought experiment, and it elegantly gives a precise form to a general approach to fairness that has been invoked for a long time in the ethical literature. But such hypothetical choices are not easy to use in practice for actual comparisons of utility, and the main merit of the approach is purely conceptual.

21. The content of the set of possible utility functions corresponding to a given choice behavior would depend on the type of measurability that is presumed (e.g., ordinal, cardinal, ratio-scale). Interpersonal comparison of utilities requires "invariance conditions" being imposed on the combinations of utility functions of different persons from the Cartesian product of their respective sets of possible utility functions. On these matters, see my "Interpersonal Aggregation and Partial Comparability," *Econometrica* 38 (1970), reprinted in my *Choice, Welfare and Measurement* (1982), and *Collective Choice and Social Welfare* (1970). See also K.W.S. Roberts, "Interpersonal Comparisons and Social Choice Theory," *Review of Economic Studies* 47 (1980). Such "invariance conditions" cannot be obtained from observed choice behavior.

22. On this issue, see Franklin M. Fisher and Karl Shell, *The Economic Theory of Price Indices* (New York: Academic Press, 1972). This issue was also raised in

Herb Gintis's Harvard University Ph.D. thesis, "Alienation and Power: Toward a Radical Welfare Economics" (1969).

23. The basic results in the literature on real-income comparisons are surveyed and scrutinized in my "The Welfare Basis of Real-Income Comparisons: A Survey," *Journal of Economic Literature* 17 (1979), reprinted in my *Resources, Values and Development* (Cambridge, Mass.: Harvard University Press, 1984; reprinted 1997).

24. The diversity of influences on personal welfare have been studied in depth in the "Scandinavian studies" on living standards; see, for example, Robert Erikson and R. Aberg, *Welfare in Transition* (Oxford: Clarendon Press, 1987).

25. See particularly Glen Loury, "A Dynamic Theory of Racial Income Differences," in *Women, Minorities and Employment Discrimination,* edited by P. A. Wallace and A. Lamond (Lexington, Mass.: Lexington Books, 1977), and "Why Should We Care about Group Inequality?" *Social Philosophy and Policy* 5 (1987); James S. Coleman, *Foundations of Social Theory* (Cambridge, Mass.: Harvard University Press, 1990); Robert Putnam, R. Leonardi and R. Y. Nanetti, *Making Democracy Work: Civic Traditions in Modern Italy* (Princeton: Princeton University Press, 1993); Robert Putnam, "The Prosperous Community: Social Capital and Public Life," *American Prospect* 13 (1993); and "Bowling Alone: America's Declining Social Capital," *Journal of Democracies* 6 (1995).

26. Adam Smith, *An Inquiry into the Nature and Causes of the Wealth of Nations* (1776). See also W. G. Runciman, *Relative Deprivation and Social Justice: A Study of Attitudes to Social Inequality in Twentieth-Century England* (London: Routledge, 1966), and Peter Townsend, *Poverty in the United Kingdom: A Survey of Household Resources and Standards of Living* (Harmondsworth: Penguin Books, 1979).

27. On this see my "Gender and Cooperative Conflict," in *Persistent Inequalities: Women and World Development,* edited by Irene Tinker (New York: Oxford University Press, 1990), and the literature cited there.

28. Indeed, in some contexts, such as explanation of famines (and policy analysis for famine prevention), the lack of income of potential famine victims (and the possibility of regenerating their incomes) may occupy a central position in the investigation. On this see my *Poverty and Famines* (1981).

29. Rawls, *A Theory of Justice* (1971), pp. 60–5. See also his *Political Liberalism* (1993).

30. In a related line of argument, Ronald Dworkin has argued for "equality of resources," broadening the Rawlsian coverage of primary goods to include insurance opportunities to guard against the vagaries of "brute luck" (see his "What Is Equality? Part 1: Equality of Welfare" and "What Is Equality? Part 2: Equality of Resources," *Philosophy and Public Affairs* 10 [1981]).

31. On this see my "Equality of What?", in *Tanner Lectures on Human Values,* volume 1, edited by S. McMurrin (Cambridge: Cambridge University Press, 1980), and "Justice: Means versus Freedoms," *Philosophy and Public Affairs* 19 (1990). There is, however, some ambiguity about the exact content of "primary goods" as defined by Rawls. Some primary goods (such as "income and wealth") are no more than means to real ends (as Aristotle famously noted at the very beginning of the *Nicomachean Ethics*). Other primary goods (such as "the social basis of self-respect" to which Rawls makes an explicit reference) can include aspects of the social climate, even though they are generalized *means* (in the case of "the social basis of self-

respect" means to achieving self-respect). Still others (such as "liberties") can be interpreted in different ways: either as means (liberties permit us to do things that we may value doing) or as the actual freedom to achieve certain results (the latter way of seeing liberties has been particularly used in the social choice literature, for example in my *Collective Choice and Social Welfare* [1970], chapter 6). But the Rawlsian program of using primary goods to judge individual advantage in his "Difference Principle" is mainly motivated by his attempt to characterize general-purpose means, and thus is subject to interpersonal variations in the conversion of means to the freedom to pursue ends.

32. See Alan Williams, "What Is Wealth and Who Creates It?" in *Dependency to Enterprise*, edited by John Hutton et al. (London: Routledge, 1991); A. J. Culyer and Adam Wagstaff, "Needs, Equality and Social Justice," Discussion Paper 90, Centre for Health Economics, University of York, 1991; Alan Williams, *Being Reasonable about the Economics of Health: Selected Essays by Alan Williams,* edited by A. J. Culyer (Cheltenham, U.K.: Edward Elgar, 1997). See also Paul Farmer, *Infections and Inequalities: The Modern Plagues* (Berkeley, Calif.: University of California Press, 1998); Michael Marmot, Martin Bobak and George Davey Smith, "Explorations for Social Inequalities in Health," in *Society and Health,* edited by B. C. Amick, S. Levine, A. R. Tarlov and D. Chapman Walsh (London: Oxford University Press, 1995); Richard G. Wilkinson, *Unhealthy Societies: The Afflictions of Inequality* (New York: Routledge, 1996); James Smith, "Socioeconomic Status and Health," *American Economic Review* 88 (1998), and "Healthy Bodies and Thick Wallets: The Dual Relationship between Health and Socioeconomic Status," *Journal of Economic Perspectives* 13 (1999). Much insight can also be obtained from studies of specific health problems; for example, see Paul Farmer, Margaret Connors and Janie Simmons, eds., *Women, Poverty and AIDS: Sex, Drugs and Structural Violence* (Monroe, Me.: Common Courage Press, 1996); Alok Bhargava, "Modeling the Effects of Nutritional and Socioeconomic Factors on the Growth and Morbidity of Kenyan School Children," *American Journal of Human Biology* 11 (1999).

33. See A. C. Pigou, *The Economics of Welfare,* 4th edition (London: Macmillan, 1952). See also Pitambar Pant et al., *Perspectives of Development: 1961–1976, Implications of Planning for a Minimal Level of Living* (New Delhi: Planning Commission of India, 1962); Irma Adelman and Cynthia T. Morris, *Economic Growth and Social Equity in Developing Countries* (Stanford: Stanford University Press, 1973); Amartya Sen, "On the Development of Basic Income Indicators to Supplement the GNP Measure," *United Nations Economic Bulletin for Asia and the Far East* 24 (1973); Pranab Bardhan, "On Life and Death Questions," *Economic and Political Weekly* 9 (1974); Irma Adelman, "Development Economics—A Reassessment of Goals," *American Economic Review,* Papers and Proceedings 65 (1975); A. O. Herrera et al., *Catastrophe or New Society? A Latin American World Model* (Ottawa: IDRC, 1976); Mahbub ul Haq, *The Poverty Curtain* (New York: Columbia University Press, 1976); Paul Streeten and S. Javed Burki, "Basic Needs: Some Issues," *World Development* 6 (1978); Keith Griffin, *International Inequality and National Poverty* (London: Macmillan, 1978); Morris D. Morris, *Measuring the Conditions of the World's Poor: The Physical Quality of Life Index* (Oxford: Pergamon Press, 1979); Graciela Chichilnisky, "Basic Needs and Global Models: Resources, Trade and Distribution," *Alternatives* 6 (1980); Paul Streeten, *Development Perspectives* (London: Macmillan, 1981); Paul Streeten, S. Javed Burki, Mahbub ul

Haq, N. Hicks and Frances Stewart, *First Things First: Meeting Basic Needs in Developing Countries* (New York: Oxford University Press, 1981); Frances Stewart, *Basic Needs in Developing Countries* (Baltimore: Johns Hopkins University Press, 1985); D. H. Costa and R. H. Steckel, "Long-Term Trends in Health, Welfare and Economic Growth in the United States," Historical Working Paper 76, National Bureau of Economic Research, 1995; R. C. Floud and B. Harris, "Health, Height and Welfare: Britain 1700–1980," Historical Working Paper 87, National Bureau of Economic Research, 1996; Nicholas F. R. Crafts, "Some Dimensions of the 'Quality of Life' during the British Industrial Revolution," *Economic History Review* 4 (1997); Santosh Mehrotra and Richard Jolly, eds., *Development with a Human Face: Experiences in Social Achievement and Economic Growth* (Oxford: Clarendon Press, 1997); A. P. Thirwall, *Growth and Development*, 6th edition (London: Macmillan, 1999); among other contributions.

34. United Nations Development Programme, *Human Development Report 1990* (New York: Oxford University Press, 1990), and the subsequent yearly reports. Mahbub ul Haq's own account of this innovative departure can be found in his *Reflections on Human Development* (New York: Oxford University Press, 1995). See also the applications and extensions illuminatingly presented by Nicholas F. R. Crafts, "The Human Development Index and Changes in the Standard of Living: Some Historical Comparisons," *Review of European Economic History* 1 (1997). The United Nations Children's Fund (UNICEF) has also been a pioneer in issuing annual reports on the lives of children; see UNICEF, *The State of the World's Children* (New York: Oxford University Press, 1987), and other annual issues. Mention must also be made of the informationally rich *World Development Reports* produced by the World Bank, with its increasing attempt to cover more ground on living conditions. The health conditions received extensive attention in the *World Development Report 1993* (New York: Oxford University Press, 1993).

35. Aristotle, *The Nicomachean Ethics*, translated by D. Ross (Oxford: Oxford University Press, revised edition 1980), book 1, section 7, pp. 12–14. On this see Martha Nussbaum, "Nature, Function and Capability: Aristotle on Political Distribution," *Oxford Studies in Ancient Philosophy* (1988; supplementary volume).

36. Smith, *Wealth of Nations* (1776), volume 2, book 5, chapter 2.

37. Smith, *Wealth of Nations* (1776), volume 2, book 5, chapter 2, in the edition by R. H. Campbell and A. S. Skinner (Oxford: Clarendon Press, 1976), pp. 469–71.

38. See my "Equality of What?" in *Tanner Lectures on Human Values*, volume 1, edited by S. McMurrin (Cambridge: Cambridge University Press, 1982; Salt Lake City: University of Utah Press); reprinted in my *Choice, Welfare and Measurement* (1980); also in John Rawls et al., *Liberty, Equality and Law*, edited by S. McMurrin (Cambridge: Cambridge University Press, and Salt Lake City: University of Utah Press, 1987), and in Stephen Darwall, ed., *Equal Freedom: Selected Tanner Lectures on Human Values* (Ann Arbor: University of Michigan Press, 1995). See also my "Public Action and the Quality of Life in Developing Countries," *Oxford Bulletin of Economics and Statistics* 43 (1981); *Commodities and Capabilities* (Amsterdam: North-Holland, 1985); "Well-Being, Agency and Freedom" (1985); (jointly with Jean Drèze) *Hunger and Public Action* (Oxford: Clarendon Press, 1989); and "Capability and Well-Being," in *The Quality of Life*, edited by Martha Nussbaum and Amartya Sen (Oxford: Clarendon Press, 1993).

39. On the nature and pervasiveness of such variability, see my *Commodities and Capabilities* (1985) and *Inequality Reexamined* (1992). On the general relevance of taking note of disparate needs in resource allocation, see also my *On Economic Inequality,* chapter 1; L. Doyal and I. Gough, *A Theory of Human Need* (New York: Guilford Press, 1991); U. Ebert, "On Comparisons of Income Distributions When Household Types Are Different," Economics Discussion Paper V-86-92, University of Oldenberg, 1992; Dan W. Brock, *Life and Death: Philosophical Essays in Biomedical Ethics* (Cambridge: Cambridge University Press, 1993); Alessandro Balestrino, "Poverty and Functionings: Issues in Measurement and Public Action," *Giornale degli Economisti e Annali di Economia* 53 (1994); Enrica Chiappero Martinetti, "A New Approach to Evaluation of Well-Being and Poverty by Fuzzy Set Theory," *Giornale degli Economisti* 53 (1994); M. Fleurbaey, "On Fair Compensation," *Theory and Decision* 36 (1994); Elena Granaglia, "More or Less Equality? A Misleading Question for Social Policy," *Giornale degli Economisti* 53 (1994); M. Fleurbaey, "Three Solutions for the Compensation Problem," *Journal of Economic Theory* 65 (1995); Ralf Eriksson and Markus Jantti, *Economic Value and Ways of Life* (Aldershot: Avebury, 1995); A. F. Shorrocks, "Inequality and Welfare Comparisons for Heterogeneous Populations," mimeographed, Department of Economics, University of Essex, 1995; B. Nolan and C. T. Whelan, *Resources, Deprivation, and Poverty* (Oxford: Clarendon Press, 1996); Alessandro Balestrino, "A Note on Functioning-Poverty in Affluent Societies," *Notizie di Politeia* (1996; special volume); Carmen Herrero, "Capabilities and Utilities," *Economic Design* 2 (1996); Santosh Mehrotra and Richard Jolly, eds., *Development with a Human Face* (Oxford: Clarendon Press, 1997); Consumers International, *The Social Art of Economic Crisis: . . . Our Rice Pots Are Empty* (Penerz, Malopia: Consumers International, 1998); among other contributions.

40. See my "Equality of What?" (1980), *Commodities and Capabilities* (1985), and *Inequality Reexamined* (1992). See also Keith Griffin and John Knight, *Human Development and the International Development Strategies for the 1990s* (London: Macmillan, 1990); David Crocker, "Functioning and Capability: The Foundations of Sen's and Nussbaum's Development Ethic," *Political Theory* 20 (1992); Nussbaum and Sen, *The Quality of Life* (1993); Martha Nussbaum and Jonathan Glover, *Women, Culture, and Development* (Oxford: Clarendon Press, 1995); Meghnad Desai, *Poverty, Famine, and Economic Development* (Aldershot: Edward Elgar, 1994); Kenneth Arrow, "A Note on Freedom and Flexibility," and Anthony B. Atkinson, "Capabilities, Exclusion and the Supply of Goods," both in *Choice, Welfare and Development,* edited by K. Basu, P. Pattanaik and K. Suzumura (Oxford: Clarendon Press, 1995); Stefano Zamagni, "Amartya Sen on Social Choice, Utilitarianism and Liberty," *Italian Economic Papers* 2 (1995); Herrero, "Capabilities and Utilities" (1996); Nolan and Whelan, *Resources, Deprivation, and Poverty* (1996); Frank Ackerman, David Kiron, Neva R. Goodwin, Jonathan Harris and Kevin Gallagher, eds., *Human Well-Being and Economic Goals* (Washington, D.C.: Island Press, 1997); J.-Fr. Laslier et al., eds., *Freedom in Economics* (London: Routledge, 1998); Prasanta K. Pattanaik, "Cultural Indicators of Well-Being: Some Conceptual Issues," in *World Culture Report* (Paris: UNESCO, 1998); Sabina Alkire, "Operationalizing Amartya Sen's Capability Approach to Human Development" (D. Ph. thesis, Oxford University, 1999).

41. Even the elementary functionings of being well-nourished involve significant

conceptual and empirical issues, on which see, among other contributions, Nevin Scrimshaw, C. E. Taylor and J. E. Gopalan, *Interactions of Nutrition and Infection* (Geneva: World Health Organization, 1968); T. N. Srinivasan, "Malnutrition: Some Measurement and Policy Issues," *Journal of Development Economics* 8 (1981); K. Blaxter and J. C. Waterlow, eds., *Nutritional Adaptation in Man* (London: John Libbey, 1985); Partha Dasgupta and Debraj Ray, "Adapting to Undernutrition: Biological Evidence and Its Implications," and S. R. Osmani, "Nutrition and the Economics of Food: Implications of Some Recent Controversies," in *The Political Economy of Hunger*, edited by Jean Drèze and Amartya Sen (Oxford: Clarendon Press, 1990); Partha Dasgupta, *An Inquiry into Well-Being and Destitution* (Oxford: Clarendon Press, 1993); S. R. Osmani, ed., *Nutrition and Poverty* (Oxford: Clarendon Press, 1993).

42. These issues are discussed in my Tanner Lectures included in my *The Standard of Living*, edited by Geoffrey Hawthorn (Cambridge: Cambridge University Press, 1987), in which see also the contributions of Geoffrey Hawthorn, John Muellbauer, Ravi Kanbur, Keith Hart and Bernard Williams, and my response to these comments. See also Kaushik Basu, "Achievement, Capabilities, and the Concept of Well-Being," *Social Choice and Welfare* 4 (1987); G. A. Cohen, "Equality of What? On Welfare, Goods and Capabilities," *Recherches Economiques de Louvain* 56 (1990); Norman Daniels, "Equality of What: Welfare, Resources or Capabilities?" *Philosophy of Phenomenological Research* 50 (1990); Crocker, "Functioning and Capability" (1992); Brock, *Life and Death* (1993); Mozaffar Qizilbash, "Capabilities, Well-Being and Human Development: A Survey," *Journal of Development Studies* 33 (1996), and "The Concept of Well-Being," *Economics and Philosophy* 14 (1998); Alkire, "Operationalizing Amartya Sen's Capability Approach to Human Development" (1999). See also the symposia on the capability approach in *Giornale degli Economisti e Annali di Economia* 53 (1994), and in *Notizie di Politeia* (1996; special volume), including contributions by Alessandro Balestrino, Giovanni Andrea Cornia, Enrica Chiappero Martinetti, Elena Granaglia, Renata Targetti Lenti, Ian Carter, L. Casini and I. Bernetti, S. Razavi, and others. See also the related symposium on entitlement analysis in *Journal of International Development* 9 (1997), edited by Des Gasper, which includes contributions by Des Gasper, Charles Gore, Mozaffar Qizilbash, and Sabina Alkire and Rufus Black.

43. When numerical representation of each functioning is not possible, the analysis has to be done in terms of the more general framework of seeing the functioning achievements as a "functioning n-tuple," and the capability set as a set of such n-tuples in the appropriate space. There may also be considerable areas of incompleteness as well as fuzziness. On this see my *Commodities and Capabilities* (1985). The recent literature on "fuzzy set theory" can be helpful in analyzing the valuation of functioning vectors and capability sets. See particularly Enrica Chiappero Martinetti, "A New Approach to Evaluation of Well-being and Poverty by Fuzzy Set Theory" *Giornale degli Economisti,* 53 (1994), and her "Standard of Living Evaluation Based on Sen's Approach: Some Methodological Suggestions," *Notizie di Politeia,* 12 (1996; special volume). See also Kaushik Basu, "Axioms for Fuzzy Measures of Inequality" (1987); Flavio Delbono, "Povertà come incapacità: Premesse teoriche, identificazione, e misurazione," *Rivista Internazionale di Scienze Sociali* 97 (1989); A. Cerioli and S. Zani, "A Fuzzy Approach to the Measurement of Poverty," in *Income and Wealth Distribution, Inequality and Poverty,* edited by

C. Dagum et al. (New York: Springer-Verlag, 1990); Balestrino, "Poverty and Functionings" (1994); E. Ok, "Fuzzy Measurement of Income Inequality: A Class of Fuzzy Inequality Measures," *Social Choice and Welfare* 12 (1995); L. Casini and I. Bernetti, "Environment, Sustainability, and Sen's Theory," *Notizie di Politeia* (1996; special volume); among other contributions.

44. The relevance of the capability perspective in many different fields has been well explored, inter alia, in a number of doctoral dissertations done at Harvard that I have been privileged to supervise, in particular: A. K. Shiva Kumar, "Maternal Capabilities and Child Survival in Low-Income Regions" (1992); Jonathan R. Cohen, "On Reasoned Choice" (1993); Stephan J. Klasen, "Gender, Inequality and Survival: Excess Female Mortality—Past and Present" (1994); Felicia Marie Knaul, "Young Workers, Street Life, and Gender: The Effects of Education and Work Experience on Earnings in Colombia" (1995); Karl W. Lauterbach, "Justice and the Functions of Health Care" (1995); Remigius Henricus Oosterdorp, "Adam Smith, Social Norms and Economic Behavior" (1995); Anthony Simon Laden, "Constructing Shared Wills: Deliberative Liberalism and the Politics of Identity" (1996); Douglas Hicks, "Inequality Matters" (1998); Jennifer Prah Ruger, "Aristotelian Justice and Health Policy: Capability and Incompletely Theorized Agreements" (1998); Sousan Abadian, "From Wasteland to Homeland: Trauma and the Renewal of Indigenous Peoples and Their Communities" (1999).

45. See the rather extensive literature on this, referred to in my *On Economic Inequality* (Oxford: Clarendon Press, expanded edition, 1997), with a substantial annex jointly written with James Foster. See also the references given in notes 38–44, above, and also Haidar A. Khan, *Technology, Development and Democracy* (Northampton, Mass.: Edward Elgar, 1998); Nancy Folbre, "A Time (Use Survey) for Every Purpose: Non-market Work and the Production of Human Capabilities," mimeographed, University of Massachusetts, Amherst, 1997; Frank Ackerman et al., *Human Well-Being and Economic Goals;* Felton Earls and Maya Carlson, "Adolescents as Collaborators: In Search of Well-Being," mimeographed, Harvard University, 1998; David Crocker and Toby Linden, eds., *Ethics of Consumption* (New York: Rowman and Littlefield, 1998); among other writings.

46. This approach is called "elementary evaluation" of the capability set; the nature and scope of elementary evaluation is discussed in my *Commodities and Capabilities* (1985). See also G. A. Cohen's argument for what he calls "midfare," in "On the Currency of Egalitarian Justice," *Ethics* 99 (1989); "Equality of What? On Welfare, Goods and Capabilities" (1990); and *Self-Ownership, Freedom, and Equality* (Cambridge: Cambridge University Press, 1995). See Richard Arneson, "Equality and Equality of Opportunity for Welfare," *Philosophical Studies* 56 (1989), and "Liberalism, Distributive Subjectivism, and Equal Opportunity for Welfare," *Philosophy and Public Affairs* 19 (1990).

47. These issues have been discussed extensively in my *Freedom, Rationality and Social Choice* (forthcoming). See also Tjalling C. Koopmans, "On Flexibility of Future Preference," in *Human Judgments and Optimality,* edited by M. W. Shelley (New York: Wiley, 1964); David Kreps, "A Representation Theorem for 'Preference for Flexibility,' " *Econometrica* 47 (1979); Peter Jones and Robert Sugden, "Evaluating Choice," *International Review of Law and Economics* 2 (1982); James Foster, "Notes on Effective Freedom," mimeographed, Vanderbilt University, presented at the Stanford Workshop on Economic Theories of Inequality, sponsored by the

MacArthur Foundation, March 11–13, 1993; Kenneth J. Arrow, "A Note on Freedom and Flexibility," in *Choice, Welfare and Development*, edited by Basu, Pattanaik and Suzumura (1995); Robert Sugden, "The Metric of Opportunity,"
Discussion Paper 9610, Economics Research Centre, University of East Anglia,
1996.

48. On this see my *Commodities and Capabilities* (1985) and "Welfare, Preference, and Freedom," *Journal of Econometrics* 50 (1991). On various proposals on
assessing the extent of "freedom," see also David Kreps, "A Representation Theorem for 'Preference for Flexibility' " (1979); Patrick Suppes, "Maximizing Freedom
of Decision: An Axiomatic Analysis," in *Arrow and the Foundations of Economic
Policy*, edited by G. R. Feiwel (London: Macmillan, 1987); P. K. Pattanaik and
Y. Xu, "On Ranking Opportunity Sets in Terms of Freedom of Choice," *Recherches
Economiques de Louvain* 56 (1990); James Foster, "Notes on Effective Freedom"
(1993); Kenneth J. Arrow, "A Note on Freedom and Flexibility," in *Choice, Welfare
and Development*, edited by Basu, Pattanaik and Suzumura (1995); Carmen Herrero, "Capabilities and Utilities"; Clemens Puppe, "Freedom, Choice, and Rational
Decisions," *Social Choice and Welfare* 12 (1995); among other contributions.

49. On these issues see my *Commodities and Capabilities* (1985); *Inequality
Reexamined* (1992); and "Capability and Well-Being" (1993).

50. See Rawls, *A Theory of Justice* (1971) and *Political Liberalism* (1993). In
analogy with Kenneth Arrow's famous impossibility theorem, various "impossibility
theorems" have been presented in the literature about the existence of satisfactory
overall indices of Rawlsian primary goods; see Charles Plott, "Rawls' Theory of Justice: An Impossibility Result," in *Decision Theory and Social Ethics*, edited by H. W.
Gottinger and W. Leinfellner (Dordrecht: Reidel, 1978); Allan Gibbard, "Disparate
Goods and Rawls's Difference Principle: A Social Choice Theoretic Treatment,"
*Theory and Decision* 11 (1979); Douglas H. Blair, "The Primary-Goods Indexation
Problem in Rawls' *Theory of Justice*," *Theory and Decision* 24 (1988). Informational limitations play a crucial part in precipitating these results (as in the case of
Arrow's theorem). The case *against* imposing such informational limitations is dis-
cussed in my "On Indexing Primary Goods and Capabilities" (mimeographed, Harvard University, 1991), which reduces the rub of these alleged impossibility results,
applied to Rawlsian procedures.

51. Analytical correspondences between systematic narrowing of the range of
weights and monotonic extension of the generated partial orderings (based on
"intersections of possible rankings") have been explored in my "Interpersonal
Aggregation and Partial Comparability" (1970) and *Collective Choice and Social
Welfare* (1970), chapters 7 and 7*; and in Charles Blackorby, "Degrees of Cardinal-
ity and Aggregate Partial Ordering," *Econometrica* 43 (1975); Ben Fine, "A Note on
Interpersonal Aggregation and Partial Comparability," *Econometrica* 43 (1975);
Kaushik Basu, *Revealed Preference of Government* (Cambridge: Cambridge Univer-
sity Press, 1980); James Foster and Amartya Sen, "*On Economic Inequality* after a
Quarter Century," in my *On Economic Inequality*, expanded edition (1997). The
approach of intersection partial orderings can be combined with "fuzzy" represen-
tation of the valuation and measurement of functionings, on which see Chiappero
Martinetti, "A New Approach to Evaluation of Well-being and Poverty by Fuzzy Set
Theory" (1994), and also her "Standard of Living Evaluation Based on Sen's
Approach" (1996). See also L. Casini and I. Bernetti, "Environment, Sustainability,

and Sen's Theory," *Notizie de Politeia* 12 (1996), and Herrero, "Capabilities and Utilities" (1996). But even with an incomplete ordering many decision problems can be adequately resolved, and even those that are not fully resolved can be substantially simplified (through the rejection of "dominated" alternatives).

52. This issue, and its connection with both social choice theory and public choice theory, are discussed in my presidential address to the American Economic Association, "Rationality and Social Choice," *American Economic Review* 85 (1995).

53. T. N. Srinivasan, "Human Development: A New Paradigm or Reinvention of the Wheel?" *American Economic Review,* Papers and Proceedings 84 (1994), p. 239. In presenting this argument, Srinivasan quotes, in fact, from Robert Sugden ("Welfare, Resources, and Capabilities: A Review of *Inequality Reexamined* by Amartya Sen," *Journal of Economic Literature* 31 [1993]), whose skepticism of the possibility of valuing different capabilities is clearly less intense than Srinivasan's (as Sugden puts his own conclusion, it "remains to be seen whether analogous metrics can be developed for the capability approach," p. 1953).

54. Paul A. Samuelson, *Foundations of Economic Analysis* (Cambridge, Mass.: Harvard University Press, 1947), p. 205.

55. I have tried to address this issue in my presidential address to the American Economic Association in 1995 and in my Nobel lecture in 1998; see "Rationality and Social Choice," *American Economic Review* 85 (1995), and "The Possibility of Social Choice," *American Economic Review* 89 (1999).

56. These approaches have also been discussed in the new annex (authored jointly with James Foster) in the enlarged (1997) edition of my *On Economic Inequality.*

57. It is tempting to consider distribution measures in different spaces (distributions of incomes, longevities, literacies, etc.), and then to put them together. But this would be a misleading procedure, since much would depend on how these variables relate to one another in interpersonal patterns (what may be called the "covariance" issue). For example, if people with low incomes also tend to have low literacy levels, then the two deprivations would be reinforced, whereas if they were unrelated (or "orthogonal"), this would not happen; and if they are oppositely related, then the deprivation in terms of one variable would be, at least to some extent, ameliorated by the other variable. We cannot decide which of the alternative possibilities holds by looking only at the distribution indicators separately, without examining collinearity and covariance.

58. In a study on poverty in Italy, in the European context, undertaken by the Bank of Italy and led by Fabrizio Barca, it is mostly this supplementary approach that is used and applied.

59. On this see Angus Deaton, *Microeconometric Analysis for Development Policy: An Approach from Household Surveys* (Baltimore: Johns Hopkins University Press for the World Bank, 1997). See also Angus Deaton and John Muellbauer, *Economics and Consumer Behaviour* (Cambridge: Cambridge University Press, 1980), and "On Measuring Child Costs: With Applications to Poor Countries," *Journal of Political Economy* 94 (1986). See also Dale W. Jorgenson, *Welfare,* volume 2, *Measuring Social Welfare* (Cambridge, Mass.: MIT Press, 1997).

60. See Hugh Dalton, "The Measurement of the Inequality of Incomes," *Economic*

*Journal* 30 (1920); A. B. Atkinson, "On the Measurement of Inequality," *Journal of Economic Theory* 2 (1970).

61. Particularly in my *Commodities and Capabilities* (1985); "Well-Being, Agency and Freedom" (1985); and *Inequality Reexamined* (1992).

62. Some of the more technical issues in the evaluation of freedom have been investigated in my *Freedom, Rationality and Social Choice: Arrow Lectures and Other Essays* (forthcoming).

### Chapter 4: *Poverty as Capability Deprivation*

1. This view of poverty is more fully developed in my *Poverty and Famines* (Oxford: Clarendon Press, 1981) and *Resources, Values and Development* (Cambridge, Mass.: Harvard University Press, 1984), and also in Jean Drèze and Amartya Sen, *Hunger and Public Action* (Oxford: Clarendon Press, 1989), and in Sudhir Anand and Amartya Sen, "Concepts of Human Development and Poverty: A Multidimensional Perspective," in *Human Development Papers 1997* (New York: UNDP, 1997).

2. These claims and their implications are more fully discussed in my "Poverty as Capability Deprivation," mimeographed, Rome: Bank of Italy.

3. For example, hunger and undernutrition are related both to food intake and to the ability to make nutritive use of that intake. The latter is deeply affected by general health conditions (for example, by the presence of parasitic diseases), and that in turn depends much on communal health care and public health provisions; on this see Drèze and Sen, *Hunger and Public Action* (1989), and S. R. Osmani, ed., *Nutrition and Poverty* (Oxford: Clarendon Press, 1993).

4. See, for example, James Smith, "Healthy Bodies and Thick Wallets: The Dual Relationship between Health and Socioeconomic Status," *Journal of Economic Perspectives* 13 (1999). There is also another type of "coupling" between (1) undernutrition generated by income-poverty and (2) income-poverty resulting from work deprivation due to undernutrition. On these connections, see Partha Dasgupta and Debraj Ray, "Inequality as a Determinant of Malnutrition and Unemployment: Theory," *Economic Journal* 96 (1986); "Inequality as a Determinant of Malnutrition and Unemployment: Policy," *Economic Journal* 97 (1987); and "Adapting to Undernourishment: Biological Evidence and Its Implications," in *The Political Economy of Hunger,* edited by Jean Drèze and Amartya Sen (Oxford: Clarendon Press, 1990). See also Partha Dasgupta, *An Inquiry into Well-Being and Destitution* (Oxford: Clarendon Press, 1993), and Debraj Ray, *Development Economics* (Princeton: Princeton University Press, 1998).

5. The large contribution of such handicaps to the prevalence of income poverty in Britain was sharply brought out by A. B. Atkinson's pioneering empirical study, *Poverty in Britain and the Reform of Social Security* (Cambridge: Cambridge University Press, 1970). In his later works, Atkinson has further pursued the connection between income handicap and deprivations of other kinds.

6. On the nature of these functional handicaps, see Dorothy Wedderburn, *The Aged in the Welfare State* (London: Bell, 1961); Peter Townsend, *Poverty in the United Kingdom: A Survey of Household Resources and Standards of Living* (Harmondsworth: Penguin Books, 1979); J. Palmer, T. Smeeding and B. Torrey, *The Vulnerable: America's Young and Old in the Industrial World* (Washington, D.C.: Urban Institute Press, 1988); among other contributions.

7. I have tried to investigate the perspective of capability deprivation for analyzing gender inequality in *Resources, Values and Development* (1984; 1997); *Commodities and Capabilities* (Amsterdam: North-Holland, 1985); and "Missing Women," *British Medical Journal* 304 (March 1992). See also Pranab Bardhan, "On Life and Death Questions," *Economic and Political Weekly* 9 (1974); Lincoln Chen, E. Huq and S. D'Souza, "Sex Bias in the Family Allocation of Food and Health Care in Rural Bangladesh," *Population and Development Review* 7 (1981); Jocelyn Kynch and Amartya Sen, "Indian Women: Well-Being and Survival," *Cambridge Journal of Economics* 7 (1983); Pranab Bardhan, *Land, Labor, and Rural Poverty* (New York: Columbia University Press, 1984); Drèze and Sen, *Hunger and Public Action* (1989); Barbara Harriss, "The Intrafamily Distribution of Hunger in South Asia," in Drèze and Sen, *The Political Economy of Hunger*, volume 1 (1990); Ravi Kanbur and L. Haddad, "How Serious Is the Neglect of Intrahousehold Inequality?" *Economic Journal* 100 (1990); among other contributions.

8. On this, see United Nations Development Programme, *Human Development Report 1995* (New York: Oxford University Press, 1995).

9. See W. G. Runciman, *Relative Deprivation and Social Justice: A Study of Attitudes to Social Inequality in Twentieth-Century England* (London: Routledge, 1966); and Townsend, *Poverty in the United Kingdom* (1979).

10. On this see my "Poor, Relatively Speaking," *Oxford Economic Papers* 35 (1983), reprinted in *Resources, Values and Development* (1984).

11. The connection is analyzed in my *Inequality Reexamined* (Oxford: Clarendon Press; and Cambridge, Mass.: Harvard University Press, 1992), chapter 7.

12. Jean Drèze and Amartya Sen, *India: Economic Development and Social Opportunity* (Delhi: Oxford University Press, 1995).

13. See the collection of papers in Isher Judge Ahluwalia and I.M.D. Little, eds., *India's Economic Reforms and Development: Essays for Manmohan Singh* (Delhi: Oxford University Press, 1998). See also Vijay Joshi and Ian Little, *Indian Economic Reforms, 1991–2001* (Delhi: Oxford University Press, 1996).

14. These arguments are more fully developed in Drèze and Sen, *India: Economic Development and Social Opportunity* (1995).

15. See G. Datt, *Poverty in India and Indian States: An Update* (Washington, D.C.: International Food Policy Research Institute, 1997). See also World Bank, *India: Achievements and Challenges in Reducing Poverty*, report no. 16483 IN, May 27, 1997 (see particularly figure 2.3).

16. Adam Smith, *The Theory of Moral Sentiments* (1759; revised edition, 1790); republished, edited by D. D. Raphael and A. L. Macfie (Oxford: Clarendon Press, 1976).

17. John Rawls, *A Theory of Justice* (Cambridge, Mass.: Harvard University Press, 1971). See also Stephen Darwall, ed., *Equal Freedom: Selected Tanner Lectures on Human Values* (Ann Arbor: University of Michigan Press, 1995), with contributions by G. A. Cohen, Ronald Dworkin, John Rawls, T. M. Scanlon, Amartya Sen and Quentin Skinner.

18. Thomas Scanlon, "Contractualism and Utilitarianism," in *Utilitarianism and Beyond*, edited by Amartya Sen and Bernard Williams (Cambridge: Cambridge University Press, 1982). See also his *What We Owe Each Other* (Cambridge, Mass.: Harvard University Press, 1998).

19. See, for example, James Mirrlees, "An Exploration in the Theory of Optimal

Income Taxation," *Review of Economic Studies* 38 (1971); E. S. Phelps, ed., *Economic Justice* (Harmondsworth: Penguin Books, 1973); Nicholas Stern, "On the Specification of Modes of Optimum Income Taxation," *Journal of Public Economics* 6 (1976); A. B. Atkinson and Joseph Stiglitz, *Lectures on Public Economics* (London: McGraw-Hill, 1980); D. A. Starrett, *Foundations of Public Economics* (Cambridge: Cambridge University Press, 1988); among many other contributions.

20. A. B. Atkinson, "On the Measurement of Inequality," *Journal of Economic Theory* 2 (1970), and *Social Justice and Public Policy* (Brighton: Wheatsheaf; Cambridge, Mass.: MIT Press, 1983). See also S. Ch. Kolm, "The Optimum Production of Social Justice," in *Public Economics*, edited by J. Margolis and H. Guitton (London: Macmillan, 1969); Amartya Sen, *On Economic Inequality* (Oxford: Clarendon Press, 1973; expanded edition, including an annex with James Foster, 1997); Charles Blackorby and David Donaldson, "A Theoretical Treatment of Indices of Absolute Inequality," *International Economic Review* 21 (1980), and "Ethically Significant Ordinal Indexes of Relative Inequality," *Advances in Econometrics*, volume 3, edited by R. Basmann and G. Rhodes (Greenwich, Conn.: JAI Press, 1984).

21. In my paper "Inequality, Unemployment and Contemporary Europe" (presented at the Lisbon conference on "Social Europe" of the Calouste Gulbenkian Foundation, May 5–7, 1997, published in *International Labour Review,* 1997), I have discussed the relevance of this contrast for contemporary policy issues in Europe. The importance that the unemployed themselves attach to the loss of freedom and capability as a result of unemployment is illuminatingly analyzed (with Belgian data) by Eric Schokkaert and L. Van Ootegem, "Sen's Concept of Living Standards Applied to the Belgian Unemployed," *Recherches Economiques de Louvain* 56 (1990).

22. See the literature cited in my "Inequality, Unemployment and Contemporary Europe" (1997). On the psychological and other "social harms" of unemployment, see Robert Solow, "Mass Unemployment as a Social Problem" in *Choice, Welfare and Development*, edited by K. Basu, P. Pattanaik and K. Suzumura (Oxford: Clarendon Press, 1995), and A. Goldsmith, J. R. Veum and W. Darity Jr., "The Psychological Impact of Unemployment and Joblessness," *Journal of Socio-Economics* 25 (1996), among other contributors. See also the related literature on "social exclusion"; good introductions to the literature can be found in Gerry Rodgers, Charles Gore and J. B. Figueiredo, eds., *Social Exclusion: Rhetoric, Reality, Responses* (Geneva: International Institute for Labour Studies, 1995); Charles Gore et al., *Social Exclusion and Anti-Poverty Policy* (Geneva: International Institute for Labour Studies, 1997); Arjan de Haan and Simon Maxwell, *Poverty and Social Exclusion in North and South,* special number, *Institute of Development Studies Bulletin* 29 (January 1998).

23. A. B. Atkinson, Lee Rainwater and Timothy Smeeding, *Income Distribution in OECD Countries* (Paris: OECD, 1996).

24. The need for new policy initiatives is particularly strong at this time. See Jean-Paul Fitoussi and R. Rosanvallon, *Le Nouvel âge des inégalités* (Paris: Sevil, 1996); Edmund S. Phelps, *Rewarding Work: How to Restore Participation and Self-Support to Free Enterprise* (Cambridge, Mass.: Harvard University Press, 1997). See also Paul Krugman, *Technology, Trade and Factor Prices,* NBER Working Paper no. 5355 (Cambridge, Mass.: National Bureau of Economic Research, 1995); Stephen Nickell, "Unemployment and Labor Market Rigidities: Europe versus North

America," *Journal of Economics Perspectives* 11 (1997); Richard Layard, *Tackling Unemployment* (London: Macmillan, 1999); Jean-Paul Fitoussi, Francesco Giavezzi, Assar Lindbeck, Franco Modigliani, Beniamino Moro, Dennis J. Snower, Robert Solow and Klaus Zimmerman, "A Manifesto on Unemployment in the European Union," mimeographed, 1998.

25. Data from M. W. Owen, S. M. Teutsch, D. F. Williamson and J. S. Marks, "The Effects of Known Risk Factors on the Excess Mortality of Black Adults in the United States," *Journal of the American Medical Association* 263, number 6 (February 9, 1990).

26. On this see my *Commodities and Capabilities* (1985). UNDP's *Human Development Report*s have provided important information and assessment regarding this way of seeing poverty, especially in *Human Development Report 1997*. See also Sudhir Anand and Amartya Sen, "Concepts of Human Development and Poverty: A Multidimensional Perspective" (1997).

27. Drèze and Sen, *India: Economic Development and Social Opportunity* (1995); Amartya Sen, "Hunger in the Modern World," Dr. Rajendra Prasad Memorial Lecture, New Delhi, June 1997; and "Entitlement Perspectives of Hunger," World Food Programme, 1997.

28. For sources of this information and of other information used in this section, see Drèze and Sen, *India: Economic Development and Social Opportunity* (1995), chapter 3 and statistical appendix. The picture here focuses on 1991, for reasons of data availability. There has, however, been a considerable increase in literacy just reported in the latest Indian National Sample Survey. There are also some important policy departures announced by some of the state governments, such as West Bengal and Madhya Pradesh.

29. See C.J.L. Murray et al., *U.S. Patterns of Mortality by County and Race: 1965–1994* (Cambridge, Mass.: Harvard Center for Population and Developmental Studies, 1998), table 6d, p. 56.

30. The severity of India's failure to devote resources and efforts to social development is convincingly and movingly discussed by S. Guhan, "An Unfulfilled Vision," *IASSI Quarterly* 12 (1993). See also the collection of essays in his honor: Barbara Harriss-White and S. Subramanian, eds., *Illfare in India: Essays on India's Social Sector in Honour of S. Guhan* (Delhi: Sage, 1999).

31. This is taken from table 3.1 in Drèze and Sen, *India: Economic Development and Social Opportunity* (1995). See also Saraswati Raju, Peter J. Atkins, Naresh Kumas and Janet G. Townsend, *Atlas of Women and Men in India* (New Delhi: Kali for Women, 1999).

32. See also A. K. Shiva Kumar, "UNDP's Human Development Index: A Computation for Indian States," *Economic and Political Weekly*, October 12, 1991, and Rajah J. Chelliah and R. Sudarshan, eds., *Indian Poverty and Beyond: Human Development in India* (New Delhi: Social Science Press, 1999).

33. See World Bank, *World Development Report 1994* (Oxford: Oxford University Press, 1994), table 1, p. 163.

34. On this see the extensive comparison made by Peter Svedberg, *Poverty and Undernutrition: Theory and Measurement* (Oxford: Clarendon Press, 1997). Svedberg also scrutinizes alternative approaches to measuring undernutrition, and the conflicting pictures generated by different statistics, but arrives at a firm conclusion against India in terms of undernutrition vis-à-vis sub-Saharan Africa.

35. See World Bank, *World Development Report 1993* (Oxford: Oxford University Press, 1993), table A.3. Mortality rates have worsened with the spread of the AIDS epidemic.

36. See Svedberg, *Poverty and Undernutrition* (1997). See also C. Gopalan, ed., *Combating Undernutrition* (New Delhi: Nutrition Foundation of India, 1995).

37. See Nevin Scrimshaw, "The Lasting Damage of Early Malnutrition," in R. W. Fogel et al., *Ending the Inheritance of Hunger* (Rome: World Food Programme, 1997). See also the papers of Robert W. Fogel, Cutberto Garza and Amartya Sen in the same volume.

38. This is not to deny that each of the standard criteria of undernourishment admits some room for doubt, but indicators based on health and physique do have some advantages over measures that simply look at food input. It is also possible to make use of the available medical and functional knowledge to improve the criteria to be used. On these and related issues, see Dasgupta, *An Inquiry into Well-Being and Destitution* (1993); Osmani, ed., *Nutrition and Poverty* (1993); Scrimshaw, "The Lasting Damage of Early Malnutrition," and Robert W. Fogel, "The Global Struggle to Escape from Chronic Malnutrition since 1700," in Fogel et al., *Ending the Inheritance of Hunger* (1997).

39. See Svedberg, *Poverty and Undernutrition* and the literature cited there. See also United Nations Development Programme, *Human Development Report 1995* (New York: Oxford University Press, 1995).

40. Africa also suffers from a much greater burden of international debt, which is now gigantic. There is also the difference that African countries have been much more subjected to dictatorial governance, partly as a result of being caught in the cold war, with the West and Soviet Union both being willing to provide support to military coups and other takeovers by their nondemocratic allies. The penalties of dictatorship in terms of loss of voice by the vulnerable underdog and loss of transparency and accountability will be discussed in chapters 6 and 7. Even the inclination to run into heavy debt to meet military and other priorities is encouraged by dictatorial rules.

41. The UNDP has produced since 1990 interesting and important detailed data on the nature of deprivation in the different parts of the world in its annual *Human Development Report*s, initiated by Dr. Mahbub ul Haq. They have also proposed and presented some aggregate measures, in particular the Human Development Index (HDI) and the Human Poverty Index (HPI). These aggregate indices have tended to draw much more public attention than the detailed and diverse empirical pictures emerging from the tables and other empirical presentations. Indeed, getting public attention has clearly been a part of UNDP's objective, particularly in its attempt to combat the overconcentration on the simple measure of GNP per head, which often serves as the only indicator of which the public takes any notice. To compete with the GNP, there is a need for another—broader—measure with the same level of crudeness as the GNP. This need is partly met by the use of the HDI, just as the HPI has been offered by the UNDP as a rival to the standard measures of income poverty. It is not my intention to question the merits of such competitive use, in the context of getting public attention (I have, in fact, provided technical help to the UNDP to devise both these indices). The fact remains, nevertheless, that the *Human Development Reports* are much richer in relevant information than can be

obtained from an exclusive concentration on the aggregative indicators such as HDI and HPI.

42. Amartya Sen, "Missing Women" (1992).

43. See also my *Resources, Values and Development* (1984); Barbara Harriss and E. Watson, "The Sex Ratio in South Asia," in *Geography of Gender in the Third World,* edited by J. H. Momson and J. Townsend (London: Butler & Tanner, 1987); Jocelyn Kynch, "How Many Women Are Enough? Sex Ratios and the Right to Life," *Third World Affairs 1985* (London: Third World Foundation, 1985); Amartya Sen, "Women's Survival as a Development Problem," *Bulletin of the American Academy of Arts and Sciences* 43, number 2 (1989), pp. 14–29; Ansley Coale, "Excess Female Mortality and the Balances of the Sexes in the Population: An Estimate of the Number of 'Missing Females,' " *Population and Development Review* 17, number 3 (1991), pp. 517–23; Stephan Klasen, "Missing Women Reconsidered," *World Development* 22 (1994).

44. See I. Waldron, "The Role of Genetic and Biological Factors in Sex Differences in Mortality," in *Sex Differences in Mortality,* edited by A. D. Lopez and L. T. Ruzicka (Canberra: Department of Demography, Australian National University, 1983).

45. On this see my "Women's Survival as a Development Problem," *Bulletin of the American Academy of Arts and Sciences* (November 1989); revised version, "More Than a Hundred Million Women Are Missing," *The New York Review of Books,* Christmas number (December 20), 1990.

46. See Drèze and Sen, *Hunger and Public Action* (1989), table 4.1, p. 52. See also my "Missing Women" (1992).

47. Coale, "Excess Female Mortality."

48. Stephan Klasen, "Missing Women Reconsidered," *World Development* 22 (1994).

49. Chen, Huq, and D'Souza, "Sex Bias in the Family Allocation of Food and Health Care in Rural Bangladesh" (1981), p. 7; Sen, *Commodities and Capabilities* (1985), appendix B, and the empirical literature cited there (also Coale, "Excess Female Mortality," 1991).

50. See particularly Atkinson, *Social Justice and Public Policy,* (1983), and his *Poverty and Social Security* (New York: Wheatsheaf, 1989).

51. Harry Frankfurt, "Equality as a Moral Ideal," *Ethics* 98 (1987), p. 21.

52. I have discussed different aspects of this distinction in "From Income Inequality to Economic Inequality," *Southern Economic Journal* 64 (1997).

53. On this see my "The Welfare Basis of Real Income Comparisons," *Journal of Economic Literature* 17 (1979), reprinted in *Resources, Values and Development* (1984).

## Chapter 5: *Markets, State and Social Opportunity*

1. I have tried to present some attempts at scrutiny in my *On Ethics and Economics* (Oxford: Blackwell, 1987), and further in "Markets and Freedoms," *Oxford Economic Papers* 45 (1993); "Markets and the Freedom to Choose," in *The Ethical Foundations of the Market Economy,* edited by Horst Siebert (Tübingen: J.C.B. Mohr, 1994); and "Social Justice and Economic Efficiency," presented at a seminar on "Philosophy and Politics" in Berlin, November 1997.

2. On the distinction between "culmination outcomes" and "comprehensive

outcomes," see my "Maximization and the Act of Choice," *Econometrica* 65 (July 1997). The comprehensive outcome takes note not merely of the end-states, but also of the *process* of choice itself.

3. There is a separate but important issue as to what kinds of relations can be appropriately seen as fit for marketing and commodification, on which see Margaret Jane Radin, *Contested Commodities* (Cambridge, Mass: Harvard University Press, 1996).

4. See Robert W. Fogel and Stanley L. Engerman, *Time on the Cross: The Economics of American Negro Slavery* (Boston: Little, Brown, 1974). See also chapter 1 above.

5. See G. A. Cornia with R. Paniccià, *The Demographic Impact of Sudden Impoverishment: Eastern Europe during the 1986–1996 Transition* (Florence: International Child Development Centre, UNICEF, 1995). See also Michael Ellman, "The Increase in Death and Disease under 'Katastroika,' " *Cambridge Journal of Economics* 18 (1994).

6. Friedrich Hayek, *The Road to Serfdom* (London: Routledge, 1944). See also Janos Kornai, *The Road to a Free Economy: Shifting from a Socialist System* (New York: Norton, 1990), and *Visions and Reality, Market and State: Contradictions and Dilemmas Revisited* (New York: Harvester Press, 1990).

7. On this see my "Gender and Cooperative Conflict," in *Persistent Inequalities: Women and World Development*, edited by Irene Tinker (New York: Oxford University Press, 1990); see also the extensive references, cited there, to the empirical and theoretical literatures on this subject.

8. On this see Ester Boserup, *Women's Role in Economic Development* (London: Allen & Unwin, 1970); Martha Loutfi, *Rural Women: Unequal Partners in Development* (Geneva: ILO, 1980); Luisella Goldschmidt-Clermont, *Unpaid Work in the Household* (Geneva: ILO, 1982); Amartya Sen, "Economics and the Family," *Asian Development Review* 1 (1983), *Resources, Values and Development* (Cambridge, Mass.: Harvard University Press, 1984), and *Commodities and Capabilities* (Amsterdam: North-Holland, 1985); Irene Tinker, ed., *Persistent Inequalities* (1990); Nancy Folbre, "The Unproductive Housewife: Her Evolution in Nineteenth Century Economic Thought," *Signs: Journal of Women in Culture and Society* 16 (1991); Naila Kabeer, "Gender, Production and Well-Being," Discussion Paper 288, Institute of Development Studies, University of Sussex, 1991; Lourdes Urdaneta-Ferrán, "Measuring Women's and Men's Economic Contributions," *Proceedings of the ISI 49th Session* (Florence: International Statistical Institute, 1993); Naila Kabeer, *Reversed Realities: Gender Hierarchies in Development Thought* (London: Verso, 1994); United Nations Development Programme, *Human Development Report 1995* (New York: Oxford University Press, 1995); among other contributions.

9. The need to see the working of the market mechanism in combination with the roles of other economic, social and political institutions has been stressed by Douglass North, *Structure and Change in Economic History* (New York: Norton, 1981), and also—with a different emphasis—by Judith R. Blau, *Social Contracts and Economic Markets* (New York: Plenum, 1993). See also the recent study by David S. Landes, *The Wealth and Poverty of Nations* (New York: Norton, 1998).

10. There is by now quite a substantial literature on these and related issues; see Joseph Stiglitz and F. Mathewson, eds., *New Developments in the Analysis of Mar-*

*ket Structure* (London: Macmillan, 1986), and Nicholas Stern, "The Economics of Development: A Survey," *Economic Journal* 99 (1989).

11. See Kenneth J. Arrow, "An Extension of the Basic Theorems of Classical Welfare Economics," in *Proceedings of the Second Berkeley Symposium of Mathematical Statistics,* edited by J. Neyman (Berkeley, Calif.: University of California Press, 1951), and Gerard Debreu, *A Theory of Value* (New York: Wiley, 1959).

12. The modeling of the market economy in the recent development literature has substantially broadened the rather limited assumptions made in the Arrow-Debreu formulation. It has particularly explored the importance of economies of large scale, the role of knowledge, learning from experience, prevalence of monopolistic competition, the difficulties of coordination between different economic agents and the demands of long-run growth as opposed to static efficiency. On different aspects of these changes, see Avinash Dixit and Joseph E. Stiglitz, "Monopolistic Competition and Optimum Product Diversity," *American Economic Review* 67 (1977); Paul R. Krugman, "Increasing Returns, Monopolistic Competition and International Trade," *Journal of International Economics* 9 (1979); Paul R. Krugman, "Scale Economies, Product Differentiation and the Pattern of Trade," *American Economic Review* 70 (1981); Paul R. Krugman, *Strategic Trade Policy and New International Economics* (Cambridge, Mass.: MIT Press, 1986); Paul M. Romer, "Increasing Returns and Long-Run Growth," *Journal of Political Economy* 94 (1986); Paul M. Romer, "Growth Based on Increasing Returns Due to Specialization," *American Economic Review* 77 (1987); Robert E. Lucas, "On the Mechanics of Economic Development," *Journal of Monetary Economics* 22 (1988); Kevin Murphy, A. Schleifer and R. Vishny, "Industrialization and the Big Push," *Quarterly Journal of Economics* 104 (1989); Elhanan Helpman and Paul R. Krugman, *Market Structure and Foreign Trade* (Cambridge, Mass.: MIT Press, 1990); Gene M. Grossman and Elhanan Helpman, *Innovation and Growth in the Global Economy* (Cambridge, Mass.: MIT Press, 1991); Elhanan Helpman and Assad Razin, eds., *International Trade and Trade Policy* (Cambridge, Mass.: MIT Press, 1991); Paul R. Krugman, "History versus Expectations," *Quarterly Journal of Economics* 106 (1991); K. Matsuyama, "Increasing Returns, Industrialization and the Indeterminacy of Equilibrium," *Quarterly Journal of Economics* 106 (1991); Robert E. Lucas, "Making a Miracle," *Econometrica* 61 (1993); among other writings.

These developments have very substantially enriched the understanding of the process of development, and in particular of the role and functioning of the market economy in that process. They have also clarified the insights of earlier economists on development, including Adam Smith (especially on economies of scale, division of labor and learning from experience), but also Allyn Young, "Increasing Returns and Economic Progress," *Economic Journal* 38 (1928); Paul Rosenstein-Rodan, "Problems of Industrialization of Eastern and South-eastern Europe," *Economic Journal* 53 (1943); Albert O. Hirschman, *The Strategy of Economic Development* (New Haven, Conn.: Yale University Press, 1958); Robert Solow, "A Contribution to the Theory of Economic Growth," *Quarterly Journal of Economics* 70 (1956); Nicholas Kaldor, "A Model of Economic Growth," *Economic Journal* 67 (1957); Kenneth J. Arrow, "Economic Implications of Learning by Doing," *Review of Economic Studies* 29 (1962); and Nicholas Kaldor and James A. Mirrlees, "A New Model of Economic Growth," *Review of Economic Studies* 29 (1962). Fine accounts of the major issues and results can be found in Robert J. Barro and X. Sala-i-Martin, *Economic*

*Growth* (New York: McGraw-Hill, 1995); Kaushik Basu, *Analytical Development Economics: The Less Developed Economy Revisited* (Cambridge, Mass.: MIT Press, 1997); Debraj Ray, *Development Economics* (Princeton: Princeton University Press, 1998). See also Luigi Pasinetti and Robert Solow, eds., *Economic Growth and the Structure of Long-run Development* (London: Macmillan, 1994).

13. For an elementary, expository discussion of the results and their ethical implications, see my *On Ethics and Economics* (1985), chapter 2. The results also include the "inverse theorem" that guarantees the possibility of reaching, through the market mechanism, *any one* of the possible Pareto optima, from a suitable initial distribution of resources (and a corresponding set of generated prices). The need to establish the identified initial distribution of resources (for realizing the desired result) does, however, call for enormous political power and sustained administrative radicalism in bringing about the needed redistribution of assets, which can be quite drastic (if equity figures prominently in the choice between different Pareto optima). In this sense, the use of the "inverse theorem" as a justification of the market mechanism belongs to the "revolutionary's handbook" (on this see my *On Ethics and Economics*, pp. 37–8). The direct theorem, however, does not make any such demand; any competitive equilibrium is shown to be a Pareto optimum, given the required conditions (such as the absence of particular types of externalities), for *any* initial distribution of resources.

14. See my "Markets and Freedoms," *Oxford Economic Papers* 45 (1993).

15. There are also other ways of seeing effective freedom, which are discussed and scrutinized in my *Freedom, Rationality and Social Choice: Arrow Lectures and Other Essays* (Oxford: Clarendon Press, forthcoming); see also the literature cited there.

16. On this see also Kenneth Arrow and Frank Hahn, *General Competitive Analysis* (San Francisco: Holden-Day, 1971; republished, Amsterdam: North-Holland, 1979).

17. While the form of the preferences does impose restriction on what the individuals are assumed to be seeking, there is no further restriction on *why* they are seeking what they are seeking. For a scrutiny of the exact requirements and their relevance, see my "Markets and Freedoms" (1993). The basic point here is that the efficiency result—as extended to apply to substantive freedoms—relates directly to *preferences,* irrespective of the reasons for those preferences.

18. On this see my "Poverty, Relatively Speaking," *Oxford Economic Papers* 35 (1983), reprinted in my *Resources, Values and Development* (1984), and "Markets and Freedoms" (1993).

19. See, for example, A. B. Atkinson, *Poverty in Britain and the Reform of Social Security* (Cambridge: Cambridge University Press, 1970). See also Dorothy Wedderburn, *The Aged in the Welfare State* (London: Bell, 1961); Peter Townsend, *Poverty in the United Kingdom: A Survey of Household Resources and Standards of Living* (Harmondsworth: Penguin, 1979).

20. See Emma Rothschild, "Social Security and Laissez Faire in Eighteenth-Century Political Economy," *Population and Development Review* 21 (December 1995). Regarding the Poor Laws, Smith saw the need for social safety nets, but criticized the restrictions imposed by these laws on the movements and other freedoms of the poor thus supported; see Adam Smith, *An Inquiry into the Nature and Causes of the Wealth of Nations* (1776; republished, edited by R. H. Campbell and A. S.

Skinner, Oxford: Clarendon Press, 1976), pp. 152–4. Contrast Thomas Robert Malthus's severe attack on the Poor Laws in general.

21. Vilfredo Pareto, *Manual of Political Economy* (New York: Kelley, 1927), p. 379. See also Jagdish N. Bhagwati, *Protectionism* (Cambridge, Mass.: MIT Press, 1990), who quotes and cogently develops this argument. On related issues, see also Anne O. Krueger, "The Political Economy of the Rent-Seeking Society," *American Economic Review* 64 (1974); Jagdish N. Bhagwati, "Lobbying and Welfare," *Journal of Public Economics* 14 (1980); Ronald Findlay and Stan Wellisz, "Protection and Rent-Seeking in Developing Countries," in David C. Colander, *Neoclassical Political Economy: The Analysis of Rent-Seeking and DUP Activities* (New York: Harper and Row, 1984); Gene Grossman and Elhanan Helpman, *Innovation and Growth in the Global Economy* (Cambridge, Mass.: MIT Press, 1991); Debraj Ray, *Development Economics* (1998), chapter 18.

22. Dani Rodrik has pointed to an important asymmetry that may to some extent help the advocates of tariff, to wit, that this brings in money for the government to expend ("Political Economy of Trade Policy," in *Handbook of International Economics*, volume 3, edited by G. M. Grossman and K. Rogoff [Amsterdam: Elsevier, 1995]). Rodrik points out that in the United States, in the period 1870–1914, tariffs contributed to more than half of all revenues that the U.S. government earned (the proportion was even higher—more than 90 percent—before the Civil War). To the extent that this feeds a restrictionist bias, it has to be reckoned with, but to recognize a source of a bias is itself a contribution in the direction of countering it. See also R. Fernandez and D. Rodrik, "Resistance to Reform: Status Quo Bias in the Presence of Individual-Specific Uncertainty," *American Economic Review* 81 (1991).

23. Smith, *Wealth of Nations*, Campbell and Skinner edition (1976), volume 1, book 11, pp. 266–7. In modern interpretations of Adam Smith's opposition to the state's regulatory intervention, there may be an inadequate recognition of the fact that his hostility to such regulations related closely to his reading that these regulations were most often aimed at catering to the interests of the rich. Indeed, Smith expressed himself quite unequivocally on this subject (in Smith, *Wealth of Nations* [1976 Campbell and Skinner edition], pp., 157–8):

> Whenever the legislature attempts to regulate the differences between masters and their workmen, its counsellors are always the masters. When the regulation, therefore, is in favour of the workmen, it is always just and equitable; but it is sometimes otherwise when in favour of the masters.

24. On this see Emma Rothschild, "Adam Smith and Conservative Economics," *The Economic History Review* 45 (February 1992).

25. On this see my "Money and Value: On the Ethics and Economics of Finance," the first Paolo Baffi Lecture of the Bank of Italy (Rome: Bank of Italy, 1991); republished in *Economics and Philosophy* 9 (1993).

26. Adam Smith not only saw the banning of interest as mistaken policy, but also pointed out that such a prohibition would increase the cost of borrowing for the needy borrower.

> In some countries the interest of money has been prohibited by law. But as something can every where be made by the use of money, something ought

every where to be paid for the use of it. This regulation, instead of preventing, has been found from experience to increase the evil of usury; the debtor being obliged to pay, not only for the use of money, but for the risk which the creditor runs by accepting a compensation for that use. (Smith, *Wealth of Nations* [1976 Campbell and Skinner edition], volume 1, book 2, chapter 4, p. 356.)

27. Smith, *Wealth of Nations* (1976 Campbell and Skinner edition), volume 1, book 2, chapter 4, pp. 356–7. The term "projector" is used by Smith not in the neutral sense of "one who forms a project," but in the old pejorative sense.

28. Letter, 1787, of Jeremy Bentham, "To Dr. Smith," published in Jeremy Bentham, *Defence of Usury* (London: Payne, 1790).

29. Smith does not give any evidence of having been convinced by Jeremy Bentham's argument, even though Bentham felt convinced that he had indirect evidence that he had persuaded Smith to abandon his own earlier position (Smith's "sentiments," Bentham felt convinced, "with respect to the points of difference are at present the same as mine"). In fact, though, the subsequent editions of *The Wealth of Nations* did not include any revision whatsoever of the passage of which Bentham had been critical. On this odd debate, see Smith, *Wealth of Nations* (1976 Campbell and Skinner edition), pp. 357–8, footnote 19. See also H. W. Spiegel, "Usury," in *The New Palgrave: A Dictionary of Economics*, edited by J. Eatwell, M. Milgate and P. Newman, volume 4 (London: Macmillan, 1987).

30. Smith, *Wealth of Nations* (1976 Campbell and Skinner edition), volume 1, book 2, chapter 3, pp. 340–1.

31. In Smith, *Wealth of Nations* (1976 Campbell and Skinner edition), pp. 26–7.

32. There are various distinct concerns about the limitations of the market economy. For illuminating analyses of different types of worries, see Robert E. Lane, *The Market Experience* (Cambridge: Cambridge University Press, 1991); Joseph Stiglitz, *Whither Socialism?* (Cambridge, Mass.: MIT Press, 1994); Robert Heilbroner, *Visions of the Future: The Distant Past, Yesterday, Today and Tomorrow* (New York: Oxford University Press, 1995); Will Hutton, *The State We Are In* (London: Jonathan Cape, 1995); Robert Kuttner, *Global Competitiveness and Human Development: Allies or Adversaries?* (New York: UNDO, 1996), and *Everything for Sale: The Visions and the Limits of the Market* (New York: Knopf, 1998); Cass Sunstein, *Free Markets and Social Justice* (New York: Oxford University Press, 1997).

33. See particularly Alice H. Amsden, *Asia's Next Giant: South Korea and Late Industrialization* (New York: Oxford University Press, 1989); Robert Wade, *Governing the Market: Economic Theory and the Role of Government in East Asian Industrialization* (Princeton: Princeton University Press, 1990); Lance Taylor, ed., *The Rocky Road to Reform: Adjustment, Income Distribution and Growth in the Developing World* (Cambridge, Mass.: MIT Press, 1993); Jong-Il You and Ha-Joon Chang, "The Myth of Free Labor Market in Korea," *Contributions to Political Economy* 12 (1993); Gerry K. Helleiner, ed., *Manufacturing for Export in the Developing World: Problems and Possibilities* (London: Routledge, 1995); Kotaro Suzumura, *Competition, Commitment and Welfare* (Oxford: Clarendon Press, 1995); Dani Rodrik, "Understanding Economic Policy Reform," *Journal of Economic Literature* 24 (March 1996); Jomo K.S., with Chen Yun Chung, Brian C. Folk, Irfan ul-Haque, Pasuk Phongpaichit, Batara Simatupang and Mayuri Tateishi, *Southeast*

*Asia's Misunderstood Miracle: Industrial Policy and Economic Development in Thailand, Malaysia and Indonesia* (Boulder, Colo.: Westview Press, 1997); Vinay Bharat-Ram, *The Theory of the Global Firm* (Delhi: Oxford University Press, 1997); Jeffrey Sachs and Andrew Warner, "Sources of Slow Growth in African Economies," Harvard Institute for International Development, March 1997; Jong-Il You, "Globalization, Labor Market Flexibility and the Korean Labor Reform," *Seoul Journal of Economics* 10 (1997); Jomo K.S., ed., *Tigers in Trouble: Financial Governance, Liberalisation and Crises in East Asia* (London: Zed Books, 1998); among other writings. Dani Rodrik has provided a helpful overall account of the need for an appropriate combination of public intervention, markets and global exchange; the chosen combinations may vary from country to country; see his *The New Global Economy and Developing Countries* (1999). See also Edmond Malinvaud, Jean-Claude Milleron, Mustaphak Nabli, Amartya Sen, Arjun Sengupta, Nicholas Stern, Joseph E. Stiglitz, and Kotaro Suzumura, *Development Strategy and the Management of the Market Economy* (Oxford: Clarendon Press, 1997).

34. James D. Wolfensohn, "A Proposal for Comprehensive Development Framework," mimeographed, World Bank, 1999. See also Joseph E. Stiglitz, "An Agenda for Development in the Twenty-First Century," in *Annual World Bank Conference on Development Economics 1997*, edited by B. Pleskovi and J. E. Stiglitz (Washington, D.C.: World Bank, 1998).

35. On this see chapters 1–4 above; also Amartya Sen and James D. Wolfensohn, "Let's Respect Both Sides of the Development Coin," *International Herald Tribune*, May 5, 1999.

36. On this see Jean Drèze and Amartya Sen, *India: Economic Development and Social Opportunity* (Delhi: Oxford University Press, 1995). See also my "How Is India Doing?" *New York Review of Books* 21 (Christmas number, 1982), reprinted in *Social and Economic Development in India: A Reassessment*, edited by D. K. Basu and R. Sissons (London: Sage, 1986).

37. In this context see Isher Judge Ahluwalia and I.M.D. Little, eds., *India's Economic Reforms and Development: Essays for Manmohan Singh* (Delhi: Oxford University Press, 1998). See also Vijay Joshi and I.M.D. Little, *India's Economic Reforms, 1991–2001* (Delhi: Oxford University Press, 1996).

38. See the classic analysis of "market failure" in the presence of public goods in Paul A. Samuelson, "The Pure Theory of Public Expenditure," *Review of Economics and Statistics* 36 (1954), and "Diagrammatic Exposition of a Pure Theory Public Expenditure," *Review of Economics and Statistics* 37 (1955). See also Kenneth J. Arrow, "The Organization of Economic Activity: Issues Pertinent to the Choice of Market versus Non-market Allocation," in *Collected Papers of K. J. Arrow*, volume 2 (Cambridge, Mass.: Harvard University Press, 1983).

39. The nature of uncertainty in health is a further issue that makes market allocation problematic in the field of medicine and health care, on which see Kenneth J. Arrow, "Uncertainty and the Welfare Economics of Health Care," *American Economic Review* 53 (1963). The comparative merits of public action in the field of health care have much to do with the issues identified by Arrow as well as Samuelson (see the preceding note); on this see Jean Drèze and Amartya Sen, *Hunger and Public Action* (Oxford: Clarendon Press, 1989). See also Judith Tendler, *Good Government in the Tropics* (Baltimore: Johns Hopkins University Press, 1997).

40. The literature on this is quite vast, and while some contributions have

concentrated on institutional diversities needed to deal with the problem of public goods and related issues, others have concentrated on redefining "efficiency" after taking note of the costs of transaction and collusion. The need for institutional enhancement beyond the reliance only on traditional markets cannot, however, be escaped by redefinition, if the object is to go beyond achieving what the traditional markets can actually achieve. For an illuminating account of the various issues discussed in this vast literature, see Andreas Papandreou, *Externality and Institutions* (Oxford: Clarendon Press, 1994).

41. Smith, *Wealth of Nations* (1976 Campbell and Skinner edition), volume 1, book 2, p. 27, and volume 5, book 1, f, p. 785.

42. See my "Social Commitment and Democracy: The Demands of Equity and Financial Conservatism," in *Living as Equals*, edited by Paul Barker (Oxford: Oxford University Press, 1996), and also "Human Development and Financial Conservatism," keynote address at the International Conference on Financing Human Resource Development, arranged by the Asian Development Bank, on November 17, 1995, later published in *World Development*, 1998. The discussion that follows draws on these papers.

43. Undernourishment does, of course, have many complex aspects—on which see the papers included in S. R. Osmani, ed., *Nutrition and Poverty* (Oxford: Clarendon Press, 1992)—and some aspects of nutritional deprivation are more easily observed than others.

44. See the discussion of this issue in Jean Drèze and Amartya Sen, *Hunger and Public Action* (Oxford: Clarendon Press, 1989), chapter 7 (particularly pp. 109–13). The empirical observations come from T. Nash, "Report on Activities of the Child Feeding Centre in Korem," mimeographed (London: Save the Children Fund, 1986), and J. Borton and J. Shoham, "Experiences of Non-governmental Organisations in Targeting of Emergency Food Aid," mimeographed, report on a workshop held at the London School of Hygiene and Tropical Medicine, 1989.

45. On this see Drèze and Sen, *Hunger and Public Action* (1989). See also Timothy Besley and Stephen Coate, "Workfare versus Welfare: Incentive Arguments for Work Requirements in Poverty-Alleviation Programs," *American Economic Review* 82 (1992); Joachim von Braun, Tesfaye Teklu and Patrick Webb, "The Targeting Aspects of Public Works Schemes: Experiences in Africa," and Martin Ravallion and Gaurav Datt, "Is Targeting through a Work Requirement Efficient? Some Evidence from Rural India," both published in *Public Spending and the Poor: Theory and Evidence*, edited by Dominique van de Walle and Kimberly Nead (Baltimore: Johns Hopkins University Press, 1995). See also Joachim von Braun, Tesfaye Teklu and Patrick Webb, *Famine in Africa: Causes, Responses and Prevention* (Baltimore: Johns Hopkins University Press, 1998).

46. It won't help those who are too old, or too disabled, or too ill to work in that way, but as was mentioned earlier, such people can be easily identified in terms of these capability handicaps and supported through other—complementary—schemes. The possibility and actual experiences of such complementary programs were discussed in Drèze and Sen, *Hunger and Public Action* (1989).

47. On this see Sudhir Anand and Martin Ravallion, "Human Development in Poor Countries: Do Incomes Matter?" *Journal of Economic Perspectives* 7 (1993). See also Keith Griffin and John Knight, eds., *Human Development and the International Development Strategy for the 1990s* (London: Macmillan, 1990). In the

specific context of famines, see also Alex de Waal, *Famines That Kill: Darfur 1984–1985* (Oxford: Clarendon Press, 1989).

48. See my *On Economic Inequality* (1973), pp. 78–9.

49. These issues are discussed more fully in "The Political Economy of Targeting," my keynote address to the 1992 Annual World Bank Conference on Development Economics, published in van de Walle and Nead, *Public Spending and the Poor* (1995). See also the other essays in that illuminating volume.

50. On the general problems underlying asymmetrical information, see George A. Akerlof, *An Economic Theorist's Book of Tales* (Cambridge: Cambridge University Press, 1984).

51. See John Rawls, *A Theory of Justice* (Cambridge, Mass.: Harvard University Press, 1971), pp. 440–6. Rawls discusses how institutional arrangements and public policies can influence "the social bases of self-respect."

52. See particularly William J. Wilson, *The Truly Disadvantaged* (Chicago: University of Chicago Press, 1987); Christopher Jencks and Paul E. Peterson, eds., *The Urban Underclass* (Washington, D.C.: Brookings Institution, 1991); Theda Skocpol, *Protecting Soldiers and Mothers: The Politics of Social Provision in the United States, 1870–1920* (Cambridge, Mass.: Harvard University Press, 1991). I first encountered the argument (like many others) in a conversation with Terence (W. M.) Gorman at the London School of Economics around 1971, though I don't believe he ever wrote on this.

53. Michael Bruno, "Inflation, Growth and Monetary Control: Non-linear Lessons from Crisis and Recovery," Paolo Baffi Lecture (Rome: Bank of Italy, 1996). See also his *Crisis, Stabilization, and Economic Reform* (Oxford: Clarendon Press, 1993).

54. Bruno, "Inflation, Growth and Monetary Control," pp. 7–8.

55. Bruno, "Inflation, Growth and Monetary Control," pp. 8, 56.

56. Bruno, "Inflation, Growth and Monetary Control," p. 9.

57. Even though the World Bank was rather slow in recognizing the role of the state in East Asian economic success, it did eventually acknowledge the importance of the states' particular roles in promoting the expansion of education and human resources; see World Bank, *The East Asian Miracle: Economic Growth and Public Policy* (New York: Oxford University Press, 1993). See also the Asian Development Bank, *Emerging Asia: Changes and Challenges* (Manila: Asian Development Bank, 1997), and Nancy Birdsall, Carol Graham and Richard H. Sabot, *Beyond Trade-Offs: Market Reforms and Equitable Growth in Latin America* (Washington, D.C.: Inter-American Development Bank, 1998).

58. See Hiromitsu Ishi, "Trends in the Allocation of Public Expenditure in Light of Human Resource Development—Overview in Japan" (Asian Development Bank, 1995).

59. The nature of this connection was discussed in Drèze and Sen, *Hunger and Public Action* (1989). See also the analysis presented in World Bank, *The East Asian Miracle* (1993), and the extensive list of empirical references cited there. Also see the papers presented at the International Conference on Financing Human Resource Development, arranged by the Asian Development Bank, on November 17, 1995; many of the papers have been published in *World Development*, 1998. Fine analyses of contrasting experiences can be found in Nancy Birdsall and Richard H. Sabot, *Opportunity Forgone: Education, Growth and Inequality in Brazil* (Washington,

D.C.: World Bank, 1993); James W. McGuire, "Development Policy and Its Determinants in East Asia and Latin America," *Journal of Public Policy* (1994).

60. On this see Jere R. Behrman and Anil B. Deolalikar, "Health and Nutrition," in *Handbook of Development Economics*, edited by H. B. Chenery and T. N. Srinivasan (Amsterdam: North-Holland, 1988).

61. However, because of the impossible burden of international debt, some countries, especially in Africa, may not be able to exercise much choice at all in determining their fiscal priorities. On this issue the need for "visionary" international policy as a part of "realistic" economic possibilities is forcefully advocated by Jeffrey D. Sachs, "Release the Poorest Countries from Debt Bondage," *International Herald Tribune*, June 12–13, 1999.

62. On this, see UNDP, *Human Development Report 1994*.

## Chapter 6: *The Importance of Democracy*

1. The first part of this chapter draws much on my paper "Freedoms and Needs," *New Republic*, January 10 & 17, 1994.

2. Quoted in John F. Cooper, "Peking's Post-Tiananmen Foreign Policy: The Human Rights Factor," *Issues and Studies* 30 (October 1994), p. 69; see also Joanne Bauer and Daniel A. Bell, eds., *The East Asian Challenge for Human Rights* (Cambridge: Cambridge University Press, 1999).

3. The analysis presented here and the discussions that follow draw on my earlier papers "Freedoms and Needs" (1994); "Legal Rights and Moral Rights: Old Questions and New Problems," *Ratio Juris* 9 (June 1996); and "Human Rights and Asian Values," Morgenthau Memorial Lecture (New York: Carnegie Council on Ethics and International Affairs, 1997), published in a shortened form in *The New Republic*, July 14 & 21, 1997.

4. See, among other studies, Adam Przeworski et al., *Sustainable Democracy* (Cambridge: Cambridge University Press, 1995); Robert J. Barro, *Getting It Right: Markets and Choices in a Free Society* (Cambridge, Mass.: MIT Press, 1996). See also Robert J. Barro and Jong-Wha Lee, "Losers and Winners in Economic Growth," Working Paper 4341, National Bureau of Economic Research (1993); Partha Dasgupta, *An Inquiry into Well-Being and Destitution* (Oxford: Clarendon Press, 1993); John Helliwell, "Empirical Linkages between Democracy and Economic Growth," Working Paper 4066, National Bureau of Economic Research (1994); Surjit Bhalla, "Freedom and Economic Growth: A Vicious Circle?" presented at the Nobel Symposium in Uppsala on "Democracy's Victory and Crisis," August 1994; Adam Przeworski and Fernando Limongi, "Democracy and Development," presented at the Nobel Symposium in Uppsala cited above.

5. On this see also my joint study with Jean Drèze, *Hunger and Public Action* (Oxford: Clarendon Press, 1989), part 3.

6. On this see my "Development: Which Way Now?" *Economic Journal* 93 (December 1983) and *Resources, Values and Development* (Cambridge, Mass.: Harvard University Press, 1984; 1997).

7. It could be argued that at the time of the Irish famines in the 1840s, Ireland was part of the United Kingdom, rather than a colony. However, not only was there a great cultural gulf between the Irish population and the English rulers, with deep English skepticism of the Irish (going back at least to the sixteenth century—well reflected in Edmund Spenser's sharp-tongued *The Faerie Queene*), but also the divi-

sion of political powers was extremely uneven. For the purpose of the point at issue, Ireland was governed in a way not unlike the colonies ruled by alien governors. On this see Cecil Woodham-Smith, *The Great Hunger: Ireland 1845–1849* (London: Hamish Hamilton, 1962). Indeed, as Joel Mokyr has noted, "Ireland was considered by Britain as an alien and even hostile nation" (*Why Ireland Starved: A Quantitative and Analytical History of the Irish Economy, 1800–1850* [London: Allen & Unwin, 1983], p. 291).

8. Fidel Valdez Ramos, "Democracy and the East Asian Crisis," inaugural address at the Centre for Democratic Institutions, Australian National University, Canberra, November 26, 1998, p. 2.

9. An important factor is the reach of deliberative politics and of the utilization of moral arguments in public debates. On these issues, see Jürgen Haberman, "Three Normative Models of Democracy," *Constellations* 1 (1994); Seyla Benhabib, "Deliberative Rationality and Models of Democratic Legitimacy," *Constellations* 1 (1994); James Bonham and William Rehg, eds., *Deliberative Democracy* (Cambridge, Mass.: MIT Press, 1997). See also James Fishkin, *Democracy and Deliberation* (New Haven, Conn.: Yale University Press, 1971); Ralf Dahrendorf, *The Modern Social Contract* (New York: Weidenfeld, 1988); Alan Hamlin and Phillip Pettit, eds., *The Good Polity* (Oxford: Blackwell, 1989); Cass Sunstein, *The Partial Constitution* (Cambridge, Mass.: Harvard University Press, 1993); Amy Gutman and Dennis Thompson, *Democracy and Disagreement* (Cambridge, Mass.: Harvard University Press, 1996).

10. This is discussed in Drèze and Sen, *Hunger and Public Action* (1989), pp. 193–7, 229–39.

11. It is also worth noting that the environmental challenges, when adequately grasped, raise some of the central issues of social choice and deliberative politics; see my "Environmental Evaluation and Social Choice: Contingent Valuation and the Market Analogy," *Japanese Economic Review* 46 (1995).

## Chapter 7: *Famines and Other Crises*

1. The first part of this chapter draws on my keynote address to the Inter-Parliamentary Union in the Italian Senate on the occasion of the World Food Summit in Rome, Italy, November 15, 1996. The analysis derives from my *Poverty and Famines: An Essay on Entitlement and Deprivation* (Oxford: Clarendon Press, 1981), and my joint study with Jean Drèze, *Hunger and Public Action* (Oxford: Clarendon Press, 1989).

2. For an exposition of "entitlement analysis" see my *Poverty and Famines* (1981), and also Drèze and Sen, *Hunger and Public Action* (1989); Drèze and Sen, eds., *The Political Economy of Hunger* (Oxford: Clarendon Press, 1990), and its shortened version, Drèze, Sen and Athar Hussain, *The Political Economy of Hunger: Selected Essays* (Oxford: Clarendon Press, 1995).

3. For examples of famines arising from different causes, with little or no reduction of food output and availability, see my *Poverty and Famines* (1981), chapters 6–9.

4. On this see my *Poverty and Famines* (1981). See also Meghnad Desai, "A General Theory of Poverty," *Indian Economic Review* 19 (1984), and "The Economics of Famine," in *Famines,* edited by G. A. Harrison (Oxford: Clarendon Press, 1988). See also Lucile F. Newman, ed., *Hunger in History: Food Shortage, Poverty,*

*and Deprivation* (Oxford: Blackwell, 1990), and going further back, Peter Garnsey, *Famine and Food Supply in the Graeco-Roman World* (Cambridge: Cambridge University Press, 1988).

5. A major critical survey of the literature on famines can be found in Martin Ravallion, "Famines and Economics," *Journal of Economic Literature* 35 (1997).

6. On this see my *Poverty and Famines* (1981), chapters 7 and 8.

7. The Bangladesh famine of 1974 is analyzed in my *Poverty and Famines* (1981), chapter 9, and also in Mohiuddin Alamgir, *Famine in South Asia* (Boston: Oelgeschlager, Gunn & Hain, 1980), and in Martin Ravallion, *Markets and Famines* (1987).

8. On this see Ravallion, *Markets and Famines* (1987).

9. The fact that Ireland was exporting food to England during the famines is sometimes cited as evidence that food output had not declined in Ireland. But that is an erroneous conclusion, both because we have direct evidence of a decline in Irish food output (associated with the potato epidemics), and because the movement of food is determined by relative prices, and not just by the size of food output in the exporting country. Indeed, "food countermovement" is a common phenomenon in a "slump famine" in which there is a general economic decline, which can make demand for food go down even more than the reduction of supply (on this and on related matters, see my *Poverty and Famines* [1981]). In the Chinese famines too, a much larger proportion of the reduced food output of rural China was being taken out into the urban areas as a result of official policy (on this see Carl Riskin, "Feeding China: The Experience since 1949," in Drèze and Sen, *The Political Economy of Hunger* [1989]).

10. There were also other factors behind the differential mortality in the Bengal famine of 1943, including the governmental decision to shelter the urban population in Calcutta through food rationing, price control and fair-price shops, leaving the rural poor thoroughly unprotected. On these and other aspects of the Bengal famine, see my *Poverty and Famines* (1981), chapter 6.

11. It is not uncommon, in general, for the rural people to suffer more from famines than do the economically and politically more powerful urban population. Michael Lipton has analyzed the nature of the "urban bias" in a classic study: *Why Poor People Stay Poor: A Study of Urban Bias in World Development* (London: Temple Smith, 1977).

12. On this see Alamgir, *Famine in South Asia* (1980), and my *Poverty and Famines* (1981), chapter 9. The analyses of food prices (and other causal factors) are extensively explored by Martin Ravallion, in *Markets and Famines* (1987). Ravallion also shows how the rice market exaggerated the extent of the future decline of food supply in Bangladesh, making the anticipatory price rise a good deal steeper than it need have been.

13. *Encyclopaedia Britannica*, 11th edition (Cambridge, 1910–1911), volume 10, p. 167.

14. See A. Loveday, *The History and Economics of Indian Famines* (London: G. Bell, 1916), and also my *Poverty and Famines* (1981), chapter 4.

15. On this see Alex de Waal, *Famines That Kill* (Oxford: Clarendon Press, 1989). See also my *Poverty and Famines*, appendix D, on the pattern of famine mortality in the Bengal famine of 1943.

16. The analysis here utilizes my essays "Famine as Alienation," in *State, Mar-*

*ket and Development: Essays in Honour of Rehman Sobhan,* edited by Abu Abdullah and Azizur Rahman Khan (Dhaka: University Press, 1996), and "Nobody Need Starve," *Granta* 52 (1995).

17. On this see Robert James Scally, *The End of Hidden Ireland* (New York: Oxford University Press, 1995).

18. See Cormac O Grada, *Ireland before and after the Famine: Explorations in Economic History, 1800–1925* (Manchester: Manchester University Press, 1988), and *The Great Irish Famine* (Basingstoke: Macmillan, 1989).

19. Terry Eagleton, *Heathcliff and the Great Hunger: Studies in Irish Culture* (London: Verso, 1995), pp. 25–6.

20. For analyses of the Irish famines, see Joel Mokyr, *Why Ireland Starved: A Quantitative and Analytical History of the Irish Economy, 1800–1850* (London: Allen & Unwin, 1983); Cormac O Grada, *Ireland before and after the Famine* (1988) and *The Great Irish Famine* (1989); and Pat McGregor, "A Model of Crisis in a Peasant Economy," *Oxford Economic Papers* 42 (1990). The issue of landlessness is particularly serious in the context of famines in South Asia and to some extent sub-Saharan Africa; see Keith Griffin and Azizur Khan, eds., *Poverty and Landlessness in Rural Asia* (Geneva: ILO, 1977), and Alamgir, *Famine in South Asia* (1980).

21. On this see Alamgir, *Famine in South Asia* (1980), and Ravallion, *Markets and Famines* (1987). See also Nurul Islam, *Development Planning in Bangladesh: A Study in Political Economy* (London: Hurst; New York: St. Martin's Press, 1977).

22. On food "countermovement," see Sen, *Poverty and Famines* (1981); Graciela Chichilnisky, "North-South Trade with Export Enclaves: Food Consumption and Food Exports," mimeographed, Columbia University, 1983; Drèze and Sen, *Hunger and Public Action* (1989).

23. Mokyr, *Why Ireland Starved* (1983), p. 291. On different aspects of this complex relationship, see R. Fitzroy Foster, *Modern Ireland 1600–1972* (London: Penguin, 1989).

24. See Mokyr's balanced assessment of this line of diagnosis in *Why Ireland Starved* (1983), pp. 291–2.

25. On this see Cecil Woodham-Smith, *The Great Hunger: Ireland 1845–1849* (London: Hamish Hamilton, 1962); also O Grada, *The Great Irish Famine* (1989), and Eagleton, *Heathcliff and the Great Hunger* (1995). Ireland's subsequent history has also been deeply influenced by the famine and thus by the treatment it received from London; see Scally, *The End of Hidden Ireland* (1995).

26. See Andrew Roberts, *Eminent Churchillians* (London: Weidenfeld & Nicolson, 1994), p. 213.

27. Quoted in Woodham-Smith, *The Great Hunger* (1962), p. 76.

28. The relevance of moral reasoning in the prevention of hunger and famines has been illuminatingly analyzed by Onora O'Neil, *Faces of Hunger: An Essay on Poverty, Justice and Development* (London: Allen and Unwin, 1986). See also P. Sainath, *Everybody Loves a Good Drought* (New Delhi: Penguin, 1996); Helen O'Neill and John Toye, eds., *A World Without Famine? New Approaches to Aid and Development* (London: Macmillan, 1998); Joachim von Braun, Tesfaye Teklu and Patricia Webb, *Famine in Africa: Causes, Responses, Prevention* (Baltimore: Johns Hopkins University Press, 1999).

29. There is a large literature on this, which is discussed and critically assessed in Drèze and Sen, *Hunger and Public Action* (1989), chapter 9. See also C. K. Eicher,

*Transforming African Agriculture* (San Francisco: The Hunger Project, 1986); M. S. Swaminathan, *Sustainable Nutritional Security for Africa* (San Francisco: The Hunger Project, 1986); M. Glantz, ed., *Drought and Hunger in Africa* (Cambridge: Cambridge University Press, 1987); J. Mellor, C. Delgado and C. Blackie, eds., *Accelerating Food Production in Sub-Saharan Africa* (Baltimore: Johns Hopkins University Press, 1987). See also the papers of Judith Heyer, Francis Idachaba, Jean-Philippe Platteau, Peter Svedberg and Sam Wangwe in *The Political Economy of Hunger,* edited by Drèze and Sen (1990).

30. See Drèze and Sen, *Hunger and Public Action* (1989), table 2.4, p. 33.

31. On this see Drèze and Sen, *Hunger and Public Action* (1989), chapter 8, and the papers of Drèze in Drèze and Sen, *The Political Economy of Hunger* (1990).

32. On the mechanics of such procedures see Drèze and Sen, *Hunger and Public Action* (1989), chapter 8, and the papers of Jean Drèze in Drèze and Sen, *The Political Economy of Hunger* (1990).

33. On this see Drèze and Sen, *Hunger and Public Action* (1989), chapter 8.

34. On this and related issues, see my *Poverty and Famines* (1981), and Drèze and Sen, *Hunger and Public Action* (1989).

35. The comparative picture is presented in Drèze and Sen, *Hunger and Public Action* (1989), chapter 8.

36. See Basil Ashton, Kenneth Hill, Alan Piazza and Robin Zeitz, "Famine in China 1958–61," *Population and Development Review* 10 (1984).

37. See T. P. Bernstein, "Stalinism, Famine, and Chinese Peasants," *Theory and Society* 13 (1984), p. 13. See also Carl Riskin, *China's Political Economy* (Oxford: Clarendon Press, 1987).

38. Quoted in Mao Tse-tung, *Mao Tse-tung Unrehearsed, Talks and Letters: 1956–1971,* edited by Stuart R. Schram (Harmondsworth: Penguin Books, 1976), pp. 277–8. See also the discussion of this statement in Ralph Miliband, *Marxism and Politics* (London: Oxford University Press, 1977), pp. 149–50.

39. On this see also Ralph Miliband, *Marxism and Politics* (1977), p. 151.

40. On this see also Drèze and Sen, *Hunger and Public Action* (1989).

41. An "internal" account of the IMF's general strategy of crisis prevention and long-run reform in East and Southeast Asia can be found in Timothy Lane, Atish R. Ghosh, Javier Hamann, Steven Phillips, Marianne Schultz-Ghattas and Tsidi Tsikata, *IMF-Supported Programs in Indonesia, Korea and Thailand: A Preliminary Assessment* (Washington, D.C.: International Monetary Fund, 1999).

42. See James D. Wolfensohn, *The Other Crisis: Address to the Board of Governors of the World Bank* (Washington, D.C.: World Bank, 1998).

43. Destitution can result not only from natural catastrophes or economic slumps, but also from wars and military conflicts; on this see my "Economic Regress: Concepts and Features," in *Proceedings of the World Bank Annual Conference on Development Economics 1993* (Washington, D.C.: World Bank, 1994). On the general role of militarism as a modern scourge, see also John Kenneth Galbraith, "The Unfinished Business of the Century," mimeographed, lecture at the London School of Economics, June 28, 1999.

44. See Torsten Persson and Guido Tabellini, "Is Inequality Harmful to Growth? Theory and Evidence," *American Economic Review* 84 (1994); Alberto Alesina and Dani Rodrik, "Distributive Politics and Economic Growth," *Quarterly Journal of Economics* 108 (1994); Albert Fishlow, C. Gwin, S. Haggard, D. Rodrik and

S. Wade, *Miracle or Design? Lessons from the East Asian Experience* (Washington, D.C.: Overseas Development Council, 1994). See also the contrast with India (and South Asia in general), in Jean Drèze and Amartya Sen, *India: Economic Development and Social Opportunity* (Delhi: Oxford University Press, 1995). The lower level of inequality of this kind does not, however, guarantee the kind of equity that democratic politics can bring at times of crisis and acute deprivation. Indeed, as Jong-Il You notes, in these countries (including South Korea) "low inequality and high profit shares coexisted primarily due to the unusually even distribution of wealth" ("Income Distribution and Growth in East Asia," *Journal of Development Studies* 34 [1998]). In this, the past history of Korea, including prior land reforms, widespread development of human capital through educational expansion, and so on, seems to have played a very positive part.

## Chapter 8: *Women's Agency and Social Change*

1. I have discussed this issue in some previous works, including: "Economics and the Family," *Asian Development Review* 1 (1983); "Women, Technology and Sexual Divisions," *Trade and Development* 6 (1985); "Missing Women," *British Medical Journal* 304 (March 1992); "Gender and Cooperative Conflict," *Persistent Inequalities: Women and World Development,* edited by Irene Tinker (New York: Oxford University Press, 1990); "Gender Inequality and Theories of Justice," *Women, Culture and Development: A Study of Human Capabilities,* edited by Martha Nussbaum and Jonathan Glover (Oxford: Clarendon Press, 1995); (jointly with Jean Drèze) *India: Economic Development and Social Opportunity* (Delhi: Oxford University Press, 1995); "Agency and Well-Being: The Development Agenda," in *A Commitment to the Women,* edited by Noeleen Heyzer (New York: UNIFEM, 1996).

2. My paper "Well-Being, Agency and Freedom: The Dewey Lectures 1984," *Journal of Philosophy* 82 (April 1985), investigates the philosophical distinction between the "agency aspect" and the "well-being aspect" of a person, and attempts to identify the far-reaching practical implications of this distinction, applied to many different fields.

3. Alternative statistical estimates of the extent of "extra mortality" of women in many countries in Asia and North Africa also are discussed in my *Resources, Values and Development* (Cambridge, Mass.: Harvard University Press, 1984); (jointly with Jean Drèze) *Hunger and Public Action* (Oxford: Clarendon Press, 1989). See also Stephan Klasen, " 'Missing Women' Reconsidered," *World Development* 22 (1994).

4. There is a vast literature on this; my own attempts at analyzing and using the available evidence can be found in "Gender and Cooperative Conflict" (1990), and "More Than a Hundred Million Women Are Missing," *New York Review of Books,* (Christmas number, December 20, 1990).

5. These issues have been discussed in my *Resources, Values and Development* (1984), "Gender and Cooperative Conflict" (1990), and "More Than a Hundred Million Women Are Missing" (1990). A pioneering study of this general field was presented in Ester Boserup's classic work, *Women's Role in Economic Development* (London: Allen & Unwin, 1971). The recent literature on gender inequality in developing countries includes a number of interesting and important studies of different types of determining variables. See, for example, Hanna Papanek, "Family Status

and Production: The 'Work' and 'Non-Work' of Women," *Signs* 4 (1979). Martha Loutfi, ed., *Rural Work: Unequal Partners in Development* (Geneva: ILO, 1980); Mark R. Rosenzweig and T. Paul Schultz, "Market Opportunities, Genetic Endowment and Intrafamily Resource Distribution," *American Economic Review* 72 (1982); Myra Buvinic, M. Lycette and W. P. McGreevy, eds., *Women and Poverty in the Third World* (Baltimore: Johns Hopkins University Press, 1983); Pranab Bardhan, *Land, Labor and Rural Poverty* (New York: Columbia University Press, 1984); Devaki Jain and Nirmala Banerjee, eds., *Tyranny of the Household: Investigative Essays in Women's Work* (New Delhi: Vikas, 1985); Gita Sen and C. Sen, "Women's Domestic Work and Economic Activity," *Economic and Political Weekly* 20 (1985); Martha Alter Chen, *A Quiet Revolution: Women in Transition in Rural Bangladesh* (Dhaka: BRAC, 1986); Jere Behrman and B. L. Wolfe, "How Does Mother's Schooling Affect Family Health, Nutrition, Medical Care Usage and Household Sanitation?" *Journal of Econometrics* 36 (1987); Monica Das Gupta, "Selective Discrimination against Female Children in India," *Population and Development Review* 13 (1987); Gita Sen and Caren Grown, *Development, Crises and Alternative Visions: Third World Women's Perspectives* (London: Earthscan, 1987); Alaka Basu, *Culture, the Status of Women and Demographic Behaviour* (Oxford: Clarendon Press, 1992); Nancy Folbre, Barbara Bergmann, Bina Agarwal and Maria Flore, eds., *Women's Work in the World Economy* (London: Macmillan, 1992); United Nations ESCAP, *Integration of Women's Concerns into Development Planning in Asia and the Pacific* (New York: United Nations, 1992); Bina Agarwal, *A Field of One's Own* (Cambridge: Cambridge University Press, 1995); Edith Kuiper and Jolande Sap, with Susan Feiner, Notburga Ott and Zafiris Tzannatos, *Out of the Margin: Feminist Perspectives on Economics* (New York: Routledge, 1995); among other contributions.

6. Gender divisions within the family are sometimes studied as "bargaining problems"; the literature includes, among many other contributions, Marilyn Manser and Murray Brown, "Marriage and Household Decision Making: A Bargaining Analysis," *International Economic Review* 21 (1980); M. B. McElroy and M. J. Horney, "Nash Bargained Household Decisions: Toward a Generalization of Theory of Demand," *International Economic Review* 22 (1981); Shelley Lundberg and Robert Pollak, "Noncooperative Bargaining Models of Marriage," *American Economic Review* 84 (1994). For approaches different from that of "bargaining models," see Sen, "Women, Technology and Sexual Divisions" (1985); Nancy Folbre, "Hearts and Spades: Paradigms of Household Economics," *World Development* 14 (1986); J. Brannen and G. Wilson, eds., *Give and Take in Families* (London: Allen & Unwin, 1987); Susan Moller Okin, *Justice, Gender, and the Family* (New York: Basic Books, 1989); Sen, "Gender and Cooperative Conflict" (1990); Marianne A. Ferber and Julie A. Nelson, eds., *Beyond Economic Man: Feminist Theory and Economics* (Chicago: Chicago University Press, 1993); among other contributions. Useful collections of papers on these issues can also be found in Jane Humphries, ed., *Gender and Economics* (Cheltenham, U.K.: Edward Elgar, 1995), and Nancy Folbre, ed., *The Economics of the Family* (Cheltenham, U.K.: Edward Elgar, 1996).

7. On this see Okin, *Justice, Gender, and the Family* (1989); Drèze and Sen, *Hunger and Public Action* (1989); Sen, "Gender and Cooperative Conflict" (1990); Nussbaum and Glover, *Woman, Culture and Development* (1995). See also the

papers of Julie Nelson, Shelley Lundberg, Robert Pollak, Diana Strassman, Myra Strober and Viviana Zelizer in the 1994 Papers and Proceedings in *American Economic Review* 84 (1994).

8. This issue has started receiving considerable attention in India. See Asoke Mitra, *Implications of Declining Sex Ratios in India's Population* (Bombay: Allied Publishers, 1980); Jocelyn Kynch and Amartya Sen, "Indian Women: Well-Being and Survival," *Cambridge Journal of Economics* 7 (1983); Bardhan, *Land, Labor and Rural Poverty* (1984); Jain and Banerjee, eds., *Tyranny of the Household* (1985). The "survival problem" relates to the broader issue of neglect, on which see also the studies presented in Swapna Mukhopadhyay, ed., *Women's Health, Public Policy and Community Action* (Delhi: Manohar, 1998), and Swapna Mukhopadhyay and R. Savithri, *Poverty, Gender and Reproductive Choice* (Delhi: Manohar, 1998).

9. On this see Tinker, *Persistent Inequalities* (1990). My own paper in this collection ("Gender and Cooperative Conflict") goes into the economic and social influences that affect the divisions within the family, and discusses why the divisions vary so much between regions (for example, antifemale bias being much stronger in South Asia, West Asia, North Africa and China than in sub-Saharan Africa or Southeast Asia), and also within different areas inside the same country (for example, gender bias at this level being very strong in some Indian states, such as Punjab and Uttar Pradesh, and effectively absent in Kerala). There are also close linkages between different influences on women's relative position, such as those connecting legal rights and basic education (since the *use* of legal provisions relates to the ability to read and write); see Salma Sobhan, *Legal Status of Women in Bangladesh* (Dhaka: Bangladesh Institute of Legal and International Affairs, 1978).

10. The role of gender divisions in the sharing of hunger has been illuminatingly studied by Megan Vaughan, *The Story of an African Famine: Hunger, Gender and Politics in Malawi* (Cambridge: Cambridge University Press, 1987); Barbara Harriss, "The Intrafamily Distribution of Hunger in South Asia," in *The Political Economy of Hunger,* edited by Jean Drèze and Amartya Sen (Oxford: Clarendon Press 1990), among others.

11. Some of these issues have been discussed in the specific context of India, with comparisons *within* and *outside* India in Drèze and Sen, *India: Economic Development and Social Opportunity* (1995); see also Alaka Basu, *Culture, the Status of Women and Demographic Behaviour* (1992), and Agarwal, *A Field of One's Own,* (1995). The different sources of disadvantage are particularly important to study in analyzing the special deprivation of groups with little economic or social leverage—for example, widows, especially from poorer families. On that, see Martha Alter Chen, ed., *Widows in India* (New Delhi: Sage, 1998), and her forthcoming book, *Perpetual Mourning: Widowhood in Rural India* (Delhi: Oxford University Press, 1999; Philadelphia, Pa.: University of Pennsylvania Press, 1999).

12. On the issues involved, see my "Gender and Cooperative Conflict," in Tinker, *Persistent Inequalities* (1990), and the literature cited there.

13. See L. Beneria, ed., *Women and Development: The Sexual Division of Labor in Rural Societies* (New York: Praeger, 1982). See also Jain and Banerjee, *Tyranny of the Household* (1985); Gita Sen and Grown, *Development, Crises and Alternative Visions* (1987); Haleh Afshar, ed., *Women and Empowerment: Illustrations from the Third World* (London: Macmillan, 1998).

14. See Mamta Murthi, Anne-Catherine Guio and Jean Drèze, "Mortality, Fertility and Gender Bias in India: A District Level Analysis," *Population and Development Review* 21 (December 1995). See also Jean Drèze and Amartya Sen, eds., *Indian Development: Selected Regional Perspectives* (Delhi: Oxford University Press, 1996). Questions can certainly be raised about the direction of causation in the identified relations—for example, whether women's literacy influences the status and standing of women in the family *or* whether women's higher standing inclines a family to send young girls to school. There could be, statistically, also a third factor that correlates with both. And yet recent empirical studies suggest that most families— even in socially backward areas in India—seem to have a strong preference for educating the children, including girls. One large survey indicates that the proportion of parents who think it is "important" to send girls to school even in the states with the *least* female literacy is remarkably high: 85 percent in Rajasthan, 88 percent in Bihar, 92 percent in Uttar Pradesh, and 93 percent in Madhya Pradesh. The main barrier to the education of girls appears to be the absence of convenient schools in the neighborhood—a major difference between high-literacy and low-literacy states. See the Probe Team, *Public Report on Basic Education in India* (Delhi: Oxford University Press, 1999). Public policy, therefore, has a central role to play. There have been recent public policy initiatives with good effect on literacy, especially in Himachal Pradesh, and more recently in West Bengal, Madhya Pradesh and a few other states.

15. The 1991 Indian census indicates that the death rate per thousand in the 0–4 age group was 25.6 for males and 27.5 for females at the all-India level. The female mortality rate in that age group was lower than the male mortality rate in Andhra Pradesh, Assam, Himachal Pradesh, Kerala and Tamil Nadu, but higher in all the other major Indian states. The female disadvantage was most pronounced in Bihar, Haryana, Madhya Pradesh, Punjab, Rajasthan and Uttar Pradesh.

16. Murthi, Guio and Drèze, "Mortality, Fertility and Gender Bias in India" (1995).

17. See Jean Drèze and Mamta Murthi, "Female Literacy and Fertility: Recent Census Evidence from India," mimeographed, Centre for History and Economics, King's College, Cambridge, U.K., 1999.

18. There were, apparently, not enough data with adequate interdistrict variations to examine the impact of different forms of property rights, which are relatively more uniform across India. On an isolated basis, there is, of course, the strong and much-discussed example of the Nairs in Kerala, who have had matrilineal inheritance for a long time (an association that confirms, rather than contradicts, insofar as it goes, the positive impact of female property rights on child survival in general and the survival of female children in particular).

19. There is, it appears, a positive association between female labor force participation and under-five mortality in these fits, but this association is not statistically significant.

20. See, among other important contributions, J. C. Caldwell, "Routes to Low Mortality in Poor Countries," *Population and Development Review* 12 (1986); and Behrman and Wolfe, "How Does Mother's Schooling Affect Family Health, Nutrition, Medical Care Usage and Household Sanitation?" (1987).

21. These have been extensively discussed in my joint book with Jean Drèze, *India: Economic Development and Social Opportunity* (1995).

22. The various sources of evidence on this have been subjected to critical examination, and not surprisingly, the different empirical studies emerge with rather disparate force in these critical scrutinies. See particularly the "critical perspectives" on this issue presented in Caroline H. Bledsoe, John B. Casterline, Jennifer A. Johnson-Kuhn and John G. Haaga, eds., *Critical Perspectives on Schooling and Fertility in the Developing World* (Washington, D.C.: National Academy Press, 1999). See also Susan Greenhalgh, *Situating Fertility: Anthropology and Demographic Inquiry* (Cambridge: Cambridge University Press, 1995); Robert J. Barro and Jong-Wha Lee, "International Comparisons of Educational Attainment," paper presented at a conference on How Do National Policies Affect Long-Run Growth?, World Bank, Washington, D.C., 1993; Robert Cassen, with contributors, *Population and Development: Old Debates, New Conclusions* (Washington, D.C.: Transaction Books for Overseas Development Council, 1994).

23. On these and related general issues, see my "Population: Delusion and Reality," *New York Review of Books*, September 22, 1994; *Population Policy: Authoritarianism versus Cooperation* (Chicago: MacArthur Foundation, 1995); and "Fertility and Coercion," *University of Chicago Law Review* 63 (summer 1996).

24. See United Nations, ESCAP, *Integration of Women's Concerns into Development Planning in Asia and the Pacific* (New York: United Nations, 1992), especially the paper of Rehman Sobhan and the references cited there. The practical issues relate closely to the social conception of women's role in society and thus touch on the central focus of feminist studies. A wide-ranging collection of papers (including many classics) can be found in Susan Moller Okin and Jane Mansbridge, eds., *Feminism* (Cheltenham, U.K.: Edward Elgar, 1994). See also Catherine A. Mackinnon, *Feminism Unmodified* (Cambridge, Mass.: Harvard University Press, 1987), and Barbara Johnson, *The Feminist Difference: Literature, Psychology, Race and Gender* (Cambridge, Mass.: Harvard University Press, 1998).

25. See Philip Oldenberg, "Sex Ratio, Son Preference and Violence in India: A Research Note," *Economic and Political Weekly*, December 5–12, 1998; Jean Drèze and Reetika Khera, "Crime, Society and Gender in India: Some Clues for Homicidal Data," mimeographed, Centre for Development Economics, Delhi School of Economics, 1999. The explanations of this interesting finding can invoke cultural factors as well as economic and social ones. Though the brief discussion here concentrates on the latter, there are obvious connections with psychological and valuational questions raised by those who see a basic gender contrast in morals and attitudes, most notably Carol Gilligan; see *In a Different Voice* (Cambridge, Mass.: Harvard University Press, 1982). Importance may well be attached to the fact that the most remarkable case of humane prison reform in India came from one of that rare breed, a woman prison governor, Kiran Bedi. Her own account of the radical change and the opposition she faced can be found in Kiran Bedi, *It's Always Possible: Transforming One of the Largest Prisons in the World* (New Delhi: Sterling, 1998). I do not pursue further here the important issue of distinguishing between alternative explanations of the nature of women's leadership in social change of this type, since the analysis presented in this work does not require that we try to resolve this complex issue.

26. Oldenberg argues for the former hypothesis; but see also Arup Mitra, "Sex Ratio and Violence: Spurious Results," *Economic and Political Weekly*, January 2–9, 1993. Drèze and Khera argue for an explanation with the opposite direction of

causation. See also the literature cited there, including older studies, such as Baldev Raj Nayar, *Violence and Crime in India: A Quantitative Study* (Delhi: Macmillan, 1975); S. M. Edwards, *Crime in India* (Jaipur: Printwell Publishers, 1988); S. Venugopal Rao, ed., *Perspectives in Criminology* (Delhi: Vikas, 1988).

27. Another factor has been the use of group responsibility in seeking a high rate of repayment. On this see Muhammad Yunus with Alan Jolis, *Banker to the Poor: Micro-Lending and the Battle Against World Poverty* (London: Aurum Press, 1998). See also Lutfun N. Khan Osmani, "Credit and Women's Relative Well-Being: A Case Study of the Grameen Bank, Bangladesh" (Ph.D. thesis, Queen's University of Belfast, 1998). See also Kaushik Basu, *Analytical Development Economics* (Cambridge, Mass.: MIT Press, 1997), chapters 13 and 14; Debraj Ray, *Development Economics* (Princeton: Princeton University Press, 1998), chapter 14.

28. See Catherine H. Lovell, *Breaking the Cycle of Poverty: The BRAC Strategy* (Hartford, Conn.: Kumarian Press, 1992).

29. See John C. Caldwell, Barkat-e-Khuda, Bruce Caldwell, Indrani Pieries and Pat Caldwell, "The Bangladesh Fertility Decline: An Interpretation," *Population and Development Review* 25 (1999). See also John Cleland, James F. Phillips, Sajeda Amin and G. M. Kamal, *The Determinants of Reproductive Change in Bangladesh: Success in a Challenging Environment* (Washington, D.C.: World Bank, 1996), and John Bongaarts, "The Role of Family Planning Programmes in Contemporary Fertility Transition," in *The Continuing Demographic Transition*, edited by G.W. Jones et al. (New York: Oxford University Press, 1997).

30. See Agarwal, *A Field of One's Own* (1995).

31. See Henrietta Moore and Megan Vaughan, *Cutting Down Trees: Gender, Nutrition and Agricultural Change in the Northern Province of Zambia, 1890–1990* (Portsmouth, N.H.: Heinemann, 1994).

32. The difficulties to be overcome by women in the labor market and in economic relations in society have been plentiful even in advanced market economies. See Barbara Bergmann, *The Economic Emergence of Women* (New York: Basic Books, 1986); Francine D. Blau and Marianne A. Ferber, *The Economics of Women, Men and Work* (Englewood Cliffs, N.J.: Prentice-Hall, 1986); Victor R. Fuchs, *Women's Quest for Economic Equality* (Cambridge, Mass.: Harvard University Press, 1988); Claudia Goldin, *Understanding the Gender Gap: An Economic History of American Women* (New York: Oxford University Press, 1990). See also the collection of papers in Marianne A. Ferber, *Women in the Labor Market* (Cheltenham, U.K.: Edward Elgar, 1998).

33. There is a danger of oversimplification in seeing the issue of women's "agency" or "autonomy" in too formulaic terms, focusing on simple statistical connections with variables such as female literacy or employment. On this see the insightful anthropological analysis of Alaka M. Basu, *Culture, Status of Women, and Demographic Behavior* (Oxford: Clarendon Press, 1992). See also the studies presented in Roger Jeffery and Alaka M. Basu, eds., *Girls' Schooling, Women's Autonomy and Fertility Change in South Asia* (London: Sage, 1996).

34. See Naila Kabeer, "The Power to Choose: Bangladeshi Women and Labour Market Decisions in London and Dhaka," mimeographed, Institute of Development Studies, University of Sussex, 1998.

35. The changing role of women (and its far-reaching effects) in India since independence is discussed in an interesting collection of papers edited by Bharati Ray and

Aparna Basu, *From Independence towards Freedom* (Delhi: Oxford University Press, 1999).

36. UNDP's *Human Development Report 1995* (New York: Oxford University Press, 1995) presents an intercountry investigation of gender differences in social, political and business leadership, in addition to reporting on gender inequality in terms of more conventional indicators. See also the literature cited there.

Chapter 9: *Population, Food and Freedom*

1. Thomas Robert Malthus, *Essay on the Principle of Population, As It Affects the Future Improvement of Society, with Remarks on the Speculation of Mr. Godwin, M. Condorcet, and Other Writers* (London: J. Johnson, 1798), chapter 8; in the Penguin Classics edition, *An Essay on the Principle of Population; and, A Summary View of the Principle of Population,* edited by Anthony Flew (Harmondsworth: Penguin Books, 1982), p. 123. See also *The Works of Thomas Robert Malthus,* edited by E. A. Wrigley and David Souden (London: William Pickering, 1986), including the illuminating editorial introduction.

2. See *Commodity Market Review 1998–1999* (Rome: Food and Agriculture Organization, 1999), p. xii. See also the detailed analysis presented in that report, and also *Global Commodity Markets: A Comprehensive Review and Price Forecast* (Washington, D.C.: World Bank, 1999). In an impressive technical study of the International Food Policy Research Institute (IFPRI), it is argued that there might be very significant further decline in real world prices of food between 1990 and 2020. The study anticipates further *declines* in food prices of about 15 percent for wheat, 22 percent for rice, 23 percent for maize, and 25 percent for other coarse grains. See Mark W. Rosengrant, Mercedita Agcaoili-Sombilla and Nicostrato D. Perez, "Global Food Projections to 2020: Implications for Investment," International Food Policy Research Institute, Washington, D.C., 1995.

3. See Tim Dyson, *Population and Food: Global Trends and Future Prospects* (London and New York: Routledge, 1996), table 4.6.

4. Dyson, *Population and Food* (1996), table 4.5.

5. In this see my *Poverty and Famines: An Essay on Entitlement and Deprivation* (Oxford and New York: Oxford University Press, 1981), chapter 6.

6. Note by the Secretary-General of the United Nations to the Preparatory Committee for the International Conference on Population and Development, third session, A/Conf.171/PC/5, February 18, 1994, p. 30. See also Massimo Livi Bacci, *A Concise History of World Population,* translated by Carl Ipsen (Cambridge: Cambridge University Press, 1992; 2nd edition, 1997).

7. The arguments that follow draw on my earlier papers on the population problem, and in particular on "Fertility and Coercion," *University of Chicago Law Review* 63 (summer 1996).

8. See my "Rights and Agency," *Philosophy and Public Affairs* 11 (1982), reprinted in *Consequentialism and Its Critics,* edited by S. Scheffler (Oxford: Oxford University Press, 1988), and "Rights as Goals," in *Equality and Discrimination: Essays in Freedom and Justice,* edited by S. Guest and A. Milne (Stuttgart: Franz Steiner, 1985).

9. See my "Rights and Agency" (1982); "Rights as Goals" (1985); *On Ethics and Economics* (Oxford: Blackwell, 1987).

10. John Stuart Mill, *On Liberty;* in J. S. Mill, *Utilitarianism, On Liberty;*

*Considerations on Representative Government; Remarks on Bentham's Philosophy* (London: Dent; Rutland, Vt.: Everyman Library, 1993), p. 140.

11. I have argued elsewhere that this conflict is so pervasive that even a minimal acknowledgment of the priority of liberty can conflict with the most minimal utility-based social principle, viz., Pareto optimality. On this see my "The Impossibility of a Paretian Liberal," *Journal of Political Economy* 78 (January/February 1971), reprinted in my *Choice, Welfare and Measurement* (Oxford: Blackwell; Cambridge, Mass.: MIT Press, 1982; republished, Cambridge, Mass.: Harvard University Press, 1997), and also in, among other collections, *Philosophy and Economic Theory*, edited by Frank Hahn and Martin Hollis (Oxford: Oxford University Press, 1979). See also my *Collective Choice and Social Welfare* (San Francisco: Holden-Day, 1970; republished, Amsterdam: North-Holland, 1979), "Liberty and Social Choice," *Journal of Philosophy* 80 (January 1983), and "Minimal Liberty," *Economica* 57 (1992). See the symposium on this subject in the special number devoted to it in *Analyse & Kritik* 18 (1996), among quite a large literature that has addressed this question.

12. See Massimo Livi Bacci and Gustavo De Santis, eds., *Population and Poverty in the Developing World* (Oxford: Clarendon Press, 1999). See also Partha Dasgupta, *An Inquiry into Well-Being and Destitution* (Oxford: Clarendon Press, 1993); Robert Cassen et al., *Population and Development: Old Debates, New Conclusions* (Washington D.C.: Transaction Books in Overseas Development Council, 1994); Kerstin Lindahl-Kiessling and Hans Landberg, eds., *Population, Economic Development, and the Environment* (Oxford: Oxford University Press, 1994), among other contributions.

13. English translation by Malthus himself, from his *Essay* on population, chapter 8, Penguin Classics, p. 123. Malthus uses here the original 1795 version of Marie-Jean-Antoine-Nicolas de Caritat, marquis de Condorcet's *Esquisse d'un tableau historique des progrès de l'esprit humain*. For later reprints of that volume, see *Oeuvres de Condorcet*, volume 6 (Paris: Firmin Didot Frères, 1847; recently republished, Stuttgart: Friedrich Frommann Verlag, 1968). The passage here is on pages 256–7 of the 1968 reprint.

14. Condorcet, *Esquisse;* in the translation by June Barraclough, *Sketch for a Historical Picture of the Progress of the Human Mind* (London: Weidenfeld & Nicolson, 1955), pp. 188–9.

15. Malthus, *A Summary View of the Principle of Population* (London: John Murray, 1830); in the Penguin Classics edition (1982), p. 243. Even though Malthus remained rather obtuse on the role of reason (in contrast to economic compulsion) in reducing fertility rates, he did provide a remarkably enlightening analysis of the role of food markets in the determination of food consumption of different classes and occupation groups. See his *An Investigation of the Cause of the Present High Price of Provisions* (London: 1800), and the discussions of the lessons to be learned from Malthus's analysis in my *Poverty and Famines* (1981), appendix B, and in E. A. Wrigley, "Corn and Crisis: Malthus on the High Price of Provisions," *Population and Development Review* 25 (1999).

16. Malthus, *A Summary View of the Principle of Population* (1982 edition), p. 243; emphasis added. Skepticism about the family's ability to make sensible decisions led Malthus to oppose the public relief of poverty, including the English Poor Laws.

17. On this see J. C. Caldwell, *Theory of Fertility Decline* (New York: Academic

Press, 1982); R. A. Easterlin, ed., *Population and Economic Change in Developing Countries* (Chicago: Chicago University Press, 1980); T. P. Schultz, *Economics of Population* (New York: Addison-Wesley, 1981); Cassen et al., *Population and Development:* (1994). See also Anrudh K. Jain and Moni Nag, "The Importance of Female Primary Education in India," *Economic and Political Weekly* 21 (1986).

18. Gary S. Becker, *The Economic Approach to Human Behavior* (Chicago: University of Chicago Press, 1976), and *A Treatise on the Family* (Cambridge, Mass.: Harvard University Press, 1981). See also the paper of Robert Willis, "Economic Analysis of Fertility: Micro Foundations and Aggregate Implications," in Lindahl-Kiessling and Landberg, *Population, Economic Development, and the Environment* (1994).

19. On this see Nancy Birdsall, "Government, Population, and Poverty: A 'Win-Win' Tale," in Lindahl-Kiessling and Landberg, *Population, Economic Development, and the Environment* (1994). Also see her "Economic Approaches to Population Growth," in *The Handbook of Development Economics,* volume 1, edited by H. B. Chenery and T. N. Srinivasan (Amsterdam: North-Holland, 1988).

20. On this see John Bongaarts, "The Role of Family Planning Programmes in Contemporary Fertility Transitions," in *The Continuing Demographic Transition,* edited by Gavin W. Jones et al. (New York: Oxford University Press, 1997); "Trends in Unwanted Childbearing in the Developing World," *Studies in Family Planning* 28 (December 1997); and also the literature cited there. See also Geoffrey McNicoll and Mead Cain, eds., *Rural Development and Population: Institutions and Policy* (New York: Oxford University Press, 1990).

21. See World Bank, *World Development Report 1998–1999* (Washington, D.C.: World Bank, 1998), table 7, p. 202. See also World Bank and Population Reference Bureau, *Success in a Challenging Environment: Fertility Decline in Bangladesh* (Washington, D.C.: World Bank, 1993).

22. See, for example, R. A. Easterlin, ed., *Population and Economic Change in Developing Countries* (Chicago: University of Chicago Press, 1980); T. P. Schultz, *Economics of Population* (New York: Addison-Wesley, 1981); J. C. Caldwell, *Theory of Fertility Decline* (1982); Nancy Birdsall, "Economic Approaches to Population Growth," in *The Handbook of Development Economics,* volume 1, edited by H. B. Chenery and T. N. Srinivasan (Amsterdam: North-Holland, 1988); Robert J. Barro and Jong-Wha Lee, "International Comparisons of Educational Attainment," paper presented at a conference on "How Do National Policies Affect Long-Run Growth?" World Bank, Washington, D.C., 1993; Partha Dasgupta, *An Inquiry into Well-Being and Destitution* (1993); Robert Cassen et al., *Population and Development* (1994); Gita Sen, Adrienne Germain and Lincoln Chen, eds., *Population Policies Reconsidered: Health, Empowerment, and Rights* (Harvard Center for Population and Development/International Women's Health Coalition, 1994). See also the papers of Nancy Birdsall and Robert Willis, in Lindahl-Kiessling and Landberg, *Population, Economic Development, and the Environment* (1994).

23. Mamta Murthi, Anne-Catherine Guio and Jean Drèze, "Mortality, Fertility, and Gender Bias in India: A District Level Analysis," *Population and Development Review* 21 (December 1995), and Jean Drèze and Mamta Murthi, "Female Literacy and Fertility: Recent Census Evidence from India," mimeographed, Centre for History and Economics, King's College, Cambridge, 1999.

24. See particularly an important collection of papers edited by Roger Jeffery

and Alaka Malwade Basu, *Girls' Schooling, Women's Autonomy and Fertility Change in South Asia* (New Delhi: Sage, 1997).

25. A literate community can undergo value changes that one literate family surrounded by other (illiterate) families may not be able to achieve. The issue of choice of "unit" for statistical analysis is extremely important, and in this case may favor larger groups (such as regions or districts) over smaller ones (such as families).

26. See World Bank, *World Development Report 1997* and *World Development Report 1998–1999*.

27. Patrick E. Tyler, "Birth Control in China: Coercion and Evasion," *New York Times*, June 25, 1995.

28. On the general subject of reproductive freedom and its relation to the population problem, see Gita Sen, Adrienne Germain, and Lincoln Chen, *Population Policies Reconsidered* (1994); see also Gita Sen and Carmen Barroso, "After Cairo: Challenges to Women's Organizations" in *A Commitment to the World's Women: Perspectives for Development for Beijing and Beyond*, edited by Noeleen Heyzer (New York: UNIFEM, 1995).

29. *International Herald Tribune*, February 15, 1995, p. 4.

30. Kerala is not, of course, a country, but a state within one. However, with its population of 29 million, as I have mentioned, it would have been one of the larger countries in the world—rather larger than Canada—had it been a country on its own. So its experience is not negligible.

31. On these and related general issues, see my "Population: Delusion and Reality," *New York Review of Books*, September 22, 1994. See also Robin Jeffrey, *Politics, Women, and Well-Being: How Kerala Became a "Model"* (Cambridge: Cambridge University Press, 1992), and V. K. Ramachandran, "Kerala's Development Achievements," in *Indian Development: Selected Regional Perspectives*, edited by Jean Drèze and Amartya Sen (Delhi: Oxford University Press, 1996).

32. Kerala has a higher adult female literacy rate—86 percent—than China (68 percent). In fact, the female literacy rate is higher in Kerala than in every single province in China. Also, in comparison with male and female life expectancies at birth in China of sixty-eight and seventy-one years, the 1991 figures for Kerala's life expectancy are sixty-nine and seventy-four years, respectively. For analyses of causal influences underlying Kerala's reduction of fertility rates, see T. N. Krishhan, "Demographic Transition in Kerala: Facts and Factors," *Economic and Political Weekly* 11 (1976), and P. N. Mari Bhat and S. L. Rajan, "Demographic Transition in Kerala Revisited," *Economic and Political Weekly* 25 (1990).

33. For sources of these data and some further analysis, see Drèze and Sen, *India: Economic Development and Social Opportunity* (1995).

34. Decline in fertility can be observed to some extent in these northern states as well, though it is far less fast than in the southern states. In their paper "Intensified Gender Bias in India: A Consequence of Fertility Decline" (Working Paper 95.02, Harvard Center for Population and Development, 1995), Monica Das Gupta and P. N. Mari Bhat have drawn attention to another aspect of the problem of fertility reduction, to wit, its tendency to accentuate gender bias in sex selection, in terms of sex-specific abortion as well as child mortality through neglect (both phenomena are much observed in China). In India, this seems to be much more pronounced in the northern states than in the south, and it is indeed plausible to argue that a fertility

reduction through coercive means makes this more likely (as was discussed in contrasting the situation in China vis-à-vis that in Kerala).

35. On this see Drèze and Sen, *India: Economic Development and Social Opportunity* (1995), and the literature cited there.

36. Aside from the imperative need to reject coercive methods, it is also important to promote the *quality* and diversity of noncoercive means of family planning. As things stand, family planning in India is overwhelmingly dominated by female sterilization, even in the southern states. To illustrate, while nearly 40 percent of currently married women aged thirteen to forty-nine in southern India are sterilized, only 14 percent of these women have *ever* used a nonterminal, modern contraception method. Even the *knowledge* of modern methods of family planning other than sterilization is extraordinarily limited in India. Only half of rural married women aged thirteen to forty-nine, for instance, seem to know what a condom or an IUD is. On this see Drèze and Sen, *India: Economic Development and Social Opportunity* (1995).

37. On this see the references cited in Drèze and Sen, *India: Economic Development and Social Opportunity* (1995). See also Gita Sen and Carmen Barroso, "After Cairo: Challenges to Women's Organizations."

38. On this see Drèze and Sen, *India: Economic Development and Social Opportunity* (1995), pp. 168–71.

39. On this see the demographic and sociological literature cited in Drèze and Sen, *India: Economic Development and Social Opportunity* (1995).

40. On this see my "Population and Reasoned Agency: Food, Fertility and Economic Development," in Lindahl-Kiessling and Landberg, *Population, Economic Development, and the Environment* (1994); "Population, Delusion, and Reality," *New York Review of Books*, September 22, 1994; and "Fertility and Coercion" (1996).

## Chapter 10: *Culture and Human Rights*

1. Immanuel Kant, *Critique of Practical Reason* (1788), translated by L. W. Beck (New York: Bobbs-Merrill, 1956).

2. "Culture Is Destiny: A Conversation with Lee Kuan Yew," by Fareed Zakaria, *Foreign Affairs* 73 (March/April 1994), p. 113. See also the rebuttal of this position by a pro-democracy Asian leader, Kim Dae Jung, now the president of the Republic of Korea, "Is Culture Destiny? The Myth of Asia's Anti-Democratic Values—A Response to Lee Kuan Yew," *Foreign Affairs* 73 (1994).

3. *Information Please Almanac 1993* (Boston: Houghton Mifflin, 1993), p. 213.

4. On this see Isaiah Berlin, *Four Essays on Liberty* (Oxford: Oxford University Press, 1969), p. xl. This diagnosis has been disputed by Orlando Patterson in *Freedom*, volume 1: *Freedom in the Making of Western Culture* (New York: Basic Books, 1991). His arguments do indeed point to the political freedom in Western classical thought (especially in ancient Greece and Rome), but similar components can also be found in Asian classics, to which Patterson does not give much attention. On this see my Morgenthau Memorial Lecture, "Human Rights and Asian Values" (New York: Carnegie Council on Ethics and International Affairs, 1997), published in a shortened form in *The New Republic*, July 14 & 21, 1997.

5. See *The Analects of Confucius*, translated by Simon Leys (New York: Norton,

1997), and E. Bruce Brooks and A. Taeko Brooks, *The Original Analects: Sayings of Confucius and His Successors* (New York: Columbia University Press, 1998).

6. See the commentaries of Brooks and Brooks, *The Original Analects* (1998). See also Wm. Theodore de Bary, *Asian Values and Human Rights: A Confucian Communitarian Perspective* (Cambridge, Mass.: Harvard University Press, 1998).

7. Leys, *The Analects of Confucius* 14.22, p. 70.

8. Leys, *The Analects of Confucius* 14.3, p. 66.

9. Leys, *The Analects of Confucius* 13.18, p. 63.

10. Translation in Vincent A. Smith, *Asoka* (Delhi: S. Chand, 1964), pp. 170–1.

11. On this see Jean Drèze and Amartya Sen, *Hunger and Public Action* (Oxford: Clarendon Press, 1989), pp. 3–4, 123.

12. *Kautilya's Arthashastra,* translated by R. Shama Sastry, 8th edition (Mysore: Mysore Printing and Publishing House, 1967), p. 47.

13. See R. P. Kangle, *The Kautilya Arthashastra* (Bombay: University of Bombay, 1972), part 2, chapter 13, section 65, pp. 235–9.

14. Translation from Vincent A. Smith, *Akbar: The Great Mogul* (Oxford: Clarendon Press, 1917), p. 257.

15. In the analysis here, I draw on a paper I prepared for UNESCO, "Culture and Development: Global Perspectives and Constructive Scepticism," mimeographed, 1997.

16. Some scrutiny of the Darwinian concept of progress is provided in my "On the Darwinian View of Progress," *London Review of Books* 14 (November 5, 1992); republished in *Population and Development Review* (1993).

17. If the crusty old guard is offended at the popularity of MTV, or of Kentucky Fried Chicken, even after people have had a chance to consider the choices, there is not much comfort we can offer to the resenters, but the opportunity of examination and choice is quite a central right that each citizen should have.

18. From Rabindranath Tagore, *Letters to a Friend* (London: Allen & Unwin, 1928).

19. On this see my "Our Culture, Their Culture," *New Republic,* April 1, 1996.

20. Howard Eves, *An Introduction to the History of Mathematics,* 6th edition (New York: Saunders College Publishing House, 1990), p. 237.

21. John Stuart Mill, *On Liberty* (1859; republished, Harmondsworth: Penguin Books, 1974).

22. See the letter of Edward Jayne in *The New Republic,* September 8 & 15, 1997; my reply appeared on October 13, 1997.

23. A quick introduction to this literature can be found in *A Sourcebook in Indian Philosophy,* edited by S. Radhakrishnan and C. A. Moore (Princeton: Princeton University Press, 1973), in the section "The Heterodox Systems," pp. 227–346.

24. English translation from H. P. Shastri, *The Ramayana of Valmiki* (London: Shanti Sadan, 1952), p. 389.

25. *Brihadaranyaka Upanishad* 2.4, 12.

26. See also Chris Patten, *East and West* (London: Macmillan, 1998).

27. See Stephen Shute and Susan Hurley, eds., *On Human Rights: The Oxford Amnesty Lectures 1993* (New York: Basic Books, 1993); Henry Steiner and Philip Alston, *International Human Rights in Context: Law, Politics and Morals* (Oxford: Clarendon Press, 1996); Peter Van Ness, ed., *Debating Human Rights* (London: Routledge, 1999).

28. See Irene Bloom, J. Paul Martin and Wayne L. Proudfoot, eds., *Religious Diversity and Human Rights* (New York: Columbia University Press, 1996).

29. See Martha Nussbaum and Amartya Sen, "Internal Criticism and Indian 'Rationalist Tradition,'" in *Relativism: Interpretation and Confrontation* (South Bend, Ind.: University of Notre Dame Press, 1989), and Martha Nussbaum, *Cultivating Humanity* (Cambridge, Mass.: Harvard University Press, 1997).

30. Joanne R. Bauer and Daniel A. Bell, eds., *The East Asian Challenge for Human Rights* (Cambridge: Cambridge University Press, 1999).

## Chapter 11: *Social Choice and Individual Behavior*

1. Both the *Nicomachean Ethics* and the *Politics* of Aristotle take up the task of examining the kinds of reasoning that can be sensibly used.

2. Kenneth Arrow, *Individual Values and Social Choice* (New York: Wiley, 1951; 2d edition, 1963).

3. See particularly Friedrich Hayek, *Studies in Philosophy, Politics, and Economics* (Chicago: University of Chicago Press, 1967), pp. 96–105, and also the references cited there.

4. This line of reasoning is more fully presented in my *Collective Choice and Social Welfare* (San Francisco: Holden-Day, 1970; republished, Amsterdam: North-Holland, 1979), and *Choice, Welfare and Measurement* (Oxford: Blackwell, 1982; Cambridge, Mass.: MIT Press, 1982; republished, Cambridge, Mass.: Harvard University Press, 1997), which examine the interpretational issues as well as the constructive possibilities that exist. See also the critical survey of the literature in my "Social Choice Theory," in K. J. Arrow and M. Intriligator, *Handbook of Mathematical Economics* (Amsterdam: North-Holland, 1986), and the references cited there.

5. I have elaborated this argument further in my Nobel lecture, "The Possibility of Social Choice," *American Economic Review* 89 (1999).

6. These connections are examined in my presidential address to the American Economic Association, "Rationality and Social Choice," *American Economic Review* 85 (1995). Pioneering attention was focused in this area in the work done by James Buchanan, "Social Choice, Democracy and Free Markets," *Journal of Political Economy* 62 (1954), and "Individual Choice in Voting and the Market," *Journal of Political Economy* 62 (1954). See also Cass Sunstein, *Legal Reasoning and Political Conflict* (Oxford: Clarendon Press, 1996).

7. Indeed, technically speaking, even "maximization" does not require a *complete* ordering, since a partial ordering permits us to separate out a "maximal" set of alternatives that are no worse than any of the available options. On the analytics of maximization, see my "Maximization and the Act of Choice," *Econometrica* 65 (July 1997).

8. Adam Smith, *The Theory of Moral Sentiments* (1759; revised edition, 1790), republished, edited by D. D. Raphael and A. L. Macfie (Oxford: Clarendon Press, 1976), p. 184.

9. Adam Smith, *An Inquiry into the Nature and Causes of the Wealth of Nations* (1776), republished, edited by R. H. Campbell and A. S. Skinner (Oxford: Clarendon Press, 1976), pp. 26–7.

10. Smith, *Wealth of Nations* (in the 1976 edition), pp. 453–71. On the interpretation and role of the "invisible hand" in Smith's reasoning, see Emma Rothschild,

"Adam Smith and the Invisible Hand," *American Economic Review* 84, Papers and Proceedings (May 1994).

11. See Hayek, *Studies in Philosophy, Politics, and Economics* (1967), pp. 96–105.

12. I have argued elsewhere that there is perhaps more insight in Albert Hirschman's points about the importance of *intended* consequences that are *not* realized. See my foreword to the twentieth-anniversary edition of his *The Passions and the Interests: Political Arguments for Capitalism before Its Triumph* (Princeton: Princeton University Press, 1977; twentieth-anniversary edition, 1997). See also Judith Tendler, *Good Government in the Tropics* (Baltimore: Johns Hopkins University Press, 1997).

13. On this see my joint book with Jean Drèze, *India: Economic Development and Social Opportunity* (Delhi: Oxford University Press, 1995).

14. On this see Drèze and Sen, *India: Economic Development and Social Opportunity,* chapter 4.

15. I have discussed the issues involved fairly extensively in *Choice, Welfare and Measurement* (1982; 1997); *On Ethics and Economics* (Oxford: Blackwell, 1987); and "Maximization and the Act of Choice" (1977).

16. The classic characterization of the competitive market by Kenneth Arrow, Gerard Debreu and Lionel McKenzie has provided much insight despite the parsimonious nature of its structural assumptions. See Kenneth J. Arrow, "An Extension of the Basic Theorems of Classical Welfare Economics," in *Proceedings of the Second Berkeley Symposium of Mathematical Statistics,* edited by J. Neyman (Berkeley: University of California Press, 1951); Gerard Debreu, *Theory of Value* (New York: Wiley, 1959); Lionel McKenzie, "On the Existence of General Equilibrium for a Competitive Market," *Econometrica* 27 (1959).

17. See Hirschman, *The Passions and the Interests* (1977; twentieth-anniversary edition 1997). See also Samuel Brittan, *Capitalism with a Human Face* (Aldershot: Elgar, 1995).

18. These connections are explored in my essay "Economic Wealth and Moral Sentiments" (Zurich: Bank Hoffman, 1994). See also Samuel Brittan and Alan Hamlin, eds., *Market Capitalism and Moral Values* (Cheltenham, U.K.: Edward Elgar, 1995), and *International Business Ethics,* edited by Georges Enderle (South Bend, Ind.: University of Notre Dame Press, 1998).

19. Karl Marx (with Friedrich Engels), *The German Ideology* (1846; English translation, New York: International Publishers, 1947); Richard Henry Tawney, *Religion and the Rise of Capitalism* (London: Murray, 1926); Max Weber, *The Protestant Ethic and the Spirit of Capitalism* (London: Allen & Unwin, 1930).

20. A central issue is the importance of what Bruno Frey has called "intrinsic motivation": *tertium dater.* See his "Tertium Dater: Pricing, Regulating and Intrinsic Motivation," *Kyklos* 45 (1992).

21. Adam Smith, "History of Astronomy," in his *Essays on Philosophical Subjects* (London: Cadell & Davies, 1795); republished, edited by W.P.D. Wightman and J. C. Bryce (Oxford: Clarendon Press, 1980), p. 34.

22. Michio Morishima, *Why Has Japan 'Succeeded'? Western Technology and the Japanese Ethos* (Cambridge: Cambridge University Press, 1982).

23. Ronald Dore, "Goodwill and the Spirit of Market Capitalism," *British Jour-*

*nal of Sociology* 36 (1983), and *Taking Japan Seriously: A Confucian Perspective on Leading Economic Issues* (Stanford: Stanford University Press, 1987). See also Robert Wade, *Governing the Market* (Princeton: Princeton University Press, 1990).

24. Masahiko Aoki, *Information, Incentives, and Bargaining in the Japanese Economy* (Cambridge: Cambridge University Press, 1989).

25. Kotaro Suzumura, *Competition, Commitment, and Welfare* (Oxford and New York: Clarendon Press, 1995).

26. Eiko Ikegami, *The Taming of the Samurai: Honorific Individualism and the Making of Modern Japan* (Cambridge, Mass.: Harvard University Press, 1995).

27. *Wall Street Journal*, January 30, 1989, p. 1.

28. See the proceedings of the conference on "Economics and Criminality" in Rome in May 1993, organized by the Italian Parliament's Anti-Mafia Commission, chaired by Luciano Violante, *Economica e criminalità* (Roma: Camera dei deputati, 1993). The text of my contribution, "On Corruption and Organized Crime," analyzes, with particular reference to the Italian situation, some of the issues briefly touched on here.

29. See Stefano Zamagni, ed., *Mercati illegali e Mafie* (Bologna: Il Mulino, 1993). See also Stefano Zamagni, ed., *The Economics of Altruism* (Aldershot: Elgar, 1995), especially his introduction to the volume; Daniel Hausman and Michael S. McPherson, *Economic Analysis and Moral Philosophy* (Cambridge: Cambridge University Press, 1996); Avner Ben-Ner and Louis Putterman, eds., *Economics, Values and Organization* (Cambridge: Cambridge University Press, 1998).

30. For general analyses of the role of trust, see the essays included in Diego Gambetta, ed., *Trust and Agency* (Oxford: Blackwell, 1987).

31. On this see my "Isolation, Assurance and the Social Rate of Discount," *Quarterly Journal of Economics* 81 (1967), reprinted in *Resources, Values and Development* (Cambridge, Mass.: Harvard University Press, 1984; reprinted 1997); and *On Ethics and Economics* (Oxford: Blackwell, 1987).

32. On the nature and importance of this interconnection in general, see Alan Hamlin, *Ethics, Economics and the State* (Brighton: Wheatsheaf Books, 1986).

33. *Wealth of Nations,* volume 1, book 2, chapter 4.

34. Jeremy Bentham, *Defense of Usury. To Which Is Added a Letter to Adam Smith, Esq., LL.D.* (London: Payne, 1790).

35. I have discussed the distinction more fully in "Rational Fools: A Critique of the Behavioural Foundations of Economic Theory," *Philosophy and Public Affairs* 6 (summer 1977); reprinted in *Philosophy and Economic Theory,* edited by Frank Hahn and Martin Hollis (Oxford: Oxford University Press, 1979); in my *Choice, Welfare and Measurement* (1982), and in *Beyond Self-Interest,* edited by Jane Mansbridge (Chicago: Chicago University Press, 1990). See also my "Goals, Commitment and Identity," *Journal of Law, Economics and Organization* 1 (fall 1985); and *On Ethics and Economics* (1987).

36. In Gary Becker's important and influential "economic approach to human behaviour," adequate room is made for sympathy, rather than for commitment (*The Economic Approach to Human Behaviour,* Chicago: Chicago University Press, 1976). The maximand that the rational person pursues can include concern for others; this is quite a significant and momentous broadening from the standard neoclassical assumption of self-centered individuals. (Some further broadening of the framework of behavioral analysis can be found in Becker's later book, *Accounting*

*for Tastes* [Cambridge, Mass.: Harvard University Press, 1996].) But the maximand is also seen in this Beckerian framework as reflecting the person's self-interest; this is a characteristic feature of sympathy—not of commitment. It is, however, possible to retain the maximizing framework and still accommodate, entirely within the discipline of maximization, values other than the pursuit of self-interest (by broadening the objective function beyond the notion of self-interest); on this and related issues, see my "Maximization and the Act of Choice" (1997).

37. Smith, *The Theory of Moral Sentiments* (revised edition, 1790; republished, 1975), p. 191.

38. Smith, *The Theory of Moral Sentiments*, p. 191.

39. Smith, *The Theory of Moral Sentiments*, p. 190.

40. George J. Stigler, "Smith's Travel on the Ship of the State," in *Essays on Adam Smith*, edited by A. S. Skinner and T. Wilson (Oxford: Clarendon Press, 1975).

41. Smith, *Wealth of Nations* (1776; republished 1976), pp. 26–7.

42. Smith, *The Theory of Moral Sentiments*, p. 189.

43. See my "Adam Smith's Prudence," in *Theory and Reality in Development*, edited by Sanjay Lal and Francis Stewart (London: Macmillan, 1986). On the history of misinterpretations of Adam Smith, see Emma Rothschild, "Adam Smith and Conservative Economics," *Economic History Review* 45 (February 1992).

44. John Rawls, *Political Liberalism* (New York: Columbia University Press, 1993), pp. 18–9.

45. For examples of different types of reasoned connections, see Drew Fudenberg and Jean Tirole, *Game Theory* (Cambridge, Mass.: MIT Press, 1992); Ken Binmore, *Playing Fair* (Cambridge, Mass.: MIT Press, 1994); Jörgen Weibull, *Evolutionary Game Theory* (Cambridge, Mass.: MIT Press, 1995). See also Becker, *Accounting for Tastes* (1996); and Avner Ben-Ner and Louis Putterman, eds., *Economics, Values, and Organization* (Cambridge: Cambridge University Press, 1998).

46. Immanuel Kant, *Critique of Practical Reason* (1788), translated by L. W. Beck (New York: Bobbs-Merrill, 1956); Smith, *The Theory of Moral Sentiments* and *Wealth of Nations* (1776; republished, 1976).

47. See Thomas Nagel, *The Possibility of Altruism* (Oxford: Clarendon Press, 1970); John Rawls, *A Theory of Justice* (Cambridge, Mass.: Harvard University Press, 1971); John C. Harsanyi, *Essays in Ethics, Social Behaviour, and Scientific Explanation* (Dordrecht: Reidel, 1976); Mark Granovetter, "Economic Action and Social Structure: The Problem of Embeddedness," *American Journal of Sociology* 91 (1985); Amartya Sen, *On Ethics and Economics* (1987); Robert Frank, *Passions within Reason* (New York: Norton, 1988); Vivian Walsh, *Rationality, Allocation, and Reproduction* (Oxford: Clarendon Press, 1996), among other contributions. See also the collection of papers in Hahn and Hollis, *Philosophy and Economic Theory* (1979); Jon Elster, *Rational Choice* (Oxford: Blackwell, 1986); Mansbridge, *Beyond Self-Interest* (1990); Mark Granovetter and Richard Swedberg, eds., *The Sociology of Economic Life* (Boulder, Colo.: Westview Press, 1992); Zamagni, *The Economics of Altruism* (1995). For the rich history of psychological literature on this subject, see particularly Shira Lewin, "Economics and Psychology: Lessons for Our Own Day from the Early Twentieth Century," *Journal of Economic Literature* 34 (1996).

48. On this see my *On Ethics and Economics* (1987), and my foreword to Ben-Ner and Putterman, eds., *Economics, Values and Organization* (1998).

49. On this, see Smith, *The Theory of Moral Sentiments*, p. 162.

50. We can, however, also be led astray by "herd behaviour," on which see Abhijit Banerjee, "A Simple Model of Herd Behaviour," *Quarterly Journal of Economics* 107 (1992).

51. Frank H. Knight, *Freedom and Reform: Essays in Economic and Social Philosophy* (New York: Harper & Brothers, 1947; republished, Indianapolis: Liberty, 1982), p. 280.

52. Buchanan, "Social Choice, Democracy and Free Markets" (1954), p. 120. See also his *Liberty, Market, and the State* (Brighton: Wheatsheaf Books, 1986).

53. Kautilya, *Arthashastra*, part 2, chapter 8; English translation, R. P. Kangle, *The Kautilya Arthashastra* (Bombay: University of Bombay, 1972), part 2, pp. 86–8.

54. See Syed Hussein Alatas, *The Sociology of Corruption* (Singapore: Times Books, 1980); also Robert Klitgaard, *Controlling Corruption* (Berkeley: University of California Press, 1988), p. 7. A payment system of this kind can help to reduce corruption through its "income effect": the officer may be less in need of making a quick buck. But there will also be a "substitution effect": the officer would know that corrupt behavior may involve serious loss of a high-salary employment if things were to "go wrong" (that is, go right).

55. See *Economica e criminalità*, the report of the Italian Parliament's Anti-Mafia Commission, chaired by Luciano Violante.

56. Smith, *The Theory of Moral Sentiments*, p. 162; emphasis added. Skillful use of social norms can be a major ally of nonprofit enterprises that call for committed behavior. This is well illustrated by active NGOs in Bangladesh, such as Muhammed Yunus's Grameen Bank, Fazle Hasan Abed's BRAC and Zafurullah Chowdhury's Gonoshashthaya Kendra (Center for People's Health). See also the analysis of governmental efficiency in Latin America by Judith Tendler, *Good Government in the Tropics* (1997).

57. English translation from Alatas, *The Sociology of Corruption* (1980); see also Klitgaard, *Controlling Corruption* (1988).

58. I have tried to discuss these diverse issues in a number of papers included in the collection *Resources, Values and Development* (1984; 1997).

## Chapter 12: *Individual Freedom as a Social Commitment*

1. I heard this account from Isaiah Berlin. Since these lectures were delivered, we have lost Berlin, and I take this opportunity of paying tribute to his memory and recollecting how very much I have benefited over the years from his gentle critique of my rudimentary ideas on freedom and its implications.

2. On this subject, see also my "The Right Not to Be Hungry," in *Contemporary Philosophy* 2, edited by G. Floistad (The Hague: Martinus Nijhoff, 1982); "Well-Being, Agency and Freedom: The Dewey Lectures 1984," *Journal of Philosophy* 82 (April 1985); "Individual Freedom as a Social Commitment," *New York Review of Books*, June 16, 1990.

3. See my "Equality of What?," in *Tanner Lectures on Human Values*, volume 1, edited by S. McMurrin (Cambridge: Cambridge University Press, 1980), reprinted in my *Choice, Welfare and Measurement* (Oxford: Blackwell; Cambridge, Mass.: MIT Press, 1982; republished, Cambridge, Mass.: Harvard University Press, 1997); "Well-Being, Agency and Freedom" (1985); "Justice: Means versus Freedoms," *Philosophy*

*and Public Affairs* 19 (1990); *Inequality Reexamined* (Oxford: Clarendon Press; Cambridge, Mass.: Harvard University Press, 1992).

4. The principal issues in characterizing and evaluating freedom—including some technical problems—are considered in my Kenneth Arrow Lectures, included in *Freedom, Social Choice and Responsibility: Arrow Lectures and Other Essays* (Oxford: Clarendon Press, forthcoming).

5. Development is seen here as the removal of shortfalls of substantive freedoms from what they can potentially achieve. While this provides a general perspective— enough to characterize the nature of development in broad terms—there are a number of contentious issues that yield a class of somewhat different exact specifications of the criteria of judgment. On this, see my *Commodities and Capabilities* (Amsterdam: North-Holland, 1985); *Inequality Reexamined* (1992); and also *Freedom, Rationality and Social Choice* (forthcoming). The concentration on the removal of shortfalls in some specific dimensions has also been used in UNDP's annual *Human Development Reports*, pioneered in 1990 by Mahbub ul Haq. See also some far-reaching questions raised by Ian Hacking in his review article on *Inequality Reexamined:* "In Pursuit of Fairness," *New York Review of Books,* September 19, 1996. See also Charles Tilly, *Durable Inequality* (Berkeley, Calif.: University of California Press, 1998).

6. On this see my *Commodities and Capabilities* (1985); *Inequality Reexamined* (1992); and "Capability and Well-Being," in *The Quality of Life,* edited by Martha Nussbaum and Amartya Sen (Oxford: Clarendon Press, 1993).

7. See John Rawls, *A Theory of Justice* (Cambridge, Mass.: Harvard University Press, 1971); John Harsanyi, *Essays in Ethics, Social Behaviour and Scientific Explanation* (Dordrecht: Reidel, 1976); and Ronald Dworkin, "What Is Equality? Part 2: Equality of Resources," *Philosophy and Public Affairs* 10 (1981). See also John Roemer, *Theories of Distributive Justice* (Cambridge, Mass.: Harvard University Press, 1996).

8. This is discussed in my *Inequality Reexamined* (Oxford: Clarendon Press, 1992; Cambridge, Mass.: Harvard University Press, 1992), and more fully in my "Justice and Assertive Incompleteness," mimeographed, Harvard University, 1997, which is a part of my Rosenthal lectures at Northwestern University Law School, given in September 1998.

9. There is a similar issue relating to competing ways of judging individual advantage when our preferences and priorities diverge, and there is an inescapable "social choice problem" here too, which calls for a shared resolution (discussed in chapter 11).

10. On this see my paper "Gender Inequality and Theories of Justice," in *Women, Culture and Development: A Study of Human Capabilities,* edited by Martha Nussbaum and Jonathan Glover (Oxford: Clarendon Press, 1995). There are a number of other papers in this Nussbaum-Glover collection that bear on this issue.

11. Aristotle, *The Nicomachean Ethics,* translated by D. Ross (Oxford: Oxford University Press, revised edition 1980), book 1, section 6, p. 7.

12. On the relevance of freedom in the writings of pioneering political economists, see my *The Standard of Living,* edited by Geoffrey Hawthorn (Cambridge: Cambridge University Press, 1987).

13. This applies to *Wealth of Nations* (1776) as well as to *The Theory of Moral Sentiments* (revised edition, 1790).

14. This particular statement is from *The German Ideology*, jointly written with Friedrich Engels (1846); English translation in D. McLellan, *Karl Marx: Selected Writings* (Oxford: Oxford University Press, 1977), p. 190. See also Marx's *The Economic and Philosophical Manuscript of 1844* (1844) and *Critique of the Gotha Programme* (1875).

15. John Stuart Mill, *On Liberty* (1859; republished: Harmondsworth: Penguin Books, 1974); *The Subjection of Women* (1869).

16. Friedrich Hayek, *The Constitution of Liberty* (London: Routledge and Kegan Paul, 1960), p. 35.

17. Peter Bauer, *Economic Analysis and Policy in Underdeveloped Countries* (Durham, N.C.: Duke University Press, 1957), pp. 113–4. See also *Dissent on Development* (London: Weidenfeld & Nicolson, 1971).

18. W. Arthur Lewis, *The Theory of Economic Growth* (London: Allen & Unwin, 1955), pp. 9–10, 420–1.

19. Hayek, *The Constitution of Liberty* (1960), p. 31.

20. These and related issues in "the evaluation of freedom" are discussed in my Kenneth Arrow Lectures included in *Freedom, Rationality and Social Choice* (forthcoming). Among the questions that are addressed there is the relation between freedom, on the one hand, and preferences and choices, on the other.

21. On this and related issues, see Robert J. Barro and Jong-Wha Lee, "Losers and Winners in Economic Growth," Working Paper 4341, National Bureau of Economic Research (1993); Xavier Sala-i-Martin, "Regional Cohesion: Evidence and Theories of Regional Growth and Convergence," Discussion Paper 1075, CEPR, London, 1994; Robert J. Barro and Xavier Sala-i-Martin, *Economic Growth* (New York: McGraw-Hill, 1995); Robert J. Barro, *Getting It Right: Markets and Choices in a Free Society* (Cambridge, Mass.: MIT Press, 1996).

22. Adam Smith, *An Inquiry into the Nature and Causes of the Wealth of Nations* (1776), republished, edited by R. H. Campbell and A. S. Skinner (Oxford: Clarendon Press, 1976), pp. 28–9.

23. See Emma Rothschild, "Condorcet and Adam Smith on Education and Instruction," in *Philosophers on Education*, edited by Amélie O. Rorty (London: Routledge, 1998).

24. See, for example, Felton Earls and Maya Carlson, "Toward Sustainable Development for the American Family," *Daedalus* 122 (1993), and "Promoting Human Capability as an Alternative to Early Crime," Harvard School of Public Health and Harvard Medical School, 1996.

25. I have tried to discuss this issue in "Development: Which Way Now?" *Economic Journal* 93 (1983), reprinted in *Resources, Values and Development* (Cambridge, Mass.: Harvard University Press, 1984; 1997), and also in *Commodities and Capabilities* (1985).

26. To a considerable extent the annual *Human Development Report*s of the United Nations Development Programme, published since 1990, have been motivated by the need to take a broader view of this kind. My friend Mahbub ul Haq, who died last year, played a major leadership role in this, of which I and his other friends are most proud.

27. Smith, *The Theory of Moral Sentiments* (1759; revised edition, 1790), republished, edited by D. D. Raphael and A. L. Macfie (Oxford: Clarendon Press, 1976), book 4, chapter 24, p. 188.

# INDEX

▼

## BY NAME

## BY SUBJECT